Advance Praise for *American Leftovers*

Beautifully written and spiritually vulnerable...
one of the best books you'll read this year.
— *Margaret Feinberg,* bestselling author

American Leftovers... will challenge you, make you think,
and perhaps break your heart... opens a window to lives that are raw,
real, and beautifully broken.
— *Tom Hilpert,* pastor and bestselling mystery writer

When the truth is told this well, it reads like a novel that will keep you
flipping pages late into the night. This is a story of hope,
a call to move beyond the wounds of the past...
If you've been burned by religion or jaded by its demands,
this book is for you.
— *Steven James*, award-winning storyteller
and critically acclaimed author of *Broker of Lies*

A brilliant book... riveting... comes marinated with refreshing honesty
and served with an extra helping of humor and grace...
will leave you hungry for more!
— *Wayne Cordeiro*, pastor and author

Gripping and hopeful... keeps the pages turning
through dysfunction, abuse,
betrayal, and miracle healings... In it all, God's Spirit is at work...
— *Max Davis,* bestselling author of over 30 books

If you're starving for spiritual nourishment with authenticity,
depth, and flavor,
American Leftovers more than satisfies! Told with courageous honesty,
insightful reflection, and audacious humor, this story will resonate with
anyone reconciling a painful past
with the desire for a better future... weaves a tapestry of healing, hope,
and family bonds that cannot be broken. Highly recommended!
— *Dudley Delffs*, author of *The Faith of Dolly Parton*

T0006870

Also by Heidi Wilson Messner

Nonfiction
Advent Encounter: a Christmas Devotional

Also by Eric Wilson

Senses Series
Dark to Mortal Eyes
Expiration Date

Aramis Black Series
The Best of Evil
A Shred of Truth

Jerusalem's Undead Trilogy
Field of Blood
Haunt of Jackals
Valley of Bones

Numbers Series
One Step Away
Two Seconds Late
Three Fatal Blows

Novelizations
Facing the Giants
Flywheel
Fireproof
October Baby
Samson

Novellas
Amelia's Last Secret
Alice Goes the Way of the Maya

Nonfiction
Taming the Beast: the Untold Story of Team Tyson
From Chains to Change: One Man's Journey from God-Hater to God-Follower
Confessions of a Former Prosecutor
Six Little Words: The Untold Story of Everett Swanson (coming 2024)

Surviving Family, Religion,
and the American Dream

American Leftovers

NY Times Bestselling Author
ERIC WILSON · SHAUN WILSON
HEIDI WILSON MESSNER

chalice
PRESS

Copyright © 2023 Heidi, Eric, & Shaun Wilson
www.WilsonWriter.com

All rights reserved. For permission to reuse content, please contact Copyright Clearance Center, 222 Rosewood Drive, Danvers, MA 01923, (978) 750-8400, www.copyright.com.

Cover image: Karsten Winegeart, photographer on Unsplash.com

Scripture taken from the New King James Version®. Copyright © 1982 by Thomas Nelson. Used by permission. All rights reserved.

Print: 9780827201101
EPUB: 9780827201118
EPDF: 9780827201125

ChalicePress.com

Printed in the United States of America

TABLE OF CONTENTS

Richard and Sandi Case

~ ~ ~

You are warm and generous souls.
Holed up in your cabin in the redwoods,
we were able to churn out these pages—
and we had a "doozy" of a time.

Mark Wilson

~ ~ ~

You will always be Daddy to us.
Home is wherever we're together, and we couldn't have
completed these edits without your amazing hospitality
and your willingness to air the truth.

And So We Begin

Olympic Peninsula, Washington — June 2019

At dusk, the three of us gather blackberries in a basket made of reeds. We later make dessert in the camper while telling stories from our childhood. It is our tenth night together near glacial peaks and the roar of the mighty Pacific. We haven't been alone like this in over thirty years.

Not since everything came undone.

Here on the peninsula, we remember, argue, laugh, and cry. We jot down some of our accounts while skipping over crazier ones we can't verify. We consolidate time lines for clarity. We change a few names and some physical descriptions to avoid causing hurt or distraction. All the while we drink wine, eat Brie, and nibble on craft chocolate. We trek to the lighthouse on Dungeness Spit, hike snowy Mt. Townsend, and stand in the spray of Marymere Falls. Black bear, osprey, and harbor seals make appearances as we log over 60 miles of trails. In the flush of nature's glory, we seek healing.

Every life involves pain and we certainly haven't suffered more than the average person. We have, however, shared some experiences which helped us hang on as our evangelical framework and family crumbled.

We clung to each other. We kept breathing.

We survived the deception, the dream, and everything in between.

Three siblings, three varying sets of memories. As we talk, we sift through the debris for the truth. We search for those trapped and wounded beneath the rubble, all those who lived through these experiences with us. And we look for the fractures which caused the final collapse. Simply put, we want to better understand our part in it all.

Even now we're still trying to find our place. How do each of us hold onto what was good and move forward? How do we forgive?

This is the story of our young lives.

— *Heidi, Eric, & Shaun*

An excerpt from our mother's out-of-print cookbook, *Global Delights:*

In 1972, the Lord sent Mark and Linda Wilson on an adventure ...
As they were stretched spiritually and emotionally through their journeys,
they were also being challenged physically to adapt to
new climates and cultures.
Through this, Linda came not only to love the peoples of
the world but their cooking.

This cookbook is a small sampling of culinary delights and wisdom gleaned ...
These recipes are designed to be flexible, to encourage substitutions ...
sale items ... and leftovers.

PART 1

RAGAMUFFIN KIDS

Ragamuffin: appealing in poorness, yet lively
enough to cause trouble

A Field Guide to Street Children

Dad & Mom
cutting
wedding
cake

Dad & Mom on picnic
in Italian Alps

Mom,
Dad,
Shaun,
Eric,
Heidi in
Belgium

Eric, Heidi, Shaun
w/ guinea pig in Vienna

1

Heidi

We have only minutes to spare. Mom's red hair is the beacon we zero in on as my brothers and I race through San Francisco Airport, ages five, four, and two. Eric is the oldest, tall and observant, followed by me with my blond pigtails, and Shaun, whose stubby legs work hard to keep up.

"Where's Daddy?" I moan.

"Airplane, airplane," Shaun mutters.

"Almost there," Mom calls over her shoulder. "Hurry, kids."

Eric waits as my Goodwill tennis shoes flap on tiny feet and as Shaun drags his silky blue blanket through the terminal. A TWA attendant checks our tickets, then waves us down the ramp. It is June 4, 1972. We are on our way.

The plane accelerates down the runway, and the cabin shakes as though tearing apart. I grip my armrests. My tummy drops as we lift into the sky. Is this what going to heaven feels like? Mom says we won't have to take naps there or be sad our bunny rabbits died. But I like naps. I even like to cry sometimes.

Nudging my arm, Eric points down at the Golden Gate Bridge.

"Wave goodbye," Mom tells us. "I don't know when we'll be back."

"Are you crying?" Eric asks her.

"Oh, honey," she says softly. She shifts Shaun on her lap and squeezes each of our hands. "We're all going on an adventure with Jesus."

This adventure started months ago. Our house in Eugene, Oregon, was sold to pay off debts, and our furniture and toys went to charity. We now have only our suitcases, the clothes on our backs, and $70 to our family name. Soon, we'll be smuggling Bibles into Eastern Europe in a camper van, defying communist guards, with me and my brothers as part of the tourist disguise.

What do we know? We are kids.

Our parents, in their early twenties, are practically kids themselves.

Of course, we have no idea Dad fled America months ahead of us to avoid a felony warrant for his arrest.

2

Heidi

No, this isn't heaven, and I don't care. After switching planes in Chicago, we land in London's Heathrow Airport. From the crowd at the arrivals gate, a wiry figure comes into view. Our father has dark sideburns, darker eyebrows, and bright blue eyes over a radiant smile.

"Daddy!"

I run toward the man I love, the one who cracks jokes to cheer me up and soothes me when I skin my knees. He is everything to me, my hero. The time away from him has been way too long.

"*There* she is," Dad responds. He sweeps me into an embrace and looks into my eyes. He is larger than life and pulsing with energy, his lean arms still corded with muscle from his days as a high school gymnast. "How's my sweetie doing?"

Mom can't possibly compete with his big personality and she doesn't try. She never wears makeup or draws attention to herself. Whenever Dad takes over a room, she just giggles and laughs along with the rest of us. She adores him. Over the next three years we will travel to more than twenty countries across Europe and Asia, and even then she'll insist he is the most handsome man in the world. Her love blinds her to the troubles that simmer.

"Why'd you leave us?" I pout. "I missed you, Daddy."

"Awww, sweetie, I missed you too. And who's *this* guy?" he says, ruffling Shaun's hair. My little brother stares up with big round eyes. "I hear you turned two while I was gone."

Shaun holds up a pair of fingers, then sticks them into his mouth.

Dad gives Mom a quick kiss before pulling us all in for a family hug. "I didn't *want* to leave you guys, but I had to come find a place for us to live. For the next month or so we'll do our initiation in the Italian Alps, giving out Bibles, and then head to Vienna. You ever heard of Austria? Do you know what a Ferris wheel is?"

Though Eric rarely admits not knowing something, I shake my head.

"You'll get to ride one of the biggest in the world," Dad says. "How's that sound?"

I grin. As long as Dad's with us, it sounds perfect.

We reach Austria's capital by early July. We've already been through Holland, Belgium, France, and Germany, not to mention the alpine vistas of Switzerland. Vienna is different, though. It is known as a city of spies, hosting dozens of embassies and thousands of diplomats.

Since our family is on a secret mission for God, we blend right in.

Out to save the world. All for a higher call.

In the center of Vienna—or *Wein*, in German—fountains, statues, and palaces hint at past glories. Beneath the soaring spires of St. Stephansdom, bakeries display rows of treats, from fresh *Apfelstrudel* to *Sachertorte*, a triple-layered chocolate cake with apricot filling. I bounce on my feet, convinced I will love it here.

Our new residence isn't far from the Alte Donau, a quiet offshoot of the Danube River. Gated walls hide the two-story structure, a local base for Operation Mobilisation. Other OM team members already live here, so our family of five is relegated to a damp and dreary attic.

The children at the house seem well behaved. While they are polite and refined at meals, we are talkative and playful. They are quiet, keeping out of the way. We are constant explorers. They have playthings of their own. We do not. Our parents think we should be like the Christians in the early church, owning nothing, sharing everything.

"That's not always practical," argues one of the senior team members.

Mom smiles. "We're just trying to live as Jesus did."

At least when my brothers or I need clothing, we can rely on OM's community closet, nicknamed Charlie. If someone grows too big for their britches, as Eric does regularly, they get to visit Charlie. I, on the other hand, never seem to grow. I am the waif. I only see Charlie when my fabric wears thin from my rough-and-tumble play.

I'm still not sure about this adventure with Jesus.

And I miss my toys.

One afternoon, Eric and I decide to take matters into our own hands. We see Mom draw Shaun onto her lap as the adults gather for a prayer meeting on the first floor. Shaun is our unwitting accomplice as he rubs Mom's blouse sleeve between his fingers. She won't be going anywhere for a while.

Eric and I sneak down the hall toward the basement door. Treasures call to us from their hiding spaces below and we know just where to find them. A stair creaks beneath my foot. I can barely see. If I fall, I'll alert everyone to our escapade.

"Should we turn on the light?" I whisper.

"The grownups are already singing," Eric notes.

This means we can complete our operation undetected. The moment my hand finds the switch, the basement goods hop into view—piles of toilet paper, buckets of laundry soap, canned food, tubs of potatoes, and stacks of breakfast boxes. The cereal is our target. Each one contains a prize. Normally, whoever pours the wrapped item into their bowl is the lucky winner.

Eric and I are done waiting around for such luck.

Today, we will be the victors.

We open the box tops carefully so the flaps can be refastened. We plunge our grubby fingers to the bottom of the bags, seeking our plastic surprises, rescuing them one by one from the depths.

"Look," Eric exclaims. "A Porsche 911."

"Mine's a..." I'm not sure what to call it. While my brother can identify all the fancy sports cars, I just know what looks nice to me. "Mine has a trunk that opens."

"Is it a trunk or a boot?"

I shrug. I think I've heard people in our house even call it a bonnet. Isn't that something you put on your head? With British, Dutch, and German team members, we hear many words used in ways we don't understand. Continuing our plunder in the musty basement, we stuff toys into our pockets and close each box fastidiously so no one will notice our thievery.

What a haul.

A few weeks later the adults unearth the raided supplies and realize squalid little hands have rummaged through their food. Who is responsible? There's a big commotion, then dismayed faces glare down at my brother and me. We're the obvious miscreants. Who else? These ragamuffin Wilson kids, with their boisterous father and their spiritually-minded mother. From now on, we better toe the line if we want to continue as part of this OM team.

All Eric and I hear is, it's our fault. Twelve months later, we will wonder if we're to blame for our family's sudden dismissal.

~ ~ ~

Our journey over the next eighteen years will lead from Austria to India, to America and South America. The five of us will have wild adventures, face individual trials, and share mountaintop experiences.

When it all unravels, people will wonder how this could happen to a young, zealous, Christian family?

They want answers. Explanations.

Some obvious sin or problem to blame.

Who are we to say? We're probably too close to see the whole picture. But I can tell you this: It doesn't happen overnight. It is a death by a thousand cuts. Little compromises. Little things left unsaid. Things we take note of as we grow older.

The truth is, Eric, Shaun, and I will spend the rest of our childhoods watching, listening, and emulating the stuff our parents model for us. Our futures, our very survival, will become increasingly dependent on our ability to sift the good from bad, the truth from lies.

When all is revealed, what will we hold onto?

What will be left once everything around us is torn apart?

None of this matters to us now, of course. Our parents are all we have and we love them. To me, they're just Daddy and Mommy. We are one big happy family.

And we have some smuggling to do.

3

Eric

Our dark-green camper van rolls up, ready to go and loaded with contraband.

"Hop in," Dad calls from the driver's seat. "We're off to Romania."

Throughout Eastern Europe, drugs, weapons, and pornography are forbidden—as well as the Holy Bible. It's too revolutionary. It says to feed the poor, care for orphans and widows, and forgive your enemies.

Our parents, for obvious reasons, haven't shown us the wall's secret compartment–codenamed *gizli*, the Turkish word for "hidden." Dad and Mom aren't in this for the money. They deliver these Bibles to Christian homes for free, where the local believers could be imprisoned and tortured if caught. We don't realize that if our parents are arrested, we could become wards of a communist state.

Here's what we do know: God is love and we're making trips to help others.

My feet drag. "How far is it this time, Dad?"

"Listen, bud, I know we went over some bumpy roads in Czechoslovakia, but I've added extra bedding for you kids in the back."

I pause at the camper door. So much for our playtimes with the Banker girls, who also live in the OM house. They are a Midwestern family, quieter than ours, with no pretense. I have a secret crush on Deneen Banker, who is my age. Heidi and Debbie, they get along, testing each other's bravery on the backyard jungle gym. Shaun and Dawn, they love the household pets. All six of us play hide-and-seek.

Heidi clears her throat. "Daddy, who's going to feed the rabbits?"

"And guinea pigs?" Shaun pipes in.

"Good *grief*, guys, it's the same as before. We have other OMers to take care of the animals. Let's get going. C'mon, Eric, set the example."

I feel the usual squeeze of being the oldest and I step into the camper. Heidi follows. Shaun slides in on his belly, then finds a cushioned seat. Mom closes the panel door, and the engine fires up. Minutes later we rattle south from Vienna toward dangerous territory.

Mom settles beside me and asks, "Did you pack your swimsuit, honey?"

"Doesn't matter. We're always stuck in this camper."

"Oh, I don't know, we might go to the Black Sea this time. You'll be fine in a pair of shorts." She taps my knee. "I have something else for you."

My head tilts up.

"You'll be six in a few months. Since you've learned to play chess, Daddy and I thought you might like an early birthday present." She hands me a travel chess set.

"Is it mine to keep?"

She grins. "All yours, Eric. Hopefully, we can play a few games together."

As I cup a black knight in my hand, Shaun inches closer for a look, but I give him a view of my back. For a few minutes at least, I want this all to myself.

~ ~ ~

It is early August as our camper groans along a fringe of the Carpathian Mountains. The weather is hotter here. We've gone over 1300 kilometers, past farmland and castle ruins. Though we masquerade as tourists, our parents are risking our freedom to spread the gospel. Sightseeing is not the goal.

At twilight, we chug past men and women wearing colorful garb. Their children have dirty caps and threadbare clothing. They will be called *Roma* in the future, but for now they're simply known as gypsies.

Our camper slows as we roll by. We pull off between some fir trees to set up camp for the evening. Dad lights a small fire. Two boys catch up with us on foot and proceed to entertain us with juggling and somersaults. They play tug-of-war with their hats, then toss them back and forth over the flames, making me and Heidi chuckle. Shaun is in awe. Mom warms up lentils on a propane stove.

"Kids, over here," Dad orders.

We hesitate to turn away from our free roadside show.

"*Now.*"

We scurry toward our father's voice, afraid of getting in trouble. Instead, he directs our attention to a third boy who has crept through the woods toward the back of our camper. The boy realizes he is busted and he whistles. He and his buddies vanish in seconds, lost to the evening shadows.

"Did you catch what was going on?" Dad says. "It's called the robber's dance. As the first two pranced around, the other was trying to sneak up and rob us."

"Can't we just give them some food?" I suggest.

"*Love* your heart, bud. Those poor kids, they're just trying to survive, and Jesus wants us to be generous, doesn't He? But there's a lesson here. If you don't stay alert to the devil's schemes, he'll try to steal from right under your nose."

When bedtime comes, Mom and Dad crack the windows in the front cab. It's hot and stuffy with all five of us. We lay on top of our sleeping bags with thousands of books in the wall beside us, hidden in the gizli. My eyes remain open in the dark.

We've been taught to be thankful for everything. Each piece of clothing is a heavenly provision, each bite of food a gift from above. Why am I so blessed? I'm no better than those gypsy boys. Somewhere out there the devil is scheming, and all I have are questions:

Did the boys get any dinner? Where will they sleep tonight?

Do they know there's a God who loves them?

My thoughts flash back to a year ago. It was a Sunday evening. My parents stepped into my sister's and my bedroom, then lit a candle. They read scriptures to us, and revealed a plate of broken crackers and a cup of unsweetened grape juice.

"Jesus is the Bread of Life," Dad said. "These crackers remind us how much He loves us, how His skin was pierced and beaten as He died on the cross."

"And this juice reminds us of His blood," Mom added. The candle's flame flickered through the burgundy liquid in the cup. "Sin, no matter how big or small, deserves punishment by death. That's why Jesus paid the price to forgive us."

I sat up in my bed. "But I don't sin."

"We all do, honey."

As little kids, neither Heidi nor I seemed convinced.

Dad tried to explain. "Sins aren't just the big, bad things. God loves you, but anytime you disobey His Word, it puts a barrier between you and Him. If you lie, that's a sin. If you want what *you* want more than what *God* wants, that's a sin. Even not sharing or grabbing one of Shaun's toys from him can be a sin."

Our little brother, only a year old, seemed an unlikely mark. He was asleep in his crib in the other room.

Heidi's eyes welled with tears. She seemed to catch the seriousness of all this.

"What if I haven't?" I pressed. "I don't think I've done those things."

"Honey," my mom said, "do you know what pride is?"

I shook my head.

"Pride is thinking you are better than you are, thinking you don't need anyone else's help. That was the devil's problem. He was convinced he was as wise as God and that was the very first sin."

Mom's words peeled back something in my child's heart, and my pulse pounded. I saw clearly I was a sinner. I did selfish things. I didn't want anyone's help, and there was pride in me for sure. The guilt felt heavy in my bones, and I realized I needed forgiveness as much as any soul alive.

"I have sinned," I whispered.

"Do you want to confess that to Jesus?" Dad said. "Would you like to ask Him to forgive you so you can have a relationship with Him? He loves you so much."

I nodded. So did Heidi. We prayed with our parents there in the bedroom, then ate the salty crackers and drank from the cup. As I pictured Jesus on the cross, those nails hammered through His wrists, my tongue puckered with the tannins in the grape juice. Shivers coursed down my neck and through my arms as though I'd been plunged into cold, crystal-clear waters, and a wave of grace swept over me.

We were saved. Washed in the Blood.

Forevermore God's children.

Staring now at the camper ceiling, I am aware of a love without boundaries, a love beyond explanation, and I wonder how I can close my hands to others? How can I shun some gypsy boys just doing their best to survive?

~ ~ ~

We are in Constanța, Romania, a day later, splashing around in the Black Sea, when Dad spots jellyfish and gestures for us to get out. Heidi, Shaun, and I are having so much fun in the sand and surf that we're reluctant to respond, until Dad points out the rubbery, blue-white creatures with their lacy tentacles.

"Those things can sting," he warns us. "We're done swimming."

Back in the camper, we drive into the afternoon. We turn down a dirt road, passing a sign we can't read. Dad says we'll wait here until nightfall. The moment he kills the engine, though, he realizes something is wrong. Military vehicles careen our way from a base just over the hill. We have trespassed on government land.

Soldiers jump out, rifles in hand. Jutting their fingers, they shout.

"We're tourists," Mom explains to them in her soft, earnest voice.

"Dumb Americans," Dad agrees. "*Americanos.*"

"Go." The soldiers gesture for us to turn around. "You go now."

As though this isn't motivation enough, a fighter plane takes off from a nearby runway. We all watch it thunder into the sky. Our dad is courageous but not stupid. He's now more than willing to comply, considering the illegal cargo we carry.

An hour later, Dad finds a safer spot, and Mom takes us on a walk while he fumbles around in the back of the camper. What is he doing? We're told not to ask. While we're gone, he unloads boxes into a local pastor's barn. The pastor covers them with straw and urges my father to leave. It's not safe, he warns.

We get back on the road as shadows fall. Dad's eyes dart between his mirrors, and his knuckles tighten on the wheel. He tells Mom we are being followed.

"Are you sure?" she says. "We're less than an hour from the border."

"There's two of them back there in a black Mercedes."

"Secret police?"

Dad edges off the road. "You know, I'll just let them pass."

"They... look, they pulled over too."

I peer through the window in the camper's rear door and see the car facing us. My heart pounds. What have we done wrong? Why does Mom sound so concerned?

Our father checks the mirrors and taps his fingers, then inches forward again as the Mercedes tracks us from a distance. His agitation grows, despite Mom's mumbled prayers. "Shit," he mutters under his breath. "I mean, pardon my French, but why won't they leave us alone?"

My eyes widen. I never knew Dad spoke French.

Only later will we learn he has a history of run-ins with American cops. He doesn't trust authority and he's willing to buck the system. As a born-again Christian, he's here in Eastern Europe trying to use his bad-boy spirit for good.

There are plenty of examples of righteous defiance in the Bible. In the Old Testament, Jewish midwives hid male newborns from Pharaoh, and Daniel still prayed to his God after King Darius forbade it. In the New Testament, the apostles went back to preaching in the streets after officials arrested them for doing so.

Dad is fixated on the black car. "What're they up to?"

"They just want you to react," Mom says. "Please, can we pray together?"

"It's all a *game* to them, that's obvious. They're messing with us."

Yanking the wheel, Dad swings the camper into the gravel where a pothole jars us from our seats. Heidi's pigtails bounce. Shaun's fingers pop loose from his mouth. I pick up my fallen chess set, then fish for strewn pieces on the floor.

Mom purses her lips. "Honey, they're still back there."

The Mercedes idles right behind us. Two men in dark suits fill the front seats, their faces expressionless. Their hats look like props from a spy movie.

"When did you first see them?" Mom asks.

"Give me a minute, okay? I'm trying to think."

She looks back at us kids. "Dear Jesus, surround us with your angels."

"This is ridiculous. I'm *done* playing games." Dad throws open his door and runs at the vehicle, waving his arms. "What do you want? You have a *problem?*"

I latch my chess set. Adrenaline shoots along my arms. Heidi and I lean toward the glass, wondering what these guys will do when they realize our dad's not afraid of them. He's not afraid of anyone.

Dad's still yelling. "Don't just *sit* there, you cowards."

The men in the Mercedes stare at the flailing apparition before them.

"You want to talk?" he says. "Okay, well, I'm *right* here!"

The men, it turns out, do not want to talk. Tired of this game, they steer around him and disappear down the straightaway. Dad climbs back into the camper, exchanges a glance with our mom, then twists around to look at us.

"Hey, *hey*, kiddos. Nothing to worry about. Papa Bear to the rescue."

Though Heidi and Shaun giggle, I notice Dad's hands shaking as they settle back on the wheel. It makes no sense. He is our superhero. I refuse to believe anything else, and I look away...

Unplanned

Oakland, California — 1965-1967

He had to be the superhero. The way he saw it, he had no other choice.

Linda Guise was only sixteen when Mark Wilson caught her eye. They were juniors at Skyline High School, in Oakland. Both came from Catholic families, both the oldest of five kids. The redhead in the cashmere sweater fell hard for the boy in the black leather jacket who showed up late for class every day.

Linda saw a man of mystery, a project to take on, and Mark saw a girl both innocent and fearless. She took finishing classes. She skied and played golf. She worked hard after school, making meals and doing laundry for four siblings while her parents ran their own furniture store.

Mark started sneaking over. Linda let him through her bedroom window and more than once her father almost caught them.

It was both thrilling and terrifying.

One February night, Mark broke into the office of a used car lot on East 14th Street, where a salesman earlier in the day had snubbed his request for a test drive. He grabbed keys from the box on the wall. He found the matching car in the lot and pulled up at Linda's house in a Triumph TR-6. On an impromptu date, they crossed the Bay Bridge into San Francisco. Mark returned the car before midnight with a note beneath the wiper: *Thanks for the ride. I filled it with gas.*

Six weeks later, Linda was pregnant. It was unplanned, and Linda later insisted they didn't have actual sex. Her Catholic guilt was very real.

Though her father never caught Mark inside Linda's room, he couldn't deny the swell of his daughter's belly. As a regular churchgoer and Rotary Club member, he was appalled.

How dare she discredit the family name.

Mark decided it was time to make things right. The only sex advice he'd received at home had been: "If you get a girl pregnant, you marry her. It's the honorable thing to do."

The night Mark went to discuss elopement plans with Linda, he overheard her father shouting at her inside the house. Thuds followed. Linda wailed.

It sent Mark over the edge.

He rushed home and grabbed a rifle. Before he could make it out the door, his own father's arms clamped around him from behind. With a master's degree from Berkeley, his father was a thin and bespectacled teacher, but his muscles transformed into bands of iron.

"Let me *go.*"

"What do you think you're doing, Mark?"

"My girlfriend's pregnant, okay? Her dad's beating the shit out of her and I'm going to go *kill* that asshole."

"You're not going anywhere."

That night, the concerned parties brokered a truce. Eventually, Mark's father and Linda's mother signed the marriage papers. When the two sixteen-year-olds stood before a judge, the robed man grilled them about their decision. The more he questioned them, the more resolute Mark became.

"We have the papers," he snapped. "You have to marry us, don't you?"

"Yes, I do," the judge conceded. "But I don't want to."

On Mark Wilson's birthday, he took Linda as his lawfully wedded wife. He was now seventeen going on fourteen. She was seventeen going on twenty-one.

In late November, Eric was born.

Linda celebrated their newborn, but even Thanksgiving couldn't soften her father's heart. She had disrespected him and his morals. For this, her father cut her off, refusing to even set foot in the same room with her and her child. He fumed and made his wife suffer whenever she dared to stay in contact with their daughter.

Mark realized he was all Linda and Eric had. They were all he had, too. With Linda at his side, he hiked with his son in a backpack through Golden Gate Park. He took him to civil rights marches and peace protests, wanting to instill higher ideals. Mark figured it was up to him to be the best damn father he could be.

4

Shaun

I'm a shrimp. What can I say? I'm the youngest of three kids. We moved to Austria months ago and our dad still hasn't taken us to the Ferris wheel. Instead, we're always loading up for another trip. Then driving, driving.

I look up to my big brother Eric, literally and figuratively. If he got all my height, I took his sense of fashion. His sleeves are always too short for his arms, and his jackets rarely reach down to his belly button. Each time I get his hand-me-downs, I wear them proudly and also give them my own flair.

Heidi's closer to my size. She tries to help me eat and get dressed, which is nice of her. Sometimes, though, she just bosses me around.

Really? I'm almost three now. I can do some stuff on my own.

Even at this young age, my memories are kicking in. Most toddlers in America see the same rooms and people on a regular basis, one week of familiarity running into the next. For Eric, Heidi, and me, each day is drastically different. New places. Unfamiliar foods. Varied customs and cultures. Our senses are on high alert, kickstarting long-term memories and recording every detail to help us survive.

Bidets, for example.

My first encounter with one is here at our house in Vienna. As I push the lever beside the porcelain bowl, water geysers upward. Boy, am I impressed. I run to tell Dad about the fancy drinking fountain—and to think it's just my size.

He bursts out laughing, my first clue that something's wrong. "Oh, *buddy*, don't you ever drink from that." He tries to compose himself. "That is *not* what it's for."

The OM house has a steady stream of visitors in transit, and I often get lost in the shuffle. While Eric seems perfectly happy to withdraw to a corner, he and his long legs are hard to miss. Heidi stands out with her bright teeth, pretty hair, and cutesy comments. As for me, people say I'm adorable—in other words, not to be taken seriously—so I use my voice to command attention.

I love to sing. Sitting on Mom's lap or Dad's, I join in with the adults during group worship times. Whether we praise God in English or German, I belt out the words with the confidence of an opera singer and nobody seems to mind.

My voice also gets me into trouble.

Dawn Banker is even smaller than me and I like her, but whenever she eats ice cream, she dips her spoon in and turns it upside down on the way to her lips. Half the time she loses the bite and has to start over again. It's dumb, I tell her.

Dad shoots me a look. "Shaun, that's not nice. You need to apologize."

Apologies and forgiveness are big in our family, and Heidi and I are told to hug each other anytime we fight. But I'm not worried about nice. I want truth. The truth is, I am not sorry. If I'm always supposed to be honest, why do I get in trouble whenever I tell it like it is? Does my dad want me to lie?

Across the table, Dawn's head is down, her hands in her lap.

Maybe I really did upset her. If so, that wasn't my intention.

"Will you forgive me?" I ask her.

"For what?" my dad cuts in. "Tell her what you did wrong."

"But I was just... okay, I'm sorry I said something mean."

Dad lets it go at that and Dawn seems to forgive me, because we are soon holding guinea pigs together on the backyard's red metal bench.

Eric says I have a gift with animals. Whether it's butterflies or cats, they all seem drawn to me. People are fine, I guess, but the way I see it, animals don't play games. Good or bad, they just let you know what they want.

Here in Vienna, the Banker girls are our main human connection, completing our little Rat Pack. Both sets of parents get along too. Dad and Mr. Banker work side by side in the warehouse where the camper vans are kept, and Mom and Mrs. Banker laugh and sing together, concocting OM team meals from vegetables and rice.

One day Mrs. Banker tells Mom she is deeply bitter, strangled by an almost physical darkness from her past. Mom's a good listener. She often moves in close—a little too close, some say—and looks you right in the eye.

"Do you want to be free of it?" Mom asks Mrs. Banker.

Her friend nods. "Linda, I am so weary."

Without hesitating, Mom rests a hand on her shoulder and prays. She doesn't raise her voice or whip up fake emotion. She calls on the name of Jesus, and just like that, Mrs. Banker says the darkness disappears.

I'm too little to care, but faith and prayer seem to work for our mom.

~ ~ ~

Eric and Heidi have trouble sharing their stuff at times. Sharing's easy for me, but there are some things not worth passing around. I learn this the hard way when all six of us kids give each other lice.

"Kerosene's the fastest way to kill the critters," claims an older American man on the OM team. "Gotta get rid of the nits as well."

"There are newer and gentler treatments," says Mrs. Banker.

"Sure, and while you're saving up to pay for 'em, lice will be spreading through the house. Is that really what you want?"

Positioned on towels near the door, Eric, Heidi, and I follow the exchange and try not to itch. The Banker girls look equally miserable beside us.

I raise my hand. "What's kerosene?"

"It's tried and true," the man says. "It'll knock 'em dead."

At his insistence, a kerosene shampoo is concocted. We kids are at its mercy. Mom tells Eric to show us how it's done and I watch my older brother lean over in the yard to get his head doused with the formula. He moans, blinking hard, and says it burns. Tears stream down Heidi's cheeks as she takes a turn, then lets Mrs. Banker work a nit comb through her thick curls.

All for one and one for all. Our entire Rat Pack suffers this torture. When my turn comes, I feel the liquid seep into my scalp and I expect a moment of agony, but there's nothing. What's the big deal? Okay, maybe a little tingle here and there. No reason to act like babies about it.

"Doesn't it hurt?" Heidi asks.

I shrug. Being the youngest, I guess I just came out a little tougher.

~ ~ ~

I spend most of our trips in the back of our camper, trapped with a box of crayons. Heidi and I often sing together, and Eric lets me look through his stamp collection. When Dad's not driving, he is slipping out at night on secret errands. During these times, Mom holds me on her lap and reads *Over in the Meadow* or my *Bee Happy* book out loud to me. I love the smiling bee hero and his lessons for the day.

My parents are very different. Dad is outgoing, always looking for ways to connect with others. He makes you feel like the most special person in the world—until the next person comes along. Mom is principled, patient, and restrained. She doesn't need the limelight. She reads books to me and plays Snakes and Ladders with us, putting in the time.

This evening we are traveling once again through the Czech countryside, the lights of Prague in the distance. I wiggle in my seat. Potty training is important at my age—how to go all by myself and warn my parents before it's too late. In Austria, the neighbor boys say, "*Ich muss.*" I must. That always gets the adults' attention. I now tell Mom I have to go, but she asks me to hold it since we're almost there.

Where is *there*? Things are getting desperate, made worse by each bump.

I tug again on Mom's sleeve. "Ich muss."

Dad realizes then it is serious. He pulls off and Mom throws open the rear door. She says I can stand on the camper's tailgate this once and pee out the back.

"But people'll see me."

"No, they won't."

"Yes, they will, Mommy."

"Here, I'll stand guard in the doorway while you stand right behind me and aim between my legs." Mom posts herself in the gap. "See, you'll be fine."

It's my best option—either that or wet my pants—and at least she is blocking my shrimpy body from view. I undo my clasps, drop my overalls to my knees, and shuffle into position. No sooner have I fired off a stream then a pair of teenage girls stroll by and turn their heads my way.

Oh, no. Can they see me?

The stream begins to wobble, splattering on the pavement.

The Czech girls realize what they are witnessing and break into raucous laughter. They point right at me. I'm scandalized. My cheeks are on fire, and anger swells in my chest. Mom said no one would see me. She was wrong, wrong, wrong.

I yank up my overalls and dive headfirst onto the seat cushions.

5

Heidi

Shrouded in darkness, our family arrives at another border crossing on our way into Hungary. Every car, truck, and camper stops. Occupants are told to step out while vehicles are searched. Mom explains that if the contents are deemed permissible—meaning no drugs, American music, blue jeans, or religious material—the vehicles will be waved through. Otherwise, violators will be pulled aside for interrogation.

In front of us, a restricted item is found and two guards drag away the driver. Where are they taking him? What will they do?

Our camper is waved forward. We're next.

Though Dad plays it cool in the driver's seat, Eric looks up nervously from the pages of *Tintin in Tibet*.

Mom appears serene. She believes the Bible contains the power of life and she's committed to our cause. "God will protect us," she tells me and my brothers. "No need to be afraid." Her deep faith and boldness fill us in that moment.

Winter is coming, and chilly air snatches our breath away as our family of five lines up outside. I watch uniformed guards climb into our camper, run hands over the seats, feel between creases, open drawers, and explore all the places they imagine contraband could be. One guard zeroes in on the gizli, knocking on the wall.

I'm not sure what they're looking for, but all their activity makes me uneasy and I burst into song. Maybe it's because Mom tells us, when we don't know what else to do we should worship. Perhaps the words are already running through my thoughts and often the stuff in my head comes tumbling from my mouth. Whatever the reason, I hold nothing back.

"Jesus loves me, this I know, for the Bible tells me so..."

Mom shushes me, realizing the very name of Jesus might stir trouble.

"Little ones to Him belong. They are weak but He is strong..."

Dad sets a hand on my shoulder, squeezing gently.

The already suspicious guard jumps from the camper, marches my way, and stops directly in front of me just as I get the hint to stop. His eyes narrow. He takes me in from head to toe, then back up to my blond ringlets. As he tilts his head to one side, a smirk appears on his lips, and he proclaims, "Brigitte Bardot."

Dad throws me a glance and a wink.

When the guard repeats the name even louder, the other guards cease their searching and emerge from our vehicle. They direct me to keep going.

"Sing, sing, Brigitte Bardot."

I've not yet heard of the famous French sex symbol known for her shape and blond tresses. I don't know who she is or how these staunch communists might be familiar with such a woman, but they are all urging me along.

I belt out the words: "Yes, Jesus loves me. Yes, Jesus loves me..."

Slapping one another on the shoulders, the guards smile and laugh as I sing to Jesus at the top of my little lungs. In the moment, I relish the attention.

Grown men in uniform are transfixed by my performance. I finish, and my parents' urgent warnings give way to stunned amazement when we're told we are free to go.

"Heidi," my mom says, a couple kilometers down the road, "do you realize God used you to protect us? He used your voice to do His will. I believe God's called you for something special."

Special isn't what I've always observed.

Everywhere I go, I feel men's eyes sliding over me, sometimes leaving the residue of a grubby pair of hands. I am a foreigner, different than those around me. And I am a child, expected to comply without saying a word. Most agonizing, I am a girl. My brothers don't get corralled and controlled the way I do. Boys are clearly more privileged, while females seem dispensable, often objects for others' service and pleasure.

These are not God's views, nor my parents'. I know that. Nevertheless, they define my identity and it will take years to undo these early imprints.

~ ~ ~

This is 1973, and the underground church is a mystery to communist officials. These Christians meet in secret, at random times and locations. Are they living like vermin? Do they actually go underground? Like rats, they seem to grow in numbers even as they face imprisonment and torture. Often, an entire congregation shares a tattered Bible, and one family might cherish a single page cut carefully from God's Word before handing it off to the next.

As we'll later learn, Dad and Mom's work is clandestine. The OM leaders take this seriously, and before each trip they make our parents file a sealed letter, addressed to the American embassy, should they get caught and need political intervention.

In other words, things can go bad in a hurry.

Most deliveries take place without any advance communication. During a particular visit to Budapest, a woman is horrified when our parents try to make contact after dark. Without a word she scurries off, slamming the door behind her.

This is the right address, isn't it? What's wrong?

Our deliveries are usually met with excitement. Tokens of appreciation range from hot tea and coffee to hand-carved plaques and knitted doilies. Tonight, though, our contact seems upset by our presence.

The woman returns a minute later with her husband. He's visibly shaken. A respected veterinarian, he's been arrested and tortured more than once for his faith. He runs his gaze up and down the block. He explains in halting English that his fourteen-year-old daughter has friends over for the night, and the path leading to where he hides the Bibles is through a roomful of rowdy girls.

"Please move your vehicle until 3 a.m.," he begs our parents, to ensure everyone has fallen asleep. He scans the block again, a facial tic tugging at his eyelid.

Dad and Mom nod. No problem.

When the clock strikes three, we return. Our parents struggle to keep quiet, tiptoeing with heavy boxes on multiple trips across a floor strewn with teens and blankets. One girl stirs, and they freeze, wondering what elaborate story might excuse their stealthy maneuvers. The girl turns over, snuggles under her covers, and they continue. Once the delivery is complete, Mom returns to our locked camper where my brothers and I are nestled into sleeping bags. She never leaves us more than a few minutes and if we wake up we know not to turn on the lights.

"Hippity hop to bed," she sings to us.

Still in the house, Dad hopes to say farewell. He follows voices down to the kitchen and finds the veterinarian in the midst of a meltdown, cowering on the floor, crying and thumping his head against the wall while his wife kneels beside him. She turns, almost angry, her gaze telling our father it's time to go.

He is torn with emotion. As risky as these missions are for our family, they are much riskier for those on the receiving end. The veterinarian's fears are real, his scars as psychological as they are physical.

"Honey, what's wrong?" Mom says when our dad returns.

He wipes at his eyes. His Adam's apple protrudes as words catch in his throat. Mom feathers her fingers down his arm and he rests his head back against the seat.

"These precious people," he says, eyes closed. "We have no idea."

It is an era without cell phones or GPS. Our parents deliver literature to memorized addresses, usually after sunset, deep in unknown territory. Stalin-era buildings aren't always numbered, and signage in rural areas is often missing altogether. They often drive unmarked roads, trusting intuition and divine direction. Dad's memory is atrocious. To avoid endangering an operation, he makes coded dots in his personal Bible to remind him of his destinations and guide him on his way.

One night in a Romanian village, Dad struggles to locate a pastor's home. He circles in our camper, searching for street signs, and is spotted by a prefect on foot. The official heads our direction and Dad steers off to the left. Running in pursuit, the prefect rounds the corner as we weave through side streets and rutted alleyways. We pull close to a courtyard wall. Dad kills the lights but keeps the engine idling.

"What do we do now?" he huffs.

Mom's answer is always the same. "Pray."

While they ask God to guide and protect us, a blanket of fog descends, cloaking our camper before the prefect can track us down. The air's water pressure dampens sound, scattering its energy, reducing the distance at which we can be heard. In moments, we are virtually undetectable.

Dad noses the vehicle forward, then stops. "Here, you think?"

Mom purses her lips. "Sure, honey, let's try it."

He goes up to a metal gate. Nearly lost in the mist, he raps loudly. A few minutes later, a door in the gate creaks open.

"*Biblia*," our dad ventures.

A smile erupts across the face peering through. "*Mulțumesc, Doamne,*" the man says, swinging the gate wide. He wants us to bring the camper into the courtyard where it'll be sheltered from prying eyes. "*Mulțumesc.*"

"Yes, thank you, Lord," Dad agrees. We have found the pastor.

We barely remember America. It's a name in our heads, a mythical place. Eric, Shaun, and I are chameleons. We shift settings often, so we know how to adapt and change colors. Our style–or lack of it–changes each time we visit Charlie.

We want a stable place, though. One spot we feel secure.

Will Vienna be it?

Our parents don't give us any indications. We are going on blind trust. We love them, and as long as we are together, we believe we'll be okay.

Dad seems to like it here and Mom tries to fit in, cooking *Apfelkuchen* and wearing a *Dirndl*, a traditional dress which contrasts nicely with her red hair. My brothers and I pick up German phrases as we play with the neighborhood kids. We like eating Weetabix and Nutella, things they don't have yet back in the States. Eric reads comic books. He and Shaun kick the soccer ball, except it's called football here. Shaun and I love feeding our pets. We all relish our time with the Banker girls.

I picture how things might be someday. Our Rat Pack will all grow up here in Vienna, and then we won't be foreigners any longer. Eric and Deneen will get married. Shaun and Dawn will, too. Debbie and I will be best of friends. We'll get Austrian passports to go with our U.S. passports–and then we will truly belong.

Of course, this isn't the way things turn out.

A recipe from *Global Delights*: **APFELKUCHEN**

filling:
1/4 cup dried currants
1/4 cup rum or rum flavoring
1/2 cup bread crumbs
2 tablespoons melted butter
6 apples, peeled and sliced

pastry:
2 cups flour
1/4 lb plus 4 tablespoons softened butter
4 egg yolks
2 tablespoons sugar
2 tablespoons grated lemon peel

custard:
2 egg whites
2 egg yolks
1/3 cup sugar
1 ¾ cup heavy cream
2 tablespoons sugar combined with 2 tablespoons melted butter

*Let currants soak in rum 20 minutes. Make pastry by mixing flour and butter,
beat in egg yolks one by one, then add sugar and lemon peel.
Use fingers to press pastry into 8x8x2 pan. Mix filling butter and bread crumbs,
sprinkle evenly over pastry. Spread in apples next. Drain currants, saving rum.
Scatter currants over apples. Bake 10 minutes at 350 degrees.
Beat custard eggs and sugar until thick, add saved rum and cream.
Pour half over apples, bake another 20 minutes. Add remaining custard mix,
bake another 30 minutes. Sprinkle top with sugar and butter mixture.
Bake 15-20 minutes until light brown.

6

Shaun

We are going to the place with the Ferris wheel. About time. Until now, our trips into Eastern Europe have kept us hopping from country to country, and OM prohibits taking cameras, since photos could reveal our stopping points and be construed as acts of espionage. At least in Austria, we're allowed to be tourists.

Heidi loves Schönbrunn Palace

Eric's favorite is Kreuzenstein Castle.

Now I get to ride the Ferris wheel—the *Riesenrad* they call it in German, rolling the r's deep in the throat.

Mom and Mrs. Banker take all six of us kids there, to the old city park called the Prater. It covers fifteen hundred acres, with the giant Reisenrad guarding its entrance. The metal monstrosity rotates slowly, over sixty meters high, with entire railroad cars carrying people inside. I like trains, but I've never seen anything like this. Talk about making a three-year-old feel small.

The crowds thicken as we enter the park. I run across the grass, laughing, ready to face the wheel.

"Not that way," Mom says. "We don't have the money for it."

Hanging my head, I slip my fingers into my mouth. I refuse to cry.

We walk all around the Prater, and Mom buys us candy with her last few coins. All I can think about are those train cars turning past the clouds. By the time we head back to the parking lot, my legs are tired, and my shoes kick up gravel on the path. Our moms split into separate cars, with kids following. There go Eric and Deneen into the Wilson vehicle, while Heidi, Debbie, and Dawn follow Mrs. Banker.

I stop for one last look at the Ferris wheel.

Will I ever get to go on a ride?

Weeks earlier, one of our visitors at the OM house promised to bring me here, but he left soon after and never followed through. If kids shouldn't lie, I don't think grownups should either. I hear it again, though. And again. Empty promises and nice words, smiles and lots of talk. Even as a little boy, I see right through it. The next time a person pats me on the head or tries to butter me up, I will cross my arms and tell them, "I don't believe you. You should tell the truth."

Oops, we're supposed to be going. I turn back toward the parking area and spy only vacant spaces. I blink hard. Maybe my eyes deceive me. Nope, both the Banker and Wilson cars are gone.

They've left me, just like that.

Am I surprised? Not really. Getting overlooked is normal for me. I am definitely scared, though, and I don't know what to do. Wide-eyed, I wait. I'm sure Mom will reappear any second, realizing I'm gone and not in the Bankers' car. She'll spin back to find me. Even if I get blamed, at least I won't be stuck out here all alone.

Alone is a funny word, considering how many people are around.

I watch for red hair. Still no sign of my mom.

A lady frowns and bends down, firing questions at me in German. I say a few words, then switch to English. She says, "*U.S.A.,*" though it sounds like, "*Ooo, ess, ahh.*" She waves down a passing patrolman.

"*Wie heissen Sie?*" he asks me.

"Shaun," I answer.

He wants my parents' names as well and I tell him Daddy and Mommy, since that's what I always call them. Neither their real names nor their OM code names will mean much to this patrolman. He leads me to a wooden booth and picks up a phone. I know only playground German, so I can't understand him.

Does he think I'm a runaway? Will he put me in jail? What is taking Mommy so long? I've been scolded recently for my attitude, for talking back to adults. Maybe she figures I'm just too much trouble.

No, she will definitely come back.

Eric will insist on it. Heidi will cry if she doesn't.

By the time Mom does track me down, her eyes wet with relief, the patrolman has already consoled me with pieces of a Milka chocolate bar. I'm pretty much over it, anyway. If I don't want to be forgotten from now on, I realize it will be up to me.

~ ~ ~

Summer arrives, along with some friends from Oregon, Mike and Debbie Monaghan. They were part of my parents' youth group in the U.S. They got married and now they've come to smuggle Bibles also. They will be a part of our lives for decades to come, Mike with his infectious laugh and Debbie with her nurturing ways. She often holds me on her lap. I like her.

The days turn warm and sunny, giving me plenty of opportunities to ride my birthday present from Dad and Mom.

My own tricycle.

It's brand new, not one of those old rusty things. It's red with a yellow cart attached to the back and I pedal it up and down our street.

The neighbor boys take notice. They step into my path one afternoon. With Eric nowhere in sight, it's two against one, and the bigger kid pushes me off my trike as the other hops on. He is too heavy, causing the metal to bow. My fists clench, but he just sneers. He thinks it's hilarious when the trike's frame buckles and the back tires splay. He's ruined my most valued possession.

No one even listens when I stomp inside. Instead, our parents tell us we are heading off to England for the annual OM conference. Eric and Heidi grumble. We all went last year, a long drive through Germany, Luxembourg, and Belgium, plus a ferry ride across the English Channel. Do we have to break up our Rat Pack again? This isn't fair.

Then Dad delivers the real shocker:

"Sorry, kids, we won't be living here anymore. Our time in Vienna is over."

Eric slouches and wears a frown. He's probably mad about leaving Deneen. We will all miss playing with the Banker girls.

Heidi's lip quivers. "Is it because we stole toys from the cereal boxes?"

"Oh, not at *all*, honey. For security reasons, the leaders say it's best if we make a change. It has nothing to do with you kids."

Still angry, I say, "That's dumb. Why do they get to tell us what to do?"

"Now, Shaun." Mom takes my hand. "Who knows what the Lord has ahead? I promise He's full of wonderful surprises and all we can do is trust."

I'm not so sure about that. After all, my trike just got smashed.

7

Heidi

"Are you ready to see the Crown Jewels?" Dad toggles an eyebrow at us.

We are at the Tower of London, a tourist stopover on our way to the OM conference. My little legs are stiff from our long journey here. This place is supposed to help me and my brothers forget about leaving Vienna, our friends, and our pets.

Instead, I think my heart will burst.

Where will we live now? Will there be kids our age? I mull the questions, wallowing in the drama of it all. The answers will depend on how God leads Dad and Mom during the conference starting tomorrow.

Outside the tower, our family waits in a long line as funnily clothed men called Beefeaters stand guard on either side. They protect the Jewel House. Everyone quiets as we crowd inside. Behind security glass, gold crowns and scepters glimmer with emeralds, rubies, and diamonds. Photos show Queen Elizabeth in full regalia, so proper with shoulders pulled back. This collection, we're told, is worth over a billion pounds.

I tug on my father's sleeve. "Daddy, how many pounds am I?"

He chuckles. "It's confusing, isn't it? No, pounds are what they call their money here. Anyway, you're my little princess. You are *priceless*."

I stand a bit taller, like the queen in her royal pictures. Even if I'm still sad, I trust my parents will always be my home, no matter where we live.

~ ~ ~

Eric

Heidi seems fine with all this, but I just want to settle somewhere long enough to learn the language and fit in. I can't even guess where we'll end up next. Our parents say they'll make those big decisions here at the conference, in this large Episcopalian church. I don't know how any decisions can be made amid all this noise. The place swirls with activity, a barrage of stimulation.

A speaker, at long last, steps to the microphone and asks for quiet.

Attendees from dozens of countries find their seats. Stained glass windows and dark wooden pews create a somber atmosphere, which matches how I feel since leaving Austria. Shaun crawls onto Mom's lap. Heidi and I watch motes of dust float through colored sunbeams while the speaker at the podium starts rambling.

"Why can't we go back to Bible Club?" I moan to my mom.

Yesterday our parents took us to a Bible club put on by a local English physician at her nearby home. We learned with other OM children about biblical characters on a flannel storyboard. We made bookmarks and memorized verses. I even tried Marmite on bread and liked it—salty, yeasty, and strong.

"We think you kids ought to be in here with us today," Mom replies.

"It's just a lot of talking."

"Honey, please, your brother and sister listen to every word you say. And who knows? Maybe Jesus has a surprise up His sleeve."

My shoulders slump.

Mom slips me and my sister some pens and paper. Heidi draws while I link words across the page. Shaun comes up with his own form of entertainment.

"Mommy?" He tugs on her arm. "I have to go to the toilet."

"Okay, Shaun, but come right back."

Walking around the sanctuary releases some pent-up energy, and Shaun loves it when people nod at the cute little guy with the smile and big attitude.

"Mommy," he says a short time later, "I have to go again."

This happens every fifteen minutes until Mom catches on. When she walks all the way to the bathroom with him, Shaun says he no longer has to go. I doubt our mom is getting much from the conference while dealing with the three of us.

During a break, she says to Dad, "I'm taking the kids outside for some—"

Shouts cut her off, echoing across the large conference space.

"Mark, Mark!"

I turn to see a wiry young figure running toward us. He looks like our dad with lighter hair. He catapults over the pew and falls, laughing, into Dad's arms. They almost tumble to the floor. Heidi, Shaun, and I all smile. We already like this man.

"Hey, kids, remember Uncle Paul." Dad says. "He's my younger brother."

We're too little to recall meeting any of our relatives, and with Gramps Wilson now living on the island of Guam and Grandpa Guise still refusing to talk to us, we have nebulous notions, at best, about family. We think it's just the five of us.

"What're you doing here?" Dad says.

"My wife and I..." Paul pulls a brunette into view. "Here, let me introduce you. Mark and Linda, this is Val."

"The *newlyweds*." Dad squeezes them both in a hug.

"We've joined OM," Paul continues. "Didn't you get our letters?"

"You kidding." Dad rolls his eyes. "We've been all over the place these last fifteen months. Our mail's *still* trying to catch up."

Uncle Paul picks up my little sister. "Wow, you kids have grown. Val, this is Heidi." He bounces her ringlets in his palm.

"Well, hi there," our new aunt says. "I've heard so much about you."

Val wears a short, colorful skirt and knee-high boots. She has styled, shoulder-length hair, like something from the movie posters I saw in central London. We kids can't keep our eyes off these relatives as our uncle explains their plans to work aboard the *Logos,* a ship carrying Christian literature to ports around the world.

"What about you guys." Paul pries. "You have plans."

"We're on our way to India," Mom confides. "The Lord's made it so clear."

I cross my arms and frown. It's the first I have heard of it, but I guess there's no use arguing. When it comes to knowing what God wants, Mom seems to have a hotline to heaven. Even Dad rarely challenges her.

"India?" Val gasps. "With three little kids?"

"They're little adventurers," Dad says. "Travel is a great teacher."

Smiling, Mom brushes back her thick locks. "And since many of the precious Indian women do not cut their hair, I'm letting mine grow. God needs disciples. Seeing all these countries has given us such an appreciation for the States, but we can't go back there to stay, not when others are being robbed from experiencing Jesus for themselves. We must take up our crosses daily and follow Him."

"I've heard India is a tough place," Paul warns. "Don't rush into it."

"Oh, Paul, the Lord's given us such love for the Indian people and culture. We know there'll be trials, but we are purified by the testing of our faith."

"Well, let's just hope you guys are going by plane."

"On an OM budget?" Dad scoffs. "We'll be driving overland from Belgium, at least seven thousand kilometers. Once we get there, Linda and I will be helping an Indian couple establish house churches in a city called Ajmer."

Val smiles. "That sounds beautiful, it really does. If the *Logos* stops in India, perhaps all of us can get together again."

This is the only thing which keeps us from blubbering as the conference comes to an end. We love our new aunt and uncle. We feel connected in deeper ways than we understand, woven into a family fabric we barely knew existed until now.

"If all goes as planned, we'll see you sometime next year," Val tells us.

Paul hugs us, his green eyes watering. "We'll stay in touch, we promise. We'll record a tape onboard the ship and send it to you soon as we can, okay."

Though we nod, we have a hard time turning frowns into smiles.

We are so tired of goodbyes.

~ ~ ~

Shaun

Here we are, at a dusty old OM warehouse in Zaventem, Belgium. This will be our launching pad to India. The windows are grimy, framing rain clouds and smokestacks as September comes to a close.

Dad's gone much of the time, helping pack and load Christian literature for shipments across Europe. In his spare time, he studies Indian history and reads the Bhagavad Gita. The British have colonized India and many other lands, while missionaries have too often forced their beliefs upon others. Dad reminds us we are not going there to trample tradition, but to love unconditionally.

Mom has a list of team kitchen duties. She puts Eric to work peeling carrots and potatoes–and often his fingertips. Heidi sweeps and mops the floors until her little arms are stiff. My hands turn red as I rinse cups to be run through the industrial dishwasher. We're all in this together, as a family.

Anyway, if you don't work, you don't eat.

That's straight from the Bible.

At long cafeteria tables, OMers gather for meals, and our ears perk up at the accents from across Europe, South America, Africa, and Asia. Mommy says these people are so smart, able to speak more languages than most Americans. We try to assimilate a host of new words and sounds. We giggle when people call a truck a lorry. We know a woman named Laurie.

One by one, members of our India team show up. Meanwhile, in the garage bays, our seven-ton Bedford trucks—one red, one blue—are prepped for our marathon journey ahead. The goal is to strip away anything we don't need, for the sake of space, weight, and fuel consumption.

Radios? Unnecessary. We can sing instead.

Heavy padded seats? Goodbye. Hard seats will have to do.

Heaters? Who needs them? We should be passing through Eastern Europe at the end of their summer and through Asia in early fall.

There are no gizlis, of course. We have nothing to smuggle on this trip.

The back of each seven-ton beast is a metal shell. Supplies are loaded in layers, with boxes of books and tracts on the bottom. Spare tires are stacked in next, with sacks of rice, tins of oil, and cans of peanut butter. Next, come cooking supplies, medical goods, water reserves, and clothes selected from Zaventem's Charlie. Mattresses and bedding top it off, leaving one meter of wiggle room beneath the ribbed roof. We will all sleep side by side, with two sealed windows to offer our only lighting.

We have sixteen people total, split between both Bedfords: Darrell, our team leader, a good-natured ventriloquist; Faroe, our stoic mechanic; nine other men and women; and the five of us Wilsons.

At last, in late October, we pose for departing photos by the trucks.

Mom nuzzles up to Dad. "Don't you think this is romantic?"

He rolls his eyes and slaps a huge tire. "Sure, if you call sleeping in this diesel *rust* bucket romantic. No hanky-panky allowed."

"Oh, honey," she snuggles closer.

"If you have any doubts, Linda, now is the time to speak up."

"The Lord often requires something from us that is difficult, but the moment we do what He asks, He fills us with so much more. I've already begun growing my hair to fit into another culture. I've felt the Lord's tugging the same as you have."

"Then there's no turning back," he exclaimed. "We are going to India..."

Undaunted

Woodland, California — 1967-1968

Romantic movies usually end with a happily-ever-after.

Life is not so simple.

In the year they would have graduated from high school, Mark and Linda moved into a small Woodland home, north of Sacramento. Being a hero was no easy task, Mark realized, as he worked a listless grocery-clerk job. He was able to buy a black VW Bug and cover costs on rent and diapers, but he was disturbed by the things he saw in his own workplace, an adult world of backstabbing, cheating, and flagrant racism. As for Linda, her second pregnancy was proving difficult.

The marriage was also struggling. They both felt ignored and misunderstood. When they argued, they put Eric in the other room to protect his little ears. He was already showing sensitivity to conflict and noise.

Feeling frustrated one night, Mark completed his work week and stayed out late drinking. He stumbled back to the house and tried not to wake his wife and toddler. Linda was only a month or so from her due date.

Mark cracked open another cold one and flipped on a thirteen-inch TV. He saw some young guy in a suit and tie waving around a Bible.

Great, just what he needed. More God-talk.

Before meeting Linda, Mark had already rejected religion as out of touch, shallow, and fake. He had seen its stifling effects and wasn't impressed.

Mark's mother was a smart, willowy woman who was also a functioning alcoholic. Rather than tend to her offspring, she let the Catholic church do her job for her. She dropped them off at St. Jarleth for Mass, then went home to pour herself a glass of liquor from a Bols Ballerina bottle. Upon retrieving her children, she undercut their religious lessons with callous comments. Even when she encouraged the development of mind and spirit, she had nothing of the heart to give.

Mark, after completing catechism, decided to become an altar boy. He didn't have any spiritual aspirations. What he did have was his mother's taste for alcohol, and cleaning up after the Eucharist gave him a chance to drain the dregs in the communion cup. As soon as the priest learned of this sacrilege, Mark's altar-boy duties were over. Perhaps fearing her own addiction might be discovered, Mark's mother dropped off her brats the next week at St. Bernard Church instead.

In this new church, Mark noticed roped-off chairs where the hearing-impaired used earpieces to listen to the priest give the liturgy. As a recent convert to the thrills of rock and roll, he spotted an opportunity.

At the next service, he moved directly to the roped-off section and grabbed a seat. Beneath his sweater, a transistor radio filled his chest pocket. He slid in the earpiece, turned on the radio, and nodded along with the music. Why squirm in a pew while a priest recited Latin, when he could listen to the Beatles sing about love?

It worked like a charm.

A few weeks into this charade, he was drumming his hands on his legs when everyone stood for the Prayers of the Faithful. He hopped up quickly to join them. As he did so, the cord loosened in its socket.

The priest, from the pulpit, mentioned an item for supplication.

"Lord, hear our prayer," the congregants responded.

As the priest mentioned a second item, the cord from Mark's headset fell free and an entirely different sound blared through the sanctuary:

"I wanna hold your *haaaaand*... I wanna hold *yooour* hand!"

Clearly not one of the faithful, Mark knew his youthful ruse was up.

In Woodland now, half-drunk before his tiny TV, Mark Wilson felt that old spark of rebellion. As a disillusioned Catholic, he would watch this Protestant preacher who called himself Billy Graham. Anyway, there was something different about the man. He spoke with conviction. He said God the Father knew the things in your past but still wanted a relationship with you.

Mark blinked through his stupor.

This was heavy stuff. Was it in the Bible? Why hadn't he heard it before?

He scooted closer and felt the preacher staring into his soul, unlocking the abuse and accusations he held inside. Sobered by the man's message, his armored heart opened wide—and he wept.

Washed raw by his tears, Mark heard Billy Graham ask him to join in a prayer for salvation. Right there on the living room floor, Mark fell to his knees and gave his heart to a God full of love and compassion. This God was nothing like the harsh one of Mark's past. That God seemed diabolical, as distant as his irritable father and as untouchable as his drunken mother. That God didn't interest him.

But this? This was completely new.

Still on his knees, Mark sensed years of falsehoods falling away. Though his former deeds and misconceptions would come back to haunt him, he had no doubt he was a changed man—born again, set free, and radically transformed. He flipped through the entire New Testament that weekend, learning all he could about this Jesus character. How could he keep it to himself?

At his next work shift, Mark refused to sell booze or cigarettes to shoppers in his line. He told them it was time to be free of addiction. It was time to get saved.

After a few warnings, his boss let him go.

Even Linda found it hard to trust this man who only days earlier was drinking and carousing. To prove his sincerity, Mark slicked back his hair, wore ties and white dress shirts, and tried to clean up his language. He told her, "We need to get married the right way, standing before God as believers."

In March, the two eighteen-year-olds renewed their vows at a nearby chapel. They arrived in their VW Bug, its panels covered in Christian slogans and peace symbols which Mark had painted. They had conceived their second baby in this vehicle, and since Linda was eight months pregnant, she was told by the priest to wear a black wedding dress—one more shame she would have to carry.

In April, Heidi was born. She had curly hair and a healthy set of lungs.

"Mark, what're we going to do?" Linda prodded. "What about our bills?"

"Hang on, okay? I know something good's just around the corner."

Barely holding on after the birth, Linda sank into postpartum depression. She felt fat and unattractive. She wished she was better able to cuddle and nurture growing Heidi, even as Eric lost himself in a world of Legos and Tonka trucks.

Mark remained undaunted. He had a cause, a gospel message, and he would tell the whole world if he could.

8

Heidi

Our cross-continental journey is set to begin. Dad and Faroe mark our route on a large world map. Together we sing "He's Got the Whole World in His Hands."

Here we go.

Our family is assigned to the red truck. My brothers and I are stuck side by side, kilometer after kilometer, with the diesel fumes in the cramped space atop the supplies. At times, we can barely breathe. I have my paper dolls, draping them in ornate outfits and imagining them at a ballroom dance. Eric has his chess set, plus red knitting needles Mom gives him to keep him occupied. Shaun has crayons and paper.

Dad and Mom are firm believers in education. There's no conflict between science and faith, as far as they are concerned. If God made the world, we should be able to learn about Him by studying how plants grow, canyons form, and stars twinkle in the sky. They also encourage us to appreciate all the differences we encounter—new foods, cultures, and people who don't look like us. Our world is fluid and wide open, full of unexplored mysteries and scientific wonder.

We're taught not to view things in only black and white.

No, there's a whole range of technicolor.

I'm kindergarten age and Eric's old enough for first grade. Our mom, a former Girl Scout and editor of her school newspaper, doesn't want us falling behind as we travel. She handwrites lessons and equations for us. She buys an old abacus to help us conceptualize math. Our windows become portholes to the passing world.

Shaun's as smart as any of us, picking up knowledge at every turn. He absorbs sights, smells, and sounds. With the framework of his young life constantly shifting, he has to be strong to stand on his own.

We pass through Luxembourg and Germany into Austria. I draw the delicate petals of an Edelweiss, with flower pods inside of them. Shaun cuddles next to Mom, rubbing the sleeve of her jacket while she tells us about Wolfgang Amadeus Mozart. She has to project her voice over the rumbling engine.

"Like a gang of wolves," I comment. "What a funny name. But wolves are called a pack, aren't they, Mommy?"

"Yes, they are, Heidi."

I grin ear to ear, hoping Eric is impressed.

She continues. "Mozart was born here in Salzburg and wrote music in all the genres of his day. His talents were universal, meaning he excelled at many things."

"I'll be universal too someday."

"Well, honey," Mom says, "you just might be. Yes, you just might."

Vienna is getting closer, our old stomping grounds. Snowcapped peaks and idyllic towns ease us toward stately opera houses. Over the weekend at our old OM house, our trucks get maintenance checks while we take showers and do laundry. We cry out as our Rat Pack reunites, and we dash into the backyard with Deneen, Debbie, and Dawn. The jungle gym groans beneath our combined weight.

When our father interrupts us, our hearts sink.

Time to leave already?

"Tomorrow," Dad admits. "But right now we're going somewhere special, just the five of us. What do you say, we all take a ride together on the Ferris wheel?"

Squealing, we dash over and cling to his legs, Eric on one, Shaun and I on the other. Dad lurches across the grass, lifting his left foot, then his right. We urge him to keep going and he huffs along. Left foot, right foot. Trying to maintain his balance. Finally, he collapses with us in a tangle of limbs and giggles.

"Good *grief,*" he gasps. "You kids, you're growing way too fast."

The Reisenrad is everything we imagined. It's huge. It ferries us above the treetops and provides views across all of Vienna. A quiet awe falls over us. Daddy and Mommy hold hands. Safe and out of reach, I know trouble cannot touch us here.

~ ~ ~

Eric

Another departure. Separation anxiety might not yet be a term, but Heidi, Shaun, and I feel it anyway—fitting in, making friends, then leaving again. Faster than you can say *auf Wiedersehen,* we leave the Bankers, and we won't see them again for seven years. Instead, we cross the border into a land of goulash and paprika.

"It's making me Hungary," I say, trying to lighten the mood. "You get it?"

Mom scrunches her nose. "Very punny, honey."

We have gone from Belgian factories, to towns built with Germanic order, to Hungary's drab, Russian-era buildings. Next we enter Yugoslavia, with its bell towers, steep-roofed barns, and handmade crafts sold in villages.

Inspired, Heidi draws the pretty little bells of the national flower.

Mom drapes her hair over her shoulder and takes a peek. "I love it. Are those lilies of the valley? You know, the real ones might smell good, but you should never eat their red berries. The berries will make you sick and many things which look nice can get you into trouble. Did you know the Bible calls the devil an angel of light?"

I look up. My sister and I both shake our heads.

"He often seems dark and scary, making us think he's more powerful than he is. Jesus is the Good Shepherd, watching over us. When the devil realizes he cannot scare us, that's when he likes to disguise himself as something good instead."

"The devil's a liar," Heidi interjects. "Lying is bad."

I furrow my brows. "How do we know if he's tricking us?"

"Well, Eric, he'll either tempt you to do things you shouldn't be doing or distract you with nice things so you'll ignore the Shepherd's voice."

This confuses me. "If they are good things, how can they be bad?"

"Eric, things are just things, neither good nor bad. The devil likes to take advantage when you love something too much or you let it control you."

~ ~ ~

Summer gives way to the colors of autumn, and it's early November when we move into Bulgaria. The weather isn't the only thing changing as we move east. People's skin turns swarthy, and there's strange lettering on the road signs. Mom calls it Cyrillic. Buildings are no longer angular but rounded and smooth. In Sofia, I'm mesmerized by the churches with their blue, green, and gold onion domes.

The changes are even more dramatic in Turkey, the bridge between east and west. Muslims here who convert to Christianity face pressure and death threats. We meet a young Turkish believer who has barely survived being poisoned by his father.

When we reach Istanbul, Dad and I go exploring. He never saunters. He walks with purpose, with speed, unlike Mom who approaches life at a snail's pace. Together, Dad and I climb steep streets, dodging feral cats and listening to vendors shout out their wares while taxis honk and swerve. Calls to Muslim prayer ring out from minarets, exotic and beautiful to my ears. I've been reading C. S. Lewis, and this city reminds me of Tashbaan from *The Horse and His Boy*.

We meet up with Mom, Heidi, and Shaun at the Grand Bazaar, a warren of rugs, trinkets, sandals, and spices. Mom points out baskets holding thousands of hazelnuts placed carefully in spiraling patterns. Dad shows us ribbed beef and pork on butcher hooks, and the aroma of meat skewers is tantalizing. We stick close together in the bustling walkways, drinking bottles of Fanta and eating hot shish-kebabs. I've never tasted anything so delicious. I could eat this every day.

But if I like something this much, will the devil take advantage?

Just don't let it have control, I remind myself.

The only thing better than shish-kebabs and the bazaar's mysterious recesses is a long, low bridge flanked by the Bosphorus Strait. The breeze off the water is cool, tugging at our clothes as domes and spires change color in the setting sun.

Before bed, Dad tells us he wants to record a tape cassette for our pastor, the one who prayed over us and sent us out from his church in Eugene, Oregon. Dad pushes a button on the recorder and asks us, "Do you remember Roy?"

The name sounds familiar, though we can't be sure.

"Roy Hicks, Jr. Is he the one who sweeps the church?" Dad tests us, trying to help us remember. "No, he's the pastor at Faith Center, isn't he?"

"We went to his house," Heidi recalls.

"That's right" Dad turns to Shaun. "Hey, bud, what did *you* see today?"

"Cows and pigs," Shaun mumbles.

Of all the sights we passed at the market, my little brother remembers the animals at the butcher shop. He doesn't often cry or show pain, but he feels deeply for living things. That same passion comes out as he and my sister follow Dad in song, belting words into the microphone: "Blessing and honor and glory be Thine..."

I can't compete, so I listen. Heidi and Shaun's voices make me happy.

~ ~ ~

Shaun

Trouble awaits us as our team piles back into our truck the next day, Faroe and Dad in the cab, the rest of us wedged into the back. It's cramped here, barely any room between us and the roof. My bedding is level with one of the truck's windows, and through it I watch the city fade as our truck grinds eastward.

It's mid-November. At a petrol station in Ankara, Faroe shoves his hands into his mechanic overalls and fields questions about the gathering storms.

"Snow coming," he mutters. "In the mountains."

"Least our truck's reliable," Dad says. "A diesel's a good engine."

"Bad roads. Cliffs and ice. No guardrails."

Dad's eyes flicker my way. "Okay, so we'll have to hurry instead and beat the weather. I'll take shifts through the night. The real problem might be our weight."

"Seven tons," Faroe says. "This means good traction."

I tug on Dad's pants. "How far is India?"

"Weeks away, bud. If we're lucky. We've still got fifteen hundred kilometers to Tehran and another three or four thousand from there through the Khyber Pass."

"We don't need luck," Mom says, joining the group. "God will go before us, just as He did with the Israelites out of Egypt. Now back into the truck, Shaun. I have peanut butter sandwiches waiting."

"Thanks, Linda." Dad gives her a wink.

Nobody can predict just how bad the road will be, a winding, climbing trail between the Pontic Mountains on the north and the Taurus Mountains on the south. The coming blizzard will turn this usual three-day section of dangerous road into a two-week struggle to survive.

When we take off, Eric sits beside me, cross-legged on his sleeping bag and lost in a book. His head brushes the truck's roof as he reads and chews on a fingernail.

"You're doing it again," Mom chides him. "You're biting down to the nub."

"I am not. I'm fine."

Eric's not the only one with a nervous habit. I pluck my own hand from my mouth. I like sucking on fingers, especially when I don't have my silky blanket to rub.

"If it helps you, just sit on your hands," Mom suggests to Eric. "There are germs under your nails and you'll get sick if you're not careful. That's why *warshing* is so important." She pronounces it the way her Pennsylvanian grandparents did.

Eric seizes on this. "It's not warshing. It's washing."

Heidi sits up in her sleeping bag. "Mommy, I need to wash my hair."

"Showers will have to wait till Tehran," Mom says. "Still a couple days away."

I pluck at Eric's sleeve and gesture out the window. Glad for the diversion, he crawls over and we stare out, shoulder to shoulder, at a pair of mangled vehicles. One car is on its side like a beetle, oil and gas oozing onto the rocks. A group of men in loose wool pants and hats rock the car until it thuds back down in a cloud of dust. There aren't any cheers or high fives. They act like this is routine.

Eric puts his arm around me. "Don't worry. Dad's a safe driver."

"And Faroe," I say.

Darrell, our team leader, likes to joke and make his ventriloquist dummies talk, with their flapping mouths and jerky eyes. Faroe's the one I trust, though. He doesn't say much. There's a verse Dad quotes about being swift to hear and slow to speak. I take that to heart. The less people talk, the more I believe them when they do.

I start fidgeting. "Mommy, when're we going to get out?"

She grins and says, "Looks to me like someone has ants in his pants."

"I don't have ants in my pants."

"Mommy," Heidi jumps in, "I miss Uncle Paul and Aunt Val. Are they really going to meet us in India? That's what they said, right?"

"If the *Logos* drops anchor there, I'm sure we'll see them, but we will be up in the north. You remember the pictures I showed you of the Taj Mahal? We might get to go there. Wouldn't that be fun? Where we'll be staying in Ajmer, you will have a yard to run around in and you'll probably see monkeys too."

I squirm on my bed, trying to get comfortable. "I want another trike," I say.

"Well, Shaun, you pray about that, okay? Who knows what'll happen? We'll have lots of work to do and there's never a dull moment serving Jesus."

Eric and Heidi seem to eat this up. Not me. This is a dull moment. What is she talking about? At this rate, I'll be four by the time we get to India.

Outside, the clouds darken.

9

Eric

The temperature drops. Our Bedford trucks rumble onto the mountain fringes. The views turn charcoal-gray, and my nose nearly freezes to the glass. I pull back. My siblings and I burrow under blankets, our breath visible in the cold.

The engine whines. Gears crunch. And still we climb.

We left Ankara yesterday and haven't seen another city for hours. I have to use the toilet, but I've learned to hold it. With two vehicles and sixteen people on this trek, I don't want to be the one who slows things down.

"Are you okay, honey?" Mom asks, recognizing the look. "Dad and Faroe will switch driving soon. It won't be much longer."

Our headlights weave through the gathering darkness. Snowflakes appear, drawing us to the windows, and I entertain thoughts of sleds and ice skates, just like back in Vienna when we played on the frozen Alte Donau.

We pull over at the next turnout and I pee against the mountainside. Snow tickles my nose. I scoop up a handful and touch it to my tongue.

"Hello," a voice calls from my right. When Darrell appears on my left, I realize he's used ventriloquism to trick me. "Just don't eat the yellow snow," he chortles.

Dad smiles and points at the truck. "Better climb back in, buddy. Faroe needs some rest and it's my turn behind the wheel. We've got a long night ahead."

"Dad, you'll freeze up there."

"Keeps me from falling asleep. Anyway, Faroe and I have been driving in our sleeping bags. I can still work the pedals with my feet. In you go, Eric."

By daybreak, the deep valleys below are blanketed in white. Dad and Faroe alternate between sleeping and driving, never turning off the engine. Peaks and ridges hem us in. Wind blasts through the vehicle every time the rear door slides open for toilet stops and driver changes. We dip through rustic villages. Tires shift on slick spots before gripping the road again.

Mom helps us safely down to the pavement during our next stop. She is not about to leave us alone near these precipitous drop-offs.

"Eric," she whispers. "Eric, can you...?"

I see her wobble on her feet and grab at the air. She faints, crumpling beside the truck. The altitude and sub-zero weather are too much for her. She regains consciousness in Dad's lap, with him smoothing her long hair. I'm worried about her.

When I wake the next morning, it is still dark. We later learn it's twenty degrees below zero. My teeth chatter so hard I think they'll break. My three-year-old brother wears a dazed look beside me. My sister's eyes are closed, her lips purple.

"Heidi, can you hear me?" I croak.

She doesn't answer. There is frost on her eyebrows.

"Heidi?" I try again. "Should I get a hot-water bottle?"

She whimpers, then sits up.

That's when we realize just how far the temperature has plummeted.

~ ~ ~

Heidi

Jolted from my dreams by my brother's voice, I sit up. Pain shoots through my skull and a sticky substance drips down my forehead. "Mommy!" I cry out.

A flashlight blinds me and an audible gasp escapes my mother's lips. Her hands clamp around both sides of my jaw. "Don't move," she says. "What'd you do."

My head throbs and tears stream down my face.

Why's it hurt so bad? I wonder. What's wrong?

"Jesus, help us," Mom gasps. She knocks on the metal wall between us and the cab. "Mark! Mark, I'm going to need some help in here."

The brakes screech, the rear door slides open, allowing gray light and bitter wind inside, and my father's shadowy figure appears. Along the ribbed truck's roof, icicles glisten, formed by condensation from our breath during the night. They look deadly and strangely beautiful, like something from a Narnia book.

"It's her head," Mom says. "An icicle is lodged in her scalp."

"What do you *mean*? No, that's impossible."

"Listen to me, Mark. She sat straight up into it and it's not good. We need something to stop the bleeding while I pull this thing out."

"What, are you *kidding*? No, no, no." Grabbing a cloth, he scrambles up.

I feel myself growing dizzy and my eyes began to close.

"Heidi, sweetie, keep them *open*. You *need* to stay awake."

Dad's strong arms wrap around me and I pry my eyelids open. Mom's hands move to the top of my head. Excruciating heat radiates through my skull as she tugs the ice free. She applies the cloth to the wound, and my agony turns into screams.

"Jesus, help Heidi," Mom prays. "Seal this wound. We need you."

I am trying to obey my dad, but my eyelids are weighty. My mom's hands support the weight of my head while my dad keeps my body upright.

Prayers and whispers and people.

Movement. Darkness. Stabs of light.

I feel as though someone is hammering on my head. The pounding won't stop. I am still blubbering. Everything whirls around me and I yearn for peaceful escape.

Mom intercedes for me using her spiritual language. She's told us the Holy Spirit can pray through us when we don't know the words to say and this will strengthen our faith. As mysterious as it sounds, the soothing vowels and consonants wash over me. Other voices swell in unity, penetrating my haze:

"Move the flashlight closer. Look, the bleeding has stopped."

"Clean up the blood."

The intensity recedes to a dull ache, unbearable heat replaced with welcome coolness.

"Is that a scab?"

"Sure looks like it. It seems to be closing up."

"Thank you, Lord. Help there be no permanent damage."

The amens continue through another round of prayers.

"Can I go back to sleep now, Daddy?" I ask.

His embrace tightens. "You might want to stay up a little longer, sweetie."

"Maybe we can read a story now," Mom says. "Would you like that? How about *Babar Loses His Crown*? It's one of your favorites."

I nod. "Yes, please, and can I have some water? I'm really thirsty."

"My little princess," Dad says, "you can have *whatever* you want."

My scalp will bear a scar into adulthood. Under normal circumstances, such an injury takes months to heal, with the possibility of permanent damage. Some will say the cold slowed the bleeding and closed the wound. It is possible. Others call it a miracle, a speeding up of the natural healing process—a description which certainly fits. All I know is, the restoration happens within minutes and is confirmed by multiple witnesses.

~ ~ ~

Eric

Heidi feels better, but Mom faints a second time. Doctors later say it is triggered by bad circulation from a bout with rheumatic fever years before. To add to our fears, both Bedfords trucks begin stalling sporadically. Every ten to twenty kilometers or so, the diesel turns gummy and stops flowing through the lines.

"How's it even possible?" Dad asks our mechanic.

"Diesel. Sub-zero." Faroe shrugs. "It is normal."

"What do we do?"

Faroe lights a blowtorch. In wool cap, coat, and coveralls, he slides beneath the truck and runs the flame along the metal tank to warm the fuel. Dad has taught us to keep fire away from gasoline, so this diesel-thawing process terrifies us.

Raised on the Faroe Islands between Norway and Iceland, Faroe seems impervious to the cold. Where others can barely endure thirty seconds outside, he is exposed for minutes at a time, risking frostbite, knowing he'll repeat the task a half hour later. He does this for hours on end. Without him, we would be trapped forever in the Turkish mountains, statues of ice, like victims of the White Witch's wand.

The journey is tedious, three days, then four. We seem to get nowhere. Ice forms on the road's tight turns and inclines, further reducing speed.

We kids cry quietly under our blankets. Mom is sickly, her lips cracked and bleeding. We are numb to the marrow in our bones, too miserable to talk, sing, color, or play games of I Spy. Even reading is hard, with my eyeballs cold in their sockets.

In the cab, Dad is much colder. He is layered in sweaters and coats, cocooned in the sleeping bag, but he still needs his hands and feet to function.

A flat tire means yet another stop. Dad flashes his lights at the truck ahead, and both vehicles nudge up against the mountain. Traffic is minimal here, but the men are about to change a tire and there is a cliff on the other side of the road. Dad slips on ice, gets his footing, and opens the back door. We huddle deeper in our blankets. Darrell tugs a spare tire from the bottom of the supply pile, another man grabs a jack and tire iron, and Faroe fires up his blowtorch.

Mom and we three kids stare out the back door. Along this bend in the road, pebbles are all that stand between the pavement and nothingness.

The truck lurches on the jack. Huge tires are swapped around. The chassis settles back down and metal screeches in thin air as lug nuts go back on. Almost done. I've watched them do this before and imagine every maneuver.

The skid backward is gradual. Only a meter or so, at first.

Dad barks at Faroe to get out from underneath. He and the other guys throw themselves against the back bumper, trying to stop any further retreat. Darrell hops into the cab, revs the engine, and puts it into gear. Instead of pushing the vehicle up the incline, the tires spin on the ice, and the rear slides sideways.

We are slipping faster now. Mom's face turns ashen.

"Try again," someone yells.

Though the engine revs and the tires whir furiously, none of it works. The ice slickens beneath the rubber, creating a chute toward the drop-off. The men all push, leaning hard, trying not to fall beneath the tires. We children are trapped inside with all the food, the bedding, the supplies—and our sickly mom.

"Lord, help," someone cries out. "We need you!"

The truck still skids backward, seven tons of gross vehicle weight. A handful of exhausted men jump aside, unable to defeat the laws of physics and gravity.

One of them calls up to us. "Kids, hurry down. We'll get you out."

Heidi says she's too scared and Shaun doesn't make a sound. Deciding to set the example, I scramble down the boxes, ready to take the man's hand. As the truck gains momentum, he reaches for me and misses. He yells at me to jump, but all I see is that nothingness drawing nearer. My thoughts and reactions turn to mush.

"Dear Jesus," my mom croaks, "put your angels all around us."

"Jesus," others echo.

The truck's rear end dangles over the edge, giving us views of treetops, mist, and crags far below. We will die in free fall. Only seconds away.

The diesel roars again and belches exhaust. Suddenly, the tires claw and find unlikely purchase on the pebbled roadside. Like a bull pawing the ground, the vehicle shudders, stops, then makes a charge up the grade. Cries of relief are followed by opened and slammed doors, the men throwing themselves into the cab. Dad launches himself through the back, pulls down our door, and gathers us on top of the bedding. His hands are bone-white, and ice crystals glisten in his hair.

"I just watched everything I love almost slip away," he cries, pulling us into a family embrace. His eyes meet each of ours. "I love you, Shaun. I love you, Heidi. I love you, Eric. You all mean the *world* to me, I hope you know that." Gently, he pulls Mom closer. "Linda, I love you. If there's such a thing as miracles, we just saw one."

"He gives His angels charge over us," she responds.

"He did *something*, alright. I was sure you were all goners."

~ ~ ~

I believe it is divine intervention. I'm even willing to call it a miracle.

This doesn't mean all our prayers are suddenly answered and our troubles disappear. In fact, the next day we have a head-on collision while

Darrell is behind the wheel. We are close to Ağri, ready to call it a night, and neither vehicle is going fast on the slippery pavement. It is nobody's fault, just two drivers floundering in darkness and snow. No one is badly hurt, but our radiator is *kaput*, which forces us to hunker down in this eastern outpost.

An accident, that's all it is. Things happen, plain and simple.

But why didn't the angels who stopped us from going over a cliff also protect us from a collision? Were they tired? Or just busy elsewhere? Shaun and I earlier saw the burnt-out hulls of vehicles. Sometimes people crash and die. Or get sick and waste away. If there's heavenly intervention for some, why not for others?

At almost seven years old, these deeper issues lodge in my brain. When and where does God work? Why and why not?

Like Jacob with the angel, I start wrestling with the questions.

I probably always will.

PART 2

RUNNING ON FUMES

Who will I be
when I have nothing else to hold on to?

Henri J. M. Nouwen

Eric, Dad, Heidi, Mom, Shaun, Darrell, Faroe w/7-ton truck in Zaventem

Shaun in floaties, Eric diving in Tehran pool

Eric, Heidi, Shaun at northern Indian home

Dad developing stress sores in India

10

Heidi

It is early December. Dad tells the OM team we'll need replacement parts and the quickest way to get them is by placing a collect call from Ağrı, Turkey, to the Bedford factory in England. Darrell lurches the truck into town, down a dirt road to a hotel. While we check in, our mechanic dials from the lobby phone.

"Yes," Faroe says. "Yes... hoses and clamps... Thank you."

We are all anxious for a timeline.

"One week," he tells us after hanging up. "Maybe two."

Dejected, the single women and single men file into separate rooms. Our family takes a third room. Darrell's family—he, his wife, and his ventriloquist dummies—take the fourth. The shared toilet and sink are located at the end of a long hallway, a bit of a hike for my little legs.

We have a late lunch at a hole-in-the-wall place, with exotic food and music. Dad savors the Turkish coffee. It looks like black sludge, but it smells good. The Americans in our group talk about missing Thanksgiving, and my mouth waters as they describe pumpkin pie topped with whipped cream. I love whipped cream.

Later, Mom brings almonds and hazelnuts to our room for us to munch on while we study. She says mechanical delays are no excuse for skipping school.

The first night at the hotel, a bloodcurdling scream from the distant bathroom awakens us. Our single guys explode into the hallway and rescue one of our single women from an ambush by local men. She has red hair like our mom, which we find out is highly coveted here. The male team members decide the females can no longer go anywhere unattended.

I fold my arms and pout. "Why do Eric and Shaun get to do whatever they want? I can't even go out of our room."

"We should be thankful," Mom tells me. "It's for our safety."

"What if I want to take a shower? Do I still have to wait till Tehran."

"Sweetie, be patient. Daddy and I have plans to take you somewhere special tomorrow."

My mood brightens. "Does it have a bathtub?"

"Even better."

Turkish bathhouses are called *hammams*, and the one in Ağrı is elaborate, a huge marble bathing pool with gold-covered faucets and showers. The men head off to their own area, the women to another. The colors in this place are as varied and vivid as the water options. There are steam baths, ice baths, and mineral baths. I think of Queen Esther in the Bible and I feel pampered.

"Mark, that was amazing," Mom exclaims as we return to the hotel, her thick hair still wrapped in a towel. "First a luxurious bath, then a massage. I've never felt so relaxed."

Dad huffs. "I could do without the karate chops they inflicted on me."

"Karate chops?"

"And they call that a *massage*. Then I was offered a shave by some guy with a blade and leather strop. No, thank you. It wasn't just for the face, if you catch my meaning. The nuts? *C'mon*. Talk about too close for comfort."

Eric looks up from his book. "Mom, those hazelnuts were really good."

"Sure," Dad agrees, "the nuts were good. And I'd like to *keep* mine, thank you very much."

Mom wears a pained expression. "Honey, there are little ears listening."

~ ~ ~

Ten days later, the Bedford parts arrive. From the warmth of the hotel lobby, we watch Faroe work in the courtyard. He secures the radiator behind the front grill, attaches the hoses, and tightens the clamps. Everyone's anxious to leave since the weather is turning. Our mechanic finishes up and tops off fluids. Our parents shuffle us to the doors as team members heft belongings back to the trucks.

Darrell whispers, "Don't look behind us."

In a pretense of kneeling to tie a shoe, Dad eyes the men gathered with rocks and clubs at the courtyard entrance. "Not good," he says. "That's our only way out."

A chill runs down my neck. Are they waiting for us?

"We'll have to make a run for the trucks," Darrell says, "to protect the women and children. I already paid at the desk."

"Okay, good." Dad is in full control. "Linda, keep your hair covered with the hat I gave you, and once you're all in the truck, pull the doors down as quickly as you can. Eric, use your body to block Heidi from sight, you understand me?"

My brother nods. My heart is thumping.

Dad gives me a reassuring wink. "Now... *go.*"

Our dash to the vehicle feels like a race through sinking sand. No matter how fast my legs move, I don't seem to get anywhere. The mob near the entrance comprehends our plan and sprints toward us. Shadowed by the males on our team, the single women leap into the back of one truck. Mom, Shaun, and Darrell's wife hurry to the other. Eric shields me all the way and we arrive right behind them. As soon as we climb up, Mom yanks down the door. We are safe for the moment, huddled in our cave.

We hear Dad and Darrell jump into the cab, locking themselves in with Faroe. The newly repaired engine roars to life, then dies.

The mob is right outside. They pry at the door.

Mom and Darrell's wife stand on top of the interior handles.

Dad tries the engine again. Like my heart, it falters. Terrified, I crawl to our bedding on top and peek out the window. Men circle our truck, banging clubs against the sides. They can't get in, Mom assures us, but she is trembling. The men drop their weapons and begin rocking the vehicle in an attempt to tip us over.

The engine roars again.

Please, Jesus. My pulse pounds in my ears. Please.

Our truck lurches forward, shedding attackers who fall to the ground. Some scream, shaking their fists. A few give chase, throwing rocks. A large one hits with a heavy thud and causes me to jump back into the blankets as we speed away.

The next hour is as silent as the attack was deafening.

~ ~ ~

Once again, Faroe crawls beneath the diesel tanks with his faithful blowtorch. Dad lifts the door high enough to join Eric at the back and together they pee off the bumper. Shaun refuses to join in, afraid of being seen.

"Watch, buddy," Dad says, chuckling with Eric, "the pee freezes before hitting the ground. If you wiggle it a little, it creates a layered effect."

Fascinated, I scramble from my sleeping bag.

"No, Heidi, you wait until they're finished," Mom says.

"When will I be able to use a toilet? I really have to go."

"It's too cold for a princess," Dad says, coming back for me. "You have to bundle up. Here, put on this hat. Wrap some scarves around your neck and your face. *There* you go. You ready?"

"Mm-hmm."

He hurries me outside, holding me close to his chest for mutual warmth. He points. "You see that over there, way off in the distance? That's Mt. Ararat, a dormant volcano and the highest mountain in Turkey. It's mentioned in the Bible. Do you remember why, Heidi?"

I squint through my layered aperture. Even from here, I can tell the mountain is big and wide, cloaked in snow, with clouds scraping the double-crested peak. "Is that where Noah's Ark landed after the Flood?"

"You got it. I'm impressed."

"Is it still up there?"

"Some people think so. We don't know for sure. Here's a good spot." He sets me down around a bend in the road, sheltered from the icy wind and the view of the trucks. He turns away.

I squat carefully and do my business. "All done."

Dad scoops me into his arms again.

"Look," I say, pointing up. "It's like the moon on the Turkish flag."

"A crescent moon. Mom's been teaching you guys a lot, hasn't she?"

As we near the truck, I note the big dent in the side panel and recall the thud of the striking rock. I burrow in closer to my dad. That dent is a permanent reminder of something ugly and I have questions I don't know how to ask.

Dad props me inside the truck, then jumps in beside me. "Hey, hey, everything okay."

I shrug.

He closes the door. "You still thinking about those men today?"

I nod.

"Well, listen, they're long gone."

"Why were they chasing us? They were yelling."

Mom joins our conversation. "Sometimes," she says, "men want what they don't have. Since most women in Turkey have dark hair, those men liked the way our lighter hair looked. In the moment, it made them dangerous."

"I didn't like it."

"Neither did I, sweetie. But we know God still loves those men, doesn't He? Even you and I can be dangerous when we let our own desires take control. We can cut others down with just our words."

"We all wrestle with different things," Dad says. Then a shadow passes over his face and his gaze drifts off. "If we're not careful, our desires can lead us to hurt even those we love the most."

It'll be years before I recognize this as a confession. He is a man still running from his past. In the moment all I know is, he's my daddy and I love him. I have no reason to start questioning him and a thousand and one reasons to trust him. Even later when this trust is broken, I will still hold onto the fact he loves me. Most men see me as something to possess and do with as they will. They do not see me as my dad does, as a treasured princess.

~ ~ ~

Before bed, my parents thank God for our safety and pray for sweet dreams.

"Love you, cutie." Mom kisses me before climbing under her own covers.

"You know what these are?" Dad rubs his nose against mine. "Eskimo kisses. Eskimos live in places even colder than this, so they get all wrapped up for protection, covering even their lips. Touching noses, that's how they connect."

"Eskimo kisses." I giggle. "They feel funny, Daddy."

"Well, 'a merry heart does good like medicine...' That's straight out of God's Word."

"Do I have to take medicine?"

"You just keep laughing," he says. "I love you, Heidi. Goodnight."

11

Eric

By the time our trucks reach Iran, Belgium seems a world away. Stuck in this diesel-belching truck, we still have a long way to go before reaching India. I turned seven a week ago, in Ağri, and my parents apologize now for there being no celebration. With sixteen team members, things got lost in the shuffle. I tell them it's okay.

As we roll into Tehran, our whole group is sniffly and feverish.

While fighting the flu, I gather more postal stamps for my collection. This is the land of the Persian Empire. I love stamps with pictures of the Shah, his tanks, and camouflaged jets. My dad explains how the Shah helped bring this Muslim nation into the modern age, but some don't trust his ties to the U.S. I notice many Westerners here living in fancy homes. They work in the oil industry. They smoke, go to movies, and drive American muscle cars, such as the Mustang Mach 1.

Mach 1 is the speed of sound. Are Mustangs even faster than Porsches?

Once our group is done with the flu, we travel from Tehran to Shiraz, where we visit the Vakil Mosque with its carved pillars and ornate designs. It's a rare tourist detour for us, and a few of our team members insist we are dishonoring God by praising such profane artistry. My parents want to stay but don't argue the point.

This confuses me. Is it wrong for people to make something so beautiful? Isn't God the one who gives us our talents?

I catch up with Dad. "Why can't we stay in Iran?"

"What about India, bud? We're going to live in the north, in the land of kings. You will absolutely *love* it there."

If Dad says it, I believe it, and I dutifully climb back onboard. I realize, of course, we'll face more troubles en route, but I have no idea they will include bites, stings, and gunshots. And I certainly don't expect the trials awaiting our family when we reach our destination. Every superhero wrestles through a dark night of the soul, and for our dad this will happen in India.

~ ~ ~

Heidi

Afghanistan is just ahead. As our truck nears the Taybad border crossing in early afternoon, we overhear our team members talking of a recent political coup and of a *New York Times* article which describes the country as, "moving at a hesitant, almost grudging, pace into the twentieth century." My brothers and I aren't sure what a coup is, but we do notice all the grownups are on edge.

I shift onto my side. "Mommy, why's everyone being so quiet?"

"Things are uncertain in Afghanistan right now. They're almost medieval."

"Evil is bad," Shaun says, trying to touch the ceiling with his feet.

"We don't want anything to do with evil," Mom agrees. "But medieval is the word for a period in history. According to the news, going into Afghanistan right now is like going back in time."

Eric listens, biting at his thumbnail.

I squint into pale sunlight as we arrive. We've been to plenty of borders before and our Iranian departure should go smoothly. The entry into Afghanistan is the real test. My eyes are glued to the window.

Our truck halts. Seconds later, an illegal refugee sprints toward us from the Afghan side of the border and ducks under a cross-arm. Iranian guards yell for the man to stop. When he fails to comply, they pursue and tackle him to the ground. Blood pools beneath his head as they beat him senseless, and I shrink back.

This was supposed to be the safe side. Is this my first glimpse of medieval?

Dad is up front, I remind myself. He'll get us through this. Even so, I'm nervous as our passports are stamped and we are waved through Taybad to the Afghan checkpoint. I can't see the refugee anymore. For all I know, he's dead. We have now moved into a land of ancient laws and traditions.

In the lane beside us, Afghan guards search a shiny Ford Mustang.

"Another Mach 1," Eric tells me.

These guards wear heavier boots, thick belts, and rifles slung over their shoulders. The British driver of the Mustang, probably an off-duty oil worker, folds his arms, muttering as a pair of soldiers march around his sporty vehicle. One guard narrows his eyes and sniffs the air at the back of the car. This new Afghan regime wants to make a statement, ending Westerners' mad dash to Kabul for drugs.

"Hashish," the guard barks. "Hashish!"

The British man stiffens. "No, actually, that's—"

The guard shouts in Pashto and fires his rifle into the trunk. I'm in shock. I have never heard a weapon go off this close to me and the sound is more primal than I expect. It hurts my ears and rattles my bones. What is going on? Why would someone shoot a car? Later our dad explains to us diesel is the predominant fuel in these parts, and the guard confuses the unfamiliar odor of petrol with that of certain drug components.

The driver freaks out. "Bloody hell, that's petrol! Stop shooting, you imbecile, or you'll incinerate the lot of us."

Whether or not he is allowed to drive through the border in his bullet-pocked car, I don't know. It is our turn for scrutiny, with a separate pair of armed men telling us to get out and unload our trucks for inspection. My brothers and I stand next to Mom. Dad seems loose and relaxed, talking louder than normal, hoping to be understood by the guards. He pleads for leniency and motions to his wife and kids.

The guards' eyes harden. They don't care.

Resigned to their task, our team members stack items one by one on the ground and try to keep things organized, but the soldiers are impatient.

"What's that? What's that?" they demand, poking things with their rifles.

Darrell's ventriloquist dolls are stored in two violin cases.

"What's that?" the younger guard asks, thumping a case.

"A dummy," Darrell explains.

Since the guard's English is minimal, he doesn't think to take offense. He uses his rifle barrel to lift the latches and lid. If he expects a harmless string instrument, he's in for a surprise. He stiffens when he sees a slack-jawed doll staring up at him.

This is a good time, Darrell figures, to lighten the tension and throw his voice, making the dummy talk. The guard jumps back in terror and our leader chuckles. Failing to get the joke, the guard raises his weapon, shouts at the resident of the case, and blows it to smithereens. Bits of hard plastic scatter across the pavement.

I tuck myself behind Dad's legs. Mom is holding my brothers' hands.

Before us, our team leader is no longer laughing.

"Least it was the dummy," Dad says, tight-lipped, "and not *you*, Darrell. What about that guy we saw back there trying to sneak across the border?"

So, I'm not the only one who witnessed the bloody mess.

Our OM leader and the rest of the team cooperate fully after the doll's demise, and the guards stamp our passports. We spend another half hour reloading the trucks in the dark. It's almost midnight when we settle into our hotel in Herat.

"We're not in Kansas anymore," Darrell notes.

~ ~ ~

Despite the confidence we have in God and in Dad, Eric and I are still restless before bed. Shaun is passed out on the floor, sucking on two fingers. Our parents go into the bathroom, their voices low and urgent. Are they arguing? As a rule, they keep their disagreements out of sight and earshot, believing it will cause us kids less stress.

When Dad comes back out, he gives me a wink. "What a day, huh? How're you feeling, little princess?"

I bite my lower lip.

"How about *you*?" he says, turning to Eric.

"Why'd they have to shoot Darrell's dummy?" my brother asks.

"Completely unnecessary, agreed. But *boy*, were you two brave."

We have no context for the things we witnessed today. In trying to escape trouble on one side of the border, the refugee ran into just as much trouble on the other side. And those soldiers, what made them so afraid of a lifeless doll?

Mom explains to us how some people believe if you throw your voice the way Darrell does, you must have a demon living in your belly. This is not what we believe, of course, and according to the Bible, God does not give us a spirit of fear.

"Why don't you two brush your teeth?" Dad says. "I want you to know, your mom and I are proud of how you handled things out there."

We didn't exactly have a choice. We had nowhere to go, nothing to say.

Eric scowls. "It made me angry," he admits.

"Oh, *buddy*, that's understandable. Me, too."

"It made me sad," I say, pursing my lips.

Mom takes my hand. "The best thing we can do, Heidi, is try to love and forgive. It doesn't mean you'll forget what you saw. It was wrong. But so many people have no knowledge of Jesus' love. They are full of anger and guilt." She turns to my brother. "And, Eric, when you get mad back at someone, does it really help anything? No, your lack of forgiveness keeps you trapped in the unpleasant memory."

"What if they did something wrong?"

"Honey, we have to be so careful not to judge others. James 1:20 tells us, 'The wrath of man does not produce the righteousness of God.'"

"Someone should've stopped them from hitting that man on the ground."

"It's no fun feeling helpless, is it?" Dad says.

We brush our teeth. We pray. Eric and I finally fall asleep.

Blood. Demons. Dolls shot full of holes.

My dreams tonight are troubled, punctuated by gunfire in my memories and in the actual city streets below.

~ ~ ~

Eric

Two days later, we drive through Kabul into the Khyber Pass. Steep slopes and sparse terrain dwarf our trucks on either side. Many vehicles go over the cliffs here every year. We stop for hot soup and drinks at a roadside inn, gathering round a long table.

"Listen, bud," my dad says. "You should go use the toilet."

He lets me head off alone, which makes me feel all of seven years old.

When I get back, Dad and Mom are beaming and the group surprises me by singing "Happy Birthday." Even the bearded Afghan men at a nearby table turn and raise their mugs. All this attention makes my cheeks turn warm. An object sits at my place, bundled in old newspaper, Dad's giftwrap of choice. When I peel the paper open, I can't even speak. It's a painted tin car the size of my hand.

I haven't been forgotten, after all.

Shadows turn black in the chasm outside the windows, softened only by smudges of cloud. Inside, a coal fire burns, the lights are dim, the air is smoky—and to me, it's all magical.

12

Shaun

Mom shifts her braided hair over her shoulder and addresses the Pakistani official at the bare wooden table. As usual, her voice is barely more than a whisper, but it's also firm and unwavering, a steel cable wrapped in brushed wool.

"Our visas are good," Mom says. "See, right here."

The man snatches our passports from her, eyeing us kids over his glasses.

I stare right back from our hard chairs across the room.

Eric and Heidi write in their school notebooks, knowing our mom expects their work to be done. I can't sit still. It's much warmer down here at the base of the Khyber Pass. After our six weeks in icy weather, this abrupt heat causes beads of sweat to run down Dad's forehead into his dark sideburns. He stands at an open window, profiled by the sun. He says we're going to the city of Peshawar.

A buzzing sound draws my attention to the upper corner, where a clump of dry dirt clings to the wall. Even if Eric and I had a mud fight, I couldn't throw it that high. The buzzing continues. From a hole in the dirt, two wasps crawl into view.

Dad notices the look on my face and follows my gaze. "I haven't seen those for a few months, not in the cold. Those are mud wasps."

"Do they sting?"

"Why, Shaun? Do they scare you?"

Even though they fascinate me, I'm gripping the edges of my chair.

"Listen, bud, it's better to stay relaxed. When you're afraid, your body releases a chemical that makes you seem like a threat. That's when they want to attack."

One of the wasps appears to be listening. No sooner has the warning been issued, it shoots down with its curved abdomen and stinger. Mom is still chatting with the official, unaware of the trouble. The wasp aims straight for me and hovers.

Yep, I am frightened. I can't help myself.

Eric and Heidi gawk, scattering papers as they scoot away.

The wasp drops to my forearm, its sting coming hard and fast. Just as quickly the creature is gone, back to its corner, to its hole. What a coward. Already, the venom is spreading hot, hot, hot beneath my skin. It hurts and I'm embarrassed as a tear wells in my eye. Stupid, stupid. Don't be weak. I focus instead on the swollen wound, fascinated by the damage a single wasp can inflict.

Even more vivid than the pain is the realization my dad was absolutely right.

He sweeps me up in his arms. "Oh, Shaun, are you *okay*? I'm so sorry. It's my fault. I should've *never* said a word. C'mon, let's put some mud on it to draw out the poison." He rushes me outside and spits into the dirt. "Please forgive me, Shaun."

What do I need to forgive him for? He was right, wasn't he?

He spreads the wet dirt on my wound and it dries quickly in the arid conditions. I don't understand how this is supposed to help, but if he knows about wasps and fear, he must know about poison and mud.

"You're smart," I say. "You tried to tell me."

"Which probably made you even more afraid. You're a brave little kid, you know that? Or maybe *not* so little, the way you handled that sting."

"It only got me once."

"See there? See, that's what I'm talking about."

He pulls me in tight and I clasp my arms around his neck. This is a bonding moment I will never forget, his wisdom highlighted by my dull, throbbing pain.

~ ~ ~

Eric

Peshawar is a dangerous place, with Pakistani men and teens toting semi-automatic rifles in the streets. Dad and I are on foot, passing storefronts where kids clean and reassemble AK-47s and cheap knockoffs. My dad seems confused. I know he wants to tell others about new life in Christ, but it's death which seems prominent here.

"Not death," a young man tells us on the street. "Honor. If someone kills a member of my family, I am obligated to avenge the death. This is how it works."

"I don't understand." Dad shakes his head. "If you kill someone, doesn't that keep the cycle going? Now they have to kill one of your family members, then you have to kill one of theirs, and so on and so on. When does the killing *end?*"

"The end is not important. Honor is important."

"Even if it means more death?"

The man hefts his weapon. "Yes." No hesitation.

Dad tries again. "You know, Jesus was more than a prophet. He is God's Son, the Lamb of God, and He died to free us from all this hate."

The man bristles. "Then your God must avenge His Son's death."

"It was His Father who *allowed* Him to die. For *you.* For *me.* He died and came back to life, ending this need for vengeance. He told us to *love* our enemies."

"This is impossible."

"With God, nothing is impossible," Dad declares.

The young man is unconvinced and I see my dad's spiritual bravado falter. Sure, he can rattle off Christian answers, but what if nobody's even asking the questions? What if they've accepted life just the way it is?

~ ~ ~

Our stop in Peshawar is supposed to last only a few days. This timeline is undone by what happens to me during our stay with Dr. Fields.

Dr. Fields, a British man who stands gangly and thin as Narnia's Puddleglum, hosts our family at his house while our other team members settle into Christian homes scattered about this Muslim enclave. It's nice for our family to be in a place with toilets and running water. This is luxury after months in a truck.

"You'll keep the gates locked, won't you?" Dr. Fields asks our parents. "No one in or out while I'm at university."

"Oh, what a glorious treat to be here," Mom says.

"We'll keep it all to ourselves," Dad responds. "What about your German shepherd? All three of our kids love animals. Is he safe?"

"Ah, he's a bit testy, that one. A guard dog. He's been known to nip, especially at children. If any of them wish to pet him, I really ought to be present."

"Good to know."

While my siblings nap, Mom lets me into a backyard protected by walls higher than my head. I'm happy to play alone. I carve roads in the dirt, then race my tin car along them. I wear corduroy pants and a gray T-shirt. My skin tingles in the heat.

The moment Dr. Fields returns from work and the gate creaks open, the German shepherd sounds a welcome from the other side of the house. I trot around the corner. The dog is on his chain, shaded beneath the overhang.

"Would you like to pet him?" asks Dr. Fields.

He crouches beside his guard dog, a hand resting on his head as I approach. The dog's ears are straight up, his nose pointed my way. Shaun may be the animal whisperer, but I also care for all creatures great and small and expect my love to be reciprocated. Even the meanest cat or dog just needs to know someone cares.

Kneeling, I face the German shepherd. He is nearly as tall as I am, and I notice his nose is dry. I let him sniff my hand before stroking his head. Admiring his black and tan fur, I look up—and our eyes lock.

His lips curl, his fangs drop into view, and he snarls.

Before Dr. Fields can grab hold of the chain, the dog attacks. His jaws clamp onto my face, canines hooking into my left eyebrow and right nostril. I tear away, scrambling backward on my bottom.

He comes after me. Spittle flies. Blood is spilling over my eye. I sprint around the house before hearing the poor dog choke as the chain snaps him back.

"Dad," I yell. "Daddy, the dog bit me."

I burst through the door with Dr. Fields close behind. Red droplets splatter the entryway tiles and I search my dad's eyes as he rushes from his bedroom. Though even-keeled, he is alert and full of concern. Behind him, Mom's hand is over her mouth, and Dad tells her to keep Heidi and Shaun away while he takes care of this.

"He bit my nose," I squeal. "I was just petting him."

"I'll fetch the bandage strips," Dr. Fields says, hurrying off.

"He certainly did." Dad leads me into the toilet. "Don't look in the mirror."

"Why not?"

"Well, you looked awfully funny the way you came in here, red all over your face like a clown. I just can't have you *laughing* in such a serious moment."

I grin despite everything.

"Now, sit here by the sink while I clean things up. Does it hurt?"

I nod, more aware each second of the shredded tissue and skin. The water makes me wince and pink liquid swirls down the drain. My T-shirt is dotted with blood stains as dark as mud. Dad prays as he works, conversational in tone. His calm faith infuses me with strength. Once the wound is flushed, he presses a towel to my nose and tells me to hold it to stop the bleeding. He presses another to my eyebrow.

Dr. Fields rejoins us. "We've no bandages, but perhaps this'll do."

"Mercurochrome? That'll work," Dad says. "And electrical tape? Why not?"

He has me lift the towel as he applies drops of cleansing solution. Next, he peels off strips of black tape and tells me to stay very still. With one hand, he pieces together my flaps of hanging skin. With the other, he tapes them back in place. Pain shoves tears to my eyes as he applies four pieces over my nose and on my eyebrow.

"All done, Eric. That should hold till we get you to the hospital."

"What're they going to do to me?"

"At a *clown* hospital, they'd paint a smile back on your face, but at *this* one they'll make sure there's no infection." He pretends to ignore my laughter. "*Very* serious stuff, of course, but with the Good Physician on our side, you'll be A-okay."

Dad and I ride with Dr. Fields to Lady Reading Hospital, where a Pakistani doctor examines the bites. He says my dad's strips of tape are working better than stitches. I should keep them on for the next five to seven days and stay nearby in case there are complications. I'll have scars, but the wounds will heal. He gives me a tetanus shot and I'm done.

I say, "Dad, I was just being nice to the dog."

He lifts his shoulders. "You know, Eric, there are just times when you *can't* win a person or an animal over. You do your best and it still backfires."

"That doesn't happen to you."

"It did just the other day in the street. That young man, remember? I actually wondered if your mom and I made the right decision bringing you kids all this way." Dad swallows hard before his voice finds solid ground again. "But you know, our trust is in the Lord, isn't it? He will never leave us nor forsake us."

I marvel at his composure over the past few hours. Where does he get so much faith? It's as though my dad talks to God and expects an answer...

Unlocked

Eugene, Oregon — 1968-1972

After Mark Wilson lost his job at the grocery store, his faith wavered. He had bills stacking up and he needed to do something. With his inexhaustible desire for knowledge, he also wanted to learn all he could about his Christian beliefs.

"Linda, let's pray," he said. "I want to provide for you and the kids, I do. I just can't stop telling others what Jesus has done for me. You get that, don't you?"

"I'm exhausted," she said. "But as your wife, I will go wherever you go."

"Where does *He* want us to go, that's what I'm trying to figure out."

In the other bedroom, Eric was having alone time on a blanket. Heidi was getting fussy in her crib. The cupboards were mostly bare. Mark and Linda dropped to their knees by the couch and sought God's direction.

Someone knocked at their door.

That was odd. Mark answered at the second knock and found a preacher on the front step, inviting neighbors to come visit his church. Did they have any particular needs? Why, yes, they did. Mark introduced himself, shared his testimony, and explained how desperate he was for guidance.

The man leaned back. "Mark, I'm in no position to play God."

"Aren't you a pastor? Since He sent you here, He must be saying *something*."

"Seems to me you've had a religious conversion experience. Let me ask you this. Have you ever considered going to a Bible college?"

"Are there any in the United States?"

The pastor grinned. "There's one up in Eugene, a day's drive from here."

Within weeks, Mark moved his family to Oregon and found a new job. He enrolled at Northwest Christian College, and when his professor told the story of the prodigal son, Mark fell to his knees in the classroom and sobbed. Linda's depression began to lift. Eric and Heidi got along, except for squabbles over bowls of popcorn.

Shaun was the final addition. The only one actually born in Oregon, he was full of bravado from the get-go, ready to take on the world.

The Wilson family was now complete. They climbed Spencer Butte and watched deer graze near the rhododendron garden at Hendricks Park. They made day treks to the coast, stopped at the Gingerbread Village, visited fish hatcheries, and camped by alpine lakes. Nature was their friend. The kids loved ferns and mushrooms, as well as chipmunks and salamanders. They tramped barefoot through puddles when they could get away with it, and nothing smelled better than fresh rain.

Borrowing the down payment from his father, Mark bought a house in Eugene, on Barrett Avenue. He picked up hitchhikers and handed out cards with his new address, inviting one and all to come over for food, conversation, and a place to crash. With the Jesus Movement in full swing, the Wilsons let their house became a refuge for wayward kids, hippies, drug addicts, and the mentally ill. Dozens gave their lives to God. Many gave up their drugs and alcohol and some went on to become pastors. Eric, Heidi, and Shaun trudged out in their pajamas each morning, never knowing who might be sacked out in the living room.

It was at this house Eric and Heidi downed crackers and grape juice.

Here, Shaun learned to walk and say his first full sentence.

Mark and Linda also began helping at a local church, pastoring teens such as Mike and Debbie Monaghan–who later followed them to Vienna. But the Wilsons were a bit radical for the religious folk. They carried around Bibles, believed every word was true, and prayed in a spiritual language. Well, that was just too much.

The Wilsons were kicked out of the church and ended up at Faith Center, where an intense little man named Roy Hicks, Jr., pastored a ragtag group. When it came to teaching from the Bible, Roy pulled no punches and played no games.

It was the perfect fit.

Mark and Linda especially admired men and women who left their pampered cultures and comfort zones to serve God in other countries. When they read *God's Smuggler*, about a man who secretly delivered Bibles in communist territory, they both felt inspired to do the same.

Mark wondered, though, was he worthy of such a task? What if people knew his secrets? What if they saw his inner struggles? Then again, God was the Father of prodigals, wasn't He? Didn't He work through the worst of sinners?

13

Shaun

Here we are, a young family in India. It's January 1974. Though Dad and Mom work for Operation Mobilisation, they don't have any formal missions training and don't know any local languages. Dad has a few Bible courses under his belt, that's it. Mom now has flowing red hair down to her waist, which she hopes will earn her respect from the Indian women. Our parents have come with big hearts and little else.

We drive for what seems like forever through the Punjab into the state of Rajasthan. It is warm and dusty. Skinny cows walk over cracked earth. Men wear turbans as insulation and the sun's heat radiates through our truck, turning it into a slow-cook oven.

This is India, huh?

We've endured the past three months with India dangled in front of us. We've been promised Ajmer will be a place to stretch our legs and play for days on end. It will be an oasis, with monkeys, sunshine, and yummy drinks called mango *lassis*.

That's what our parents have told us. Well, I have my doubts.

"It'll get better," Mom promises as she fans us with her Living Bible.

My stomach burbles. I'm almost four and just want some food. The other OM team members are also famished.

When the trucks pull over, Darrell and his wife stumble down from the cab, and Faroe looks ready for a cold drink. We're at a restaurant in the middle of nowhere, a mud structure with a canopy stretched over tables and chairs. Crates of empty Coca-Cola bottles stand outside the door. A sign in Sanskrit looks like scribbles to me.

Dad tells us to play while he orders food. "I'm not sure there'll be anything for you three kids here. Mom might have to make you some sandwiches."

"I'm tired of peanut butter," Heidi grumbles.

"I'll see what we can get you guys," Dad says. "As long as it's not too hot."

"We're already hot." Eric fans his neck.

"You can change into shorts to be more comfortable. And I meant spicy hot," Dad clarifies. "We'll make sure it's mild, so you kids don't burn your tongues."

I trust him since he was right about those mud wasps. "We want lots to eat, Daddy. We're hungry." I don't say starving because I know not to exaggerate.

"What about something to drink?" Heidi says.

"Sure thing, princess. I'll grab some Cokes too."

Darrell and the others are already seated. Dad follows. I see him talk to an Indian server, a short woman in a *sari*. Mom owns a bright pink and gold sari. She wears it to fit in, which she says is important since we are the outsiders and not here to change other people's ways. Sounds like *sorry* to me, which I think is funny.

"Here, go play while you wait," she says, tossing down a ball. "Eric, make sure everyone stays close by."

We change clothes, then kick the ball around in the truck's shadows. My brother and sister chase a lizard through the dirt around the tires. Mom seems thankful for the warm weather and at least she isn't fainting anymore. That scares me. I like that Mom never whines, no matter what. Dad calls her resilient.

He returns now, empty-handed. "Sorry, kids, no drinks. You'll be sick as all get-out if I buy them here." Shaking his head, he glances at Mom. "You should *see* it, honey. They're refilling bottles and glasses without even washing them."

"It's simply a matter of education," Mom responds. "In these rural areas, it's doubtful they've ever seen germs under a microscope. I'll tell the kids to warsh up."

I point toward the canopy. "Is that our food?"

An Indian woman catches our eyes, plates in hand, wobbling her head as we rush to a table. She sets things down. She has a kind face with golden-brown eyes.

Mom waits till the woman is gone, then says, "Are you sure it's safe?"

"The kids have been waiting for this, Linda."

We thank the Lord and dive in, knowing this Indian meal will be the first of many to come. No more stale bread and marmalade. Even more thrilling, we can eat with our hands—only with the right hand, though, since the left is unclean. We will do it the way the Indians do, cupping our fingers to shovel bites into our mouths.

"Hubba *hubba*," Dad's eyes widen. "And they call that *mild?*"

Before he can stop us, we each take a bite.

In seconds, my tongue erupts as though stung.

Despite the mildest local flavoring, the Tandoori chicken is spicier than anything we have ever tasted. I spit mine out, blinking against the pain. Eric and Heidi jump up and run off, tears spurting from their eyes. Of course, nothing is chasing them, but if they think they are running from wasps, I can't blame them.

Why did our dad tell us it wouldn't burn our tongues?

While Mom tries to calm my brother and sister, Dad decides to keep eating and claims his childhood experiences in Mexico will give him greater tolerance. "Plus," he says, "these spices'll kill any germs."

Not this time, though. Not here.

Our truck is lumbering again through the desert when the effects of the meal hit our dad. Beads of sweat pop out on his forehead, and his nose drains. This isn't the worst part. He grabs a roll of toilet paper and disappears around the side of the vehicle to deal with his other problems. Ten minutes later, he makes another stop. And another. It's pathetic, and he isn't the only team member who has trouble.

"Maybe it's good we spit out the food," Eric comments.

"Daddy was right," I say. "It's not for kids."

~ ~ ~

From New Delhi, our team splits in various directions. It is the last time we will ever see Darrell, Faroe, or the others. Why do we even waste time making friends?

As our family travels through Jaipur toward Ajmer, dead pigs catch my attention with their bloated bodies and their legs in the air. Nearby, people stand in bus-stop queues while others sip milky *chai* at open-air cafes. None of them seem to notice the carcasses. Dogs and goats mill about, and water buffalo cool themselves in ponds of dark-brown water. It's a lot to assimilate. Nearly impossible to forget.

Some sections of road are also lined with human bodies. Men in turbans stack them onto wooden carts while chanting in their local tongue.

"Are those people dead?" I want to know.

"Dear Jesus," Mom whispers. "The disease and starvation are terrible."

Later, Dad explains that funeral pyres are common here since the soil is hard to dig graves in and since fire burns off disease and infection.

"But where do they go?" I ask. "Do they go to heaven?"

"Did all those bodies scare you?" He wraps an arm around me. "Bud, I'm sorry. That's not something little boys should have to see."

This land we've heard so much about seems like a land of death to me. While my parents believe in Jesus, as do my brother and sister, I'm still not sure what I believe. Maybe I'm too little to know yet. If I can't trust the stuff adults tell me, how can I trust in Jesus? I've never even seen Him.

"Daddy," I say, "if a body's already burned, does it still have to burn in hell?"

His forehead crinkles and his eyes cloud. Whether he is angry or sad, I can't tell. "Where'd you hear about that, Shaun?"

"From the men in our trucks. Is there really a lake of fire?"

"You know I love you, right? I am your father. God's your Heavenly Father and He loves you even more than I do. You don't need to worry, okay?"

My questions are mostly forgotten by the time we reach our destination. With a quarter million people, Ajmer is small by Indian standards but bustling with ox carts, rickshaws, buses, taxis, bikes, motorcycles, animals, and people.

Dusk is upon us and bats track insects through the air. Tree leaves whisper as we turn off Jaipur Road into a walled compound. We pass houses and huts, then stop at a domed earthen structure. Eric, Heidi, and I dash around the place. We find a cracked tennis court with a drooping net. A barren field stretches beyond the dirt road. Inside, high ceilings and stone floors keep things cooler.

The toilet situation is unique. Palm-sized spiders crouch behind the overhead water tank with its rusty chain. When I flush, water sprinkles me from above. *Drip, drip, drip...* Even worse, the plumbing can't handle toilet paper and in standard Indian fashion I'm supposed to wipe myself with my left hand—wipe with your left, eat with your right. Touching a person with your left hand is just plain rude.

Thankfully, Mom doesn't trust my washing abilities. For hygiene reasons, she decides to wipe all three of us kids with her own hand. Even years later when we get annoyed with her, we think back to her sacrifices and all the crap we put her through.

Yuck.

From the Zaventem warehouse to the Domes in Ajmer, we have reached our new house at last. We will live here off and on for the next year.

14

Heidi

In India, we encounter a land of color and contrasts. Brilliant yellow and scarlet hues brighten dreary landscapes. Beggars stand in the shadows of opulent temples, mosques, and shrines. Hindi is spoken everywhere, while Muslims converse in Urdu, and Sikhs in Punjabi. Men wear *dhotis*—loose-fitting, light sarongs—while women drape themselves in elegant saris. Black charcoal is used to make teeth white.

Mom teaches us to evaluate each situation and embrace the good, instead of judging and rejecting.

"It's so important," she urges, "to let Jesus fill us each day with grace."

As the only girl, I notice males are the masters. They converse loudly in market squares, strutting while their wives trail at a respectful distance. If a man rides a donkey, his children walk alongside while his wife carries the firewood. A widow sometimes climbs atop her husband's funeral pyre to die an honorable death.

"The surprising thing," Mom tells me, "is how men here handle the message of Jesus. When they discover He wants them in close relationship with their spouses, they are so joyous. Many of them want to lead their kids with love instead of the rod."

Dad has always been a loving father to us, the man we look up to. Recently, though, the rod has become an option. Spanking, he has decided, is a biblical form of discipline. Eric and I get occasional swats, but Shaun has an attitude and seems to get the brunt of it. Our little brother is like a turtle, so sensitive inside. If the only way to reach him is to break that outer shell, I wonder what it will do to him.

Can a turtle live with a broken shell? Does he go and find a harder one?

~ ~ ~

When Dad brakes our OM vehicle to a halt and starts picking at his forehead, I lean forward and tap my mom's shoulder. "What's wrong, Mommy?"

"We're waiting for a cow. It's lying in the middle of the road."

The creature is chewing her cud. "Can't someone make her move?" I ask.

"Well, sweetie, Hindus believe in something called reincarnation. This cow could be their dead grandmother, so why would they want to upset her?"

Shaun looks perplexed. "The cow is someone's grandma?"

Mom turns. We have no A/C and the temperature is boiling, causing sweat to bead on her face, but she prefers the heat over the cold any day. She says, "Some people think they'll be punished or rewarded in their next life by coming back in a new form. As a toad maybe, or an elephant. Even as a lesser god. This has many of them bound in guilt and fear, while making others feel prideful. It's a system all based around karma."

"Reaping what you sow," Dad comments. "That's what the Bible calls it."

Mom rests her hand on his shoulder. "No matter how many good deeds we do, we cannot save ourselves. Our forgiveness only comes through Jesus."

Dad touches a sore on his cheek, stares off, then bangs his palm on the dash. "*C'mon.* This is a complete waste of time." His eyes are on the obstruction ahead, so I figure this is what he is talking about. I'm too young to fathom the deeper issues he wrestles with, an existential crisis churning at his core.

"You mean, we don't have to do nice things?" Eric says.

"Doing them doesn't make Jesus love us more," Mom clarifies. "We do them because we want to please Him. The problem with karma is, it gives you an excuse to ignore others who are suffering. It must be their fate, just paying for past mistakes."

"What about him?" I gesture to a man beside our vehicle.

Traffic hasn't moved and a gnarled form drags himself by on a wheeled slab of wood. His hands paw the ground. His upper body is bare and skeletal, his torso wrapped in a diaper-like cloth. His legs are scaly, thick as tree trunks.

Shaun lifts his nose over the lip of the open window. "Why's he look like that?"

"He's got elephantiasis," Dad responds. "Tiny worms get under the skin and multiply, making the extremities swell up."

Tears well in my eyes. "But worms don't belong inside a person."

Ahead, the cow rises and saunters into a ditch. There's a rush of commotion now that the road is clear. Weaving through cars, an impatient rickshaw driver nearly knocks the man off his board, and my brothers and I frown at each other. The people in front of us seem more worried about the cow than about this human being contorted in pain.

~ ~ ~

My mind is racing as I watch Mom cook *chapatis* over a fire. The aroma of the Indian flatbread makes my mouth water, but I can't shake the images of the man with the swollen legs. He matters. He deserves love. "Mommy," I say, bouncing on my toes. "I want a whole roomful of chapatis, with mango lassis to wash them down."

"That seems very selfish, honey. Some people have no food at all."

"But in heaven I can share, even with the man we saw today."

"Oh, I see what you're saying." She watches the salted dough bubble, then flips it over. She also heats mild curry for us kids. "I'm sure in heaven you'll have a whole mansion full of chapatis and lassis."

"Then I can share with the whole wide world." I twirl, arms spread wide.

Mom laughs. "Yes, you can. Now please go call your brothers for lunch."

1 medium diced onion	*Slowly stir in 4 cups chicken broth & 2 cups diced, boiled chicken. Simmer 20 minutes. Thicken with flour or cornstarch, if needed. Serve over rice. For beef curry,
1/2 chopped green pepper	
5 cloves garlic or equivalent garlic powder	
*On medium heat, fry ingredients in oil until golden brown, then sprinkle in:	
1/2 teaspoon basil	
1 teaspoon chili powder	use beef & beef broth. For egg curry, use sliced, hard-boiled eggs & chicken broth.
2 teaspoon cumin	
1/2 teaspoon marjoram	
1/4 teaspoon sage or savory, optional	

Eric

Chewing my nails is a habit I cannot break. Between Shaun's fabric fetish and my oral fixation, I'm sure we are candidates for some twisted Freudian diagnoses, but we don't know about Freud yet. It all seems pretty simple, actually. Shaun, a toddler with a topsy-turvy life, holds onto whatever is constant and comforting. And I'm always hungry. Since I don't want to burden my parents for food, the act of chewing serves as temporary relief, whether I'm nibbling on erasers, pencils, or fingernails.

Dad and Mom discuss our habits, I'm sure. They often lie out on a table, watching the burnt-orange sun go down. They talk about the day and various family issues. Recently, their voices have grown more intense. Dad often seems upset. Thankfully, their conversations are interrupted by appearances of monkeys, bats, and camels. Insects are the most common distraction. We kids sleep under mosquito nets.

"Eric, you can't keep biting your nails," my mom tells me one morning as we sweep the communal living area. "You're exposed to trouble every time you go out on the streets, every time the women pinch your cheeks and tug at your hair."

"I just look different. They don't mean anything by it."

"Germs spread, honey, and each time you put your hands near your mouth, you're taking a risk. Let's make a deal. If you can go a full day without biting your nails, I'll let you have a whole mango or papaya just for yourself."

"Can't God protect me?"

"He gives you a *brain*," Dad jumps in, "and expects you to use it. If you know about hygiene and choose to ignore it, well, that's not very smart, is it?"

I try to stop. I do. But anytime I'm playing marbles or jacks with my brother or kicking the ball with our friends around the Domes, I start nibbling again.

One day, a shipment arrives from Vienna. Dad opens the mysterious box and assembles the white metal tubes, wires, and chain. It's a bicycle, he tells us. For all of us kids to share. Mom explains how Debbie Monaghan insisted on sending it, since the neighborhood bullies ruined Shaun's red tricycle.

Shaun tries lifting a leg over the center bar. "It's too big," he says with a frown.

"Try to be thankful," Mom says. "You'll grow into it soon enough."

Even Heidi is too small for the bike, leaving me to ride through the compound gates into the streets of Ajmer. It's a thrill, a sensory overload. My eyes, ears, and nose can barely take it all in. Soon, my hand is near my mouth again.

Later, Mom catches me nibbling at a finger. "You're still doing it, Eric."

I feel guilty. Dirty. I dash outdoors and up the stone stairs to the roof of our house. Heidi and Shaun aren't allowed up here. This is my hideaway. I lean back against the curve of the dome, feeling its warmth through my thin T-shirt. As the sun dips below the mountains, I wipe at my eyes, mad at my mom and at myself.

At seven years old, I have learned to fit in everywhere, knowing I don't truly belong anywhere. I love this country, but if India is to be my lifelong residence, will I ever be seen as a local? I'm neither Hindu nor Muslim. I'm a tall, light-haired, pale-skinned apparition who can't yet speak the language.

Blending in is my goal. I just want to find common ground.

~ ~ ~

As my nail-biting continues, Mom tries positive reinforcement, but I've never been motivated by gold stars on a chart, and as much as I love mangos and papayas, even they aren't incentive enough. After her efforts fail, Dad tries a different tactic.

He calls it negative reinforcement.

I call it hot sauce.

He bastes my fingers in the stuff, staining my fingertips. The local spices burn my hangnails and raw cuticles. My tongue blazes and my eyes water each time I chew. My attempts to wash off the sauce lead him to use thicker applications. All things considered, I don't blame him for thinking it might cure me.

Instead, I develop a love for spicy things and rarely get sick.

Mom figures I've developed a cast-iron stomach during our travels. She calls me her human garbage can. I gobble up the leftovers and always tell her thanks.

Shaun also has a hard time breaking his habit. He sucks on his fingers and fondles any soft material he can find. Unfortunately, he becomes the focus of our dad's simmering frustration and he feels each spanking on a deeply personal level.

What's wrong with Dad, anyway? He looks so thin.

Mom doesn't say a word. She simply tilts her head and squints her eyes. I guess she's trusting Jesus to fix it all.

15

Shaun

It's March, and the days are getting hotter. By the time I finish my breakfast of *aloo paratha*—potato-stuffed chapati—the sun is already baking the earth. I dash outside to play and find Eric in shorts and no shirt standing over a toad. The poor creature looks dead, like a scrap of elephant skin on the ground.

"Tried pouring water over it," Eric says. "It hasn't even moved."

"Maybe it's old."

"Should we put it out of its misery?"

With no idea what he has in mind, I watch him pick up a rock and bring it down on the toad's head. He does this two more times, then begins crying. I am in shock and my stomach churns. I watch my brother hop onto our white bike and pedal away.

We have no indoor showers at the Domes. We stand in our underwear in a basin along the back of the house, using three scoops of cold water as we bathe—one for getting wet and lathering, one for rinsing our hair, and one for rinsing our bodies. Our entire compound relies on water containers filled daily at the community pump.

This morning, Vikay Peter steps into the outdoor basin. We love Vikay. He's one of the single men in the compound and he plays tag and football with us. His broad white smile stands out against deep-brown skin, which results in him being snubbed for coming from southern India. No matter where we go, from Austria to India, people find reasons to look down on those who don't look or sound just like them.

Vikay is lathering and washing up when I hear him shout.

Already unsettled by the toad's death, I run to see what's wrong.

"Out. You are not belonging here," he says, swatting at a yellow-tailed bird. The bird darts about his head. "No, no, you go now. You must be leaving me alone." Another swat catches the bird midair and she tumbles onto the hot dirt. She tries to stand. Her feathers are ruffled, one wing at a strange angle.

Birds are plentiful here, in all shapes and sizes. I don't like to see even one of them hurt. We love animals. Eric was just trying to ease the toad's pain, even if he did the wrong thing. And Heidi cried even harder while playing with a lizard whose tail came off between her fingers. I promised her a new one would grow in its place.

Now it's my turn to watch a living thing suffer.

I drop to my knees beside her. "Hey, little birdie. You're okay." She isn't, though. Her tiny chest is all that moves. "Vikay Peter didn't mean to hurt you. He was just scared, that's all." Vikay is already gone, oblivious. I pet the bird's soft head.

"Shaun!" My dad yanks me up by the arm. "What're you *doing?*"

I dangle beside him, startled.

"You don't *ever* touch a bird, especially if it's sick or dead. Those things're full of disease, you hear me. What're you *thinking*?"

"I wasn't—"

"I *saw* you. Don't you dare lie to me." He plops me down in the basin. "Now clean yourself up and scrub those hands." He makes certain his instructions are followed before marching around to the front of the Domes where people gather for an OM prayer meeting. His pants barely cling to his bony hips.

I shake myself off. Soon, the heat will dry my clothes.

Why'd Daddy yell at me? Eric and Heidi didn't get in trouble for messing with the toad or the lizard. I was helping this dear creature and my dad wouldn't listen.

With sounds of voices and guitars carrying around the property, I go back to the bird. Her chest is no longer moving. Her wings are still. I pluck nearby flowers and sprinkle petals around her. If she dies, I want things to look pretty for her.

Not even sure what I believe, I whisper, "Jesus, you love this bird. Make her all better."

She doesn't move.

"Please, Jesus," I try again. "You did stuff like this in the Bible."

The bird suddenly shakes, catching me off guard. Dirt and petals scatter as she hops up on both legs. She fluffs and sticks out her chest, spreads her feathers. Her little beak points up at me as she tests her wings. Then she flies away. Whether she is healed through my prayers or just needed a few minutes, I don't know. In this moment, though, I feel like someone actually listened to me—and I feel peace.

There's still life in this land where I have seen so much death.

~ ~ ~

Heidi

"Heidi, look," Mom exclaims. "It's a wedding betrothal."

Two baby elephants parade along, carrying a boy and a girl dressed in silk. Towering over them, enormous parent elephants are draped in gold chains and jewels, while two adult couples ride on top in brightly adorned boxes.

"Who are they, Mommy?"

"Two kids and their rich families, I suppose. Once they're old enough, they'll have a big celebration and live as husband and wife, same as Daddy and me."

"When are they old enough?"

Mom grins. "Aren't you the little romantic? Well, it depends, sweetie. Usually when they're capable of having children. The groom often builds another story on top of his parents' house, and they live there. It's part of the culture, families staying together to help each other out. It's wonderful, don't you think?"

"If I have to go live with my husband's family, then I'm never getting married," I protest. "I want to stay with you guys."

She hugs me. "One day, Heidi, you'll get to form a family of your own."

Back at the Domes, Dad calls us together for a family meeting. We sit cross-legged on the threadbare rug. This must be a special occasion because Mom is serving up fried, syrupy dough balls called *gulab jamun*. These are a rare treat.

"Are you guys ready for a change of scenery?" Dad asks, then presses on since we have full mouths and sticky lips. "It's going to get extremely hot here in the next few months, so after we renew our visas, we'll go into the mountains to a town called Mussoorie. Hey, *hey*, no long faces. We'll come back once the temperatures drop."

"Isn't Missouri one of the fifty United States?" I venture.

Mom pats my head, proud of her little student.

"They sound similar," Dad agrees. "But this is eighteen hundred meters high, in the foothills of the Himalayas. We'll still be in India, but it'll be much cooler."

"Will we see Mt. Everest?" Eric sounds hopeful.

"Sorry, bud, that's near Tibet. You will see Tibetan monks, though."

Eric takes another bite of gulab jamun.

"Before we go, we are making two side trips. The first is to Agra, to a place that'll *blow* your minds." He raises his hands to stop our questions. "Hold on. In a minute, you can try to guess. In even bigger news, we're going to southern India where the *Logos* will be anchored for two weeks. Can you guess what *that* means? You are going to see Uncle Paul and Aunt Val again."

First, our mouths drop. Then we scream, jumping up from the floor.

"I know, I know," Dad laughs. "I'm excited, too."

~ ~ ~

The five of us climb into a taxi at the Domes, carrying one bag each—all of our earthly belongings—and ride down Jaipur Road. The train station is a madhouse. Mom holds me tightly as we thread through the masses. Dad carries Shaun, with Eric at his side. In each train car, two, three, even four people occupy the same seat, while others spill out the windows, clinging to the sides and squatting on the roof.

We shove our way up the steps onto the train. Holding third-class tickets, our family squeezes into two seats.

We are going to the Taj Mahal. I can't wait.

The train platform is a microcosm of India itself. The caste system regulates society here. People are born into their caste and their only hope of moving up is to do good, affording the possibility of a better situation in the next life. We have learned there are four main castes, in descending order:

Brahmin, the priests and academics.

Kshatriya, the warriors and kings.

Vaishya, the merchants, artisans, and landowners.

Shudra, the commoners, peasants, and servants.

A fifth group, the *Dalits* or the Untouchables, aren't even considered worthy of being human. They are the outcasts—the out-of-caste, literally—

the street sweepers, the dung gatherers, being punished for their sins from a previous life. They can't use the public wells. They can only drink from rough earthenware vessels.

"Oh, these precious people." Mom's voice softens. "I can't help but think of Second Corinthians, where it says, 'We have this treasure in earthen vessels...'"

Shaun speaks up, "A girl behind the Domes, she picks up cow poop."

"Yes, she's an Untouchable. She dries it to use as fuel for the fire. But kids, she is a treasure. Jesus loves her as much as He loves you and me. None of us are worthy. We're only worthy by walking with Him, as part of His church, His bride."

We are stiff and sore, dripping with sweat, by the time we reach Agra hours later. A bus takes us the final leg to one of the Seven Wonders of the World.

At the Taj Mahal, we are nearly blinded by the sun's glare off a long, shallow pool set between gardens and minarets. We walk with other tourists toward the huge, glistening shrine. Inside, we wear special slippers to protect the floors as a guide gives us an overview of this white-marble structure inlaid with thousands of precious stones. Its chambers reflect all the shades of the sky.

"Taj Mahal means 'Crown of the Palace,'" the guide explains to our group. "The emperor had it built as a burial site for Mumtaz, his favorite wife. They were married for nineteen years, and her name meant 'jewel of his palace.' She traveled with him and assisted him in his work and his military campaigns."

"I'll be the jewel of my husband's palace," I whisper to my dad.

Next to me, Eric gawks at the intricate tiles and archways.

"I'm sure you will be, my little princess." Dad gives my shoulder a squeeze.

The guide continues. "During the birth of her fourteenth child, Mumtaz suffered hard labor and hemorrhaging. On her deathbed, she had four final wishes: that her husband erect a symbol to their love, that he never marry again, that he be kind to their children, and that he visit her tomb each year. It took twenty thousand laborers nearly seventeen years to complete the Taj Mahal's main mausoleum."

Spurred by curiosity, I step forward. "What about her baby?"

Mom raises a long finger to her lips. "Shhh, let him finish."

The guide gives me a head bob and a grin. "She lived a long healthy life."

"I knew it," I say with a smile.

He turns back to the group. "The emperor was paralyzed by heartache. As he grew gravely ill, his sons vied for his throne. One son claimed he was unfit to rule and had him locked up at Agra Fort. For years, the emperor could only view this noble shrine from the fort, unable to visit his beloved's tomb as he'd promised her."

My eyes well up. A few other tourists look sad as well.

"The Taj Mahal is over three hundred years old, a lasting tribute," our guide concludes, "signifying romance and beauty. It was built to be symmetrical in every way. Only the emperor's coffin, laid just off center from his wife's, breaks the rule."

"Isn't it an incredible picture of Jesus?" Mom says as we return to the station.

Dad frowns. "I doubt that's how anyone *here* sees it."

"We are His bride," Mom continues, corralling her long hair over the shoulder of her sari. "He's gone to prepare a place in heaven for each one of us, more beautiful than anything here on earth."

"Even the Taj Mahal?" I draw in a breath.

"Oh, sure." Dad gestures at the throng. "But what about all these people?"

"Jesus loves them," Mom says.

"Most of them have never even *heard* of Him. If they have, He's just another god to them. So that's it, they're just shit out of luck? Jesus loves them but they're going to hell anyway, cursed for praying to the wrong gods?"

"Honestly, honey. Is that really what you think?"

"I don't know, Linda. I don't know *what* to think anymore."

Eric's eyes darken as he chews on a finger. Shaun reaches for the hem of Mom's sari.

She scrunches her eyes and steps closer to Dad. "Isn't this why we've been sent here? How will these dear people ever know if we don't tell them the good news? What a glorious privilege to be God's messengers."

"*Fantastic.* So it's all on us. And if I don't do my job right, they burn for eternity."

"The Holy Spirit is the one who changes hearts and minds."

"Then why, for crying out loud, are we even *wasting* our time?"

Mom moves to put her arm through his, but he's already pacing ahead. My brothers and I hurry after our dad as our mom tries to catch up. I peer over my shoulder and see beads of sweat on her brow. Headed back to the railway depot, we look like a typical Indian family, the man leading as the woman takes her place at the back. This is not normal for us. Dad's eyes are hooded and dark.

What's wrong, Daddy? I want to ask, but I worry it'll make him mad...

Uncertain

North and South India — 1973-1974

Mark's anger simmered even as he tried to tamp it down and focus on his work. He partnered with an Indian couple to run prayer meetings and Bible studies for locals. He went by truck on supply runs to New Delhi and by train to seminars in Mumbai. He supplied Indian men and women with Christian literature to distribute.

Each day, though, presented new questions and dilemmas.

Mark was in a crisis of faith.

He had come halfway around the world to share the gospel, to get people saved. He had been told the Good News must be preached to every person in every nation, only then could Jesus return. Having now seen the enormity of this task, with over a billion souls in India alone, he felt overwhelmed. He couldn't do it all, he just couldn't. Most of them knew nothing about Jesus. There were thousands of gods here, millions. Disease was rampant. Children died daily.

Ill-prepared to deal with his doubts, Mark locked them inside, and his health began to deteriorate. Food was scarce, and more than once he chipped his teeth on rocks in the rice—rocks increased the weight and raised the market price. Skinny already, he turned skeletal. His moods became unpredictable.

What was he doing here? Had he made a mistake?

Were his crimes back in America blocking God's favor?

At twenty-four, Mark wasn't used to failure. He had dragged his family across two continents to make a difference. He'd left everything behind to share God's forgiveness with others and to alleviate his own shame in the process. Now, when all was said and done, he felt basically helpless. He'd be lucky to save a few.

Did these smiling, beautiful people deserve the fires of hell for not knowing the white American gospel? Was it their fault they weren't born into Christian families? If God was love, did any of this make an iota of sense?

The pressure of it all bore down, a psychological weight, and Mark's physical body reacted. Sores broke out in his forehead and his hair fell out in dark clumps.

16

Heidi

Though Dad's face is still gaunt and his head bears sores, his anger fades in the days after the Taj Mahal. He has worked nonstop for months. What he really needs is to do something fun. Doesn't he say laughter is like a medicine? I believe it's true, because whenever he puts his head back and laughs, it seems nothing in the world can stop him.

Seeing his brother Paul will be good for him.

Mom thinks so too.

From Agra, we have a two-day railway journey to reach the *Logos*. At the Hyderbad depot, passengers crowd the platform and jockey for their places. Various odors assault our noses. Our clothes are sticking to our backs. While we wait for our train, our parents buy us *samosas* from a vendor. We also stop to watch a chai *wallah* siphon milk and water from a metal canister, mix and heat it with spices, then serve up sweet cups of tea.

All I'm really thinking about are my relatives. I can still see my uncle diving over a pew to hug Dad. I see my aunt sashaying in her fashionable skirt.

"Will Uncle Paul and Aunt Val remember us?" I want to know.

"What? They *love* you," Dad says. "They got the tape you kids sent them, and they sent one back. Didn't you like their story about seeing whales and flying fish?"

"But we listened to that in Belgium."

"Okay, so six months ago. They're still your family. You know, Paul and I used to fight like cats and dogs. And now look at me, dying to see him because I love him so much. Believe me, little princess, they'll be ecstatic to see you."

We finish our samosas and chai, then fight our way onto a train bound for Pondicherry–which will one day be known as Puducherry. As we wait for departure, the heat inside is suffocating and we lower our windows.

A man in a turban appears outside and meets my eye. "For you," he says, pushing up a colored basket with a domed lid. "You look inside, yes?"

He wants an audience, a customer with U.S. dollars, but I don't realize this. I simply admire the basket's shades of blue and green. "Mommy, look, this man's showing us something."

"What's he want?" She pulls me closer and tugs at the basket's lid.

I lick my lips, thinking there might be chapatis inside.

As the top works loose, a coiled shape bobs into view. The movement resembles the noncommittal head wobble we get from the Indian people. How many times have we seen it in response to a question? We've been taught to *let your yes be yes, and your no be no*, but here direct answers are hard to come by.

A weaving shape rises hypnotically in front of me. I stare into beady black eyes and hear the hiss of a darting tongue.

"Heidi, watch out!"

Mom slams the lid over the cobra's head, locking it back in its hole, and shoves the basket out the window. Though the snake charmer scowls, my mom wants none of this. Let someone else discover the basket's wonders.

Moments later, the mighty engine awakens and the train begins to move. Mom pulls Shaun and me onto her lap. Dad is beside us with Eric on his knee. We're off on another leg of our trek. The heat will grow more unbearable, the humidity more soupy as we move south, but we are going to see our relatives.

"I love you, Daddy," I mouth.

He winks and mouths it back. Hope glimmers in his eyes.

~ ~ ~

Eric

The *Logos*, built in Denmark in 1949, is nearly 90 meters long. She has been refurbished and her gleaming white profile greets us, boasting multiple masts and a covered poop deck. She is anchored offshore from Pondicherry, lapped by the Bay of Bengal. Thousands of Indians will visit her onboard bookstore, hear teachings from the Bible, and watch films about Jesus.

Our parents check in at a registration table. As OMers, they're handed name badges. They will attend sessions and volunteer at the literature tables.

"Can you check the crew list for me?" Dad says. "We're looking for Paul Wilson."

A woman rifles through some papers. "I don't see him listed."

"He came aboard last year, he and his wife Val."

"There's no Val Wilson either."

Dad turns serious. "The crew's, what, a hundred people or so? *C'mon*, if you find me a crew member, I'm sure they'll know who I'm talking about. Paul's my brother, for heaven's sake."

Mom pulls us kids closer. She's praying under her breath.

"Mr. Wilson," the woman says, "I am a crew member. I joined the ship a few ports back, which means Paul and Val Wilson must have left by February. I apologize for your frustration, but is it possible they tried to call or send news by mail?"

Dad shakes his head. "*Unbelievable*. I'll find someone who knows what they're talking about." He marches off, his sideburns pointing him toward a ship's steward.

"They have to be here," Heidi wails. "You guys promised."

"I'm sorry, sweetie, but it sounds like we might not see them," Mom says. "If they sent a letter, it must've been lost between here and Tehran."

Shaun's fingers are in his mouth and I'm chewing the skin around my thumbnail. Too young to comprehend all of my dad's internal struggles, I still have questions of my own.

Is God involved in daily matters? When and where does He intervene?

We watch our father's shoulders slump as the steward confirms the bad news. We have traveled over 1800 kilometers by train. We are hungry and thirsty, sweaty and stiff. The weather here is hot and sticky. Having reached our destination, we are exhausted, running on fumes of hope–and we've come up empty.

We have nothing left.

For the next two weeks, Dad and Mom overwork themselves to combat their disappointment. This will become a long-running pattern, leaving personal issues unattended as they partner in public ministry. They confine us to a ship cabin for hours on end, where we look out the porthole and catch glimpses of Sri Lanka. We mope for the first day or two, but this doesn't make our aunt and uncle appear, so we start bouncing Superballs off the walls–nearly breaking a picture and a lamp–and we concoct fake medicinal drinks for each other using anything we can scrounge out of the cupboards, from birdseed to coconut milk to hot sauce.

Shaun also turns four years old while we are onboard.

Resourceful as always, Mom makes birthday cupcakes from the limited ingredients at her disposal. She throws in beets to sweeten the mix and it actually tastes good. We sing to Shaun, and he is given a pair of neon swim goggles. Since the heat is oppressively humid, there's a kiddie pool on the poop deck for all the children on the ship. Shaun dons his new goggles and splashes around with a vengeance.

In the sweltering conditions, we three kids stand at the railing and watch some of the ship's crew toss aside shoes and shirts and jump off the lower deck into the sea. We wave at them and they wave back, squinting into the sun.

"Jellyfish," someone shouts from the upper deck.

Onlookers gesture wildly at the water, where Portuguese man o' wars are floating by. They're huge compared to what we saw at the Black Sea. Their venomous blue tentacles drag like nets, a potential threat, and the crewmen in the sea scurry back up the anchor chain.

As our time on the *Logos* concludes, we say farewell to our latest group of friends from around the world–none of whom we'll ever see again. They will sail for other ports and fly off to distant lands while we will head off for the Himalayas.

~ ~ ~

Shaun

Over the next three days we travel another 2500 kilometers, riding the trains, fleeing the heat by going north toward Mussoorie. I am lulled to rest by the rhythm of wheels on the tracks—*chh-chh-chh-chuhhh, chh-chh-chh-chuhhh.*

Along the way, my brother shows me pictures from a book about one of his latest heroes, Sadhu Sundar Singh. After Singh became a follower of Jesus, his father rejected him and his own brother tried to kill him.

Hmm. I would never do that to my brother.

"Mark, you admire Sadhu Sundar Singh. Why don't you tell the kids what you've learned about him?" Mom prods.

Dad's gaze is fixed out the window. He doesn't even turn.

Undeterred, Mom says, "Singh was such a beautiful man of God. He shared the Good News with other Indians and told them they didn't need to adopt the

British clothing and customs which had nothing to do with Christianity. When they heard this, some of the people got mad at him and released venomous snakes into his house."

"Did they bite him?" I want to know.

"Jesus was watching over him and he escaped."

Certain Christians, we've been told, go into a country and force their ways on others. Some do mean, ungodly things under religious pretenses. Our parents don't hide these realities from us, but they remind us of Jesus who left heaven and came to earth as a man. He went through all the hardships of a regular person. He got tired and dusty, and His feet felt sore, and He took potty breaks just like I do.

He is our example.

He humbled and sacrificed Himself.

"Our family's goal," Mom states, "is to do the same."

She tells us stories of other larger-than-life characters, godly men and women such as William Carey and Amy Carmichael, who spread the love of God in India.

"And Mother Teresa is still here," Mom explains. "As a young woman, she left her home in Albania and committed her life to this country. We left America to come here too. We give out literature free of charge, and the times we do present the love of Jesus, we act only on the wishes of those who express a sincere interest."

Inspired by these heroes of the faith, I have no idea Mother Teresa herself will take me under her wing fourteen years from now as she works with needy orphans.

Beside me, Dad is quiet. Seems he needs someone to care for him.

"I miss Uncle Paul too," I tell him.

He blinks and turns toward me. "Aww, buddy, I really wish you could've seen him. I guess he and Aunt Val decided the ship wasn't the right fit for them. Listen, I've been busy moping and not even *thinking* about how *you* feel. I am so sorry."

"It's okay, Daddy."

Mom looks pleased. She always says, since God has forgiven us, we must also forgive others. The two go hand in hand.

"I haven't been myself lately," Dad adds. "I promise to do better, okay?"

He means it, I know he does. But I'm not holding my breath.

17

Eric

We reach the base of the Himalayas, the world's highest mountain range. We drive up curvy roads and switchbacks from the hill station of Deradhun to Mussoorie.

"You know, Eric," Dad says, glancing at me in the rearview mirror, "we've arranged for you to take some classes at Woodstock School. You'll meet international children your own age, maybe even some Americans."

"I'm an American, right?"

"Absolutely. People from all over the world want the privileges of the red, white, and blue. Not that our country always gets it right. There are lots of people upset at us for the war in Vietnam and for the ways we still treat Black people."

"But God made everyone."

"He did, and this world would be awfully drab without color. In India *we're* the minority, which is why the ladies pinch your cheeks. You're like a ghost to them."

"What's the red, white, and blue?" I ask.

"You remember the U.S. flags you saw in Tehran?"

"Oh." As I picture the colors of the stars and the stripes, it all makes sense.

"Now keep your eyes focused out the window so you don't get carsick."

An hour later we enter Mussoorie, which offers a respite from the summer heat for tourists, missionaries, relief workers, and diplomats. It's a privilege to be here, our parents tell us. We shouldn't ever take things for granted. Even our hand-to-mouth existence is lavish to most Indians.

As our car threads through narrow streets to reach the OM property, we pass Hindu shrines, Buddhist temples, and homes stacked on top of each other. Bright banners and gaudy advertisements line the route, then give way to trees whose branches droop from the hillsides and over the road to touch guardrails along the cliffs. The air is cooler here, crisp and clean.

"This is it, kids, our house for the next few months." Dad parks outside a single-story structure with screened windows and a low roof. Trees surround the property–walnuts, cedars, and West Himalayan firs.

"Swings," Heidi shouts. "Like we had in Vienna."

"All yours. Why don't you guys pose over there for a picture?" Dad waits till we are hanging off the structure, then snaps a photo with a cheap Kodak. "Now, Mom and I are going in to check the house. You can play out here, but *do not* wander."

The swing set is only steps from a fenced drop-off. We can see far into the distance, looking over treetops, down mountain paths, to the haze of hot, flat India. We shiver in the evening breeze. We lose interest in the swings and explore the yard, coming across an old bathtub full of rainwater.

"Is that a scorpion?" Heidi asks me.

Using a stick, I fish the reddish creature from the scummy depths and set it on the tub's edge. "It's not moving. It probably drowned."

Our parents find the three of us hunched over the pincered form.

"Mommy, are we going to take baths out here?" Shaun says.

"Hey, *hey.*" Dad snatches my brother away. "That's a scorpion, buddy."

"It's dead," I say.

Heidi peers closer. "It looks like some of the spiders at the Domes."

"I *mean* it," Dad snaps. "Stay back. Any of you touch that tail and you could still get stung." He uses the pointy end of my stick to cut off the tail, which he then kicks across the dirt and down the slope. "It's scorpion season, so keep an eye out. We'll have to be really careful up here, Linda."

This is our first scorpion but not our last.

I see one on the bathroom wall while my hair is foamy with shampoo. Dad leaves his desk one night to get a drink and finds a large black scorpion skittering past when he returns. We learn to shake out clothes and shoes before putting them on. We check cups and plates as we lower them from the cupboards.

Scorpions, I realize, aren't the only things that sting here in Mussoorie.

In my class at Woodstock the next week, a British teacher strikes my palm with a ruler for each word I get wrong on a spelling test. Hating the sting of the ruler, I ace the next test. The teacher flashes a wicked grin, hands me the ruler, and tells me it's now my job to distribute punishment to each of my classmates.

I refuse.

"Then you will be punished for each of their mistakes," says the teacher.

I still refuse.

As soon as Dad and Mom hear of this, my time at the international school is over. Though my studies continue under Mom's tutelage, I have more free time to strike out and see orange-robed monks at the Tibetan monastery, chase skinks along the village paths, and wander goat trails into the valley. Goat milk's not my favorite.

Along these paths, I suffer a third type of sting when I come across a pair of Western kids from the school. They are older, bigger. They know about my ruler incident and tease me for being too nice to mete out discipline.

"Here's what happens to the weak kids." Laughing, they shove me into stinging nettles.

I scramble to my feet, trying to ignore the fiery rash along my arms, and speed back up the slope through a grove of trees.

That's when I spot the camera. It sits on a stump all alone. It is black, with buttons marked by numbers and colored dots. I pick it up, look through the viewer, and see tiny focal lines. I'm holding a Nikon 35mm. It feels heavy, fancy. This isn't just some piece of junk.

"Hello?" I call out, but no one answers.

The flare of pain in my arms is subsiding. I point the camera down the path, peeking again through the viewer. I pretend I'm scanning for treasure through a periscope, like Captain Nemo or Jacques Cousteau.

"Did someone lose their camera?" I call again, with no response.

Should I keep it? I wonder. How long has it been out here? Leaving it where I found it is one option. If whoever lost it never comes back, though, it will sit here and rust. Another option is hiding it back at the house. Is it stealing if I'm not really taking it from anyone? *Finders, keepers...* as Dad likes to say.

The best thing, I decide, is to go and ask permission to keep it. I'm sure my parents will honor my honesty.

Confident, I loop the strap around my neck and head back.

But Dad is working when I walk through the door and Mom doesn't respond as hoped. She tells me Nikons are expensive, someone will miss it, and I should go put it where I found it. Furious, I storm back outside. My ears ring as I bound down the steps and follow the stone embankment.

"I hate you," I scream.

With all my might, I swing the camera by its strap into the embankment. The lens cracks, knobs fly, and it shatters into dozens of pieces. My outburst feels naughty, tapping something dark in me–and it feels good, even satisfying.

When I return to the house near dinnertime, my face is no longer flushed, but the unfairness of it still weighs on my back.

"Eric, come here a minute," Dad says.

I take a cautious step his direction. Oh no, am I in trouble?

"Listen, bud, your mom told me about the camera you found. It was a mature thing of you to do, bringing it to her. That wasn't easy, was it? Well, we talked it over. Since you told us the truth, we want to reward you with a big responsibility. Your mom and I have decided to let you keep the camera."

All I can do is mutter a thank you.

Losers, weepers...

Decades later, I will have two major regrets about my childhood overseas. First, our family never stays any place long enough to learn the language. We pick up some German and Hindi, but never become conversational. In a largely multilingual world, my own ignorance will always embarrass me.

Second, we have very few pictures. We are barred from taking them during our Eastern European travels, and our Kodak is barely up to the task here in India. When I finally have a chance at owning a quality camera, I literally throw it away. Knowing this, knowing what I did in a fit of rage, that is the worst sting of all.

~ ~ ~

Heidi

"You want to kick the ball with me?" Shaun asks.

"Sure."

Last night, while playing with beetles in the dirt, I was called indoors and met by a chorus of "Happy Birthday." Mom appeared with a six-candled cake. My gift was a rubber ball, dusted in a swirl of blues, oranges, and pinks, reminding me of an Ajmer sunrise.

I bound into the yard with it now. Shaun and I aren't supposed to venture past the fence and embankment. Beyond, narrow paths snake down into the valley. Vultures circle beneath us, their screeches echoing from the neighboring ridge. Whatever falls down there becomes food for the birds. Against orders, though, we have sneaked down the switchbacks a few times. After we came face-to-face with a king cobra, we ran all the way back up and decided to heed our mom's warnings.

Shaun and I now play happily with my ball. Mom watches us from the back porch and says I am good at sharing, especially since this is my new present. When Shaun and I aren't arguing, we actually have fun together. Eric, as usual, is exploring the area on his own or hiding indoors with a book.

For fun, Shaun and I start tossing the ball to each other through the swing set bars. Sometimes it bounces off in crazy directions and we have to chase it down. In the midst of our giggling, my brother kicks the ball toward me through the A-gap at the top of the bars. I reach up to catch it. The ball flies through the gap, catches the corner, then angles away.

We both sprint after it as it floats over our fence.

"No," I cry out.

My gift sails downward, riding the wind currents, and disappears.

I bawl as my parents try to console me. Mom and Eric even go down the paths in hopes of finding my treasured toy. When they return empty-handed, I am distraught. I'm not sure I'll ever let anyone touch my stuff again. I shared my rubber ball, my beautifully colored birthday gift, and my little brother didn't take care of it.

Why does our family have to make all the sacrifices?

Will we ever get back to America?

Things sound safe there, rich and stylish. Some of the kids on the *Logos* talked about the coolest fashions, the latest rock and roll—and we didn't understand a word of it. We don't dress like other Americans. We don't own a house or a car. I can't name one Beatles song. We're nomads, that's all we are. We're like my ball, lost out here on an adventure and so far from home.

~ ~ ~

One afternoon, Shaun and I are in the yard, racing each other on foot in the long driveway, when I spot a pack of furry shadows coming up the hill.

"Shaun, run." I am frantic. "Get inside."

Small monkeys called rhesus macaques like to terrorize Mussoorie by smashing and stealing items in their path. Troops of macaques have killed grown adults in other cities. Out of honor for the monkey god, *Hanuman*, the locals do little to stop the pillaging.

My brother turns and notices the threat. "The house is too far. Just climb, Heidi." In seconds, he scrambles up a tree. He can ascend just about anything and he is high in the branches by the time I get to the tree's base.

"What're you doing?" he shouts. "Hurry up."

The raucous creatures nearly drown out his voice. I clamber up as fast as I can, barely making it into the lower branches as the macaques crest the embankment onto our property. They seem as big as we are. We cannot fight these things.

An object zings over my head at the beasts. It looks like a small grenade, and a monkey picks it up for inspection. More grenades cruise past and I realize Shaun is throwing walnuts from the tree. The macaque studies a nut, cracks it between his teeth, and stuffs another in his cheek. His companions scoop up some of the loot for themselves, chattering at us and scanning the yard. Seemingly placated, they angle back down the incline.

Mom hurries out, catching us as we hop down from our perches. She has witnessed the whole thing through the kitchen window. She pulls us into a joint hug, squeezing so hard it hurts.

"Thank you, Jesus," she gasps. "Thank you."

My brother puffs his chest. "I'm the one who threw the walnuts."

"You sure did."

"That was smart of you," I tell him.

"Yes, Shaun," Mom says, "the Lord gave you wisdom in that moment."

I'm pretty sure Shaun thinks he saved us all by himself.

18

Shaun

Our time ends all too fast and we must return to Ajmer. Back to water from a village pump. Showers in a basin. Spiders behind the toilet. Mosquito nets and candles at night instead of cool air and electric light bulbs.

Dad seems refreshed after our months in the mountains. He tucks us in at night and tells us Bible stories, his blue eyes sparkling. He's had time away from the crowds and the pressing questions of eternal damnation. He's almost back to his old self. We are one big happy family again and we love him.

Then I get sick.

I am dehydrated, down in weight, vomiting, with a severe case of diarrhea. Dad prays for me, but I only get worse and his calm begins to fray. He's seen me running around in the dirt fields behind the Domes and also seen cows peeing and pooping in places I use as a playground. He is sure I've been contaminated by sucking on my fingers and he wants to believe he can call on God to be a healer.

I'm not getting better, though. Worse, in fact.

And Dad starts scratching at his sores again.

Though Mom seems suspicious of hospitals, Dad believes they are used by God to heal us. He rushes me to a clinic in Ajmer. The doctor says I have amoebic dysentery and they must replenish my fluids quickly. Nurses poke an IV needle at my arm, then my stomach. They can't locate a vein, which is fascinating to me. Their probing makes my belly button pull tight. Concerned, they watch for my reaction.

Crying seems weak to me. Actually, I think it's funny and I laugh.

The nurses stare at me like I've gone crazy.

Later, Dad brags to Vikay Peter about how well I tolerate pain. This confuses me since he also says crying is nothing to be ashamed of. He often gets emotional when ministering to people. Am I supposed to be tough or misty-eyed?

I am released the next day, feeling stronger. Dad tells me he wants to spend more time together. He cycles around the compound with me perched on the back. When I complain about being too small to pedal, he reminds me of the man with elephantiasis. Least I'm still able to walk and run. I have nothing to gripe about.

Until the day my dangling foot gets caught in the spokes.

The white bike lurches and flips. Dad and I go tumbling. He grimaces, uttering a few off-color words as he gets up. It is the last time he takes me riding.

Me and my short legs. Stupid, stupid.

"You'll be okay," says Vikay Peter. "You are a smart, precocious child, Shaun, you and your brother and sister. You are also having a soft heart, like your father. "

At the window one morning, I suck my fingers and watch my brother pedal around while my sister weaves through the arbor, trying to tag him with a tennis ball. They get to do whatever they want. I drop down from my perch feeling sorry for myself. Voices from the communal area let me know the OM prayer meeting is going on. The doors are closed, the hallway dark, as I huddle and tears roll down.

Footsteps round the corner. My dad is coming.

I stiffen, wondering if this is the wrong place to be. Will he be mad at me?

His shadow nears. "Shaun, buddy, what's going on? You're... are you crying?" He takes a seat on a step and pulls me onto his lap. "Aww, tell me what's wrong."

"It's not fair."

"What's not fair, bud?"

Sniffling, I hope the darkness hides my face. "Those mean boys ruined my trike in Vienna, and now we got a new one but I can't ride it, and I always have to stay inside while Eric and Heidi play with the big kids. There's nobody my size."

"That's a lot to be upset about. You know, I was little too once. We had bullies who did mean things to me and my brother. It made me mad and afraid. And very sad." Dad's eyes meet mine. "You know, when you're lonely you can talk to Jesus."

"I can't see Him."

"He's here right now, Shaun." Dad's voice is tender. "He loves you and wants to be your friend. People make mistakes. They promise things and then forget. They get angry. They fight. Jesus is the *only* one who is perfect. He will *never* leave you."

Sure, I've heard these words before. My parents talk to others about Jesus and we sing songs about Him, but my own beliefs are not solidified. Daddy and Mommy have never forced me to make a decision, since they think each person must choose for themselves. In this moment, my dad's words reach deep inside.

My tears keep rolling. "I want Jesus to be my friend," I say.

"Do you want to pray with me, asking Him to come into your heart?"

When I nod, Dad hugs me and whispers a prayer which he has me repeat. He doesn't feed me scary words about hell. He says I can talk this way to Jesus anytime and He wants to be part of my life. The truth of it wells up in my chest and spreads. I feel lighter, my sadness gone, and at four I know Jesus as my savior and friend.

"Look, Daddy, the hallway's not dark anymore. It's all yellow and bright."

He follows my pointing finger. "You're not *kidding*. It really is."

My childlike faith will be put to test the next week when I start preschool, and Heidi starts first grade at the nearby government building.

~ ~ ~

Heidi

A dry, weed-ridden expanse separates the Domes from the school where we will learn both English and Hindi grammar. Whereas Mom will instruct Eric with her interactive teaching style, this place will be strict and regimented.

Which causes problems even sooner than we expect.

The first morning, Shaun and I duck under a wire fence and walk across the field, dodging thorns and cow patties. At the school entryway, we are ordered to take off our shoes. This is also our habit at the Domes, to keep things clean. The school's cement floor feels cool beneath our toes, a blessing in this heat.

Shoeless, I look around to see where I go next. Other students move toward a low table lined with small statues and incense. Some kids kneel in front of the display while others sit cross-legged, all bowing their heads before going to class.

Shaun tugs on my shirt. "What're they doing?"

"Praying, I guess."

We've heard our parents talk about the many Hindu gods. The three main ones stand in the center of the table—*Brahman*, the supreme god and creator; *Vishnu*, the protector; and *Shiva*, the destroyer. Other statues crowd around this trio. One resembles an elephant, another holds a flute, and one has four arms.

Shrugging, Shaun and I walk to our respective classrooms.

My first daily requirement is to write my name and the date directly on my slate desk. I'll also use this for solving math problems and practicing Devanagari script. My natural tendency is to write left-handed–the culturally unclean hand–but this is corrected with the smack of a ruler and an eventual scar on my knuckles.

After school, we tell our mom about our day. When she hears of the children bowing to gods, she pulls out her green and gold edition of The Living Bible.

"Do you know the story of Shadrach, Meshach, and Abednego?" When we shake our heads, she tells us of three Hebrews who refused to bow to a huge statue. When the king of Babylon threatened to throw them into a fire if they didn't bow, they responded, "If we are thrown into the flaming furnace, our God is able to deliver us... But if he doesn't, please understand, sir, that even then we will never under any circumstance serve your gods or worship the gold statue you have erected."

"Did they die?" Shaun asks. "I bet they died."

"You've seen what that looks like, haven't you, sweetie?" Mom links her arm through his. "Oh yes, the king was furious. He told the guards to throw the Hebrew boys into the roaring inferno and he expected them to fall over dead. Instead, they walked around unharmed in the flames, joined by a mysterious fourth figure."

I bounce on my knees. "Who was it?"

"Some believe God sent His angel to protect them. When Shadrach, Meshach, and Abednego came out of that furnace, their hair wasn't burned and their clothes didn't even smell of smoke. The king decided their God was the most powerful of all."

This story emboldens me and my brother. The next morning, we take off our shoes at the school's front entrance and walk over to the table of Hindu gods. While others bow, we stand like those three Hebrew boys.

A figure thunders toward us. The principal grips our tiny arms and marches us down the hall, her sari swishing with every step. In her office, the heat is stagnant. Bees swarm around a hive on the ceiling. After rattling off a lecture, the principal paddles us both using a breadboard drilled with holes to increase the pain.

We stand, unflinching, in what becomes a daily ritual.

I'm willing to stand for God, but what I can't stand is the person stealing my shoes from the front pile. More than once I'm left barefoot for the thorny walk back to the dull tan structure of the Domes.

"Stealing is wrong," I gripe to my mom. "I hope they get caught."

"It is," she agrees, sponging my heels. "Remember, though, some of the kids you play with don't have any shoes at all. Some don't even have indoor toilets at home. We are sooo fortunate to live where we do."

I frown, realizing she is right.

"Heidi, don't you think you ought to pray for them instead of being angry?"

I remember her words to us in Turkey: *The best thing we can do... is try to love and forgive... when you get mad back at someone, does it really help anything? No, your lack of forgiveness keeps you trapped...*

I take a deep breath and pray.

Mostly, I guess, I don't feel trapped anymore.

~ ~ ~

Shaun

Heidi and I take a stand for God at school, but it doesn't stop us from getting fevers a few weeks later. We are put to bed in the middle of the day, with curtains drawn. A lizard zigzags along the wall as a fan wobbles overhead, drawing hot air toward the domed ceiling. Eric isn't sick. He's on the floor in the communal area, doing schoolwork while watching for frogs which often hop through the room. He likes to take care of them as pets, probably making up for what he did to the toad.

"Shaun, you should keep your covers on," Heidi tells me from her bed.

"I don't want them on," I react from my bottom bunk. "I'm already hot."

"The heat's good, though. It helps burn away the fever."

I roll away from her. I don't have to listen to a thing she says.

A low whispering gets my attention. Is she still trying to talk to me? It sounds nonsensical, a hissing without any words I can pick out.

"Heidi, just be quiet," I say.

"I'm not even talking," she shoots back.

Seconds later, the whispering starts again. Does she think this is funny? I turn back over to tell her this is a stupid argument, stop messing around.

"Shaun." Her voice is strained. "Look at that."

We both see it, an ethereal form near the ceiling. It seems to beckon us, and its alluring movements don't match any of the shadows coming through the window.

Heidi sits up. In a loud voice, she calls out, "Jesus."

The moment she speaks, the form wavers and changes shape. It now looks to me like a misshapen goat's head, horns and all. We know all about the enemy of our souls. Mom's warned us about the devil disguising himself as an angel of light. He's a liar and a thief. He's also an accuser, pointing fingers and trying to make us feel bad.

Even though we aren't supposed to be afraid, Heidi and I are freaked out. We leap up and run outside. We locate our parents, sipping tea in the shade with their Indian friends and work partners.

"What're *you* two doing out of bed?" Dad demands. "You should be resting."

"Satan's in there," I blurt out.

Heidi nods. "I saw it too, Daddy."

Maybe our fever has caused us to hallucinate. Or maybe our stance against the gods at school has stirred a spiritual confrontation. We've heard Ephesians 6:12: "For we do not wrestle against flesh and blood, but against principalities, against powers... against spiritual hosts of wickedness in the heavenly places."

Either way, our parents sense our urgency.

They put us to bed in another room, but as Dad wraps us in blankets, there's something unsettling in his eyes. He looks shaken. He's not supposed to be afraid, is he? He's our protector. He puts on his best face and kisses our cheeks.

"You two get some rest," he says.

When Mom suggests we pray together, Dad takes a deep breath. I've seen him do this before. Though he believes in his heart as she does, in his head he puts up barriers. Not to be dissuaded, Mom speaks quietly for a moment in her spiritual language before praying in English over my sister and me.

"Jesus," she says, "in your name we rebuke any evil spirits in this house. We rejoice that our names are written in heaven, in the book of life. We ask you to fill this place with a peace that surpasses all understanding and we plead your cleansing blood over Heidi and Shaun, so they might–"

"And Eric," I interject.

"Yes." She gives me an almost desperate squeeze. "So they can get some rest."

When Heidi and I open our eyes, our dad is already gone from the room.

19

Eric

Dad's health worsens as we go into the fall. Dark bags appear beneath his eyes. His skin is peeling in places and his hair is coming out in clumps.

"I've lost thirty pounds," I hear him tell Vikay Peter. *"Thirty."*

"Your body, Mark, it is dwindling."

"These dang *pants*, they barely stay up when I walk."

"A new belt we can be getting you. It is your faith I think is dwindling."

Dad is too weary to challenge this diagnosis. "I don't know what to do, Vikay. I can't sleep. All these thoughts just keep spinning through my head."

At only twenty-five years of age, Dad has a wife and three children. If he is too young to be falling apart, he doesn't seem to know it. He feels old. He still feels the crush of all these lost souls, and he's trying to reconcile this reality with his concepts of heaven and hell. Will these precious people burn for eternity if he fails to deliver the gospel? Is God the Old Testament God who sends out Israelite armies to slay men, women, and children? Or is He the God of love who puts the needs of the world above the life of His only Son? I think about these questions, too.

Sitting quietly in a corner, nose buried in a book, I catch snippets of adult conversations and hear an ugly word spoken in reference to my dad:

Breakdown.

The meaning is both clear and ominous. I've seen OM cars and Bedford trucks in need of repair. Some problems are easy to fix. Others need labor, tools, and parts. I've also seen vehicles left to rot and rust. What is wrong with our dad? He can still be fixed, can't he? What will happen to our family if a breakdown does occur?

As the oldest, I don't tell Heidi or Shaun any of this stuff I've heard.

Soon after, some OM leaders take action. Even though our family has time left on our renewed visas, we are strongly encouraged to head back to Iran for an indefinite time of rest and recharging. The plan makes sense to my young brain.

Without a break, an actual breakdown will occur.

~ ~ ~

It's early September when we arrive in the capital city. It is still warm in Tehran, and Dad surprises me by taking me to a large stadium where athletes from many nations compete in the Seventh Asian Games. The energy in the air is electric, and I'm mesmerized during the track and field events, applauding the winners. At one point, Dad gestures across the arena and asks if I recognize anyone.

There, in attendance with his wife, sits the Shah of Iran.

A real-life ruler, in person.

Afterward, to celebrate the event, our OM hosts in Tehran give me rare commemorative stamps which became the highlight of my collection.

Going into October, we are still at our place of retreat, the private home of a Christian couple from the States. Large windows overlook a blue-tiled swimming pool, with an *ichthus*, the Christian fish symbol, painted in the deep end. I spend hours playing with Heidi and Shaun, pretending I am a shark sneaking up on them. I grab their knees or ankles and they squeal. Heidi loves doing cannonballs. Shaun paddles about in yellow floaties.

Today, Mom joins us in the sun, but Dad is indoors with a week's worth of stubble. He thumbs through tomes on religion and philosophy, reading Kierkegaard and Sartre, sipping Turkish coffee, and trying to make sense of his own beliefs.

We kids splash about while a number of other OMers stop by to join us for a swim. Voices carry over the water, bouncing off the backyard walls. One of the men teaches us to do jackknifes, can openers, and swan dives. Maybe someday I can compete in the Olympics or in the Asian Games. Maybe the Shah will even be there, watching from the stands.

"Look, he's... he's underwater," someone calls. "Is he swimming?"

At pool level, I twist and don't see anything. What're they talking about?

"No, over there. I think he's... he's sinking!"

One of our day visitors rockets out of his poolside recliner. Fully clothed, still in his shoes, the man dives toward the deep end. He emerges seconds later, shouldering my brother to the surface.

Shaun coughs up water. His hair is drenched, his eyes bleary.

"His floaties popped," the man calls. "Or maybe deflated, I don't know. I just saw he was going under."

Mom can't stop thanking my little brother's rescuer.

When our dad hears of the incident, he is beside himself. What if no one had even noticed? What if Shaun had drowned? He holds my little brother tightly and tells him how sorry he is for not being there to save him.

"I'm okay," Shaun says. "I just gulped lots of water."

"What if nobody had seen you? I don't *even* want to think about it."

"My floaties stopped working. It's not your fault."

"I should've been there for you."

"It's okay, Daddy. That other guy jumped right in."

Dad swallows hard while these words settle over him. The tension in his jaws dissipates. His eyes brighten. There is a bigger lesson here about lost souls and the need for a savior. Dad's been blaming himself, thinking all the weight is on him, when in actuality others are also willing to hop up, dive in, and shoulder the load.

Dad alone does not need to save the world.

"Well, thank God," he responds to Shaun. "I'm so glad we didn't lose you."

~ ~ ~

Everything changes in mid-December, when Dad gets a letter from America. He slices through the envelope with an ivory letter opener, reads carefully, then lets out a whoop.

"What is it, Mark?" our mom wants to know.

"It's time to go home," he shouts. "We are going home."

I will be almost twenty years old when he finally sits me down and reveals all the details. Today, though, he learns from a county clerk in Eugene, Oregon, that his felony charges have been dropped, and his arrest warrant dismissed. A judge has heard of his work in Eastern Europe and India. In the judge's words: "Mr. Wilson has already done his time through community service overseas."

God's grace is defined by some as getting something we *don't* deserve, and His mercy as *not* getting what we *do* deserve.

Dad's unexpected letter delivers a dose of both.

A gift of grace. And an act of mercy.

Our mom has no idea about the felony, the warrant, or the crack in our family's foundation. All she knows is her husband's mood is exuberant and he is ready to return to the States–for the sake of his marriage and kids.

We came here with nothing, and we're going back with nothing. During our time with Operation Mobilisation, mail has been unreliable, and we've had very limited support from our church in Oregon. We'll need to book the cheapest flights available, even if it means lots of layovers. Getting to American shores is the goal.

Clear-eyed and clean-shaven, Dad leads us on our long journey home, which starts with a trip to Tashkent, deep in the Soviet Union. From Tashkent to Moscow, we fly through snow flurries in a dual-propeller Aeroflot plane. The windows and overhead cabinets rattle from takeoff till landing.

"What a *death* trap," Dad says. "Bet this thing flew in World War Two."

The other passengers are less than amused by his comments.

We touch down behind the Iron Curtain, in the heart of the communist empire. We kids are directed to hard airport chairs, where we tuck our bags under our feet. The waiting area is unheated. Our numb hands draw pictures in our notebooks while our parents negotiate with dismissive ticket agents. The hours pass. We have nowhere to go. We are trapped in Moscow without hotel reservations or airline tickets. We have traveled in trains, hovercrafts, jet planes, ferries, lorries, and automobiles. The years of world travel have left us worn out.

After the agents change shifts at the counter, Dad and Mom try all over again. They flash what little cash they have in hopes of buying tickets. Please, can't someone find us a deal? I am hungry as always, chewing on my nails. Heidi is whimpering in the cold. Shaun is blank-eyed, two fingers in his mouth.

"For you," a gray-haired gentleman says. "Please, you take."

We glance up.

"Do not be afraid," he tells us softly.

Our parents are still pleading with the agents, unaware of our elderly visitor. The man holds up small gift bags, one for each of us. Shaun and I lean forward. Heidi looks skeptical since her last offer from a stranger came in the form of a cobra.

"Take them," the man implores us. His eyes glow with an inner light and his smile seems genuine. "God gives good gifts to His children, *da?*"

We accept the bags. Peering inside, we find packaged Matchbox cars and Manner hazelnut wafers. The gloom lifts and our mouths drop in wonder.

"Mommy," Heidi calls. "Look at what that old man gave us."

She hurries over. "What old man? What're you talking about?"

"There," the three of us say in unison.

He's gone, though. Across the vast waiting area, there isn't a single person visible. There are no flights boarding or arriving at this time. We are alone.

"He gave us these." Heidi holds up her bag. "He was right here, Mommy."

She marvels at our gifts. "They're perfect, something fitting for each of you. You know what I think? I think you kids just met an angel."

"He was wearing a long gray overcoat," I counter.

"We're not making it up," Shaun insists.

"Oh, I believe you. The Bible calls angels messengers and ministers. We can be visited by one, completely unaware, and I think that's what just happened." Mom leans in. "God wants you to know He cares for you. Look around. If that wasn't an angel, who else could have given you these bags? I haven't seen Matchbox in ages, and do you remember these Austrian wafers? You and the Banker girls loved them."

In this moment, the treats taste downright heavenly.

"Good news." Dad rushes over from the counter. "I finagled a bit and we've got a flight out of here. We have to hurry, though. There are connections through London, with a ferry from Dover to Holland. We'll fly standby out of Amsterdam. Three or four days from now, we should be back in the U.S. of A."

"America, here we come," Heidi cheers.

This is it. We crossed the Atlantic three years ago to find our dad, and now he is going back with us. The breakdown did not happen. I smile as we race through the terminal. Everything is fine. Everything will be perfect. After 40,000 kilometers through twenty-three nations across two continents, we are returning to North America. We kids aren't really sure what this country will look like or if we'll even have places to lay our heads, but this third continent is the land of our births.

Until now, home has always been just the five of us–Dad, Mom, Eric, Heidi, and Shaun. For the first time, though, home will also mean a physical location.

Both definitions will be severely tested before we are through.

PART 3
HOME FIRES BURNING

Home's where you go
when you run out of homes.

John le Carre

Heidi concentrating on her card game

Shaun, Dad, Eric, Heidi, Mom on Disneyland trip

Heidi, Mom, Shaun, Eric, Dad ready for Halloween

Dad & Mom chatting in the backyard

20

Shaun

We are at JFK airport in New York City, our first steps back onto American soil. Everything seems bigger here, shiny and clean. It's unfamiliar to us, overwhelming. But this is home, that's what Dad and Mom tell us. This is where we belong.

As Dad sets off with my brother in search of food, Mom plants me and my sister in a row of lobby chairs. Mom listens to a public announcement, then says, "Don't move. I'll be five steps away, checking departures."

"When's our next plane?" Heidi asks.

"Just pray we don't get stuck here overnight."

We won't actually be going anywhere, but we don't know this yet.

If we think all the darkness has been left overseas, we are wrong. The darkness is here too and will reach into our personal lives. Betrayal. Abuse. Sexual predators. Shame. For the next twelve years, we will chase healing and forgiveness, even as others put us on a pedestal and call us the all-American Christian family.

What do we know? We are kids.

Our parents, in their mid-twenties, are practically kids themselves.

Of course, we have no idea of the battles our parents will face, unable to shake off the demons of their pasts.

Steps away from me, Mom is still studying the big departure board. Though her back is turned, I can't miss her long red hair. I shift my attention to the escalator, where travelers go up and down without even lifting their legs. I've never seen moving stairs before. My mechanical mind wants to know more.

I slip from my seat. My mom is still close by.

Almost five now, I kneel by the down escalator and set my right palm on a metal step. The step descends, flattens, and I move my palm to the next step. Pretty cool. This one also descends in a consistent motion, driven by a purring motor.

A passing traveler tells me to get up and stop playing around. I lift my chin. People are rushing past–businessmen, Orthodox Jews, a clown carrying balloons, and a woman pushing a stroller. They block the view of my mom. Where is she? Diverted, I forgot to lift my hand from the descending step.

The motor reacts instantly.

Urrrr-urh-urrrr-urh...

The metal steps slow as my right hand gets caught in the bottom grill. I stare in shock, not yet feeling pain. I rip my hand free and know right away it isn't good. Two fingers, part of my palm, and the meat along the side of my hand are torn. There isn't much blood, which fascinates me. It looks like ground beef.

"Shaun?" My mom cries out. "Shaun, where are you?"

With my hand behind my back, I rush toward her voice and tug on her pants.

"Don't wander off," she scolds me. "It looks like we've been delayed again."

My stomach feels weird. I lift my chin to meet her eyes.

"What's wrong?" she says. "Honey, talk to me."

I bring the mangled hand into view, and as I do, blood wells through the shredded skin, streaks down my arm, and *drip-drip-drips* on the floor.

Mom scoops me into her arms and sprints down the airport corridor toward the nearest bathroom. She sets me on the counter, puts my hand under the tap, and turns on the cold water. Until now the pain hasn't kicked in. The moment the water hits, the agony explodes through my body, worse than anything I've ever felt. Tears turn everything blurry, a collage of swirls, yellow dots, and throbbing crimson.

The world tilts. Goes black.

When my eyes finally open, my family is gathered around in an empty first-class lounge. Airport medical staff have come to my aid, cleansing the wound, applying antibiotic cream, wrapping it in thick gauze. I receive a tetanus shot. At last, a doctor arrives to give his prognosis.

"The muscle and nerve damage are significant," he tells my parents. "Even stitches won't do much good since there are no viable folds of remaining skin to suture. Truth is, your son will never again have full use of his hand."

"Yes, I will," I declare.

"Son," the doctor says, "you have sustained severe lacerations."

"Jesus will heal me."

"Excuse me, but I've been doing this for—"

"Daddy and Mommy say God's healed people before."

The doctor whips toward my parents. "You two have brainwashed this kid with your nutcase beliefs. You're not doing him any favors, you know? Face reality."

I feel sorry for the man. Being a doctor, he thinks he knows everything. I realize I am badly hurt. I'm not stupid. I also know this doctor can believe whatever he wants, but he shouldn't try taking away the faith of a little boy.

We spend the night at JFK, using airline blankets and pillows in a lounge that smells of stale cigarettes. Not exactly the grand homecoming we envisioned. Eric twists himself into a pretzel to get comfortable in a chair. Heidi folds herself easily between the armrests. My parents barely sleep as I moan for hours on end.

~ ~ ~

Days before Christmas 1974, we arrive with our five bags in Eugene, Oregon, welcomed by old friends Ray and Dodie Kelly into their place on River Road. This drafty house with weeds visible through the floorboards is our new home.

We will live here for the next four years.

The following evening, I'm put into the bath and told to keep my wrapped hand out of the water. Mom goes back to the living room to share her overseas adventures with Dodie and a women's church group. Dodie likes to laugh. Her name sounds funny to me, like dhoti, the men's clothing in India. Settling my hand into the bubbles, I move it like a fin along the surface. The bathwater turns lukewarm. My bandages absorb water, unwind, and work themselves loose. I study my exposed skin. It's smooth and pink, no scars. Besides being extra itchy, it feels fine.

"See," I mutter. "I knew it."

Mom pokes her head in. "How are you doing?"

"Look." I lift my arm. "Jesus healed me."

Her hands fly to her cheeks. "Oh, Shaun, your hand, it's all better." She rushes me into the living room, my body dripping water, and shows me around to the ladies. "Look at how it's closed up. It's gone! It's like nothing ever happened."

I am mostly embarrassed. I'm naked, after all.

Anyway, why is she so surprised? She's the one who always says Jesus heals.

21

Eric

Though we kids haven't met our great-grandmother yet, we feel her influence. Granny is the Wilson matriarch, a widow whose husband graduated from law school, argued before the Supreme Court, and served in the Marine Corps during World War II. She views science as a guide and religion as an obstacle. While she thinks it "simply asinine," the way her grandson dragged his wife and children around the globe on some spiritual escapade, she decides paying for us to attend private school is better than subjecting us to one of those "horrid public schools."

In early 1975, Heidi, Shaun, and I are enrolled at Eugene Christian School, off Amazon Parkway. It is on the south end of town, far from where we live, but we are surrounded by kids who look and believe as we do.

Or so we think.

At first, I feel welcome, greeted warmly by my teacher in American English. When I spell color as *colour* and center as *centre*, she doesn't get upset. When I pronounce airplane as *aeroplane*, she just smiles.

No rulers on my wrist? No shouting? No uniforms?

Already, I like this place.

When mealtime comes around, I and the other second-graders who can't afford cafeteria food sit at our desks with brown paper bags. Controlling my nail-biting in class has been harder than expected and I am hungry. I chomp into my sandwich as I quietly thank God for this food.

"Ummm, I'm telling." A boy points his finger at me.

Wrinkling my forehead, I set down my food.

"You didn't pray before eating," he says. "You're going to be in trouble."

"I did so pray."

"You're joshing," another kid joins in. "You didn't even fold your hands."

"I'm not joshing," I say. I have no idea what the word means, but I'm not guilty of whatever they think. "I thanked God."

"If you didn't fold your hands and close your eyes, it doesn't count."

This rule is new to me. Until our return to the States, we haven't even attended regular Sunday church services. Instead of pounding us with religious regulations, our parents focus on our attitudes and ways of treating others. Our faith is organic, lived each day through conversations and encounters and home meetings with other believers. Praying over our food is more an attitude of thankfulness than a physical posture we take.

An olive-skinned kid with black curly hair steps between me and the other boys. "Leave Eric alone," he says. "He's new."

"You can't make me, Eben. I'm telling the teacher."

Eben strolls over and sits by me. "Don't let him bug you."

I shrug and take another bite of my sandwich.

"There are nicer kids," Eben assures me. "You met Pat yet? You'll like him. I'm Jewish and he's Arabic. Everyone says we should fight, but we get along fine. Our moms do too."

Eben is an only child, raised by a single mother who also happens to work at Faith Center with Roy Hicks, Jr. Eben will be my best friend through junior high. Together, we will form spy clubs, study atoms and quasars, and play chess.

When our teacher hears of what happened at lunch, she addresses the entire class. "Please, let's all be kind to one another. Eric's just returned from living in India, so he's still adjusting to the way we do things here."

I shift in my seat, my eyes on my desk.

What does it even mean to be an American? Does this make me any smarter, richer, or better-looking? Does it qualify me as a Christian?

People here assume I will act and speak as they do. Throughout my travels, I've rarely had trouble adjusting. I am attuned to facial expressions, tones of voice, and unspoken motives. My parents have taught me to evaluate individuals by their character, not by their intelligence, wealth, clothing, or appearance.

So, what am I missing here?

I feel like a stranger in my own land.

~ ~ ~

More adjustments are made that afternoon at the corner market, where I try to barter with the guy at the register. With a depressed Oregon economy, Dad working late shifts at Caribou Campers, and Mom using food stamps to buy powdered milk, Tang, and Spam, money is in short supply in our house. I have only a few coins in my pocket and I've already promised Heidi and Shaun some candy bars.

"That'll be seventy-five cents," the clerk tells me again.

I fold my arms. "I'll give you forty for all three."

The clerk looks less than amused by my efforts. "Look, kid, the price is right there. Twenty-five each. It's not up to me."

Empty-handed, I march toward the exit and expect the clerk to call me back to negotiate. He does no such thing. My dad taught me to haggle in India, but none of my techniques are working here. I can't make sense of it. While the clerk ignores me and rings up the next customer, I slip back into the store. I glance around, stuff three new candy bars into my pants' waistband, then zip up my coat.

Out the doors I go.

At the corner of River Road and Knoop Lane, I check both ways before darting through traffic toward our ramshackle house. We live with the Kellys and their toddler, eight of us packed into the two-bedroom structure. Thick Visqueen plastic is stapled over the windows to fight the chill, but it mostly turns things dreary. We are always cold anyway, our toes perpetually numb. Dad tells us to ignore it, layer up, and wear two pairs of socks. Right now, I miss Ajmer's sunshine and heat.

As I tramp through the weeds in our yard, Dad steps onto our sagging porch.

"It didn't work," I tell him. "The clerk wouldn't haggle with me."

"Sorry, bud, doesn't work that way here. The price is fixed." He points to some solid white lines on the road. "And you see that? In America, we use crosswalks. You can't just run through the traffic. You have to press the button on the pole, then wait for a walk signal to appear. Once it does, *you* get to cross and the *cars* have to wait."

"Can't I go when I see a gap?"

"Use the crosswalks, Eric. Even then, look both ways. Which... oh, that's also different. Cars here drive on the opposite side of the road, so you need to look *left, right, left*. You got it?"

"Even if it's raining, I have to wait for the signal?"

Dad nods. "God sets authorities over us for our good. I've had my share of run-ins with the cops, but, for the *most* part, they're just trying to keep us safe."

"What if they're communists?"

"You mean our Bible smuggling? Now that you kids know about that, I hope you understand you should always honor the laws of the land unless they run counter to God's Word. In that case, God's law is the one we obey."

The candy tucked into my waistband feels conspicuous and I wonder if Dad knows what I've done. Will God understand just this once?

I excuse myself and hurry inside to deliver the stolen goodies.

~ ~ ~

Heidi

They say opposites attract. Karma is contemplative, tall and lanky, with green eyes. I am bubbly, short and muscular, with violet blues. She lives one block over, and I'm told her mother taught us both in preschool before our family left the States. I don't remember it, but who cares?

Karma and I are the exact same age. Born the same day.

The very same hour.

Despite the cold, my new best friend and I roam every foot of our half-acre on River Road. We climb cherry and plum trees, ready to pick their fruit when summer comes. We build tunnels through the sticker bushes and pluck blackberries from the brambles growing through the bathroom wall, eating them while doing our business.

I try not to notice the shinier things at Karma's place. She has a neatly stocked wooden playhouse with a store-bought kitchen play set. My parents construct a play kitchen for me using large boxes, paint, and duct tape. Yes, Mom's told me wanting what someone else has is wrong. *Thou shalt not covet* is one of the Ten Commandments.

But doesn't the Bible also say God gives us the desires of our hearts?

What if I desire my friend's stuff?

What if she desires something of mine?

Sadly, Karma and I don't attend the same school. She goes to River Road Elementary and I've just started at Eugene Christian.

I have first-day jitters as my teacher introduces me to the class then directs me to my desk. As much as I miss Karma, I look forward to discovering new things today. Science and math, of course. But also stuff about the Bible.

Pulling out a pencil, I turn to a girl beside me. "Hi, what's your name?"

"Anna Dale," she whispers.

Anna has short brown bangs, dimpled cheeks, and a grin turned up at the corners by the faintest hint of mischief. We also will be friends for years to come, a connection which will alter the courses of both our lives—and of many others as well.

"What's today's date?"

"January eighth." Her eyes shift downward.

I pencil this date on top of my desk just as I did in Ajmer. A moment later I feel a hand on my shoulder.

"Heidi, we don't talk during class," the teacher says, then her tone turns sharp. "What are you doing?"

"Writing my name and date right here on my–"

"Unacceptable, young lady. We do not write on school property. You will stay after the bell to clean that off." Shaking her head, she takes her place in front of her students. "Class, please rise for the pledge of allegiance."

Everyone stands, placing their hands on their hearts. Anna shoots me a look, wondering whether I will join in. As they all face the American flag and chant, I glance around the room, bewildered. Why are we giving allegiance to a wavy piece of cloth? How is this any different than bowing to idols in other countries?

After school, Mom explains to me the distinction between a slate desk you write on and a wooden desk you never write on. She also describes the contrast between chanting to Hindu gods and acknowledging loyalty to one's country.

The desk part makes sense. I'm not so sure about the other.

Isn't our loyalty to God alone?

I have been told things will be different here, but school is just one more place where I learn to obey and keep questions to myself. As a foundation for learning, the classroom now seems shaky. I drag myself to my desk the next morning, where I slump, arms folded, into my seat.

22

Heidi

Since material things are in short supply at our house, my brothers and I collect ladybugs, worms, frogs, and salamanders. Our parents take us to Greenhill Humane Society so we can get even larger pets. Eric picks a puppy. Shaun selects a guinea pig.

All I want is a kitty, but I can't seem to find the right one.

Mom hears of a family offering kittens for free. We find the newborns in the family's laundry room, and Mom says I can have my pick. The all-black one is biggest, the all-white is fluffiest, and then I spot a little gray-and-white striped ball in the corner.

I lift my finger. "I want that one."

"She's injured," the lady of the house notes. "She crawled into a pile of clothes in the dryer, and it got turned on. Her leg is broken. It's unlikely she'll make it."

I bring the tiny creature to my face, careful not to hurt the limb hanging at an angle. "Flower, she smells like a flower. That's her name."

The lady whispers to my mom, "Just come get another one when she dies."

At home, I talk gently to Flower and she mews pitifully as my dad straightens the broken leg and secures it with Popsicle sticks and masking tape. Mom is sensitive to dander and fleas, but she gathers old blankets for Flower's bed. I sleep with my kitten, bathe with her. I am hers and she is mine. One weekend on a windswept beach, Mom photographs me and my brothers holding our precious animals.

While our mom is mostly uninterested in pets, she does love pointing out intricate designs in nature—the veins of a maple leaf, the scales of a pine cone, the wonders of a spider web. God's fingerprints are everywhere, she tells us, if only we have eyes to see. She leads us on scavenger hunts and on day trips to the river to swim and ride inner tubes. Creating memories is her specialty. She'll stop suddenly in the forest, crouch down, and tell us we're on a Bible-smuggling mission, which means we better chew our carrot sticks quietly to avoid the KGB.

Of course, sugary foods are *verboten*. Cavities are to be avoided.

As much as we love our mom, my brothers and I miss our dad.

Since our return, he has gone from saving the world to getting secondhand highs while working the paint booth at Caribou Campers. Weekdays, he arrives home past our bedtimes. Saturdays, we alternate time alone with him, an hour or two to shoot baskets, sneak ice-cream cones, or skip rocks on the Willamette River.

Dad's our comic relief, entertainer, hero, and best friend.

Unable to spend much time with us, he comes up with unique ways of showing his love. When I lose a tooth, he sneaks in as I sleep, leaves a note beneath my pillow, then runs a string from the bedpost all through the room, leading me on a treasure hunt until I find the prize at the other end.

He's the best tooth fairy ever.

He is also our disciplinarian. A role he despises.

During the week, my brothers and I earn spankings for backtalking, lying, and fighting. Eric usually gets in trouble for refusing to admit he's wrong. Whenever I try to help Shaun, he accuses me of bossing him around–and maybe I do, just a little. He then bows and starts mocking me. "Yes, Your Highness," he says. "Stop it," I react. "Stop it," he echoes. It's not long before we are screaming at each other.

This is the mid-1970s. Corporal punishment is a thing in many homes, and popular evangelical books remind parents not to spoil their kids by sparing the rod. The principal's paddle at our Christian school has wear marks in the wood.

Dad quotes Ephesians 6:4, which says, "fathers, do not provoke your children to wrath, but bring them up in the nurture and admonition of the Lord." He says it's best to discipline us after he has cooled down. This seems to work with Eric and me. We turn teary and contrite, bending over for the inevitable.

Shaun's backbone doesn't bend so easily.

In years to come, Shaun will tell how he got the worst of it, spanked more often and more angrily. When he is slammed up against the refrigerator one evening, Eric jumps from his seat to defend him, but Mom shakes her head and waves Eric back. Best to ride out the storm. Shaun even recounts being pulled from Sunday service for beatings behind the Dumpster. While Eric and I don't witness this ourselves, we realize everyone goes through things in childhood which no one else sees. Do any of us truly know or feel what others have endured?

Shaun, in many ways, is the most tenderhearted in our family, willing to do anything for anyone. All I know is, at some point the turtle's shell cracks.

~ ~ ~

In the Wilson household, being wasteful is a no-no. Practically, a sin. We don't toss away bread crusts or apple skins. When a family friend brings over pastries and vegetables salvaged from garbage bins behind Safeway, we just cut off the moldy parts.

"In everything give thanks," Mom says, "for this is the will of God."

Dad teaches us to take seven-minute showers, a luxury compared to three cups of water in Ajmer. We save by buying clothes at thrift stores. Dad carries around a roll of TP instead of Kleenex to blow his prominent, runny *schnoz*, as he calls it.

Medical attention is in God's hands. Dad and Mom don't take us to doctors or clinics. Good thing they encourage flossing, since we never go to the dentist.

We are not poor, not really. We have seen true squalor and starvation, so this word does not apply to us. Between paychecks, though, there are days when pickings get slim. Eric, almost nine, is always hungry, and more than once he plucks grass from the backyard, stuffs it in his mouth, and starts chewing. "It has chlorophyll," he says.

I don't remind him of all the times our pets do their business out there.

One evening, the five of us sit down for dinner. There's no food at the table. None of Mom's cream of spinach soup. No peas. No rice pudding. Nothing. Still, Dad thanks God for the meal we are about to receive. As he wraps up his prayer, we hear a loud knock at the door. When we answer, there is not a soul in sight, but we find a box bulging with groceries on our front porch.

Dinner is served.

~ ~ ~

Eric

Dad's trust in God is real, yet he also fights fears we can't always comprehend.

One evening, he is driving our old Mercury along the coastal highway, headlights piercing the fog. Salty air wafts through my window and I feel sand between my toes after climbing the dunes at Honeyman State Park. We are on our way home from a camping trip with other Faith Center families. We'll later develop photos taken with various kids outside the tents and campers. These will be treasured memories, glimpses into the past.

And in one particular case, a glimpse into my future.

Now, through the rearview mirror, I see Dad's eyes grow round and white.

Mom glances over. "What is it, Mark?"

"We're being followed."

"Oh, honey, it's Highway 101. We're not the only car out here."

"In the dead of night? Sticking right on my tail? This isn't a *game*."

My mind flashes to our Bible-smuggling trips. Being tailed was common in Eastern Europe, but it doesn't make sense here in Oregon.

I adjust my sweet dog on my lap in the backseat. I call her Goodny because she's so well behaved and I have a true case of puppy love. On school days, I can't wait to get home to watch Goodny's little tan ears flap up and down as she runs around the yard. At the moment, she's curled into a ball. Heidi and Shaun are asleep with their own pets. Eben leans against my shoulder, also snoozing.

"Get off my ass," Dad hisses at his mirror, clearly still fluent in French.

"Can't you just let them go around?" I suggest.

"Eric, what're you *doing*? You shouldn't even be awake."

"I'm not little anymore."

"Well, look at Eben. He's out like a light. Now close your eyes, bud."

I obey, content to rest my head on my friend's thick curly hair. These days, Eben and I do almost everything together. We love Legos. We sword fight with fallen branches. We even play on an extracurricular soccer team together, along with Heidi, though we've lost every game so far.

My eyes pop open again as the Mercury roars toward a curve. We hit 60 mph, which Dad says is almost 100 kilometers an hour. I am still learning how to convert to U.S. measurements. I cradle Goodny to my belly as Dad rounds the corner, hits the brakes, and turns hard onto a logging road. He kills the engine and lights.

"Mark, honey," Mom says, "don't you think you're being—?"

"*Quiet.*" Dad slides down in his seat. "C'mon, duck your head." He waits two full minutes before he sits up, starts the engine, and backs onto the highway, the sparkle returning to his eyes. "You see that, bud? We lost them."

Mom rests a hand on Dad's arm. In the glow of the dash her eyes glisten with concern, and she asks, "Are you alright?"

"I'm *fine*, Linda. Stop mothering me."

She looks sad. She knows better than anyone the pain he still carries...

Unmoored

Oakland, California — 1956-1976

At seven years old, Mark Wilson lacked physical nurture and would do anything for the attention of a drunk, disinterested mother. He and his brother Paul became young pyromaniacs. At a farm, they lit baby chicks just to watch the yellow fuzz flare and fizzle. In an argument with their younger sister Laura, Paul flicked a match that caught fire and stuck to her face. Their mother ignored the screams.

Mark decided to practice his fire-building on a newspaper pile beside the neighbor's house. He was fanning the sparks when the neighbor rounded the corner.

"Young man, what're you doing there?"

"I'm... putting this out," Mark said, grabbing a rag to smother the mess. "Didn't want your garage catching fire."

"Why, that's mighty responsible of you. You're a Wilson, aren't you?" The man shrugged. "Guess you can't believe everything you hear around here." He pulled a $10 bill from his pocket. "Here you go. Consider it a hero's reward."

Impressed, Mark figured he would try the kid-to-the-rescue ploy one more time. He waited a few days, then started another fire by the same neighbor's house. This time when the man arrived and watched Mark snuff out the flames, he wasn't as effusive in his praise. He didn't even fork over a dollar.

Now Mark was upset. He crept back hours later and started a roaring inferno. By the time someone noticed, the garage was engulfed. Fire engines arrived as shotgun shells fired off from within, causing onlookers to dive for cover. The neighbor was certain Mark was involved, but Mark coughed up an alibi which his parents backed to save their own reputations in the community.

Soon after, the drinking began. Mark first watched Paul gulp down a glass of their mother's Smirnoff vodka, mistaking it for water. His brother stumbled around the house, laughing and banging into things before collapsing on the floor. That's when Mark realized alcohol could dull the feelings of neglect.

By the time he reached high school, Mark was smoking, riding a motorcycle, and running from cops who saw him speed by. Even a wife and newborn didn't stop him from playing car tag with a sheriff through Oakland's steep and winding streets. When he lost control of his vehicle on a curve and inadvertently killed the engine, he found himself facing a weapon out the window of a county cruiser. He did his jail time on weekends, permitted to work during the week for the sake of his wife and child.

Since then, Mark had been born again, and God had forgiven his past.

But the past still carried repercussions.

~ ~ ~

Before meeting and marrying Mark, Linda Guise had some dark moments of her own. She came home one evening from tennis practice and realized her beautiful canary was missing from its perch. At the dinner table, she asked her father, who was never a fan of the bird, where her pet had gone.

"What do you think you're eating?" he smirked. "Hope you like your soup."

Linda ran down the hall and flung herself, bawling, onto her bed. She swore to herself she would never love another pet. Her heart could not bear the pain.

Were her father's words spoken in jest?

If so, he never told her so.

Even to her death, Linda wouldn't say much about her interactions with her father. There were doors to her past which she would always keep locked. Some secrets were too painful to let loose.

Mark and Linda were two empathetic souls, drawn like moths to the flame of each other's affection. When they found the depths of God's love, they felt compelled to share it with others, including those in distant lands.

Now at last, they were back in America. And they felt unmoored.

They had not only carried the burden of lost souls in faraway places, but of their own small children as they crossed borders, mountains, and deserts. Mark had almost left his faith. Linda nearly succumbed to freezing weather. Eric bore scars from a dog in Pakistan, Heidi narrowly avoided sex traffickers in eastern Turkey, and Shaun survived amoebic dysentery in the heat of northern India.

Meanwhile, most people in the States were fixated on the price of gas or the latest TV show. And the glut of food here, it was too much. The unforgivable waste.

Ray and Dodie Kelly were kindred spirits. Years ago they had stayed at Mark and Linda's place on Barrett Avenue, and they were quick to offer their own on River Road in return. This was how Christians were supposed to operate, as a community, everyone helping each other. For Dodie, this meant three more children underfoot as she cared for her own toddler and as her husband completed his doctorate.

Ray proved to be a faithful friend. Wearing sideburns even wider than Mark's, he worked as a developmental chemist at Sacred Heart Hospital. Together, he and Mark watched *Star Trek* episodes, played chess, and cracked open beers—whenever Linda was gone, of course—to cheer on the Oregon Ducks basketball team.

Mark and Ray also discussed points of theology, trying to apply spiritual concepts to everyday life. How could you help the poor without enabling addiction or homelessness? Should you obey a boss who made unethical business decisions? If you stumbled morally, could you still qualify for spiritual leadership?

Ray often shrugged and said, "God always has a plan B."

A year after the Wilsons returned, Ray Kelly finished his studies and took a post-doctorate at a coroner's office in Ohio, where he would work with a forerunner in forensic pathology. The Kellys packed up their stuff, rented their house to the Wilsons, and headed east.

The loss of this friendship hit Mark hard.

To whom could he turn? Whom could he trust?

For years, both men had encouraged each other to stand strong in their spiritual convictions and to resist the bombardment of sexual temptations.

Ray wrote in a letter to Mark:

> Remember that we are redeemed... In Greek culture, a freed slave... was subject to being made a slave again unless he could produce the slip of paper which said, "For freedom I have purchased thee..." The blood of Jesus is our proof document to prove we are no longer a slave even if we look like one in some areas of our life...

Those words struck a chord.

Yes, Mark realized, people living in a land of freedom could still be imprisoned in ways no one else understood. Their chains were often forged from shame and pain. He knew these chains well, and he wanted nothing more than to help others be free.

23

Heidi

One evening in early 1976, I hear cries from the dining area. My heart lurches into my throat. I rush down the hall to find my oldest brother on his knees. Goodny, his puppy, is lying on a towel on the floor. Is she asleep? Is something wrong with her?

"Why isn't she moving? Goodny, wake up," Eric urges, cupping her head. "It's okay, Goodny, I'm right here. I know you can do it. Wake up."

Dad rests a hand on his shoulder. "I'm sorry, bud, but I don't think she can hear you. I was studying when I heard a car slam on its brakes. It's getting dark out, so I'm guessing they didn't see her till it was too late."

"No. She's not even bleeding. She's fine."

I lean closer and point. "Look, there's a cut on her back leg."

"That's deep," Dad notes. "All the way to the bone."

My brother snaps his head around. "Why didn't the car stop? Whoever it was should've tried to find us, to tell us what happened. You have to help her." He shrugs off Dad's hand. "If we hurry and do something, she'll get better."

."Listen, Eric, that cut tells me it happened instantly. There wasn't even time for any bleeding to start. Maybe her neck was broken. *Whatever* happened, I doubt she felt any pain. Goodny's not coming back."

Our dad has a knack for helping us smile through hardship and pain, and he often shows irreverence during formal events and funerals. Now, though, hearing him speak in grave tones, I know this must be real. My big brother's beloved pet is gone.

"God can heal her." Eric stands and sets his chin. "I just have to pray."

"It's too late," Dad reiterates. "She's dead, buddy."

"What about Lazarus? He was dead. We believe in the Bible, right? And didn't Jesus heal Shaun's hand?"

"He *did*. Right now, though, I just don't think—"

"I'm going to my room to pray. Goodny will start breathing again."

As my brother marches off, my dad pulls me closer. Tears spill down my cheeks. This is all part of life. It's true, Shaun's hand got better, but people and animals die, including some of our turtles and goldfish. Even at my age, I understand nothing on this earth lasts forever. Without death, why would we even need heaven?

Dad rests his hand on Goodny's chest, checking to be sure. For a moment, hope springs up in me and I await his verdict.

"Just as I thought," he whispers.

Eric bounds toward us from the bedroom, his eyes red and puffy. "Is she alive yet? Is she breathing?" He studies our faces and shakes his head. "Seven times, that's how many times Naaman had to dip in the river before he got better. That's in the Bible. I'll pray six more times and then she'll be fine."

I watch him head off again for his bunk bed. I imagine him up there, sniffling and mumbling into his pillow. Of course, he wants his puppy back. If I could fix it all myself, I would. After my brother's seventh attempt, though, he falls to the floor beside us. His voice cracks as he pleads with Goodny to rise up and take a breath.

"She was a great little mutt," Dad says. "Goodny sure lived up to her name."

"Why's she still dead?" My brother's eyes look hollow.

"We'll give her a nice burial in the backyard."

"By the big tree," I suggest. "The one where we took pictures with her."

"It doesn't make sense," Eric says. "She hasn't even moved."

"God doesn't always answer our prayers," Dad says. "Least not in the ways we expect. Typically, He's not going to defy the laws of nature He Himself put in place."

My brother grits his teeth. "I prayed. I believed."

Before Dad can say another word, Eric runs from the house, slamming the door behind him. Where he goes, I'm not sure. Maybe he's up in the red cedar tree on the corner, too high for me to follow. Sometimes, you need time alone.

Eric still looks mad when he returns for dinner.

I nudge his arm. "Goodny was such a cute little girl. She loved you, Eric."

"She did," Dad agrees. "And as your father, all I can do is love you guys when you're hurting. That's more than..." His voice catches. "More than *I* ever got as a kid."

Eric's eyes remain hooded and dark. Chewing on a nail, he doesn't say a word.

~ ~ ~

Shaun

Eric is mourning his puppy dog even as America prepares to celebrate its two-hundredth birthday. Stars and stripes are everywhere. We hear all about the Boston Tea Party and Paul Revere's ride. Flags and bald eagles appear on everything from mailboxes to lunch pails. I'm especially interested in the eagles. I've seen big ugly vultures hunched over roadkill in Asia, but eagles are both large and beautiful.

Eric, Heidi, and I get an early taste of patriotism during the Super Bowl.

"You're watching the Dallas Cowboys," Dad says. "America's team. Around here, *this* is what *we* call football. The quarterback, Roger Staubach, you know he's a born-again Christian."

We often hear America and Christianity mentioned in the same breath, and we know the pilgrims came over on the *Mayflower* to find religious freedom. We are taught that our founding fathers were all good God-fearing men.

Hold on, though. Didn't some of the early settlers kill Native Americans? And didn't some of the thirteen original colonies import slaves from Africa's shores?

Plus, I'm pretty sure Jesus was Middle Eastern.

"Our country's far from perfect," Dad agrees. "But at least we have freedom to live and worship as we choose. Just you wait till July Fourth. You kids'll *love* it. All across our country, there will be celebrations. We'll barbecue hot dogs and hamburgers, eat tons of potato chips, drink lots of pop, and watch fireworks."

Sounds fun. Coke and Mountain Dew are rare treats in our household, since our parents worry about us getting cavities. During our entire childhood, they will take us to a doctor and dentist a total of two or three times. Dad doesn't like to spend the money, and Mom doesn't trust Western medicine. She prefers natural remedies and trusts God to heal our infirmities. He is the Great Physician.

He's also Jehovah Jireh, our Provider—just not for medical bills, I guess.

"Will we get to sing?" I ask.

"You better *believe* it. Here, watch." Dad turns up the TV volume. "Before the game starts, there's always someone who belts out the national anthem."

"'My Country, 'Tis of Thee'?" Eric guesses.

"Try again."

"I know, I know." Heidi sits up straight. "'God Bless America.'"

"Both good songs. No, just listen."

We lean forward on the raggedy couch, taking our cues from our father as his eyes mist over during "The Star-Spangled Banner." His emotion is real. Sure, we have traveled all over the world, but we were born here in the U.S.A. Soldiers have fought and died to protect our freedom.

During halftime, I discover another American institution when the Dallas Cowboys cheerleaders prance onto the field. I feel something stir in me. I've never seen girls wear such skimpy outfits, certainly not in the countries we just came from.

"Mark, honey." Mom dons a worried expression as she sets homemade nachos on the coffee table. An olive rolls onto the floor. "Should the kids be watching this?"

"What? It's the Super Bowl."

"But the–"

"The girls? C'mon, so it's *my* fault guys like watching them shake their butts?" Dad chomps into a chip dripping with cheese and salsa. He turns toward us. "Can you believe these poor cheerleaders? They must be awfully cold, don't you think? They can't even afford to buy a little more clothing."

Roger Staubach and his Cowboys lose to the Steelers, 21-17.

Being a Christian doesn't guarantee you a win, I guess.

Using the football I got for Christmas, my brother and I throw spirals to each other in our long, puddled driveway. When Heidi joins us, we teach her to aim, step into a pass, and follow through. Before long, she can throw it as far as we can. We are all equals, and for the most part we get along.

We spend the next few months practicing our school bicentennial program. Eric and Eben wear stovepipe hats and quote Abraham Lincoln. Heidi and Anna Dale sing a rendition of the Ray Charles tune, "Fifty, Nifty United States." When Independence Day comes around, our family gathers with thousands of others to watch fireworks over Autzen Stadium. They take my breath away, the most amazing display I've ever seen.

America may have its issues, but I sense I am part of something special, something bigger than myself.

~ ~ ~

Fishing, I find out, is as American as football and the Fourth of July.

Our first real fishing lesson takes place with our uncles during a late summer visit to central California. Eric and I will head out with them on the delta, while Mom and Heidi go to the movies with Grandma Guise and our aunts, Mary, Teri, Laura, and Lynne. They all live here in Contra Costa County, east of Oakland. Dad's not particularly welcome on this side of the family.

I notice Mom gets quiet as she eases our car alongside a single-story house guarded by fruit trees. A yellow pickup truck sits in the driveway, with GUISE on the license plate. This is our grandparents' address. We have never been here. Though our grandma has visited us before, we don't even know what our grandpa looks like.

"Hi, kids," Grandma greets us at the curb, wearing a golf outfit and visor. "You made it. Good. Let's get a picture of you three over by Grandpa's truck, okay?" She guides us in front of the vehicle, as though it's a stand-in for our grandfather.

Eric throws his arm over my sister's and my shoulders. Heidi smiles.

Clickkk...

No, this is stupid. I want to see my grandpa, not some dumb old pickup.

"You wait here, Linda," says Grandma Guise. "It's been, what, eight or nine years? I will take the kids inside. They're his grandchildren, after all. Maybe he'll stop being so crazy in the head and finally show some sense."

We follow her into a sitting room where framed pictures of our aunts, uncles, and cousins are propped on lampstands. There's not a single picture of us. This could change today, of course. Eric, Heidi, and I have been praying for a miracle. From somewhere deep in the house, a door is thrown open. In an explosion of snarls and frowns, a large red-haired man—so this is where Mommy got her hair—blasts past us from a hallway and slams the front door on his way out.

Bammm!

Grandma urges me to chase after him, but his pickup roars to life and squeals around the corner before we can even say hello or goodbye.

Really? What'd we ever do to him?

The photos show Grandpa Guise with his other grandkids, smiling and having fun. They've created years of memories together, which means he cannot be all bad. So why be such an ogre to us? The more I dwell on it, the more it infuriates me.

Eric and Heidi stare at the door, wearing wounded expressions.

Nope, get over it, I think. He is not coming back.

"At least we tried." Grandma shrugs. "He's so gosh-darn stubborn."

By way of apology, she leads us into the kitchen, serves us bowls of Neapolitan ice cream, and shows us her owl figurines. She started this collection after she ran for local political office and won, using the tagline: *Be Wise, Vote Guise.*

Later that afternoon in an aluminum boat with an Evinrude outboard motor, Eric and I put worms on hooks and drop lines into the river. Our uncles guide us every step of the way. They provide hats, snacks, sunscreen, sinkers, bobbers, and lures. They teach us to cast without snagging each other and to net each fish we reel in. Over the years we will catch bass, trout, ling cod, flounder, even leopard shark. All of this gives me confidence, pitting myself against nature, knowing I won't go hungry.

Uncle Vinny guides our boat. He is well-educated, soft-spoken. Years ago, as we waited with our mom to fly overseas, he let us stay for a month in his college apartment despite his roommates' grumblings. Uncle Frank is a hardworking, no-nonsense guy, an elder in his church. Uncle Bobby, the youngest, wears a bushy red mustache, a Harley-Davidson t-shirt, and his heart on his sleeve.

These three uncles teach us to slow down, relax, and be patient. If love is spelled T-I-M-E, they show it to us on this first of many fishing trips.

And we catch a week's worth of salmon dinners.

As for Grandpa Guise, Mom tells us to love and keep praying for him. Okay, okay, but what does it mean to love a man who's never said a word to me? Will he ever be part of our lives?

Whenever Mom tries calling Grandpa on Easters or Christmases, he hangs up on her. She wrinkles her mouth and shrugs, but her eyes always turn watery. The moment Archie Bunker shows up on TV, from *All in the Family*, she leaves the room because she is reminded too much of her own father by Archie's harsh words and bigotry.

Mostly, it makes me sad for her.

Far as I'm concerned, he doesn't deserve to be called Grandpa, and I'm done wasting any energy on him. So what if we never see him again?

24

Heidi

As summer ends, Eric and I are transferred to public school. While Mom's not sure this is a good idea, Dad insists it will provide greater opportunities. "It won't just get you out of your Christian bubble," he assures us, "but you'll have more sports options and a much better science lab. It'll prepare you kids for the *real* world."

Have we been living in a fake world?

Sensing my confusion, he adds, "You guys have a lot of loving, caring people around you. You've been blessed. But not everyone out there is on your side."

He's right, as we'll soon find out.

I am in third grade, Eric is in fourth, and we finally feel like part of the local crew as we join neighborhood kids on the yellow school bus. Even better, I get to be with Karma every day now.

Right away, though, there are disparities between public and private school. We still pledge allegiance to the flag, but we never say prayer in class. Each grade has its own recess, instead of all ages playing together. There's also a lot of noise. Many kids keep talking even after the teachers tell us to be quiet. They yell both outside and inside the classroom, spewing words even our dad rarely utters. At least in Ajmer, classes were quiet, save the buzzing of insects and wobbly ceiling fans.

One day after school, I saunter into Dad's cramped home office. He's sniffling, blowing his schnoz into wads of TP, which lie strewn across the floor. He is focused on his Bible correspondence courses, but I spout off a rhyme I've heard on the playground.

His eyes dart up from his desk and I know I have his attention.

"What does it mean?" I ask. "The boys kept laughing as they said it, but I'm not sure why it's so funny."

"Well, Heidi, it seems there are some things I need to explain to you."

Dad picks up an EWEB—Eugene Water & Electric Board—utilities envelope. He draws pictures of boy and girl parts, which I know all about. I've passed naked children in India and seen my brothers when we take baths. As he goes into further details, though, I get confused about the mechanics. Is this how bodies work? For what purpose?

"All I'm saying, my little princess, is boys *will* notice you. They'll want to kiss you, but you don't need to kiss them. Even when they act nice, they're not always on your side, you understand? You should save yourself for someone special."

"But what's kissing got to do with these pictures?"

"You know, Heidi, you've got an awfully curious mind. Have you heard the saying, 'curiosity killed the cat'? Listen, this is important stuff, but you're only eight. We'll talk more later, okay? These bills have got to go out in today's mail."

And there it is, my intro to the mysteries of sex.

With the Kellys now gone, Eric, Shaun, and I no longer sleep in the same room. I've been moved into the laundry nook with a sheet hung up for my privacy. Is this because I have girl parts? I still sneak into my brothers' room after my parents tuck me in. Often, Eric and I stay up talking about the challenges at our new school and our thoughts about the opposite sex. It's a habit we'll continue into our teens.

"I miss Eben," Eric tells me one night. "At least you get to see Karma."

"At recess. We don't even have one class together, and I miss Anna."

"I'm the tallest kid in my class. The girls all stare at me like I'm weird, and I'm the only one not wearing bell bottoms."

"Maybe they like you. You know, some girls like tall boys. Guess what," I say, changing the subject. "I can do a flip off the bars now."

The next day at school, I decide to show Karma this latest maneuver. I climb onto the monkey bars and string my legs through. Though my mom wishes I would take ballet, I'm better suited for the strength of gymnastics and I'm confident I can do this.

"Look, Karma, it's easy. All you do is hang here and swing. See." My blond hair nearly touches the ground. "Then you just flip yourself off."

As I dismount, I don't consider the other bars in close proximity. My legs slam against the adjacent metal and my body crumples to the dirt. I try drawing in oxygen without success. My chest aches and my shins throb. My mouth opens again, but I can't breathe. Am I going to die?

There is a flurry of activity around me.

"Get her to the nurse's office. Her face is turning blue."

I feel myself scooped up, wind rushing past my face as I am jostled in someone's arms. Tears form and I still can't breathe. My body is placed on a metal table and I hear a door shut as the noise of the playground gives way to silence.

"You got the breath knocked out of you," a male voice says. He's one of the teachers. "I'm here now. You'll be alright."

I feel my pants being loosened. What is happening?

A cool hand slides downward.

While I don't know how anything down there is related to my breathing, I figure he must know what he is doing. There's sharp pain as something moves inside me. Is this what my dad was trying to draw on the utilities envelope? Tears burn trails down my cheeks, my lungs still scream, and darkness clouds my vision.

The door clicks open and someone else steps into the room. The male teacher keeps my body blocked from view and a gasp explodes from my throat as his hand slips roughly from my pants.

"Well, there you are." I recognize the nurse's steady voice. "I hear someone got the wind knocked out of her."

"She's all yours," the teacher says, edging toward the door. "She'll be alright, but I'm sure those shins will have some nasty bruises tomorrow."

He is gone.

While the fall from the monkey bars leaves me embarrassed, this violation by an authority figure fills me with dread. How do I even categorize the experience? What will my dad say if he finds out? Is this what the boys have been chanting about? Why would a teacher put his fingers there? Will I get pregnant?

Curiosity killed the cat, I remember.

I should stop asking questions.

Within the month, Eric and I are transferred back to Eugene Christian. Years later we learn our stint at public school was due to Granny's denial of financial support after she took issue with one of the private school's tenets. Thankfully, I never do get pregnant, and my brother and I are able to return to private school after some teachers gather quietly and vote to award us scholarships.

Relieved, I tuck away my shame and let my sexual questions go dark.

25

Shaun

In first grade, I realize we are lower-class kids at an upper-class school. Many of my classmates live in sprawling homes with plush carpets, fancy appliances, and multiple levels. Their cupboards are stuffed with Oreos and Hostess Ding Dongs, not just generic snacks. They have big TVs, Atari systems, and Mattel handheld games.

I'm invited for a sleepover one night. Making friends makes me happy.

I wake up to find fancy cold cereals on the breakfast bar–Cocoa Puffs and Cap'n Crunch. Shoot, there's even whole milk, which seems like a luxury. Powdered milk's all we get at home. "Why waste the stuff?" Eric often grumbles. "May as well just give us water."

I climb onto a stool beside my friend. I take one gulp of frothy white goodness–so this is what the real stuff tastes like–and wonder if I've gone to heaven.

My glass is from a set bearing DC superheroes, and I recognize Aquaman, Batman, Superman, and Wonder Woman. There's another I've never seen before, but he looks pretty cool.

"Who's he?" I ask my friend.

A cocoa puff dangles from his lip as he says, "Hell if I know."

After breakfast, we dart outside to enjoy a pause in the rain. My friend's mom and sister recline in their swimsuits, soaking up the sun. The joke in Oregon is that you don't really tan, you just rust. Well, let them rust if that's what they want.

My friend and I decide to play superheroes.

"I'm Batman," he says, donning a towel as a cape.

Shoot, that's who I was going to pick, since Eric and I love Batman. I know how it works, though. At a friend's house, they always get first dibs.

"Who are you going to be?" he wants to know.

My thoughts turn to that unfamiliar character on the DC glass. "Hellafino," I declare, then take off running around the backyard. "I'm Hellafino."

"Shaun," his mom barks. "Over here this minute."

"I'm Hellafino," I say again, speeding her direction.

"We do not use that language in our house," she informs me.

My shoulders slump. What'd I do wrong? I didn't give this superhero his name and I'm just repeating what my friend told me. Am I going to rat him out, though? Of course not. His mom's already mad enough.

I shrug. "Then I guess I'll be Aquaman. Least he can talk to dolphins."

~ ~ ~

Dynamite comes in small packages, that's what Mom tells me, and I feel powerful and confident as I stroll into my classroom. I'm not just a little kid anymore.

"I'm going to win top prize," I tell my teacher. She's pretty and I want to impress her.

"You're certainly capable, Shaun. Just do your best."

When it comes down to the final test, I practice my spelling list over and over, but lose out after missing a word–just one–having spelled *Washington* the way Mom pronounces it, with an *r* thrown in. The prize goes to a girl, and I'm so upset that I cross out her picture in our class photo. Who wants to see her mocking expression?

"Now, Shaun..." Mom pushes her hair over her shoulder and turns to the picture I've defaced. "Was this necessary? I'm sure the poor thing was simply doing her best, same as you. Don't you think you ought to forgive her?"

Maybe Mom's the one I need to forgive.

Warshington? Really?

My biggest problem forgiving people has to do with the grownups who treat me like I'm too small or dumb to be heard. During this school year, two particular people get under my skin.

The first, Mrs. Dale, is a thin woman, not much taller than me. She drives me back and forth to school, carpooling her own children and a number of others in her van. She tries to make things fun, telling us to throw our hands in the air as she races through dips and humps on Fox Hollow Road. We all squeal. Yep, she loves to goof around, and my brother and sister think she's great. Eric tries to get along with everyone, and Heidi knows Mrs. Dale from visits to Anna's house.

But Mrs. Dale has a short fuse with me. One wrong word can set her off.

After school one afternoon, Mrs. Dale spots me meandering toward her van as an elderly couple strolls by me on the sidewalk.

"What're you doing, Shaun?" she shouts. "Didn't you see those people?"

"I'm just—"

"You're on the wrong side, you disrespectful little brat. You were blocking their way." Her fingers clamp onto my head, nails digging into my scalp. "Get over here now."

I am dragged across the walkway and shoved into the vehicle. Her daughter, Anna Dale, is Heidi's friend. Anna has her face pressed to the window, but jerks her eyes the other direction as her mother shoots her a look. Mrs. Dale squeezes into the driver's seat, then tries to play things off with a silly joke and a sharp laugh.

"I don't want to go to school," I tell my parents the next day.

"School's not a choice," Dad informs me. "You'll get used to the routine."

"Do I have to ride with Mrs. Dale?"

"Grab your coat, Shaun. No excuses."

With my pleas falling on deaf ears, I turn to more drastic measures and start wetting my bed regularly. It's not a conscious decision, more of a psychological response—and it works. I wake up in warm pee, take a shower, and miss my ride.

Problem solved, for one day at least.

The second grownup who gives me grief is my global studies teacher. She's helping us learn about other countries now that our bicentennial celebration is over. She has my attention and I sit up at my desk as she names places familiar to me.

"France—"

"I've been there," I declare.

"Germany—"

"Been there, too."

My teacher peers at me over her glasses. "Shaun, let's not be disruptive."

The other students giggle and I do my best to keep my mouth shut. When it comes to India, though, I can't help myself.

"We lived there. The monkeys, they almost attacked me and Heidi."

"Shaun," the teacher barks, "come up here and apologize to the class."

"What'd I do?"

"Up here, Mr. Wilson."

When I remain in my seat, she hooks me by the wrist, pulls me to the front of the room, and gives me a couple of hard swats in front of everyone. My classmates don't say a word or come to my defense. Their silence is disappointing, but I refuse to shed a tear.

The next morning, I bring in my passport with its numerous stamps and visas. I figure this is the proof my teacher needs. She will be convinced I am telling the truth. Instead, her eyes widen briefly before that veil of superiority falls once again.

"My mistake." She gives me a curt nod. "Now take your seat."

No one else hears her admission of guilt.

There is no public apology.

I slide into my desk, fists balled. This isn't right. Then and there, I determine to stand up for my friends if any of them are ever treated this way.

~ ~ ~

My confidence is further shaken one afternoon at the local park. Out of nowhere, a group of girls ambush me between the swing sets and merry-go-round. I don't know how old they are, maybe twelve or thirteen. I don't know why they target me. They tackle me onto the sawdust and start tugging at my pants.

"Take 'em off," one of them orders the others. "Strip him."

What is going on? I'm a good wrestler, not used to being pinned so easily. I'm scared. And also oddly excited. Arching my back, I buck off my attackers, wriggle free, then race away from the park. First, it's Mrs. Dale clawing my head, and now its these girls pawing at me. Why can't they all just leave me alone?

I brush sawdust off my shirt and glance back over my shoulder. My heart pounds against my ribs. I feel that same stirring I had while watching the Cowboys cheerleaders, a flush of heat at my throat, a tightness in my gut.

What do those girls want? Why me?

I'm ashamed and humiliated and there's no one to talk to about this, not even my brother. I'm used to my sister ordering me around, but these older girls pose a threat—and temptation—which I'm not able to wrap my head around.

26

Eric

Eben and I are master spies, and we make hand-drawn business cards to prove it. These skills come in handy, since there could be kidnappers out there. I've never before been a fearful child. My parents arm me with facts, teach me confidence, and tell me staying calm is one of the best weapons. The more I hear in the news, though, the more I worry about mysterious illnesses and bad people.

At Eben's one night in south Eugene, we rig a string from the bedroom doorknob to a light switch, to an alarm clock, to a bucket. We climb smugly into our sleeping bags. Good luck messing with us. If you creep in to do something horrible to us, you will pay the price.

"You guys in bed yet?" Eben's mom calls.

She has a quick wit and easy laugh. We love her and have no intention of doing her harm. We call out a warning, but she's already pushing through the door. The string pulls taut, flicking on the light and triggering the alarm. Seconds later, the weighted bucket meant for criminals swings down hard into her breasts. She gasps, drops her head, and tries to gather herself.

Appalled and apologetic, we shoot up from our pillows.

Without even raising her chin, Eben's mom lifts a hand to acknowledge she is okay. "Well," she jokes at last, "looks like someone got caught in a booby trap."

Eben and I are still laughing as we doze off.

~ ~ ~

Nightmares become a regular part of my sleep. I am always running, seconds from being devoured by a huge stuffed boar we once encountered at the portcullis of an Austrian castle. The Wicked Witch of the West is another nemesis, reaching for me with long, warty fingers. Before bed each night, my mom reminds me of the scripture which says to resist the devil and he will flee. Fear, she tells me, is not of God.

My fears don't leave me, though. They pin me to my mattress in the dark.

Then one night, I personally face the devil in a dream.

The confrontation happens as Eben and I are leaving a church wedding. The moment we step outside, the devil and a leering cohort swagger into our path. They tell us they are going to capture us. They probably use the word *kidnap*. Eben and I glance at each other, then start tearing verses from our Bibles and flicking them with plastic spoons we kept from the wedding reception.

The devil dodges. He dances. "Oooh... awww..."

Within seconds, he and his goon are fleeing across the parking lot while we watch with satisfied grins.

My bed becomes a safer place from that point forward, my pillow a reliable refuge. The terror is gone. The nightmares morph into tales of suspense, and even the deadliest threats just add to the thrill. I have resisted and watched the devil flee.

While Mom has helped me successfully address my fears, neither she nor my dad address the sexual curiosity now burrowing into my thoughts.

I'm just entering puberty.

Like most evangelical parents in the 1970s, my parents trust a Christian school to provide a solid education as well as protection from society's wickedness. Eugene Christian is a reputable place with a strong curriculum and committed teachers. As students, we take part in scripture-memory contests run by Mrs. Raines, mother of an older student named Terri, who will one day marry the Crocodile Hunter. Even I have a crush on Terri, a free-spirited girl who sometimes smokes behind the lockers. We learn citizenship and get graded on our classroom behavior. Eben and I love being part of the soccer team which is now winning more games than it loses, with Heidi and her strong legs serving as a secret weapon. Shaun will eventually become a star player himself.

A lot of good things come from this school, they do. Not every kid is as pure as our parents might think, though.

Even ten-year-olds have free will.

I am spending the night at another classmate's house when he tells me some of the boys at Eugene Christian like shoving themselves against each other's naked bottoms. Though it sounds vaguely naughty, no one has told me this is something I shouldn't do. In the dark, my classmate and I take turns rubbing our prepubescent bodies together. We fumble about. We're kids and nothing really works. It feels funny and even pleasurable, making me tingle.

Another Christian school classmate suggests trying the same thing.

And a Faith Center pal.

After the third or fourth time, I worry someone's parents will catch us and I stop participating in these deeds done in the dark. I don't feel bad, not exactly. Mostly confused. My dad has explained the mechanics of men and women making babies, as well as the pleasure involved, but he's said nothing about this sort of activity.

My body is on alert now. A lock is undone in my young mind.

Are boys supposed to be together? Why do body parts feel good even when they're not procreating?

Since God has made me, I figure He must know the answers.

If so, the adults at church and school must think otherwise, because they do very little to clue us in. The few times they mention such topics, they cloak their words in judgment and guilt. Either they don't know about this stuff–could we kids have discovered something new?–or they don't think we can handle the facts.

Too late. We are already handling plenty.

At the time, I have no idea Heidi and Shaun are facing similar questions of their own. Each of us is bound in secrecy, feeling alone in a struggle we all share.

~ ~ ~

As Christmas rolls around, our family goes hunting for a tree on public land in the Cascade Mountains. We trek through snow with rubber-banded bread bags over our shoes. By the time we fell a six-foot silver fir, our toes are damp and cold. Back home, Dad fixes the tree in a stand. Mom pulls out a needle and thread to make popcorn strands, and we kids spend hours cutting strips of colorful construction paper to chain together and drape over the branches. An angel tops it all off.

Dad and Mom have never led us to believe in Santa Claus, figuring we'll question their statements about God if they lie to us about St. Nick. Still, they like to have fun and don't get caught up in the latest cultural debates.

Was baby Jesus actually born in December?

Wasn't this originally a pagan holiday?

Does Christ really get taken out of Christmas by shortening it to Xmas?

"God's more concerned about the motives of our hearts," Dad explains. "Do I want you kids caught up in the barrage of greed? Of course not. Materialism is out of control. But God is *love*, right? We get ourselves all twisted into knots, afraid of doing it wrong, when He just wants us to enjoy the gift of His Son."

Mom produces her big, green Bible, eager to share with us the nativity story.

"Can't that wait?" Dad says.

"Oh, Mark, it's the perfect time, while we're all here around the tree."

His mouth drops and he slaps his knee. "*Man*, am I a space cadet. I almost forgot. Hey, *hey*, kiddos–Santa's got an early surprise for you."

"Tell us, Daddy," my brother and sister exclaim.

"Well, there's a certain couple moving to our side of town. They've bought their own house and want us to come celebrate the holidays with them. What do you think, Linda? Should we tell them who it is?"

Mom frowns and lifts a shoulder. Her Bible still waits in her lap.

"Uncle Paul and Aunt Val," Dad announces.

We kids go wild. We've never had any nearby relatives, though some local friends have adopted us as their own–Grandma Louise who bakes us delicious oatmeal cookies, and Nana Shelton who introduces us to Almond Roca. They will both forever hold special places in our hearts.

This Christmas Eve we spend with Uncle Paul and Aunt Val. They give us trendy clothes, gleaming wristwatches, and an instant uptick in fashion awareness. They won't live in the area as long as we would like, but we are thankful anyway.

And soon, more of Dad's family will migrate to Eugene.

Uncle Dave and his wife Lori in their chic apparel.

Uncle John, still in his teens, wearing a faded denim jacket.

Even Val's sister, Lisa, makes the move, and we feel bonded with the two of them, since they also lived in other countries as children.

It all seems too good to be true.

We are Wilsons, and yes, we are home.

There are many wonderful things about other places, our parents tell us, but there's no better country in the world. They let us stay up late on New Year's Eve to watch the ball drop in Times Square. As fireworks go off, Dad dips Mom and gives her a kiss. She giggles like a teenage girl. Full of hope, we all whistle and cheer.

27

Heidi

When school starts up again in January 1977, my third-grade teacher stirs my imagination with an announcement. "I know we spent a lot of time last quarter focused on the U.S.A. Now we are going to study other cultures. I will give each of you a passport and you'll receive stamps in it as you write about countries you choose."

Anna and I exchange smiles. My mind is already racing.

"At the end of this quarter," our teacher continues, "we'll have a big party, during which each of you will share a display and a treat from your favorite country."

I hurry home, already sure of my final project.

On the morning before the big party, Mom works with me in the kitchen. She fills a Thermos with her hot blend of cardamom, cloves, honey, and powdered milk—not quite as rich as the real stuff, but her chai is still yummy. Next, she shows me how to cook up dried soy protein, which our family uses in place of meat. We fry wontons into golden perfection, layering and letting them cool between paper towels.

We're all ready to deliver our treats.

When my teacher calls me forward, I share my favorite Chinese food, divvying out crispy wontons to each of my classmates. Next, I declare India as my country of focus. Anna sits up, always curious. Students sip their chai, watching in wonder as I display my art project—a perfect picture of love, the Taj Mahal in all its glory.

I imagine finding my own perfect love one day.

A recipe from *Global Delights*: **CHINESE WONTONS**	
1 lb. hamburger 1 chopped garlic clove chopped green onions wonton skins	*Fry burger, onion, & garlic, place in center of skin. Fold 2 corners into center & seal by wetting finger & pressing firmly. Repeat for other corners so result is a square shape. Drop into hot oil and crisp, turning constantly until golden brown. Eat immediately.

As a romantic at heart, I see visions of love play out on the television. I'm told in America I can be anything I want to be, and I dream of being an actress. Maybe I'll get to kiss the leading men in my scenes, a thought which feels both thrilling and naughty. I've never combined these two emotions before and I marvel at their power.

Could this be the reason our dad's so strict about what we see on TV?

In the Wilson home, television is never a free-for-all. At the start of each week, Dad makes us mark the *TV Guide* with the shows we want to watch.

"Here's what's allowed." He circles the safe options for us. "You get one hour a day, after homework and chores. No wasting away your lives in front of the boob tube. I'm fine with *Batman, Little Rascals, Brady Bunch, Gilligan's Island,* and *The Lone Ranger,* but *The Flintstones,* they're out of the question."

"Fred and Barney make me laugh," Eric gripes.

"I like Pebbles and Bamm-Bamm," Shaun adds.

"Sorry, guys, still a no. Think about it. What are Fred and Barney usually doing? They're either *lying* to their wives or *sneaking* off somewhere. It's subtle, but it shows deception in marriage as a normal thing. What's God say about lying?"

"It's a sin," we answer in unison.

If we lie, Mom has been known to wash our mouths out with Dial soap.

"That's right. Now on the weekends, you'll get two full hours a day. Saturday cartoons are fine—and Heidi, I know you and Karma like *Scooby Doo*—but most evening shows are just cruddy." He scratches out *The Love Boat* and *Fantasy Island.* "On Sundays, there's always *Jacques Cousteau* and *Wonderful World of Disney.*"

"What about *Little House on the Prairie?*" I ask.

"Monday is family night. We'll watch it together, as usual."

Shaun says, "Will you cry like you did last season?"

"You know, that show gets me every time. It takes a real man to show his emotions." Dad taps his pen. "Now listen, if I catch you guys in front of the tube before your chores are done, that's it, you understand? End of weekly privileges. Same thing with ads. If you don't mute them, the TV goes off. You with me?"

We nod. I don't mention the fact I've never seen Daddy dust or do dishes. Both my brothers pitch in, but our dad disappears at the mere mention of a vacuum.

"No sneaking, either," he tells us. "That's flat-out rebellion, and the Bible tells us, 'rebellion is as the sin of witchcraft.' All this marketing, it's so calculated. You think these ad guys have any ethics or guidelines? *Hell,* no– pardon my French."

"Hell's a bad word," Shaun says.

"And so is *exploitation.* That's what these people are doing, getting paid big bucks to create ditties that stick in children's heads. Next thing you know, you think you need all this *stuff* to make you happy. It's BS, is what it is, and I don't want you kids being brainwashed. You already have trouble memorizing a Bible verse or two, but you can go around for *days* singing mindless shampoo commercials."

Despite Dad's best efforts, TV opens a disturbing door in my imagination. It happens during an episode of *Little House.*

As an avid reader, I've already finished the Laura Ingalls Wilder's books, but some scenes are even more vivid on the screen and play on repeat in my mind. This particular episode deals with a young woman whose body matures earlier than others. Her father recognizes this and wraps her breasts tightly with cloth in an attempt to hide her curves. While walking home from school one day, she is attacked by a local man. By the time her father finds her, she is in a heap, bruised and crying, and they move far away to avoid further confrontations.

My limbs shake as the episode ends. I recall the men in Ağri, trying to get at the women in our trucks. I think of the school teacher here in Eugene, touching me. At nine years old, I already hear comments about my curves and developing body.

Should I be thankful for being noticed? Or should I be ashamed?

Mom's words play through my mind: *It's wonderful, don't you think? ... One day, Heidi, you'll get to form a family of your own.*

Where is the special man who will love me as his princess?

~ ~ ~

Shaun

Is it just me, or am I always out of sync with the culture around me? There are words and jokes I don't get. There are TV shows I've never watched, hit songs I've never heard. This gets me laughed at on multiple occasions and in trouble more than once. I have a different set of priorities and I'm constantly on the outside looking in.

Do I want to be an outsider? Not really. I want to be part of things.

Uncle John is the nearest to us in age and he has a way of making me laugh. He's smart too, always coming up with creative business ventures. He is Dad's youngest–and shrimpiest–brother, which makes me feel connected to him.

One day I overhear him talking with some relatives, discussing his recent troubles at work.

"So that's it, huh? They're going to fire you?" Uncle Paul asks.

"You've never been a nine-to-five person," Dad says. "That's just not you."

"They've made up their minds." Uncle John shrugs and pulls on his denim jacket. "Listen, I should go."

Why is everyone so nonchalant about this? Being fired is no small thing. I've seen bodies piled on Indian death carts, so I know what happens to dead people. They are disposed of—with fire. Why doesn't someone stop this from happening?

"No," I cry, rushing forward and wrapping myself around my uncle's leg. "Don't let them fire you."

He pats my head. "Thanks, Shaun, but I'll be okay."

"He's getting fired," I wail. "Please, don't let him get fired."

"Shaun, bud, let go." Dad pries my fingers loose. "You *have* to let him go."

My sorrow is real, and it isn't until Uncle John stops by a few weeks later that I realize he is still alive.

Relieved and also frustrated, I am still wrapping my head around all these words with their flexible meanings. My frames of reference are European, Asian, and American. I'm hearing things from one culture and trying to apply them to another. People think I'm being difficult when all I'm trying to do is make sense of what they are saying. Is there anyone speaking my language?

28

Eric

The call comes in early summer, and I know by the way Mom purses her lips, it isn't good. She beckons me to come join her on the couch. I run a hand between us before plopping down, since I don't want to sit on any stray strands of her knee-length hair.

"That was Eben's mom," she says. "He's been fighting the chicken pox the past week. Camp Crestview's only ten days away, and if you catch it too, you can't go."

"What about Eben? Is he okay?"

"He still gets to be at camp. The contagious phase will be past by then."

"Well, I'm fine," I say. "If he's going, I'm going."

"If you get chicken pox, you won't be allowed without a doctor's release."

"I won't catch it."

This is a cry of desperation as much as a statement of faith. I'm still broken-hearted after Goodny's death and wonder why my prayers are ignored. My ears prick up any time miracles are mentioned, and I know all you need is faith like a mustard seed. Apparently, I haven't believed hard enough, so this time I double down.

"I'm going to camp," I reiterate. "God will make sure I don't get it."

"Honey," Mom says, "you don't want to be presumptuous."

"I'm not."

"Do you know what that word means?"

"Sheesh, why do you do that to me? Stop acting like I'm dumb."

Alone in my room, I look up *presumptuous* in the dictionary. My ears still ring with the languages of multiple nations, and definitions and origins fascinate me. Mom's warning now makes more sense, but I still feel no jeopardy to my health. I won't get sick. I will be safe because I have said it and believed it.

The next day, I am fine.

The day after that, I'm healthy as can be.

"See," I tell my parents at dinner. "I knew I'd be okay."

By that weekend, I am a miserable, itching child stretched out in a bath of Epsom salts. My birthday suit, the only one God gave me, is a polka-dotted affair, with hundreds of red splotches on a pale white background. They beg for attention and I have only two hands to answer their demands.

"Don't scratch," my mom cautions me. "You'll only make it worse."

"Mom, why do you do that? Don't look over here."

"I'm just getting your towel for you, honey. I can't see anything."

"Anyway, I'm still going to camp." I refuse to miss out on the outdoor games, the candy cabin, the dining-hall chaos, and camper camaraderie.

"Is this something Jesus has told you?"

"What?" I shake my head. "No. I mean, we hear about it at church, right? Isn't that what Roy preaches? God's supposed to heal and everything."

"We can pray for it, yes. If two or three gather in His name, He is there."

"Okay, so pray with me to get better."

"We'll ask Jesus," Mom agrees, "but then you have to trust Him."

"I do."

"Even if you don't get better?"

"How can I trust Him if He doesn't do what He says?"

"You've invited Him into your heart, Eric. He works uniquely in people's lives, teaching them different things, revealing Himself in different ways. Did you hear Him say you were going to camp?"

"I... I don't know."

"Oh, honey." Her voice softens. "I know how much you loved Goodny."

My throat tightens.

"Jesus," she prays, "You know Eric's heart. You know how much he wants this. Please help him heal quickly so he can make it to see his friends."

By the time I board the bus headed from Faith Center to Camp Crestview, I am no longer contagious. My wounds, however, are still dark pink, turning my stomach, back, and limbs into a mean-spirited dot-to-dot which seems to spell *stay away*.

After checking in the first afternoon, I pull on my swimsuit and head for the pool. This camp is one of my favorite places, on a hillside along the Columbia River. We'll all sing around the campfire, compete in team sports, and play pranks with the moose head in the lodge. I especially love the outdoor swimming pool.

The chants first start as I step onto the diving board.

"Hurry, get out. It's the Chicken Pox Man."

"I'm fine," I say. "I'm not contagious."

"The Chicken Pox Man. Get out, get out."

I dive in headfirst, and by the time I surface the pool is empty. Boys, girls, even some counselors scurry toward the changing rooms, a reaction I will face from most campers throughout the week. Eben remains at my side, immune and ever faithful, but other friends of mine refuse to even sit with me during mealtimes.

So, this is it, the answer to my presumptuous prayers?

Even if God has heard and helped me recover from chicken pox quicker than normal, my week at Camp Crestview is miserable.

~ ~ ~

One morning back home, personal misery nearly costs me my life. After dusting furniture and scrubbing the toilet, I wait for Heidi and Shaun to finish their chores. Thoughts of Goodny's floppy little ears and golden-brown eyes play through my mind, and a dark mood follows me out the door.

This cloud is one I'll encounter many times throughout my life. At times, it is mere annoyance, such as when my mom interrupts me while I'm focused on a pencil drawing or Lego creation.

"I can't just drop everything," I snap at her. "I need to be mentally prepared."

Other times, the cloud grows darker. Unsure how to deal with it, I've smashed a camera to bits in India and recently kicked a hole in our laundry room wall. Mom tells me depression and anger are not of God, leaving me to feel guilty for these feelings while providing no tools to handle them. The sudden drop into despair and loneliness is common among the Wilsons, but we don't talk about it.

Not yet.

We will one day, after it steals away a person we love.

I wander out to our red cedar tree, my vision turning palpably darker. A length of rope is in my hand. Using my weight, I pull a branch toward the ground.

Is this spiritual? Should I be rebuking the devil, as Mom might suggest?

Or do I just need food in my tummy?

Maybe my blood sugar's low.

I wish Heidi was out here. We would turn this yard into a world of make-believe. I might be Tintin or Zorro. She might be Amelia Earhart or Wonder Woman. With no one around, though, I play out my own scenario, looping the rope around my neck. I think of an episode of *The Lone Ranger*, the moment the masked hero shoots through the rope to save a wrongly accused man at the gallows.

There's no premeditation on my part, no intention.

Only that dark cloud.

The branch suddenly escapes my grasp, snapping upward, cinching the rope around my neck and yanking me to my tippy toes. The darkness deepens to black. Panic roars in my ears. I imagine my parents screaming in horror, cutting me loose, cradling my lifeless form in their laps.

I claw at my neck, work my fingers into the loop. With my other hand, I reach blindly overhead and find rough, sappy wood.

Using all my weight, I'm able to release the tension and free myself from the rope's deadly hold. My throat feels red and raw. I taste blood, almost smell it. Guilt sweeps over me and I run around to the other side of the house, where I hide under a hemlock tree until my sister emerges at last and calls my name.

~ ~ ~

Once July swings around, our summer takes a turn for the better—making driftwood forts at the beach, camping at Silver Falls State Park, exploring the woods together. Heidi, Shaun, and I bound from boulder to boulder, whittle bows and arrows, and crouch on ledges behind waterfalls. I read a favorite quote to them from Sadhu Sundar Singh: *God is revealed in the book of nature, for God is its author.*

For hours on end, we forget all about our sexual secrets, dark clouds, and first rumblings of puberty. We are simply kids–ten, nine, and seven–lost once again in the wonders of the forest.

It's also a summer of new technology and we will never forget standing in line for *Star Wars*. The buzz is strong with this one.

"You are *not* going believe it," Dad tells us. "They've got these weapons they call light sabers—I don't know how they do it, but, *boy*, do they look real—and the bad guys are called Storm Troopers, and you'll see some characters known as Sand People. Did I mention the scene with the trash compactor?"

Shaking our heads, we eye the movie poster.

"Oh." Dad slaps his leg. "And Darth Vader, good *grief*. How could I forget? He might seem scary, but remember, it's all costumes and special effects."

Two hours later, we are fans of Han, Luke, and Leia. We take turns trying to roar like Chewbacca, and Shaun comes closest, the most adept at imitating animal sounds.

~ ~ ~

Heidi

Though I'm only nine, my body is showing clear signs of womanhood. This becomes evident when I serve as the flower girl at a summer wedding.

The ceremony takes place on a clear, beautiful day at Owen Memorial Rose Garden. Aunt Lisa is marrying Johnny Burke, a pianist with curly black hair and ever-smiling eyes. The bride and groom look amazing. I stand with the other ladies in the bridal party, feeling quite grown up with my carefully tamed curls and kitten heels. My budding breasts press against my dress.

During the reception, Lisa tells me, "Since my sister Val's married to your uncle, she is your in-law. Well, I guess that makes me and Johnny your outlaws."

We both laugh.

Not long after the wedding, Mom's relatives drive up from California. Grandma Guise is determined to keep us all in connected, even if Grandpa still refuses to be involved. She comes with Aunt Mary, who is only seven years older than me, and with Uncle Frank and his wife and son.

Against all odds, our parents' teen romance has survived into an eleventh year of marriage, and we all gather for a photo of the Wilsons and Guises.

When Dad's brother, Uncle John, comes over for dinner a few weeks later, I can't help but notice how handsome he is with his waves of thick blond hair. He is single, only nineteen years old. He includes me as he tells jokes to my brothers. He looks me directly in the eye as he asks questions and awaits my answers.

Since Dad's still on his way home from work and Mom's still cooking dinner, Eric and Shaun dash outside to ride their bikes before dark.

"Just whistle when it's ready," they say.

This leaves me and Uncle John alone in the living room. He reads to me as I sit on his lap on our old sofa. Something hard rubs across my bottom and I squirm to get more comfortable.

"You want to be tickled?" he says mischievously. He pokes at my ribs till I fall on the floor, curling up in laughter. He scoops me up by my legs. "Oh no, you don't."

I dangle upside down, my shirt falling over my face. I wriggle loose and land on the carpet, my face still covered. The tickling continues. He holds my hands and straddles me, his hardened pelvis moving against mine. I am trapped, my newly budding chest laid bare. I work a hand free to pull down my shirt. My face is flushed. My uncle's eyes are narrow, almost sleepy, and I feel swollen down there.

I realize I'm... no, not embarrassed.

Just shy.

He grins, eyes twinkling. "That was fun, wasn't it?"

I nod, my lips pressed tight. Though I'm only in third grade, Mom has talked about getting me a bra. I'm not sure I want one now. This extra attention is nice. My young and good-looking uncle makes me feel desirable, and it's nothing like what happened in the nurse's office at public school. This, I tell myself, is entirely different.

Uncle John's visits increase. Each time I wonder: Do I want him to notice me, or do I want him to stay away? I love my family and all our relatives. If I talk, will it cause trouble? He is persistent and persuasive, and our tickle fights become anticipated events as he assures me my blossoming body is beautiful.

Even my overactive imagination cannot guess where my uncle's actions will one day lead him. I don't recognize the shadow hovering over him. Fantasy and fun are all I see, and my dreams at night are filled with pictures drawn on EWEB envelopes.

You should save yourself for someone special, Dad has told me.

Is my relationship with Uncle John a good thing? If so, why do he and I hide our flirtatious moments? We're related, I guess, but he's not much older than me, and I am drawn to his goofy humor, affectionate nature, and secretive winks.

Weddings. Family.

Babies. Desire.

Could this be the perfect love I have imagined?

29

Shaun

"Listen, kiddos, what I'm trying to do is *prepare* you for the real world," Dad tells us around the dinner table. "I won't always be around to *protect* you."

He says it like he knows something we don't. Over the years, he scatters these little comments, not because he has plans to bail on us, but to remind us how situations and relationships can sour. When our family does actually fall apart, we will look back and realize his comments were seedlings of a bitter fruit.

For now, we are oblivious. We trust our dad and our mom, believing for the most part they can do no wrong. We're still too young to know any better.

"You're our dad," I tell him. "You don't back down from anyone."

"You always protect us," Heidi agrees.

"Papa Bear, hey, *hey.*" He clears his throat. "Listen, I've been through some stuff you guys know *nothing* about. You don't have a *clue.* There are bullies out there, people with bad intentions, and if you don't stand up to these bozos, they will try to make life miserable."

"I punched Eben the other day." I say it proudly. "Gave him a bloody nose."

"Mom says he kept teasing you."

"Yep, he deserved it."

"You know, Shaun, standing up for yourself is important. A lot of it's about displaying the attitude that you won't be pushed around. Remember, though, if you can talk your way out a situation, that's *always* the best way to go. Just like it tells us in Proverbs, 'A gentle answer turns away wrath.'"

It isn't long before bullies begin making their presence known. Eric deals with them on the soccer field, in the locker room, and at school. He gets a fist to the face in the school gym and just stands there–which scares his attacker away.

I feel safe with my big brother. He's eleven now, taller than most kids his age. We ride for miles along the bike trails, often gone for hours. Right after Fourth of July, we pedal over the bridge into Alton Baker Park and collect discarded pop and beer cans worth nearly $100 in deposit. Eric buys himself a pair of coveted Nike Waffle Trainers. I get Mom some Jungle Jasmine, her favorite perfume.

Poor Heidi, though. She's not allowed to ride more than a block or two from home. She can't even walk to the store alone. No wonder she's so sullen these days.

"It's not fair," Dad admits to us. "She's a girl, though. That's just how it is."

"What about us?" I jut my chin. "You guys don't even know where Eric and I are half the time."

Mom clicks her lips together and winks. "Oh, Jesus and I, we know."

Not long after, I am boarding a city bus when a big kid comes out of nowhere and socks me in the stomach for no reason but to be mean. If Jesus knows, He does nothing to stop it. The bully strides to the back of the bus and plops down, legs spread, hard eyes daring anyone to approach. I tell Eric when he gets on and he promises for now on he will stick by me during our bus rides.

Dad goes ballistic when he hears about it. "What? Some pathetic little *sucker* hit you for no reason? Well, he's in for one *helluva* surprise."

True to his word, Dad follows us to the bus stop the next morning and waits for us to point out the bully. Dad puffs out his arms in his jacket, pulls his ballcap low, then shoves hard into the kid and hisses warnings about what will happen if he tries picking on anyone else half his size.

"You got that, you little *pissant?*"

The bully nods, afraid to look our dad in the eye. He never bugs me again.

Though I knew Daddy loved me before this, I've often felt like the object of his wrath. If anyone knows how to push his buttons, it's me, so I am glad to know he will come to my rescue when I really need it. Now Eric and I feel invincible. He can take a punch and not flinch. I can deliver a bloody nose if the moment calls for it.

And our dad has our backs.

Don't mess with us.

Our confidence wavers, though, after an afternoon visit with Mom to a food warehouse off River Road. With most things sold in bulk, shoppers have to mark their own prices with green grease pencils. Mom tells us we can go play alongside the building while she hunts for bargains inside.

Eric and I nod. Dad expects us to listen and respond whenever Mom calls. If we don't, he will deal with us when he gets home.

Outside, I spot a used grease pencil on the ground. We break it in half and face a warehouse wall already tagged with graffiti and anatomical drawings. We decide to add something positive. My brother sketches Jesus' name in the shape of a fish, and I draw a cross with lines radiating from a heart in the middle.

As we stand back to admire our work, three older boys on BMX bikes wheel into view. They angle right for us and skid to a stop, kicking up crumbled concrete.

"What're you dork-wads doing?" the leader demands.

"Nothing."

"What's all that Jesus crap and that cross? Did you draw those?"

My brother and I exchange looks. We are outsized, outnumbered, and not fast enough to outrun their bikes. "Yes," we say together.

"Good thing you homos aren't liars or we'd kick the shit outta you," the kid says. "You know it's against the law to mark up public property. You better get your sissy tongues a-lickin' till you clean off what you drew. It's either that or the cops."

So much for using gentle answers to turn away wrath or for talking our way out of this. Right now, such strategies seem worthless. I watch Eric for my cue. He squares his shoulders, balls his fists, and narrows his eyes. What's he waiting for? Doesn't he know I can hold my own? His gaze finally drops and he turns toward the wall.

"You guys aren't half as dumb as you look," the leader says.

Eric starts licking grease pencil off the wall. I do the same.

"That's right. Keep at it. All that religious mumbo-jumbo's for retards."

I tell him, "You're not supposed to call people retards."

"Say that again, dork-wad?"

Our mom's single-tone whistle cuts through the air as she pokes her head around the corner of the building. The boys throw their legs over their bikes, flip us off, then pedal away. We hurry the other direction, eyes down, tongues stained.

"Time to help load up the car," Mom says. "Are you guys alright?"

"Let's just get out of here." Eric's shoulders are slumped. He is not used to feeling small, and for the rest of the day he barely looks my way.

~ ~ ~

Soon after, Eric comes up with an idea which my sister and I think sounds fun. "This is top secret," he says, leaning toward us in the glow of the bedroom lamp. "Do you promise not to say a word to anyone? Not even Dad or Mom?"

"What about Karma or Anna?" Heidi ventures.

Eric frowns at her.

"Okay," she says. "We promise. Right, Shaun?"

"I'm not saying a word."

"I'm serious. Top secret," Eric repeats. "We're going to help our city. We're not just helpless kids, you know?" He catches my eye and I realize he is thinking of that warehouse wall. He holds up a book. "See this? In here, a kid stops all the pollution where he lives, and we can do the same here in Eugene. Just think of all the junk on the sidewalks and trails, the gum wrappers, bottle caps, and boxes."

"Superweasel?" I read the word from the cover.

"That's the kid's superhero name."

"Sounds kind of stupid."

"We'll each choose our own names," Eric says.

And we do. Eric is The Brain, Heidi the Black Widow, and I am Green Lantern. We wear towels as capes and Heidi even attaches a Band-Aid box to the inside of hers for holding pencils, paper, and a small flashlight. We tuck Pez dispensers into our waistbands, providing sugary power pellets for our mission.

The flashlight comes in handy after our parents go to bed. We sneak out the bathroom window, land in the soft ripe earth above the septic tank, plug our noses, and plod through thick weeds to a tree. We huddle under hemlock branches, then by flashlight write dozens of notes and split them into three piles.

"You guys ready?" my brother says.

Beneath a quarter moon, Eric heads one way and Heidi and I another. We creep into driveways up and down River Road, slipping our notes under neighbors' windshield wipers. We scramble away from dogs. We swear we even hear a gunshot. Mostly, we imagine the morning surprise when all these people read our messages:

Stop Pollution... That's the Solution!

Signed with our superhero names.

Over the next month, in the dead of night, we plug away at our mission, but Eric isn't pleased with the results. "It's not working. I've been checking the papers, the *Register-Guard* and *The Oregonian*, and nobody's reporting our notes."

"We'll make more," Heidi suggests. "Even a thousand."

My brother cocks his head. "Sure. But Eben and I passed them out on his side of town when I spent the night there last week. Still nothing. We must think of something bigger, something that'll really make people pay attention."

"You told Eben?" I scowl. "You said this was top secret."

"Eben's got security clearance, okay? He won't say anything."

That's right, I think, since he knows what I'll do if he opens his big mouth again.

The next evening, we avoid the lights and crosswalk as we dart across River Road. We climb into a big wooden recycling box next to the corner market. Seated on old newspapers, the three of us write for what seems like hours. We are barely able to keep our eyes open by the time we crawl back through our bathroom window with wads of notes ready for tomorrow's bigger excursion.

When the following night rolls around, Eric and I try waking Heidi up, but she's out like a light. We leave her snoozing as we trek off with our notes. After distributing them for blocks in every direction, we start the next step of our mission and wait beneath a streetlamp for a police car to go by. Cops make regular passes in this area, often answering calls at bars and nearby adult bookstores.

"Here comes one." I tug on Eric's cape.

Pressed against a tree, I watch my brother jump onto the pavement and wave his arms. The cruiser fishtails to a stop, the smell of burnt rubber hanging in the air. The officer lowers his window. He does not look amused.

"You boys should be in your beds," he says. "Is something wrong?"

"We're trying to stop pollution," Eric explains. "No matter what we do, no one seems to care, so we thought maybe you could help by driving us to the Weyerhauser plant. We want to climb up to the top and cover the smokestacks."

The policeman tips back his hat. "Are you wearing towels?"

Eric and I shrug out of our capes and wad them behind our backs.

"Will you do it?" my brother asks.

"Those smokestacks are huge. Just how do you plan to cover them?"

"Maybe you could help us load up some plywood. There's lots of it at that old house on the corner. We might even have some back at our... our clubhouse."

What clubhouse? I wonder. Oh, he means back home.

"You seem like nice young men. Why don't you climb in?" The officer makes sure we are buckled up in the back—no way to unlock the doors, I notice—before asking one last question. "Where exactly is your clubhouse?"

He clearly respects us, even calling us young men. If you talk nice to me, I will do just about anything to help, so without hesitation I lift my hand and point, spilling our exact address before my brother can stop me with an elbow.

And just like that, our environmental activism comes to an end.

Within moments, the policeman is leading us from the car and up the rotting wood steps of our house. His knock brings our parents to the door. Even at two in the morning, Dad is wide awake and he roars with laughter as he hears the officer's story, though he also vows to spank us till we cannot sit down if we ever do such a thing again. Mom, she just cries, realizing her children have been gallivanting about the streets past midnight.

I mostly feel bad for Heidi.

"You should've tried harder to wake me up," she pouts. "You guys rode in a police car and I didn't even get to see the cute cop. I never get to do the fun stuff."

~ ~ ~

Eric

Despite our failed escapade, I feel inspired. If a fictitious story about Superweasel can spur me to stop pollution, then perhaps I can write books which entertain, challenge, and spur others to action. I love books and love reading.

Now writing takes hold of me, a dream I cannot ignore.

Who am I kidding, though? I'm just a kid. I don't even own a typewriter. I'm not smart enough for Oxford and I don't wear spectacles or smoke pipes. Plus, all the big publishers are on the other side of the country, in the heart of New York City.

For now, being a writer is just a dream.

30

Heidi

As I near my tenth birthday in 1978, I am locked up in ways I don't fully understand. There is society's cage, telling me my looks define me and sexuality is a currency. There is my parents' cage, telling me I must always be on guard. And my own cage, telling me my uncle's affection is warranted even as it makes me increasingly uneasy.

Religion is another cage.

It is humanity's attempt to reach God through personal good works. It whispers to me that I'm sinful and dirty. I must do better, try harder, toe the line.

Our family of five is at Faith Center every Sunday morning, Sunday evening, and Wednesday night. As kids, we don't have much say in the matter, but we're okay with it at this young age. We help fold and pass out bulletins. We pick gum off the bottoms of sanctuary chairs and clean up trash in the parking lot. Our nighttime fight for the environment may have failed, but we do our part here at church.

Dad and Mom are a team, often the last ones out, calling upon seemingly inexhaustible reserves as they counsel and minister to people. We admire them for it. Our parents are truly shepherds, as described in the New Testament, tending to lost sheep and binding up wounds.

My brothers and I fend off our impatience by running through the church halls with other kids our age till the lights go off and only two or three cars remain in the lot.

We want to know: When are we going home? When will we get lunch?

Our parents thank us and remind us: Loving others takes time and sacrifice. Ministry is a team effort which involves the whole family and each of us play a role. Our patience makes Jesus happy.

We try not to grumble.

What choice do we have?

On Easter, our Sunday school watches *Jesus of Nazareth*. The images of His death and resurrection are too much for me. I've seen real death in Indian and Afghanistan, and by the time my parents retrieve me from class, I am sobbing. Soon after, I'm allowed to sign up for baptism since I clearly grasp the significance of Jesus' sacrifice for us. When a person takes the plunge, it symbolizes putting to death the old wicked nature and being born anew as a child of God.

I am baptized by Roy Hicks, Jr. As he raises me from the water, I want everyone to know Jesus is my lord and savior. The congregation applauds. Songs of worship fill my ears and the presence of heaven overwhelms me.

Perfect love?

Yes, this feels very real.

Wrapped in a towel, I am ushered into a side room where some of the pastors pray for me to also be baptized in the Holy Spirit and receive my spiritual language. They call on Jesus to fill me with boldness.

Boldness?

Dad is bold. Mom, in her own quiet way, shows no fear. Eric might be afraid to talk to girls, but he's not afraid of going against the flow. And Shaun's always ready for a challenge.

Me, though?

I keep quiet about many things, I carry secrets, and I'm not always sure of myself. Only time will tell if the prayers are answered, but I can't even imagine it.

~ ~ ~

My boldness is tested right away when my brother and I are cast in a children's church musical, *The Music Machine*, and the directors assign me a solo to sing. Terrified, I practice constantly. On the night of the production, I take my place on stage, stretched out under a piano with a blanket tucked around me.

This is my moment. My solo.

Not only do I have to sing, but I must act and emote as part of the play. Will the mics pick up my voice? Will I be heard in this huge sanctuary? Despite being breathy and shaky, I feel my imagination take flight, and the experience sparks something in me.

I've been bitten by the acting bug.

Eric and I begin performing for our parents. We write a skit about a married couple learning gratitude. We also do a comedy bit where I sit behind Eric, covered by a blanket draped over his shoulders, and reach my arms around as though they are his. He pretends to do typical morning preparations while I do all the actual motions without being able to see. I slather his face with shaving cream, brush his cheek with toothpaste, and pour shampoo down his nose. Mom giggles till she has tears in her eyes and Dad roars with laughter, slapping his leg.

Next, I am cast as Cinderella in a fourth-grade play.

I'm a natural, I tell myself. My acting career is taking off and it's time to dream big. Watch out, Hollywood, here I come.

It's not long, though, before I realize I've been cast in a non-speaking role. Another girl has the main role. Am I not good enough? Was my audition too timid? Did I forget a line? I will play Cinderella but only during the final ball, wearing long gloves, a gown, and hair piled atop my head. My acting will be limited to smiling, to dancing with Bruce who plays the dashing prince, and to running off and losing my glass slipper.

My worth, it seems, is once again wrapped up in beauty and silence.

Better to be seen and not heard.

~ ~ ~

Shaun

One sunny spring weekend, we go on a family outing to the Rogue River. Eric and I gaze up at Heidi, crouched on the lowest brace of an old riverbank fire tower.

"You can do it, Heidi," we call.

In her swimsuit, she clings to a rope swing. "It looks dangerous."

"You'll be fine," Eric says. "Just make sure to go out wide, then while you're in the air, climb up the rope really quick so you don't hit this stump at the bottom."

Our sister's eyes widen. Her legs are shaking. She usually tags along with us wherever we go and we coax her to join in our activities. When she's nervous, though, there's no hiding it. She wears her insecurities for all to see.

"What if I slip?"

"You're tough. Just jump."

It's our goal, I guess, to make her as fearless as any of the boys. We don't want her getting picked on, but it never occurs to us we might be the ones actually bullying her. Our parents teach each of us to act from personal conviction, and if she has a problem with something, all she's got to do is tell us no.

"No," she says. "Seriously, you guys, it's too high."

"Don't be a wimp," I shout. "We both did it."

She makes a move, then hesitates.

"You can do it, Heidi." Eric softens his tone, always the diplomat. "The longer you think about it, the worse it gets. You know, if you don't want to, that's okay."

"No, here goes." She grits her teeth. "Okay. One, two, three..."

My brother and I haven't taken into account our ten-year-old sister's maturing hips. As she swings out, knees bent, and tries to pull herself up to the first knot, gravity takes hold. We watch her rush toward us, eyes wide, hands slipping. She slides down the rope. With a *thuddd* and an *ooooof*, she hits the stump with her backside and catapults into the river.

"Ow!" She comes up spluttering, moaning. "You guys are such meanies. Why'd you tell me I could do that?"

"Sorry," Eric says. "I thought you'd make it if you didn't get scared."

"Weren't you guys scared when you did it?"

"That's what makes it fun," I pipe in.

"Well, it's not fun and it's not funny. I'm never listening to you guys again."

When she displays her black and blue bruises the next morning, Eric rushes to give her a hug. I urge her not to show our parents, knowing it might get us all in trouble. From now on, we promise not to mock or pressure our sister. As far as we're concerned, she's plenty brave enough. She has nothing left to prove.

~ ~ ~

Heidi

My newfound boldness doesn't last long. It's one thing to try something daring with my brothers at my side. It's a whole other story when I am all alone.

We no longer carpool to school, meaning we take public transportation back and forth across town each day. With a long wait between buses at the main station, we often play tag, hide-and-seek, and spy games in the nearby parking structure. One day I jump into the elevator to avoid being found by my brothers. As the door closes, a hand juts through and three teenage boys step in. One of them pushes the Close Door button.

Trapped in the enclosed space, I am shoved against the wall.

Fear immobilizes me.

The biggest kid presses against me, gyrating his hips against mine. With one sweaty hand over my mouth and the other groping my chest, he hisses in my ear, "That's right. You like this, don't you?"

I can't speak. Can't think.

"Nice tits. Here, check 'em out," he says, still covering my mouth as he steps aside and lets another kid take his place.

The Close Door button can only keep us hidden for so long, and at last an alarm screams in protest. There must be someone hitting the button outside, calling for the elevator, trying to free me from this nightmare. The door slides open, and the boys bolt, laughing maniacally. My trembling body slips to the floor.

Fear and shame render me mute. What did I do to draw these boys' attention? Am I the one to blame? If I don't mention these images, maybe they will fade away—though this has never worked before. Previous encounters overpower my thoughts and waves of emotion engulf me. The same fondling which seemed so titillating with my uncle feels like terror in this elevator.

I recall Mom's words years ago: *Even you and I can be dangerous when we let our own desires take control.*

Have I let my own desires turn dangerous?

A part of me wants to spill every detail to my parents. I want their advice and reassurance. They're so busy, though. If I interrupt Mom during one of her home prayer meetings, she'll wave me off as she does to my older brother. And if I catch Dad just as he gets home, he'll snap at me as he sometimes does to my younger brother. Where do I fit into their schedule? Are there any boundaries protecting my own time with my parents?

I need them to notice me.

It's my turn, please.

For just one minute, I want to receive the attention they so freely give to others while praying and counseling them...

Unfiltered

Eugene, Oregon — 1976-1978

Everyone knew Mark and Linda Wilson. They were always ready to listen, reaching out to the damaged souls at Faith Center.

And yes, the church was full of them. The Wilsons included.

In the 1970s, while many Christians viewed psychology as a diversion from the truths in God's Word, Faith Center featured a pastoral staff with counselors holding degrees from the University of Oregon. It wasn't enough to simply save souls. Ministry involved the whole being.

Anyone who hung around Mark recognized his ability to connect with people from all walks of life. Roy Hicks, Jr., brought him on staff as a counselor, though he had no formal training in that role. Mark was thankful for a decent paycheck, but his real concern was helping those who stepped into his office. Abuse, addiction, family and financial struggles—he could relate to them all, and he was soon the most sought-after counselor in the building.

At the dilapidated house on River Road, Linda also ministered to others. While her children were at school, she hosted women for morning tea. She prayed for those dealing with cheating husbands, wayward kids, stillborn babies, and sexual trauma. She later mentioned how she counseled with "drug addicts, prostitutes, and transvexuals."

Transvexuals?

Laughing, her children pointed out her faux pas. Their mother's innocence was nothing new. She once wanted to buy a T-shirt bearing the image of an old-fashioned radio. The words across the top read: *Twist my knobs... Turn me on*. The double entendre went right over her head.

Despite her naivety, Linda glowed with genuine love. In her trademark manner, she leaned in close, eyes brimming with concern, and spoke in gentle tones which often cut to the root of an issue.

Ultimately, of course, she wanted to point others to Jesus.

Wasn't He, alone, able to heal and forgive?

Mark began challenging certain aspects of her approach. At home, he carried around *The Pill Book*, a thick paperback listing antidepressants and prescription drugs. Many of the men and women he saw in his office dealt with withdrawals, side effects, or adverse reactions to combined medications. It was complicated stuff.

"The right pill can really help a person," he told his wife.

"Oh, but isn't your spirit grieved," Linda responded, "seeing the way these pharmaceutical companies rip people off?"

"Welcome to America. Anything to make a buck."

She pressed on, trailing her fingers down his arm. "Jesus knows us better than any doctor. He created us. He created you, Mark. He knows every hair on your head, every cell, every corpuscle."

"Aww, that tickles." He pulled away. "Listen, you know how much I *hate* all the corporate greed. Do they flat-out take advantage of the elderly and the sick? *Absolutely*. But aren't we supposed to love God with all our heart, soul, mind, and strength? There are researchers using the minds God gave them, and we have to use our brains as well. We can't just ignore physical and medical realities. That's *lunacy*."

"People get sick. Of course, they do. We live in a fallen world."

"Exactly, Linda. I know worship is good for the spirit, but I also think medicine can be good for the body, and psychology for the mind. If there are meds for warding off an illness or chemical imbalance, hey, I'm all for it."

"Pills, that's all people talk about. Don't you think we miss God's best?"

"By taking a *Tylenol*? Now you sound kooky."

"Our healing comes from the Lord. I'm sure you still believe that."

"Why can't we believe *both*? You said yourself, we live in a fallen world."

Mark and Linda Wilson had no health insurance or family doctor. They took their kids to the dentist once in twelve years. When Eric suffered a hairline fracture to his shin, he was told to pray for Jesus' help as he walked tenderly for the next few months. The Wilsons' faith seemed directly tied to the fluctuations of their household income.

~ ~ ~

Faith Center, only fifty people at one time, was now a congregation of over 2,500 people. The sanctuary was expanded for services, baptisms, weddings, funerals, and musical productions. All the Christian luminaries of the late 1970s stopped by here, from Amy Grant to Phil Driscoll to Keith Green.

Despite its phenomenal growth, Faith Center still felt like a family.

One Saturday, Mark and Linda Wilson visited a bay along the Oregon coast with Eben's mother and her new husband. Rising from the waters, a buxom female in scuba gear strolled their way over the sand, and Mark and the other husband tried not to gawk. Eben's mom gave the two men a knowing wink, then defused the situation with three simple words: "Mmm, big ones."

Such candor was missing from Mark's own marriage.

With relational and ministerial pressures mounting, he found himself living his Christian life on stage, so to speak, while often feeling isolated. He no longer had Ray Kelly to turn to with his personal issues. He desperately needed a friend who loved God the way he did and also lived raw and unfiltered.

Paul Jackson fit the role. A former drug addict, Paul was now a skilled mason. Years of mixing mortar and laying brick had broadened his chest and shoulders. Like Mark, he was from central California and knew many of the same landmarks. He now took his family to church, doing his best to put his past to rest.

Mark and Paul became close friends. They went fly fishing together. They played racquetball, taking out their frustrations on the little ball—and sometimes on each other. They talked sports, family, and religion over drinks. When they went out for Abby's or Pietro's Pizza, Paul invariably complained about something—the burnt cheese, gristly sausage, or long wait time—and earned himself a free pie.

Soon, the Wilsons and Jacksons were pitching their tents side by side at Odell Lake, Davis Lake, and Waldo Lake. Linda and Paul's wife spent hours together. Eric eventually built fireplaces with Paul, toughening up mentally and physically in the process. Heidi was precious to Paul and his wife, like the daughter they never had. And Shaun became good friends with Paul's oldest son.

It was the support structure Mark and Linda needed.

They set aside their growing differences regarding medicine and healing, intimacy and sex. There was no reason to fuss over a few cracks in their foundation. Why, they'd made it this far, hadn't they? With Jesus at the center of their marriage, certainly nothing could separate them.

31

Eric

In the summer between fifth and sixth grade, Eben and I buy plane tickets to New York. After picking strawberries on frosty mornings and mowing lawns on hot afternoons, we've saved enough money to make the trip. We will soon fly into JFK, where his Jewish grandparents will pick us up and show us the UN building, the Statue of Liberty, and Central Park. I picture stern-faced editors in New York City skyscrapers digging through slush piles in hopes of finding the next brilliant author.

Could that be me some day?

Heidi dreams of acting, Shaun likes to sing, and I want to pen bestsellers which will sit in bookstore displays. Dad and Mom tell me this is an impractical goal since there are no guarantees in publishing, but their warnings only add to my determination. If I work hard, God will help me, won't He?

And in America, can't we do whatever we set our minds to?

Thanks to my dad's friend, Paul Jackson, I begin to believe anything is possible, since he also wants to be an author. On camping trips, Paul gathers us kids round the evening fire and reads to us from his manuscript. I stare into the flames, watching his scenes come to life. I always beg for more. Though Paul doesn't speak the King's English, smoke a pipe, or dress like an Oxford don, he is truly a storyteller.

So, what's to stop me from being one?

I buy my own rolltop desk—shipped wholesale from Grandma Guise's furniture store—and sit at it for hours, steering it like a ship's captain through the waves of my imagination. My poems are tossed about by stormy seas, sometimes bobbing to the surface like messages in a bottle. My short stories crash across the bow.

These tales are alive. They are mystery.

They're magic.

And now I'm going to the Big Apple, the epicenter of the book world. Though I may not be talented or lucky enough, the dream actually feels within reach.

~ ~ ~

This journey to New York will change my life, broadening my imagination and opening two distinct doors in my mind.

Creativity. And craving.

Choosing between the two will become a lifelong challenge.

Eben and I arrive during a heat wave. The city is loud, crowded, and full of energy. By the weekend, the weather turns humid. A fire engine stops at the corner to open a hydrant, allowing kids to dash through the torrent of water and rainbow spray. Eben and I yell and splash around.

Later, we tour Ellis Island and climb to the viewpoint in the Statue of Liberty's crown. We are told our nation opens its arms to the poor and huddled masses, and my chest swells with patriotic pride. Having traveled around the world, I love the peoples of all nations and I'm happy to know they are welcome here.

Eben's grandparents take us on excursions to museums, parks, and the Knickerbocker Yacht Club. They teach us to take the helm of their sailboat and tack with the jib. We cruise around Long Island, tasting sea foam and whooping into the wind. Dad often implies that the rich are stingy and selfish, but this elderly man and woman are both kind and encouraging to me.

At their home, Eben and I sit on the back deck and write stories. Though I love bringing characters to life, and the words pour from my pen onto the page, I don't yet catch all the nuances of adult life and conversation. People say things they don't mean, and they don't say things they hope others will understand.

Am I ready for this?

Reluctant, I give Eben's grandmother one of my handwritten tales.

She reads for a few minutes, then peers at me over her sunglasses. "You're really quite good, Eric. You have the makings of a young writer."

"You seriously think so?"

"You know, hard work reaps rewards."

Could writing be something I do for a living? Could this be my purpose? If God has given me this ability, it must be for a reason.

And just like that, the first door in my imagination swings open.

~ ~ ~

A few afternoons later in Central Park Zoo, Eben and I stop at the giraffe enclosure. A younger animal, half as tall as his mother, lifts his forelegs against a tree and angles his groin against the trunk. What is he up to? As others in the crowd groan in disgust, I realize the giraffe is humping, just as our male dogs used to do on the legs of unsuspecting guests.

Eben's grandmother herds us away. "Let's go see the penguins, shall we?"

Her detour doesn't stop the memories from rushing in: Sleeping bags. Preteen boys. Furtive rubbing. Awkward chuckles.

Posters of Farrah Fawcett and Raquel Welch.

Dirty jokes in the locker room at school.

A waterlogged book behind a tree in a friend's backyard, with flesh-toned drawings of men and women in tangled positions.

Girls have been catching my attention a lot these days. I like a classmate at Eugene Christian. She's short and cute, runs track and field, and my pulse spikes whenever I see her at Skate World or Gateway Mall. We tell our friends we are going out, but we never talk. I have no idea what to say to her.

Thankfully, a few months earlier, Dad offered some helpful info when he called me to the kitchen table after my siblings were in bed. Mom sat across from him, her lips pressed tight, eyebrows angled in concern.

"You're a mature young man," he told me. "We are *proud* of you, you know that? Have you ever wondered why Grandpa Guise won't talk to us? Why he's never agreed to even seen you? Well, he's still mad because of some choices your mom and I made."

I glanced Mom's direction. She gave me a brave smile.

"We weren't married," Dad continued, "when we got pregnant with you, and that made Grandpa angry. Justifiably so. It had *nothing* to do with you, please know that. These were *our* mistakes. Do you have any idea how a woman gets pregnant?"

"Sort of, yeah. I think so."

"It's okay to say you don't." Dad drew images on a piece of paper. "Sex is a beautiful thing, a gift from God, but it must be used correctly. These are things we'll be sharing with Heidi next, but you are the oldest. Now, let me explain..."

His lesson provided more relief than embarrassment. Not only did I feel spoken to as an adult, but I finally understood some of the jokes and whispers at school, as well as the tangled positions in the book behind the tree. None of it seemed gross. The facts were just puzzle pieces fitting into a larger picture.

What about boys rubbing against boys, though? He didn't mention anything along those lines. Is that using the gift correctly?

Here now, in New York, my body is about to be awakened like never before. I have no inkling of this when Eben and I visit another of his relatives in the area. The man is nice enough, feeding us, giving us our own sleeping quarters in his loft.

The first night, I tiptoe from my bed to the bathroom. As a guest, I know from my childhood travels how to remain quiet and unobtrusive. In a basket next to the toilet sits a collection of magazines. I fish one out and find a woman staring at me from the cover. While she's posed at a discreet angle, she clearly wears no clothes.

My curiosity takes hold. The enticement is powerful.

Spreading the pages, I discover soft shapes and sensual curves. I'm not even sure what I am viewing. These pictures are more detailed than those my dad drew and in colors which make my head swim. The tingling is more intense than anything I experienced during my fumblings with guy friends. These girls look willing to share all their secrets, their eyes sleepy with desire.

And so, a second door in my imagination is kicked clear off its hinges.

The reaction in my loins is instantaneous. Blood throbs in my ears. My lips and mouth turn dry, my breath becoming shorter the longer I turn the pages. My hand moves down to curb my excitement but only intensifies things.

The release is quick.

I clean myself up and slip back to the loft. I am setting in place a pattern which will plague me for years to come, one more bad habit to add to my nail-biting. The roar and the rush subside, leaving a drowsy, empty feeling, and a sweaty sense of remorse. I feel as though I somehow took something from those girls in the photos. Or did I give something of myself away? A dark mood settles over me, darker than ever before. Doubts and questions follow me into sleep.

By the next evening, they have faded.

I wait till the apartment falls silent, then tiptoe to the bathroom again.

32

Heidi

In late-summer 1978, Dad and Mom buy our family a house of our own. We go from our weed-infested place to a fifty-year-old home at 1933 Port Street. Located in west Eugene, off Barger Drive, the two-story structure faces a gravel, potholed road, but to us it is a mansion. My brothers and I get our own rooms. Our parents have a walk-in closet. We even have a family room with a pool table, warped as it is.

This is really ours? We can hardly believe it.

I imagine living here forever, or at least until my brothers and I all marry and have kids of our own. This house will be home to multiple generations. We'll bring our children back for the holidays to visit with their grandpa and grandma.

Dad will dress up as the skinniest Santa anyone's ever seen.

Mom will bake oatmeal cookies and serve hot homemade cider.

Yes, I have it all planned out.

One of my favorite places to dream is in the bath. Upstairs, Mom loves what she calls the *pink bathroom*, with its delicate pink wallpaper, pink carpet, and claw-foot tub. This is my spot to enjoy the preteen beauty treatments she gives me while we listen to the Bible on tape. The story of Esther is one of my favorites and I envision being a Jewish queen, soaking in a milk bath, preparing for a foreign king. I want to be just like Esther, ready to save my people when the time comes.

When I'm not pampering, I am in the backyard playing with my brothers. Since it's not a big area, our house rules state that a baseball hit over the fence into the neighbor's driveway is a home run. With this in mind one Saturday morning, I step up to the plate and twist my body and bat toward the fence.

Eric's first pitch whizzes by and I jump back.

"Why're you standing crooked?" he wants to know. "I almost hit you."

"Put it right here." I wriggle the bat, providing a line for his next pitch.

He throws it so fast I don't even clip the ball.

"You got this, Heidi. You can do it," Shaun calls from our outfield.

On the third pitch, I swing hard and connect with a resounding crack. I am rounding first base toward second when I hear the shattering glass.

Shaun throws his hands up and groans.

"That's it. Game over," Eric says. "Should we count it as a home run?"

I look up and realize the ball has crashed through our parents' upstairs window. They are sleeping in, a rare privilege for them, and now a jagged hole mars the reflection of overhead clouds. Our dad has a reputation for coming out of sleep with roars and flailing arms and none of us want to see his reaction.

What excuse can I offer for breaking glass in our brand new house?

Will anything lessen the severity of my impending sentence?

My brothers and I are still frozen in place when Dad's voice booms down from the upstairs bedroom: "Hubba *hubba*. Pretty good hit for a girl."

A home run it is.

~ ~ ~

As a new school year begins, we each receive an alarm clock. Dad and Mom emphasize the importance of academic attendance, since getting straight A's won't do us any good if we never learn how to show up for a job. Showing up is only half the battle. We also need to know how to work. Meticulous as always, Mom posts a schedule, which includes daily chores for each of us to do after school.

"Breakfast is at six forty-five," Mom tells us. "I'll pack your lunches the night before. If you want a shower, set your alarm early. No latecomers to the table."

"Three-minute showers," Dad adds. "Our water bill here is *outrageous.*"

Three minutes? That sounds outrageous to me.

After breakfast time, our parents continue, we'll have a half hour for family devotions and for questions related to our personal Bible reading. Then it's off to the bus stop across from Dari Mart. There will be no goofing around.

Things proceed smoothly the first few weeks. No major disruptions. One morning, though, I run back to my room after family devotions, dissatisfied with how my clothes feel on my constantly altering figure. By the time I change and catch up to my younger brother, the bus is pulling away, fading east down Barger Drive.

"Eric left us," Shaun grumbles. "Probably wanted to teach us a lesson."

"I bet he tried getting the driver to stop. It's okay. Dad will take us."

Back at home, we find our dad enjoying his own morning routine, and he doesn't even glance up from his coffee and newspaper. "Better start walking," he says, "if you want to make it to school. You've got a long haul from here."

I can't believe he's serious. In my softest tone, I say, "Daddy, we didn't—"

"*Scoot.* You are *not* getting absences today." He presses a finger to one side of his schnoz and blows through the other into wadded TP. He is done with us.

Flabbergasted, we shuffle outside. Our anger mounts as we follow Barger to Highway 99. Though the bus route is the only one we recognize, it's certainly not the shortest way across town. Shaun adjusts his backpack and blames me for taking too long to change my clothes. I blame him for not sprinting ahead to stop the bus. Realizing how ludicrous we sound, we contemplate other options.

"We should just run away," Shaun determines.

"Where would we go?"

As passing vehicles kick up dirt, we conclude we are better off staying with our family—even if Eric did ditch us. Pretty soon we are laughing as we relive the scene of rounding the corner and watching our bus disappear in a cloud of exhaust. At least we have the lunches Mom packed, in case we don't get to school by noon. Anna and I were going to split our treats, but we'll have to do it tomorrow.

Behind us, a horn sounds and we whip our heads around.

"Jump in," Dad calls from the car. "I'm sure you've both learned your lesson, haven't you? Poor choices have consequences. Don't you *ever* forget it."

He drives us the rest of the way to school.

And we never miss our bus again.

~ ~ ~

Shaun

The weather turns damp and rainy, then stays stuck in that pattern for months. As winter sets in, our whole family turns moody, ready to escape the Willamette Valley. Thanks to a wealthy couple at church, we go on a weekend getaway to central Oregon's Inn of the Seventh Mountain. There, we check into a condominium.

Soon, Dad and Mom have locked themselves away in a bedroom.

They call it alone time.

We call it a chance to scamper about without parental supervision, skiing through ponderosa and lodgepole pines, mountain biking on snow-dusted trails. We play chess with life-sized pieces on a huge board beside the lodge, then ice skate at the outdoor rink until our faces freeze and our feet go numb.

As Eric and Heidi head for the heated pool, I aim for the hot tub. Stepping into the water, my body begins to thaw. I have the whole tub to myself.

Is this how the rich people live? Talk about feeling spoiled.

"Mind if I join you?" a female voice asks.

"Sure," I say to a lady with long, dark hair. "It's nice and hot."

"You seem like a polite young man. Where are your parents, may I ask?"

"Having alone time."

She smiles at that, as though she knows something I don't.

"And my brother and sister are right over there. We're not afraid of being on our own. We've been all around the world."

"Remarkable." She settles in by a jet. "Your parents in the military?"

"We smuggled Bibles."

Either my answer or my age disarms her, and before I know it this lady is telling me how rough things are in her life, how it all looks good on the outside even as she is dying on the inside. I nod and listen the way my parents do. As a kid at Faith Center, I've been told I am valued and have a voice. I'm still learning when and where to use it, since singing draws me closer to God, but getting mouthy often lands me in trouble. Right now seems like a perfect time to talk about Jesus' love.

The lady listens and wipes at her eyes. She even agrees to pray with me.

Overjoyed, I run barefoot in wet shorts to our resort room. "Daddy, Mommy," I cry, banging on the door. "This lady, she just invited Jesus into her heart."

They appear in their bathrobes. "She what? Slow down, Shaun. Where?"

Roped into impromptu ministry, they slip into flip-flops and follow me to the hot tub where they meet my new friend. They invite her to spend time with us over the next two days, and she will end up staying in touch with us for years to come.

A soul has been saved. My voice actually matters.

The thrill of it carries me through the weekend, then begins to fade as we head home over the packed snow on McKenzie Pass.

What about other lost and hurting souls?

Do I need to reach out to more people? Will ten be enough? A hundred?

My joy turns to despair, leaving a hollow unease in my tummy. Is this what Daddy faced in India? I remember my own moment of salvation, seated on his lap at the Domes. God loves me, I realized at that young age. So, I love Him. Everything else is extra. Nothing I do can make Him love me any more than He already does.

Gazing out the car window, I write a song which I share with my family as we drive. My parents nod in approval. A few days later, when we pull up at the home of Roy Hicks, Jr., for a staff dinner and prayer meeting, they tell me to be ready to share. Since Roy and his wife are always kind to me, I'm not one bit nervous.

"Roy," I inform him, "I wrote a song about Jesus."

He flashes a wry smile. "You know, I've written a few myself."

"'Praise the Name of Jesus.' I know that one."

"I sure hope so. Well, bub, let's hear what you've got."

Roy likes my song, called "Gladness and Joy," and has me sing it the following Sunday at Faith Center. Even with thousands watching, I feel confident.

My nerves return, though, when Amy Grant comes a few months later, just her and her guitar. Roy arranges for me to meet her during rehearsal, the young, single woman adored by every Christian boy. She's even prettier up close.

"Well, hi there," she says, focusing on me. "I hear you wrote a song."

At barely nine years old, I feel small and suddenly voiceless.

She picks me up, propping me on her hip. "Can you sing it for me? If you do, I'll even share it during tonight's concert. How about that?"

Despite her kindness, my lips won't move. This is Amy Grant.

Eventually, she sets me down, tugged away by responsibilities. I want to kick myself. Music is something I love. Using my voice is something I've enjoyed since I was two years old, cuddled on Mommy's lap during prayer meetings in Vienna. Singing to God makes me happy. And here, with a golden opportunity, I let it go to waste.

Watching Amy walk off in her easy manner, I still cannot utter a word.

33

Eric

"There you are," my dad says, as I step into the house and kick off my running shoes. "I'll be at the Faith Center offices most of the day."

"Dad, it's Saturday."

"Lots to do, bud. More appointments than I can keep up with. Good *grief*, what is that smell? Is that your *socks*? Listen, it's all part of going through puberty, but *wow*. From now on, taking shoes and socks off outside might be the best idea."

Another school year is almost over. It's spring of 1979, and I'm preparing for the all-comers' meet at Hayward Field, a facility where prestigious athletes have set numerous world records. The idea of going up against kids from Track City Track Club in their matching red singlets intimidates me. I feel outclassed.

"I ran six miles," I tell my dad. "All the way out Green Hill Road."

"There aren't any sidewalks out there."

"I'm careful." My fingers rest on my wrist. "My pulse is already down to eighty. You know, I'm training for three events—long jump, high jump, and the eight hundred. Have I shown you the Fosbury Flop? It's so cool. I—"

"To be continued, bud. Tell me more when I get home, okay?"

Tires spit gravel as he speeds off. Good luck seeing him again today. Dad doesn't even know about the meet. I'll have to take the city bus there by myself. After setting my shoes on the porch, I peel off my socks and take a whiff.

Whew, Dad wasn't kidding.

Alone in my room, I toss the laundry into the basket and plop down on my bed. Heidi's sleeping in. Shaun's watching morning cartoons. Mom's at a women's Bible study. Temptations kick in as my mind stirs up glossy images.

God, I wonder, what's wrong with me? I need your help.

Sports have become a distraction from my sexual tensions. When I'm not running, I ride bikes, climb trees, play soccer, and shoot baskets. Sometimes, all this activity only heightens my awareness of the human body. Girls dominate my thoughts. The pounding in my temples grows louder. How many times do I hurry over to Dari Mart and slip a swimsuit magazine under my sweatshirt? Or peek at the smut on the top shelf while the clerk's back is turned?

To create. Or to crave.

The two doors stand before me, worlds of imagination and wonder. Will I fuel another story or fan the flames of illicit desire? Asking God to forgive me becomes as regular as my sinning. How can I expect Him to take me seriously when I often repeat my mistakes within the same day? How can I be of any good to Him with all these bad thoughts churning through my head?

The Bible, I'm told, is my source of strength. It is a spiritual weapon, a sword. I highlight I Corinthians 10:13, which says, "No temptation has overtaken you except such as is common to man; but God is faithful, who will not allow you to be tempted beyond what you are able, but with the temptation will also make the way of escape..."

I feel overtaken, yes.

Is this common to man, though? Do others struggle the way I do?

As Eben focuses solely on music and academics, I become best friends with Tim Johnson, a newer student at Eugene Christian. Like Eben, he is the only son of a single mother and our relationship blossoms.

Tim and I like many of the same things. In our seasons of AYSO soccer together, we trade off as the team's high scorers. As a guard on our basketball squad, he feeds me the ball at the low post. We both master the Fosbury Flop, able to jump bars as high as our own heads. And don't even get us started on *The Lord of the Rings*. We spend hours drawing characters, making lexicons, and coming up with our own elvish alphabets.

We're athletic nerds, which gives us fair to good chances with the girls.

Especially good chances for Tim.

When he and I walk through the halls, the girls all turn to look at him. Even my sister shows some interest, and the two of them hold hands in the back seat of our car a few times when it seems Mom isn't looking. Tim's not big and muscular. I'm much taller. He has a presence about him, though, a refined, almost delicate appeal. Beneath dark eyelashes, his nose is sculptured art, while mine is unmolded clay.

It's not long before we are inseparable. Our parents trust us together. Our teachers trust us. Our youth pastor at Faith Center trusts us.

"Good thing we're not gay," we often joke. "We could be off doing whatever we want and no one would even care."

More than anything, we both love Jesus. We want to honor Him. Which means, considering how girl crazy we are, we need ways of escape from temptation.

Music, we discover, is a great diversion. Tim and I sit at a turntable wearing headphones the size of Bundt cakes and listen to Christian musicians. David Meece, Rez Band, and Keith Green are some favorites. Each time Keith performs at Faith Center, he draws large crowds with his tongue-in-cheek humor and hard-hitting lyrics.

Of course, secular entertainment is strictly off-limits in our household.

Or so we think, until we catch Dad singing along with hits such as Harry Chapin's "Cat's in the Cradle" and Gerry Raferty's "Baker Street." Mom, on the other hand, winces at anything other than praise and worship music.

When it comes to literature, my parents never censor my choices. I read *Lord of the Flies, Black Like Me, Siddharta,* and *The Outsiders*—which is banned from many school lists and leaves me crying for ten minutes after I turn the final page.

Incense could be another point of conflict. For me, the smell of sandalwood triggers good memories of India, but most of our Christian friends associate incense with Hindu and Buddhist worship. When I ask my dad and mom if it's okay to light some sticks in my bedroom, they barely bat an eye.

"Sure," Dad responds. "I mean, you're not doing it to honor other gods, are you? Didn't think so. Listen, it's no use majoring on minor things."

"You'll be a teenager soon," Mom adds. "We won't always be here to look over your shoulder. It's so crucial that you learn to hear Jesus for yourself. Just ask Him if you should be reading a certain book or listening to a group like Petra."

"I know you don't like them, Mom. Sheesh, I get it."

"Personally," she admits, "when I listen to their music, it gives me an uneasy feeling. What about you?"

"I love it."

"Be attuned to what Jesus says. He'll let you know, Eric."

"In other words, you don't want me listening to them. Fine, whatever."

"No, honey. For you, it may be okay. There's that voice inside, the Holy Spirit, which acts as your conscience, just like Jiminy Cricket in *Pinocchio*. What's suitable for you may not be for someone else. You may have no problem watching a war movie, while some of our friends who fought in Vietnam react strongly to scenes of violence."

I shrug. "Makes sense, I guess."

"Eric, we all fall short of God's glory. We need His wisdom every day."

Lurid images play through my thoughts, reminders of how far I have fallen, and I drop my chin. When Mom runs her fingers along my shoulder, I flinch and pull away. I've seen Dad react the same way, though I'm too young to suspect his reasons are not so different from my own.

~ ~ ~

A few weeks later as the credits roll after a matinee showing of a Pink Panther film, Mom and we three kids are cornered by another Faith Center mother. We've already eaten all the snacks Mom smuggled in with her purse and drank the bottles of Coke we tucked into our tube socks beneath bell-bottom jeans.

The woman says, "There were some real questionable parts in there, don't you think? If you had walked out, Linda, I was going to walk out as well."

"Oh, don't ever wait on me," Mom replies. "You and Jesus need to have your own relationship. You obey whatever He tells you to do."

Our mom is too innocent to have caught most of the movie's innuendos.

~ ~ ~

Summer is in full swing. Soon, I will be headed into seventh grade. I feel big and invincible until the weekend of the all-comers' meet. I transfer between city buses and get off near the University of Oregon. Ahead, world-famous Hayward Field beckons, full of fans, race officials, and red-clad Track City kids. Someone says local stars Rudy Chapa and Alberto Salazar are also here, though I cannot be certain.

Tim meets me on the track. He competes in high jump and places second in the 100-meter race. I fail to place in the high jump and I'm a full five seconds behind the winners in the 800-meter race. At least I manage to take second in the long jump.

Officials hand us ribbons, and then Track City members cheer on one of their own. He's a stranger to me from a coastal town, a lean, toned kid with calf muscles like balled steel cables. I have no way of foreseeing he will one day be my brother-in-law.

His name is Matthew Messner.

Back home, ready for a shower, I take off my stinky shoes and socks and leave them outside the front door.

34

Heidi

In early 1980, Gramps Wilson appears in our lives like a legend come to life. Until now, we haven't really had a grandpa on either side of the family. Gramps carries himself with quiet authority, an Air Force veteran of World War II and retired professor with salt-and-pepper hair. For years, he has lived with his wife and kids on Guam. Now he is divorced and back in California, in the Bay Area, where his mother, Granny, still resides.

One holiday weekend, we drive over ten hours to visit our grandpa.

Will he like us? Is he as stoic as he appears in his pictures?

Gramps treats us to oven-baked pizza at a candlelit Berkeley bistro, where he and our parents fall deep into discussion. We can't begin to fathom our dad's past hurts and his desire to win his father's love. We act like ragamuffin kids again, all manners cast aside. When we slurp our drinks and crunch our ice, Mom pastes on a smile and pinches the back of my arm. I wince, but Eric and Shaun carry on. They snuff out a candle with their fingertips and pour wax into shapes on the checkered tablecloth.

"Eric, Heidi, Shaun," Dad growls. *"Enough."*

Gramps glares our direction, eyes magnified by his thick glasses. We worry he'll run off the way Grandpa Guise does and want nothing more to do with us.

"We're just bored," Shaun confides.

Gramps blinks and his gaze softens in appreciation of this childlike honesty. "Of course you are. Let's go back to my place, shall we? I have an assortment of books for you to peruse, Eric. I hear you've an interest in writing."

"I'm working on a fantasy novel."

"A common starting place," he says. "And if you like rocks, Heidi and Shaun, I have a respectable collection of minerals and geodes, most of which my mother has purchased during her travels around the world."

I sit up. "We've been to Europe and Asia."

"Quite the education, I'm sure. No wonder your parents are proud."

~ ~ ~

Gramps, we find out, plays the cello, encouraged from childhood by his mother Granny. He uses big words to test our vocabularies, and his own thirst for knowledge is insatiable. He's our dad's father, with a grouchy edge to him, but he tries to make his wishes clear and tell us when our volume gets too high. As we flip through photo albums at Gramps' place, we are reminded of the various characters in our Wilson bloodline.

Our dad's mother, Grandma Rita, divorced Gramps years ago. She is a gaunt chain-smoker with icy eyes. She muses on nature, philosophy, and religion, her sharp intellect dulled only by the vodka pumping through her veins.

Uncle Paul grew up without his father's attention or his mother's love. He longs for the affection he never received. He and Aunt Val are now in the military, pulled apart by its demands and going through a divorce. My heart aches over it.

Uncle Dave is generous and funny, honest to a fault. He and his equally direct wife, Lori, have run into religious conflicts with our mom and decided to move down to San Diego after living in Eugene for only a short period. We'll miss them.

Uncle John is a wounded soul who uses humor to hide the pain in his eyes. I know his secrets, or at least some of them. He is a budding entrepreneur. and Eric will soon work with him in his mobile coffee cart at the county fair.

Aunt Laura is married with kids. Her tan, beautiful family will serve in various Christian ministries, from Guam to Hawaii. They send us native shells and necklaces as gifts, promising they'll come to visit someday. We cannot wait.

These are the Wilsons. Boundary pushers. Vagabonds. They try new things and travel to new places. They're neither defined nor confined by cultural ideals.

On the Guise side, convention is to be applauded. They go to universities, buy homes, and work the same jobs throughout their careers. They are stable, close-knit, all living in Contra Costa County. Grandma Guise is the nucleus around which they revolve, former mayor, Soroptimist, and business owner in her town.

It's a wonder our dad and mom ever connected.

Each of our relatives, Wilson and Guise, represent something important to us kids. They are threads of varied colors, their contrasts stark, all woven together in a beautiful tapestry.

Each thread matters.

Each one adds nuance.

And—as we'll soon find out—when one unravels, it alters the whole design.

~ ~ ~

Eric

Gramps pays us a week-long visit at Port Street. As much as I would like to have both my grandfathers in my life, at least I have one.

And I desperately want his approval. Even an attaboy will do.

Gramps is dealing with his own problems, including an alcoholic girlfriend back in California. He throws himself into home and garden improvements around our small property. He's gained lots of practical experience over the years, and I like laboring alongside him. Dirty hands, sweaty hair, and sore muscles make me feel productive. Hard work makes me happy. Truthfully, though, yards, gutters, and plants seem like distractions from all the stories I'd like to set down on paper. Shaun, being more mechanical and practical, gets the majority of the attaboys.

On the last night of Gramps' visit, I shower before bed as he and my parents settle in the living room. The lamps are low, the space filled with the dark, earthy aroma of locally-roasted coffee. They'll be up late talking, I'm sure.

"I'm ready," I say, poking my head through the door.

Dad nods. "Be right there." He and Mom like to tuck us in when they can.

Gramps glances at me through thick glasses. "I must say, Eric, good work today. Once you get started, you don't know when to stop. Quite commendable."

"Procrastination gets you nowhere," I respond, hoping my word choice will prove my credentials as a writer at thirteen years old. "Goodnight, Gramps."

He nods, then stops me with one word. "Eric..."

I pivot back through the doorway and meet his eyes.

"I love you," he says.

"Love you too."

Never before has a grandparent spoken those three words to me, not even Grandma Guise who shows rather than speaks her feelings. Each step along the hallway to my bedroom happens in slow motion. Droplets pool on my eyelids, then slide down my cheeks and touch the corners of my mouth. I ease my door shut, turn off the light, and sit on the floor with my back against the box springs.

My lips wear a wet, salty grin.

~ ~ ~

Shaun

People tell us we now look and sound like actual Americans, and thanks to Dad's job at Faith Center, our standard of living is better than ever. After school, Eric sneaks quarters from the stack of change on Dad's dresser and we run over to Dari Mart to play Ms. Pacman and Deluxe Asteroids. On weekends, we throw the Nerf football for hours.

I'm not so sure about all of this, though.

Before we returned to the U.S., we had a free-spirited lifestyle, always together as a family. Now we're in separate bedrooms. Back then, we learned about Jesus in the backs of camper vans and seven-ton trucks. We hung out with other Christians in living rooms, basements, and backyards. It all felt real. It was everyday life. Here, we go to a wood-and-brick structure and call it church.

It's a building, that's all it is.

Dad, of course, is invested in the system since he is on staff. He feels the mounting pressure of people who rely on him. He's in the office during the week and in the sanctuary all day Sunday. Isn't it okay if we take a break sometimes? Does our family honestly have to be there every time the doors open?

One winter evening, I make the mistake of voicing these questions out loud. Heidi and I are in the family room finishing a game of pool when our dad walks in.

"Can't we just skip church tonight?" I ask him.

"You kidding, bud? It's Wednesday night service, same as always."

"We just got home from school."

He comes to a stop. "That was hours ago. Listen, I just walked in the door myself. We're grabbing dinner, then hopping into the car, okay?"

"Church takes so long. And we have to go straight to bed when we get home."

"Well, you're not staying here alone. Go and get your shoes on. *Now.*"

"I'm going to be ten."

Heidi shoots me a look, which I ignore.

"And I'm three times your age, Shaun. Enough arguing," Dad barks, swinging a leg at my backside. "Time to get moving, before I lose my cool. *Go.*"

"I'm not arguing. I just don't know why we—"

Banggg!

Dad lifts me up and shoves me against the flue of our wood stove. The impact is jarring, and the residual heat permeates my skin. "So you think you're *big* now?" he barks. "You aren't the one making decisions, you got that? We are *going* to church, whether you like it or not."

I don't like it, but he's figured this out by now.

"Daddy," Heidi cries, tugging at his arm.

"Stay *out* of it," he tells her, then drops me to the floor. "Now do as you're told, Shaun. No *ifs, ands,* or *buts.*"

Stomping to the front door, I wonder what it is in me that stirs the reactions of teachers, carpool drivers, and parents? Why does love turn so quickly to anger? When I still wet my bed sometimes, is it to get my dad's attention? He can listen so patiently to a stranger for hours, only to have me push all his buttons in seconds. Is there something wrong inside of me, something I don't see?

I hear people blame God for this thing or that. They have all these big struggles, like my brother after his puppy died, these questions they shelve for later.

Not me.

My problem is with people.

With Jesus as our example, shouldn't Christians be living in honest and peaceful community? Instead, we burn others at the stake while patting ourselves on the backs for buying a homeless person a burger. Why don't we bear each other's burdens like the Bible says?

I sit through the Wednesday evening service, arms folded across my chest.

Am I the only one who sees trouble ahead?

Sure, we Wilsons have the initial appearances of success. We are climbing the ladder one rung at a time. We own a home, go to church. We're the model Christian family. Daddy and Mommy are having a positive impact on people's lives, Eric and Heidi are dreaming of what they want to be, and I'm realizing how much I like to sing and dance. In pursuit of the American Dream, we'll all reach the top of the ladder someday soon and be free from worry and woe. At least, that is the hope.

But what if it's all a sham?

What if all we find up there is the edge of a precipice?

People don't like me asking these questions. They tell me to keep my head down and do my best. Keep climbing, climbing, climbing. It's the American way.

PART 4

THE ASCENT

It's more difficult to stay on top
than to get there.

Mia Hamm

Shaun fishing w/ Uncle Vinny

Shaun, Uncle John, Mom, Heidi, Granny on family couch

Heidi, Mom, Eric, Shaun on camping trip in Trinity Alps

Northwest Faith Center after a new paint job

35

Heidi

Our house is unusually quiet. It's Saturday morning. Eric is over at Tim's house, and Shaun is exploring the ponds on the other side of Barger. Alone, I grab my basketball and head outside to our carport. Our girls' team at Eugene Christian has been eliminated from the playoffs and I'm already anxious for next season.

In the driveway, I find a big truck blocking my way to the basket. The truck belongs to a thin, frail-looking blonde whose husband uses the contraption on the back to paint road lines. I maneuver and shoot around it, wondering why it's here.

Shaun pulls up on his bike. "Where'd that thing come from?"

"I think the lady who owns it carpooled with Mom to the women's retreat."

"So it's going to be parked there all weekend? That's a pain."

"Watch this. I bet I can make it from way back here." I retreat all the way to the gravel road, choosing to ignore Shaun's smirk.

From this spot, Dad's recent purchase is visible, angled across our patch of dried grass for the whole neighborhood to see. It's a used Porsche 914 with black racing decals. "This one's a poor man's Porsch," Dad has explained to us, using the abbreviated term. "But lots of fun." At age thirty-one, he needs this reminder of his wilder youth.

"What're you doing, Heidi?" Shaun barks. "You going to shoot or what?"

Eyes narrowed, I cradle the basketball in my hands and take aim. My shot soars through the air over the contraption on the truck and swishes through the net. My jaw drops and I flick my eyes toward my brother. "You saw that, right? You're my witness." I run into the house and up the stairs. "Daddy, Daddy, I swooshed it from super far away. I swear, I'm not making this up. Shaun saw me."

He doesn't respond.

"Daddy." I turn the handle of his bedroom door, but it won't budge.

"That's *great*, sweetie," his voice calls from within. "Now leave us alone. Still trying to get some sleep here."

"Did he believe you?" Shaun asks when I trudge back downstairs.

I shrug, pondering the past sixty seconds. How long have our parents had a lock on their door? Did my dad say *us,* or did my ears play a trick on me?

Not long after, Dad bounds down the stairs and rubs my shoulder. He is his usual upbeat self. "C'mon, you two, jump in the Porsch. From what I hear, we have a new *superstar* in the house. How about some Garibaldi's to celebrate Heidi's shot?"

He eases the 914 along our gravel road. I'm in the passenger seat, with Shaun squeezed in on the center console. We're so low to the ground, I can hear and feel rocks popping beneath the chassis like popcorn. The moment we corner onto Barger Drive, Dad guns it. The engine emits a bobcat scream and jerks our heads back.

At Garibaldi's, we get the biggest ice-cream scoops ever, the size of softballs. Strawberry cheesecake is my current favorite.

By the time we return, the truck with the contraption is gone.

My teacher, Mr. Brownlee, once told us about a man convicted of murder who was proven innocent two decades later in a case of mistaken identity. He lost his family, career, and home during his time behind bars. There was no way to get back the years taken from him.

God, I pray silently, help me not judge too quickly.

Prayer is an active part of my life now. Mom encourages me to talk to God about everything, and I've set up a prayer closet under our staircase, with a journal, a Bible, and some pillows. Sometimes Karma even joins me here. This space provides the only safe haven from my disturbing bedtime dreams.

Boys pawing at me. Men throwing rocks.

My uncle's eyes full of dark desire.

On my knees, I ask Jesus to bring me peace. It's a nightly struggle. Fear and shame drag their fingers down my spine, trying to unnerve me, and these moments of meditation are often my only way to find rest.

~ ~ ~

Over the next few weeks, something seems to shift in our household. Mom acts distracted, diverted. She is normally so focused on us, her eyes soft and at peace. Now activities pull her away, as though she cannot sit still for a conversation.

Is she upset with me? Or simply too busy with everyone else?

When I was an infant, her postpartum depression drove a small wedge between us, but it hasn't stopped me from talking to her about almost anything.

She cares. I know she does.

So what's wrong?

At school, my world is expanding. I play on the soccer team, able to kick as far as most of the boys. I learn new toughness on the basketball team, my eyes watering as the ball drills me in the face more than once. No matter how much it hurts, I just play harder. Dad says getting hit in the nose must activate my superpower.

My real love, of course, is acting. This hasn't changed.

Our class, we're told, will be performing *The Hobbit* this spring, and I use my growing courage and determination to project my voice during my audition. Instead of landing a part for my looks, I am rewarded for my emoting and enunciating.

"I got it," I declare to my family over dinner. "The lead role."

"Oh, Heidi," Dad says, "that's *wonderful*."

"I'm playing Bilbo Baggins, a hobbit with hairy feet."

"Well, no wonder. If it was *stinky* feet, Eric would've gotten it."

My older brother chuckles, even as he draws his legs under his chair.

Since I want to be in movies one day, I must take this role seriously. Our parents teach us to do everything as unto the Lord, reminding us of Luke

16:10: "whoever is faithful with very little will also be faithful with very much." I practice *ad nauseam* for the next six weeks, learning my lines as well as everyone else's. During rehearsals, I am there to assist any time someone forgets a line or blocking.

Last year, my crush played the prince in *Cinderella*. This year's crush is cast as the dragon Smaug. I, Bilbo Baggins, in my belt and baggy clothing, crawl around the scaly creature, lifting his limbs until I find the ring amidst the gold upon which he slumbers. When he awakens, I find myself face to face with the fire-breathing beast. I quickly don the ring, turn invisible, and thrust a dagger into his vulnerable heart.

The scene demands extra blocking, which means more concentrated time for us to practice together—and no, I don't mind one bit.

The Hobbit is a screaming success, and the evening news shows a clip of me crawling over my crush's dragon body. Dad tells me I did great and Mom tells me she loved it, though she still seems removed from the moment in a way I cannot define.

Karma calls. "Wow, Heidi, that was amazing. I saw you on TV."

Anna also calls. "You're so lucky. The good stuff always happens for you."

What can I say? I am a local celebrity.

~ ~ ~

At home, my brushes with drama are more sobering. Into our home on Port Street, our parents welcome all sorts of long-term guests. It's the way things were back at our place on Barrett Avenue, in the early 1970s.

Jesus' love has no boundaries.

Which means our parents have none either, I guess.

Eric, Shaun, and I have little say in the matter, and soon Barbara is sharing my bed since I'm the only girl in the house. Barbara is sweet. At thirty, she suffers from leukemia—cancer of the blood—and spends most days getting chemo treatments. Once back home, she throws up in the bathroom, then rests in the living room sunlight. I practice flips on the trampoline at school, trying not to think of her wasting away like those emaciated bodies we saw overseas.

Barbara wears a brave smile. Many evenings, the two of us sing together until she's too weak to continue, then I sing to her and read scriptures while her eyes light up with gratitude. Barring a miracle, she will die. I know this. Our home is only a way-station, a place for her to be surrounded with love as she passes from this life.

Regardless, when her absence comes, it hits me hard.

My eyes pool with tears at her funeral as we lift our voices for "What a Friend We Have in Jesus." I imagine her dancing with Jesus in a body healthy and strong, her beautiful face wearing a smile as she sings to Him with boundless joy.

My nightly meditations grow more fervent, even as my dreams continue to haunt me. I want the peace Barbara displayed in pain and in death. Making my bed, I listen to Keith Green's latest album on my record player. His lyrics move me deeply.

Barbara will never sleep here again.

She is gone.

~ ~ ~

A week drags by, yet I still sense Barbara's presence and smell the fragrance of her hair. Tears stream down my cheeks as I listen to Keith Green's, "Oh Lord, You're Beautiful." I am reminded of Jesus' face, His grace, and my desire to shine His Word all around. I am twelve years old. Life is precious. I want to live each day for Him.

"Heidi, are you doing your chores?" Mom knocks, then enters.

"Already made my bed," I call out over the music.

Shaun pops his head in and kicks at a pile of my dirty clothes. "What a pigsty. It's like an Amazon expedition just to get to your closet."

"Nobody asked you. Leave."

"Yes, Your Highness."

"Mommy, make him leave."

"Mommy," he mimics, "make him leave."

I roll my eyes and turn away. Mom is at my birdcage on the other side of the room. I tell her, "I already cleaned their cage and my towels are in the dryer."

"You need to give them water."

"I did."

"No," she says, "you didn't. Please, water your birds."

I walk over and note the empty dispenser. My doves coo at me. "Weird," I mumble, almost to myself. "I know I did."

Mom glares at me. "Clearly, you did not." She stalks from my room.

When I grab the dispenser, my doves flutter and fluff their wings. I ask, "How'd you guys drink it all so fast?" I replace their water and sing along with my music.

Shaun appears in my doorway again. He smirks. "You're in trouble."

"You're a brat."

"You're a brat."

I stomp through my shin-high layer of dirty clothes, hangers, and shoe boxes. My goal is to slam the door in his face, but the impact is lessened by the impeding objects on my floor. Even with the door shut, his sneer still hovers in my thoughts.

Mom returns minutes later with an armload of towels, which she dumps on the bed. "They're dry. Now, Heidi, I told you to water your birds."

"Got it done."

"Don't. Lie. To. Me." She punctuates each word with a slap at my head.

"Owww, Mommy. Stop. Go check for yourself." Cringing, I notice her beet-red face. Since when does she lose control like this? What is going on? I storm over to the birdcage. "See." I'm almost yelling as I point my finger.

But the dispenser is nearly empty. What? Am I the one going crazy here?

Mom's nails dig into my arm. She throws open the cage, scatters the doves as she yanks out the dispenser, and drags me to the pink bathroom. She watches as I refill it, then marches me back to my room. She slows a bit, her voice turning syrupy.

"See, Heidi, isn't it better to just do as you're told?"

My blood's now boiling, same as hers. I did do it, I want to yell. What is wrong with you? If anything, Dad's the one who flies off the handle. Who are you anyway?

Ignoring my anger—or maybe because of it—she slips her hand into mine and leads me toward my bed, where she kneels to pray and encourages me to join her. When all else fails, she turns spiritual. If I don't comply, I am guilty by default.

"Jesus," she says in a saccharine whisper, "please help Heidi learn how important it is to tell the truth. Help her realize lying is not what you desire. When we're deceptive, we hurt ourselves and those around us, even if we don't see it. Thank you for loving us, even when we act in ways which cause pain and destruction."

How have I caused pain and destruction? Is she serious?

Anyway, I did give my doves their water.

"Jesus, you love us so much. Please now, forgive us our sins." Mom pauses, eyes still closed, and nudges me. "Heidi, is there anything you would like to confess?"

"Nope." I am seething. "Think you covered it."

"We love you, Jesus. Amen." She squeezes my hand. "Don't you feel better?"

"Sure," I mutter.

"Now if you fold the towels, you'll be done with your chores." As she turns to leave, she glances back at my doves. She moves closer to the cage. "Oh no, Heidi. Look, I think there's a leak in the dispenser. The water, it's nearly gone. I am sooo sorry I didn't believe you. I shouldn't have lost my temper." Tears pool in her eyes.

"It's fine, Mommy. I'm fine."

"Oh, honey." She envelops me in her arms and I lean into her. "Love hopes all things, believes all things. I shouldn't have assumed. Please, will you forgive me?"

I assure her again I am fine.

In my bed that night, I wonder what is happening to our family. It's like a snag in my nylons, barely noticeable at first, but you know it's only going to get worse.

36

Shaun

For years Mom has been our game partner, teacher, and comforter. She's shown interest in our interests, even making meals for Aunt Val and Aunt Lisa since she can't pay them money for giving us art lessons. She's also been my disciplinarian when Dad is gone. "Go get the red belt," she says in an even voice, referring to the hard plastic reins from an old toy horse. "How many swats do you think you deserve?" As though getting my input justifies the number of welts on my backside.

Recently, Mom has been raising her voice at us. Even yelling.

"You're sure pretty when you're mad," I tell her, using a line I heard on TV. She slaps me across the face.

Mom and Dad have always disagreed over little things, but their arguments are now louder, longer. These are not behaviors we've seen from our mom before. Heidi is convinced it has something to do with the truck we found in our driveway a few months back. Eric and I aren't so sure.

"You guys aren't even listening," she tells us. "Mom was gone to the women's retreat and there was someone else in the bedroom with Dad."

"That's disgusting." I turn away. "I don't even want to think about it."

"Like who?" Eric wants to know.

"Exactly," Heidi whispers.

Mom's told us before about her Catholic upbringing and the guilt which came with it. She now lets her own shame spill over onto us. Eric and I regularly show up for breakfast in our underwear. Heidi does too, in her bra and panties. We think nothing of it. We're ten, twelve, and thirteen. We're just hurrying to eat before dressing for school.

"Please," Mom says, "can't all of you wear some clothes to the table?"

"We are wearing clothes," I shoot back.

"Underclothes," Eric adds with a grin.

Mom shakes her head. "But Heidi is a young woman and—"

"Gross," I say. "She's my sister."

"Don't you think you're all too old to be wandering around half-dressed?"

"We're just as covered up as when we wear our swimsuits," Heidi says.

Mom wears a pained expression and waves us off, making her displeasure known. We clearly do not meet her standards for modesty and godliness.

The building resentments in the household seep over into my sister's and my relationship. What does it matter? Dad and Mom treat us however they want, spanking and slapping us when they believe correction is due. In previous arguments, I've done nothing other than taunt my sister when she bosses me around. Now our fights become physical. As the youngest and smallest, I'm sick of it. When she tries to lord it over me, I shove and pin her to ground, screaming in her face till she finally shuts up.

Do I feel bad? Not at all.

I might be little, but I am strong.

I'm watching *Donald Duck* in the living room one Saturday morning when Mom chases Heidi past me into the dining area. My sister turns, drops to the kitchen floor, and pleads, "I love you, Mommy. I love you, Mommy."

Mom swats at her head, screaming, "You little brat."

Despite my own fights with my sister, I'm stunned. Who has taken over our mother's body? Where is the woman who swam with us in the Black Sea and wiped our backsides in India? As the two of them hash out their differences, I go looking for my brother, then remember he is on a training run for the

Butte to Butte 10K. The Porsche is gone, which means Dad is at the counseling offices already.

Well, I sure as heck don't want to be stuck in this house.

A bus takes me to the downtown station, where I meet with some other kids. With too much time on our hands, we dart into the bank for free Dum Dums off the counter, then head back outside. Sucking on my grape treat, I hop onto a concrete structure which is supposed to be a piece of art. Nope, just concrete.

"How'd you get up there?" one of the boys asks.

"You grab onto that ledge and climb," I tell him. "It's simple."

He tries twice. Slips. "Dang," he says, "you're like a little monkey."

Small and agile, I always impress other kids this way. No one calls it *parkour*, not yet. My brother, sister, and I call it bounding—hopping from ledge to ledge, balancing on fallen trees over streams, scaling obstacles in a parking garage by bouncing from pylons to wire cables to low walls. Bounding fits my compact build and arms. When we nailed plywood in the red cedar branches at our old address, Uncle John was the only one able to scramble up and join us in our tree house.

Today, for some reason, I decide to push things a step further. Maybe I want to impress these other kids. Maybe I'm tired of being bossed around by my sister and tossed around by my dad. Maybe I'm tense from the recent conflicts at home. All I know is, I spot an easy target.

The boy is large and hunched, rocking on a bus stop bench, fingers twitching. He's a student from the center for the mentally disabled.

"Hey, get up off that bench," I snap at him.

His eyes swivel my way.

"You're a retard," I yell.

His chin lowers and his words trip over themselves. "I, I... I know... I am. But it's... it's not... my fault."

Something in his tone pierces my chest. Here I am, trying to prove myself, and he does just the opposite. He owns up to his challenges and accepts his place in the cruel pecking order. All he wants is a little dignity. Whether he's suffered a genetic defect of some sort or complications from birth, he is still a child created by God.

And what am I doing? Flinging insults at him.

Dad thinks empathy is important and he recently took us to watch *The Elephant Man*, a story about a gentle soul who suffers abuse and misunderstanding. I think of the misshapen man treated as a freak, and of this boy at the bus stop under verbal attack. God has a soft spot in His heart for the outcasts.

Tears well in my eyes and I brush my sleeve across my face. Instead of building this boy up, I have torn him down.

Pathetic.

More than anything I want to apologize, but my mouth is dry as ash.

~ ~ ~

Eric

Ash fills the air in mid-May 1980. Less than 200 miles north of us, Mount St. Helens erupts, killing fifty-seven people, leveling miles of forest like broken twigs, and sending a volcanic plume around the globe. In Eugene, people wear face masks as they walk outside and as they turn on windshield wipers to clear soot off their cars.

Friends in Austria and in India want to know if we've survived this disaster in the Pacific Northwest. Relatives call from California to check on us.

Are we okay? Yes, we're okay.

You would think it is the end of the world or something.

Within the evangelical bubble, the end times are a popular topic, and nothing fills pews and offering plates like news of coming persecution. Armageddon. Plagues. Rivers of blood. I've seen movies at church camps full of martyrs facing the guillotine. I've heard various world leaders described as the antichrist, a different one every two or three years. Credit cards and barcodes are a slippery slope toward the mark of the beast.

Over and over, pastors and self-proclaimed prophets get it wrong.

The hubbub dies down. Their book sales and numbers drop.

In Old Testament times, these religious leaders would have been stoned to death for their false prophecies, but it doesn't stop them from "prophesying" all over again a few years later.

"The Bible," Dad reminds me, "says no one except the Father knows the day of the Lord's return. Watch and pray, that's all Jesus told us to do. Not freak out and make wild, harebrained *guesses* based on a few verses taken out of context."

"Can Satan actually make us do bad things?" I wonder aloud.

"Each one of us has free will, Eric. If throwing temptation your way keeps you from God, then sure, Satan will try it. If being poor makes you curse God, great. If being rich makes you forget Him, all the better. Once you fully grasp God's love for you, why would you *want* anything else? Hell is being cut off from His presence."

Have I ever known God's love like that for myself?

Sure, there have been spiritual highs during youth-group worship times, moments I thought might lift me right off the ground. I've also experienced them at concerts having nothing to do with church, just hundreds of us swaying and singing together, joined by a sense of oneness both massive and deeply personal.

Is music its own religion, an altar of connection and artistry?

Or simply one more facet of God's personality?

~ ~ ~

Our family is still below the average household income, but Dad now has his forest-green 914—which I'll drive when I get my learner's permit—and Mom has an ugly light green Dodge Colt. Neither car fits in our rickety old garage, but we've moved up the ladder a few rungs, getting closer to the elusive dream.

Heidi seems pointed toward being a movie star.

Shaun's full of musical talent. He and my sister sing vocals together, and he can play just about any instrument he touches.

My own hopes are set on a writing career. I'm a fan of John Christopher, James Herriot, and Alistair MacLean. When I discover a steamy scene in a Ken Follett thriller, my sister and I read it silently with ever-widening eyes. Soon, I'm skimming through his other titles in search of more carnal knowledge.

"Boy," Dad exclaims after reading my latest fantasy story, "your descriptions are, *wow*, they're amazing. You sure know how to paint a picture with words."

"Someday, maybe, I'll write a bestseller."

"Tough market out there, buddy. Might be wise to pursue a degree in journalism, just to get your feet wet. An education's always a good thing."

"I like writing fiction. It's not the same."

"Good writing is good writing. Never hurts to sharpen your chops and pay your dues. But hey, who knows?" He claps a hand on my shoulder. "Just remember, you kids've had a much better upbringing than we ever had, and Luke 12:48 says, 'To whom much is given, much will be required.'"

I think of the writing he now holds in his hands. Have I given too much or too little? This spiritual pressure to do better feels more like a restriction than a catalyst.

"All comes down to free will," he adds. "One day we'll stand before God and answer for the time and talents He gave us. Did we honor *Him* or honor *ourselves*?"

Eyes glued to my typewriter, I sense I am not measuring up.

37

Eric

Shaun's voice echoes through the house: "The Bankers are coming, the Bankers are coming."

The Banker family is on a summer trip across the U.S., visiting scattered friends and family. After seven long years, our Rat Pack from Vienna is about to reunite—Deneen, Debbie, Dawn... Eric, Heidi, Shaun.

It all sounds wonderfully right in my head.

The morning drags by, though. Why aren't they here yet? My nerves are jangling, my heart skipping beats. Mom puts us to work, cleaning the walls and baseboards, dusting and vacuuming. Look at us, the responsible American family.

Will sparks fly when I see Deneen again? I once planted a kiss on her cheek while we hid in the bushes outside the OM house. She was my first crush. Shaun is similarly excited to see Dawn. He struts around the living room, a big plastic comb sticking out of his back pocket since that's what all the cool kids do these days.

"You can marry Deneen and I can marry Dawn," he tells me.

Mom doesn't exactly discourage this notion. She clicks her teeth twice and winks at both of us. "You never know what Jesus has planned."

I'm not even fourteen yet, but my parents dated at sixteen, married at seventeen, and had three kids by age twenty. While other boys seem focused on getting into girls' pants or feeling them up, I am on the lookout for my future bride. I want the real thing, the love of a lifetime.

And why not? It's worked for Dad and Mom, right?

Just last week, I spent the night at a friend's house near Eugene Christian. Early Saturday morning, we broke into the school office by prying open a louvered window. We scoured files for photos of incoming female students, finding nothing. What a bummer. I ignored my inner Jiminy Cricket as we climbed an overhang and sneaked into the teachers' break room. There, we drank their Pepsi and ate their M&Ms to ease our disappointment.

What if an alarm had gone off? Or a cop car had rolled by?

I could have been thrown into juvie, an embarrassment to my parents.

At the kitchen sink, I'm now washing dishes by hand when a reflection flashes through the window. My eyes dart across rows of mailboxes and fence lines to a station wagon kicking up dust on our gravel road.

"They're here," I call out. "The Bankers are here."

~ ~ ~

Over the next few days, we revert to our ragamuffin ways. Shaun and I want to impress, and Heidi is thankful for some girls to balance the ratio under our roof. For old times' sake, we go outside to play hide-and-seek and pet Shaun's outdoor cat, Macaroni, on the back deck. Since we live in a fully carpeted home now, we don't get to have indoor pets with all their fur and fleas.

"You remember our guinea pigs in Vienna?" Dawn says to Shaun.

"And the big swing set in our backyard?" Debbie says to Heidi.

Deneen and I exchange shy glances. I wonder if she ever thinks about that quick kiss at six years old, playful and innocent.

The Wilson and Banker parents laugh a lot during mealtimes, reminiscing about our Bible-smuggling days full of camper vans and mechanical breakdowns, gizlis and border crossings. God's Word is still verboten in Eastern Europe, Russia, and communist China. People still risk imprisonment taking literature and supplies to the underground church. It is secretive, mostly thankless work.

By the time we all part, our Rat Pack has run out of common interests. Our futures are pointed in different directions, with only the past holding us all together.

Deneen, Debbie, and Dawn now speak fluent German.

They hold dual passports. Austria is their home.

Heidi, Shaun, and I have retained only a few phrases from other languages and hold U.S. passports. Though we long for the food and cultures of our past, we belong here now. Even if we don't always fit in, we cannot rightly call any place else home.

We bid bittersweet goodbyes.

"Auf Wiedersehen."

Back in 1973, the parting of the Rat Pack was painful. Here in 1980, we know we will not be seeing each other again. We've capped off an era. Time to look ahead.

~ ~ ~

Shaun

I'm ready to earn some money of my own. My siblings and I don't get allowances and we rarely have cash on hand. I'm soon at the home of a divorcee in our congregation, clearing invasive ivy from an old tree to pocket a few bucks. I also give shoulder rubs to my mom's friends for a dollar here or there.

"He's so sweet," the women tell her. "What a doll."

Being short, I'm often treated like I'm younger than my actual age.

At least Len, who lives across the street, speaks to me like I'm an adult. Middle-aged, with thick white hair, Len is a genuinely nice person, which I find confusing since he rents out X-rated videos from behind a thick black curtain at his nearby corner market.

He offers to pay me for some yard work, though.

Who am I to refuse?

Headed out one afternoon, Len plunks some quarters in my hand to rake the thousands of leaves on his front lawn. His is the only real patch of grass on our block. I go back and forth, back and forth, piling and stuffing the leaves into big garbage bags. Not a single leaf remains on the ground.

Proud of my work, I sprint over to Dari Mart to play Ms. Pacman.

I'm met on the way back by Len's Doberman. Saber has never bitten any of the neighborhood kids, but he loves to step from behind hedges and cars to scare the crap out of us. With his pointed ears and sharp fangs, he's good at it.

"Hi, Saber," I say, a breeze tugging at my shirt. "Good boy."

That's when I notice the leaves strewn across Len's yard. Even worse, Len is at his front door with hands on hips. He'll blame me for a job poorly done, of course, and demand his money back. I hesitate, then press on, expecting a tirade.

"Would you look at this mess?" he says.

"I'm sorry, Len. I know I should've—"

"Now hold on, Shaun. I saw all those bags by the garage. With this wind, you just can't stay ahead of it. You want to come earn a couple more quarters tomorrow?"

I lift my head. "Sure, whenever you want."

"Very good then. You're a hard little worker. I like a man I can count on."

~ ~ ~

Eric

Shaun has motivated me. I'm now saving up for school clothes by working for Uncle John's mobile espresso business. We serve coffee and Italian sodas at the Saturday Market downtown and at the Country Fair out by Fern Ridge

Lake. Our customers range from hippies in tie-dye to topless nature lovers. Despite the hot, frantic work, I treasure these moments serving side by side with my uncle in cramped quarters.

Meanwhile, my training continues for the upcoming 10K run. Dad joins me for a few days, jogging around Pre's Trail. Though his goal is to get in shape after endless hours in the Faith Center counseling offices, he ends each run wheezing, red-faced, and short of breath. Only years later does he admit thinking:

What the hell? My own son's making me feel like an old man.

As insecure as I feel with acne and body odor, I'm tall for my age and entering adulthood. Like an old lion, Dad keeps a wary eye on this younger version of himself. He refuses to ever play me again after I beat him at a game of chess. He and his dad had a strained relationship, and he isn't sure where his and mine is supposed to go.

At my age, it all feels awkward. I just want my dad to approve of me.

There are other men in my life: Rob Bressi, my youth pastor, who has a way of making each kid feel special. Paul Jackson, who hires me for his masonry business, where I mix concrete, carry pallets of bricks, and scar my knuckles while scraping mortar off finished fireplaces. And Coach Russell, a former semi-pro from England, who manages our soccer team and teaches me how to play well with others.

On July Fourth, I get my Butte to Butte T-shirt, run the race in forty minutes, and see my name listed among thousands in the *Register-Guard*.

"Why, look at *you*," Dad congratulates me. "Quite the stud muffin."

"Wish you could've run it with me."

Dad shrugs. "Maybe next year, Eric. Maybe next year."

Next year, though, he won't have time for a jaunt between Spencer and Skinner Butte. He and Mom will be spearheading a new venture, which will take our family of five to great heights—before the final plunge.

"Eric, I'll run with you," Shaun chimes in. He's already fast enough to keep up.

38

Heidi

Two things happen which will later play into our lives. They seem insignificant at the time, simply coloring the edges of my seventh-grade year at Eugene Christian, when most of my memories have to do with mean girls, makeup, and cheerleading for Eric's basketball team.

First, Mom and Dad go to a pet store at Valley River Center.

Are they picking out animals for us? Maybe another kitty so Macaroni, Shaun's outdoor cat, will have a companion. Or another puppy for Eric, since he's never really had one to take Goodny's place. I know Shaun would love a snake or iguana. We all like box turtles.

Instead, they return with a green-and-yellow parakeet for Mom.

"Listen to how he sings with me," she coos.

"Remember," Dad whispers to us, "this is special to your mom. She was only twelve when she lost her pet canary."

Mom combs her hair down over her shoulder, her cheeks wet with tears of joy.

"Oh, *sweetie*," Dad says. He chokes up as he looks into her eyes.

She leans into him and they hold each other. Her mood turns brighter in the days ahead. She once again has an almost childlike glee, a characteristic we love about her. Even decades from now, in her last week of life, she will impress nurses with her red Pippi-Longstocking braids and giddy chuckle. Mom and Dad's angry words behind closed doors, their sullen looks across the dinner table, seem to be forgotten. Whatever has gone on, whatever grownup grievances have come between them over the past few months, seem to melt away.

My heart soars. Thank you, Jesus. Thank you.

I asked God for this in my prayer closet.

Perched now in his cage in our dining area, the parakeet whistles along with our mom anytime she sings tunes from *Oklahoma!* or plays Maranatha Praise albums. The bird chirps happily. Mom keeps singing.

"When you kids are at school," she says, "it's just sooo glorious as I worship Jesus and my parakeet joins in. All of creation cries out to the Lord."

The second thing has to do with a .22 lever-action rifle.

"Guess what," Shaun says, coming in from the backyard while Grandma Rita and Uncle John are visiting. "A possum was just out there behind the garage."

Dad jumps up. "Possums are no joke. Did it hiss at you?"

"I don't think so."

"Probably bared its teeth then, just to warn you away. Uglier than all get-out, those things. Listen, Shaun, you stay inside."

My brother fails to mention he was about to take a drag off one of Grandma Rita's cigarette butts outside. He saw lipstick smudges, hesitated, then puffed on it anyway. With Dad now eyeing him, he shrugs. "The thing just waddled off. I'm fine."

Not good enough for our dad. He is our hero, our protector, and he wants to eliminate the threat. Mom thinks guns are more a danger than deterrent, which means we don't have any in the house, not even pretend ones. Still, Dad has taken us target shooting out in the woods with guys from the church, many of whom hunt elk and deer to stock their freezers.

One night he borrows a small-caliber rifle and sets up in his second-floor bedroom. He waits over an hour at the window, then prays, "If you want me to kill this possum, I'm going to close my eyes and wait a minute. If it appears, I'll shoot it." When he opens his eyes a minute later, the critter is in the middle of the backyard.

Dad takes aim and fires.

One dead possum.

Though my brothers and I don't like taking the life of any living thing—except for flies and spiders, maybe earwigs too—Shaun is proud of our dad's marksmanship. Dad buries the creature, having done his duty for us. With a rifle he has guarded his kids, and with a bird he has put a smile back on his wife's face.

He returns the .22 lever-action. We won't see it or its larger-caliber buddies until a few years from now, under completely different circumstances.

~ ~ ~

Shaun

My fifth-grade year is filled with highs and lows. I'm ten and then eleven, my mind always going, and one good or bad teacher can change everything for a kid like me.

Ms. Norland, she's my music teacher at Eugene Christian. She is a good one. Tall, with flowing auburn hair, Ms. Norland is a highly trained woman who inspires students to grow in ways they never imagined. She sees me as a bonsai tree, small and valuable, in need of nurturing and careful shaping.

As the spring music festival nears, she gives her students more opportunities. She finds the right place for me, on clarinet, and teaches me everything from breath support to caring for my reeds. She also allows Eben to write and perform his own chamber ensemble along with other standouts from the school.

"What a festival," I hear parents react. "The way she had these kids playing, I was convinced I was in a symphony hall."

On Ms. Norland's recommendation, my mom drives me to South Eugene High School one weekend, where I join others from around the city in auditions for the Eugene Junior Symphony Orchestra. We stand in line and go one at a time into the band room. The director, a thin, genteel man, introduces himself.

"I see you play clarinet, Shaun. Tell me, what piece will you be performing?"

"Schubert's 'Marche Militaire.'"

"Feel free to start when you are ready. The stand is there for your use."

"I don't have any music."

"You're playing from memory?" He lifts his chin. "Fascinating."

This is my big moment. Eric and Heidi are older than me, both pursuing the things they love. Will my brother get published someday? He seems dedicated to it. And Heidi has the voice and dramatic flair for the stage. Hollywood? Why not? Well, Ms. Norland believes in my skills, even if no one else my age cares.

"Do you need anything, Shaun?" the director asks.

I shake my head. "Just playing it through in my mind. I'm ready."

My tongue wets the reed as I set it to my lips. If I win this director's approval, I will play with kids at prominent venues all over the state. I dream of earning a seat one day as an adult in the Eugene Symphony. Gramps once played cello for the San Francisco Symphony, the youngest member at the time. In America, it's all possible.

Only a bar or two into the upbeat piece, I hear the reed squeak. I keep going as I've been taught, giving Schubert my best.

"How long have you been playing?" the director wants to know.

"A year."

"Impressive. You have real talent, Shaun, and your teacher tells me you practice as hard as any student she's ever taught. Unfortunately, you're not quite at the place you need to be. Please—and I do mean this sincerely—try again next year."

Though I thank him, I feel like a failure. I slink outside with my clarinet case dangling from my fingers. Mom wants to know how it went. I tell her I stunk. She says she's proud I made the effort and promises we'll come back next time.

Soon after, Ms. Norland names me our school's Musician of the Year.

I'm done, though. No more auditions. Never, never again.

~ ~ ~

When I go to my fifth-grade class with Mrs. Cheswick, I feel even gloomier. She is heavily made up, with a mop of blue-tinted hair. Though she and Heidi got along, she and I butt heads from day one. Her fiery temper matches my obstinate nature.

Our clash occurs the day she calls Rod to the chalkboard.

"Go ahead," Mrs. Cheswick goads him. "Solve the equation for us."

He blinks through Coke-bottle glasses. I doubt he's even able to see the numbers scrawled up there in chalk. Made of toothpicks and pipe cleaners, he's a fragile little kid who wet his pants in earlier grades when teachers shoved him into the spotlight.

"Don't play dumb, Rod," Mrs. Cheswick says. "Don't act like you can't do it."

His shoulders slump. He is trembling and humiliated.

She folds her arms. "Do I have to put you in the coat closet again?"

"It's not his fault," I speak up, echoing the words I once heard from the disabled boy at the downtown mall. I turn to my friend. "Just sit down, Rod."

As he stutter-steps back to his desk, Mrs. Cheswick hits him on the head. *Whap, whap, whappp...*

"Mr. Wilson," she says, turning on me, "what gives you the right?"

I remember getting swats in first grade for claiming I lived in India. Though nobody rose to my defense then, things will be different now. "Mrs. Cheswick, all of us talked during recess, and we're not letting you treat Rod like this anymore."

"Is this true, class?" Her jowls shake as she scans the room.

Nobody moves.

Having seen a *Little House on the Prairie* episode where the students took a stand together, I expect solidarity. Eric and I always defend each other, even more so after being forced to lick a warehouse wall together. And though Heidi bosses me around, I don't let people talk bad about her. Loyalty's a big deal in our family.

"Rod, get back up to the board," Mrs. Cheswick commands.

I jump between her and him. "Don't do it, Rod."

"Do you want to get the paddle, Mr. Wilson?"

Imitating Albert from *Little House*, I put my arms out, head down, and ram into my teacher's belly. Her long dress gets tangled and we both fall. Students scream from their desks. Moments later, the principal rushes in, pulls me back, and plops me on my feet. He roars at me to go to his office.

"She's hurting Rod," I explain. "First, you have to make her stop."

A few days later, the administration calls in a student counselor from the U of O to talk with me as part of her developmental studies. Her assessment is dated May 1981:

> Shaun's parents reported that Shaun's developmental years were normal... He was characterized as being very outspoken... Shaun's teacher reported that Shaun often engages in "attention-getting" behavior i.e., uses baby-talk, shows off. Academically, she described Shaun as a strong B student but felt that he was capable of earning more A's... On the *Wechsler Intelligence Scale for Children-Revised*, Shaun performed in the superior range overall.

The first line is the one that jumps out at me.

Normal? Really?

Have my parents forgotten I lived in multiple countries by age four, exposed to widely divergent foods, languages, beliefs, and ways of doing things? Sure, most kids have hang-ups and feel out of place. I know this. But even my own dad and mom seem oblivious to the forces which have shaped me.

39

Shaun

Later in the month, Roy Hicks, Jr., announces to the Faith Center congregation that our parents, Mark and Linda Wilson, will be pioneering a church on the northwest end of town. We can no longer say we're counselor's kids. We'll be official pastor's kids.

Personally, I like the sound of it.

And I'm proud of Dad and Mom. Their dream is to serve God, and now they can put their own ideas into practice. They've worked through their recent personal disagreements and focused instead on helping others. Ministry is the glue which binds them. In a month or two, Northwest Faith Center will begin meeting not far from our house, in a gym at Clear Lake Elementary. The church reception and counseling office already occupy a rented duplex directly across Barger Drive.

"There goes all our fun," Eric says.

I snort. "What're you talking about?"

"We were MKs overseas, which made us oddballs. Now we're PKs. So much for any privacy, with everyone watching us and expecting us to be perfect."

"Who cares?"

"You don't get it, Shaun. I mean, what girls will be interested in a PK?"

"They all like you. That's what Heidi says."

"I seriously doubt it," Eric huffs. "And did you hear about Dad's 914? I get my permit in November, which means I can actually drive the Porsche. Well, so much for that. Dad's selling it. Says it's not appropriate while starting a new church."

"Got to admit, no one else on this side of town has a Porsch."

"It sucks. Can't he at least wait till after my birthday?" My brother skulks off.

He's being overly dramatic, if you ask me. During the next few weeks, though, I get glimpses of what he means about expectations.

I'm in the cul-de-sac outside the Northwest Faith Center office one day when I meet a new set of friends from the area. Being only eleven, I notice these kids are rougher than my usual crowd. No words or subjects are off limits to them.

"Your dad's a preacher?" the group leader sneers.

How does he know? I wonder. It's like I have a sign on my back. Jutting my chin the way Roy Hicks, Jr., does, I say, "I love my dad. He's awesome."

"Sure, man. Whatever." He turns to his buddy, a skinny, zit-faced kid. "Whaddya think, Shithead? I bet we get Shaun high before school's over."

I am sick of bullies. "I'm high on Jesus," I respond.

They all laugh.

"D'ya like sex?" Shithead asks. As far as I know this is his actual name, since I never hear him called anything else.

"I'm sure I will," I say, "but I'm saving myself for my wife."

"Damn, you're a prude. You ever even had a BJ?"

Not exactly sure what this is, I shake my head, and my new pals make sure to give me all the details. They swear there are girls over at Shasta Middle School who will give me one under the bleachers, and the guys guarantee they can get me laid by the end of the year.

My heart races at the thought. "No, thanks. I'm only going into sixth grade."

Shithead almost spits out the wad of chew in his lip. "I didn't think you were past third or fourth. You're short as shit."

"Shorter," I say.

"Huh?"

"Shorter than you, at least."

This gets a laugh and I feel them warming up to me. I remember Dad once suggesting: *if you can talk your way out a situation, that's* always *the best way to go.* Emboldened, I add, "I'm on the church music team. I'm good on clarinet."

"Clari-what?"

"I also play soccer. Bet I can run faster than any of you."

"Ohh-ho-ho. Okay, prove it," the leader says, then gestures to his pal. "You two, race to the stop sign and back. You gotta touch it. And no cheating, Shithead."

I outrun them all, one after one, and they also encounter my aggressive side while playing football on the lawn. Through sports and unflinching faith, I don't just earn their respect. Soon, we all become friends.

Not long after Northwest Faith Center starts meeting in the middle school gym, Shithead decides he wants to go to a Sunday service with me.

"Sure," I say. "You can help us set up."

NFC is still finding its way as a pioneer church. We have three hundred people at the first service, which leaves Dad and Mom feeling good about things. The next Sunday, only eighty show up. New to all this, our parents try to learn from their mistakes without getting discouraged. A sense of fellowship develops as more and more volunteers assist with each weekend's setup and teardown routine. This isn't some slick presentation for the masses. This is laughter, sweat, and hard work.

Shithead meets me, according to plan. We go through a complicated handshake, then walk in and gather folding metal chairs from gray rolling racks. I show him how to set the aisle seats first, establishing the distance between rows.

"You have to do this every Sunday?" he asks, lugging four at a time.

"We rent the gym for three hours. Soon as service is over, it's up to us to put everything away. Instruments, sound equipment, chairs, all of it."

"How's this look?"

"Yeah, that's good, just curve the rows as you go. My dad wants people to be able to see each other, instead of facing straight ahead like we're stuck in school."

"No kidding. Who wants more school after sitting in classes all week? Forget it."

"Ha, ha. Since when have you gone five days straight?"

He puts a finger to his lips. "Dude, not cool."

"Did I tell you I'm on the worship team? I play melody on my clarinet."

"You told me." He rolls his eyes. "Not my thing."

"We're not very good, not yet, but the point is to glorify Jesus. Last Sunday, a guy came up and told me how my playing encouraged him after a rough week."

As we are finishing, one of the church ladies veers toward us. "Good morning there. And who's your guest, Shaun? Aren't you going to introduce him?"

"Sure." I unfold and align my last chair. "This is, uh…"

"I'm Shithead," my friend announces.

Though the lady's eyes widen, she recovers quickly. "Well, everyone's welcome here. I'm Jan, and we are glad to have you today."

~ ~ ~

Eric

Summer is almost over. Soon I'll be a freshman and learning to drive, even if it won't be in the Porsche. *Raiders of the Lost Ark* is the latest craze, full of nonstop action, and Hall & Oates rule the pop charts with their single, "Kiss on My List."

At NFC, I feel put on a pedestal. All the parents seem to think I'll be a good example for their children, whereas their kids figure I'll be a stick in the mud. I want to prove I'm a red-blooded American boy. A first kiss will be a good start, especially since my romanticized notions about Deneen faded with her departure last summer.

How do I make the first move, though? What if I mess up?

Aunt Val and Aunt Lisa tell me I'm a good-looking kid, no need to be shy. When I look in the mirror, though, I'm not sure I believe them. Have they seen my nose?

Late at night, Heidi and I discuss this strange world of physical attraction and relationships. I never tell her about other boys rubbing against me. She never brings up her tickle fights with Uncle John. Instead, she tells me girls like a guy who is nice.

"Then why do they always go for the bullies and jocks?" I counter.

"Because we like confidence. The jerks, they don't seem scared."

"Well, I am scared."

"Girls are too," Heidi confesses. "You remember how you stole the ball last year against Santa Clara Christian? You dribbled it down for a lay-in and everybody was screaming, going crazy. It was just you and the basket, no one in your way."

I frown. "Yeah, and what'd I do? I banged it off the backboard and everyone groaned. I completely sucked."

"Mom doesn't like us using that word."

"I just did."

"Look at you now," Heidi presses on. "One of the best players on the team. Same with talking to girls, you keep trying and don't get down on yourself. Plus, you're building some muscles from all your work with Paul Jackson. You're not just my nerdy brother anymore, reading the dictionary and playing with his chemistry set."

Actually, I do still conduct experiments. When I find chemicals with labels warning not to mix them, I do exactly that, combining them in a test tube over an open toilet. If the tube bubbles or gets too hot, I drop it and flush it down. No wonder the plumbing is always backed up.

Grinning, Heidi continues. "Girls are noticing you, Eric."

"Like who?"

"Some of my friends, for sure."

"Quite a few of mine have been asking about you too."

When Camp Crestview comes around, Tim Johnson and I decide we've had enough of watching other guys get all the attention. We're athletes. We make good grades. Confidence is all we need here. Bravery. And thick skin.

After the bus drops us off and we get our cabins, we roam the grounds and approach every gaggle of girls we see. We introduce ourselves, ask their names, make silly comments. Tim turns heads with his fine features, and I make people laugh. If they sneer or whisper—which is most of the time—we act like it doesn't hurt and move on.

By the second day, girls are asking to sit with us at lunch. Pretty rad.

By the third evening, I get my first kiss.

Poor Penny. She lets me make the move and I hurry in. I'm no good at this, but our kisses soon improve. I now feel every word as I hum along with Hall & Oates.

I'm in shorts at a cafeteria lunch table when I feel a bare leg touch mine. It is attached to the guy next to me. I scoot over. He comes closer, skin touching mine. He tells me he's jealous of my friendship with Tim and he wants time alone with me.

He's a nice kid, not bad-looking, but I've never considered liking a guy. It's not something I've fantasized about, despite my prepubescent encounters. Plus, various youth pastors have told us homosexuality is a sin. Pretty much everything related to sex seems to be. They chuckle as they say God made Adam and Eve, not Adam and Steve—as though some cute little rhyme explains away the whole thing.

"Sorry," I tell the kid. "You can definitely hang out with us, but Tim's my best friend and that's all we are. Friends. There's nothing more to it."

By the end of camp, Tim and I have girls swarming to exchange numbers and long hugs. Up to this point I have felt like an outsider in my own country, state, and town. I am the kid who knows Tintin instead of Marvel characters, who loves Indian dahl and garlic naan over McDonald's fries. I've been the chameleon trying to blend in.

Now, for the first time, there is no pressing need to change my colors.

I can do this. Oh yeah, baby, I am ready for a new school.

40

Heidi

Our new school is in Junction City. Only fifteen miles north of Eugene, it seems a world away. Instead of malls and movie theaters, the town has cattle auctions, farm-and-seed stores, and the Scandinavian Festival. A block off the main thoroughfare sits a K-12 called Christ's Center, with maybe two hundred students in all.

At Eugene Christian, we were the poorer kids from the other side of town.

At Christ's Center, we will be the big-city kids.

My brothers and I sense opportunity. Eric's going into ninth grade, I'm going into eighth, Shaun into sixth. We're in this together and we have each other's backs.

My dad sits us down and tells us this is a fresh start for us, a chance to be role models, to set good examples. Since we are growing up, he won't even be offended if we decide to stop calling him Daddy.

"No," I insist. "I don't care if people laugh. I want them to know how much I love my parents."

At thirteen years old, though, I do want to be popular.

By summer's end, I have studied the cool kids in town and at camp. Their clothes clearly matter, they're definitely into dating, and they all act as though too aloof to care what anyone else thinks. Many girls have also pierced their ears, which my parents prohibit me from doing. I think it's ridiculous.

Not everything is at it seems, though. When I am alone with a lot of the cool kids, I see they're under constant pressure to keep up appearances. Being popular, I realize, is a lot of hard work.

This doesn't stop me. I still want the stamp of approval.

The first requirement?

Cooler clothes.

Since age nine, childcare has been my surefire money-earner. Though Mom tends to offer my services for free, people often decide to pay me. This summer, I ride my bike early each morning to the home of a single mom in our church. She heads off to work, leaving me to feed, clothe, and play with her preschooler. I also sweep, mop, vacuum, do dishes, laundry, and dinner before she returns at 6 p.m. Only then do I ride home for my own meal.

Pinching pennies, I'm able to update my wardrobe. No more Goodwill for me.

The second requirement?

Get a boyfriend.

Since fifth grade, I've had plenty of crushes, some lasting longer than others. I've also had boys ask me out. Afraid of disappointing them, I once said yes to two within hours of each other. What a mess. Eric's friend, Tim, won out and later kissed me, though our relationship faded over time. When clean-cut, well-mannered Bruce kissed me after we were in *Cinderella* together, I overcame my nervousness by using drama-class breathing techniques and kissed him back. Of course, my stint as a cheerleader has also given me pointers on raising my status.

The final requirement?

An air of confidence.

While visiting a girlfriend out of town, I learn how to apply makeup the *right way*. We doll up one night and meet with some of her friends. Mostly boys. They want to play strip poker and the loser must jump into a nearby pond. Seems like one way to overcome my insecurities.

To my surprise, I'm good at the game. Forty minutes later, I've lost my shoes and one sock while others are down to their underwear. My friend plays the final round trying to cover her bare chest. As I lace my shoes and the others redress, the loser throws himself into the water, then emerges shriveled and cold. He shakes his wet hair and lets out a whoop.

Style? Attraction? Confidence?

Check, check, check.

Our first day at Christ's Center, my brothers and I ride the bus a half hour into Junction City. Tim is going to school with us, which makes Eric happy. Anna and Karma will also be there. My chin is up, my legs shaved, and my cool clothes on. There's no question, I'll be as popular as I want to be.

~ ~ ~

Little do we realize Christ's Center operates on different guidelines than our last school. This isn't a place catering to Jewish, Arabic, and Christian families.

No, this center of education fits squarely in the evangelical box, with a bit of Pentecostal flair.

Praying in a spiritual language is encouraged. Crude language is grounds for a paddling. Boys can't wear beards or mustaches or have hair over their ears. Girls must wear dresses past the knee. Mascara and lip gloss must be modest. No earrings over an inch long. Not that it matters, since my parents won't let me pierce my ears anyway. During recess, I must wear shorts under my dress just to play foursquare and wall ball.

How silly is that?

One day I am loitering inside the classroom before free time ends. My teacher, Mr. Rice, shoots me a look and tells me to sit down. His voice has an edge.

Blinking, I look around while others wander through the door. My classmates are talking, laughing. Karma settles at her desk, green eyes staring straight ahead, even as Anna flicks her brown hair from her eyes and yuks it up loudly with some of the guys. Being a little tomboy-ish, she gets along better with most of them than with the catty girls in the class.

Why is my teacher picking on me? I wonder.

I try to calm myself and take my seat.

Christ's Center uses the PACE curriculum, a perfect match for my love of learning and my self-motivated personality. In this system, I can set daily goals for myself, complete booklets at my own speed, and take tests at the end of each section to advance. Dad and Mom have always encouraged us to make knowledge a personal pursuit, and at home we have Books of Knowledge, a twenty-four-volume set, which we often pull down and read for fun at the top of the stairs.

This morning, I have finished my first booklet and just opened a second when Mr. Rice asks me to step into the hall. What now? He seems to have it out for me.

"You know, Heidi, other kids are watching you." He fixes me in a stare. "Being popular is a big responsibility. When you do the right thing, they will follow. Time to step up and be the leader Jesus wants you to be, the leader you already are."

I look away. It's hard to believe Jesus expects anything of me, considering the things I've let boys do to me and things I've done with Uncle John.

My brothers get similar challenges from their teachers. We're all told we need to set good examples. We're not just the big-city kids, we are PKs. Students look up to us. What we do matters. To whom much has been given, much will be—

Yes, we know.

I'm starting to see why Eric dreaded all this.

A month later I have my head down at my desk, focused on my work, when a large hand grips my shoulder from behind. Principal Shear tells the rest of the class, "Cheeks on chairs and get to work," then marches me down to the teachers' lounge and directs me to a seat. "Young lady, I have a question for you. Answer honestly."

My mouth turns dry. I have no idea where this is going.

"What did you say to the other kids when you heard Mr. Rice wouldn't be teaching your class anymore?"

"Nothing," I mutter.

"Think hard, Heidi." The principal's volume rises a notch. "Don't lie to me."

Yes, there were rumors circulating through the halls the previous day, but I haven't spoken a word against Mr. Rice. It doesn't even matter to me if he—

Oh wait, I do recall something.

"Principal Shear, I told Anna I wasn't sure you should be our teacher."

"No, that is not what you said."

"I didn't mean anything by it. I just—"

"Stop lying to me, Heidi." Principal Shear's fist slams down, rattling the coffee table next to him. He takes a sharp breath and attempts to regain his composure. "You said Mr. Rice couldn't handle the class and that's why he was being moved down to teach fifth grade. That's what you said, isn't it?" When I shake my head, he towers over me. Each word gets louder until his final question is a roar. "I'll. Give. You. One. More. Chance. Tell me what you said."

"I promise, I did not say that."

"If you're lying, you will be kicked out of this school." He storms out.

My face is burning. Emotions twist my stomach. Principal Shear has always been nice to me in the halls. During chapel times he seems sincere, even if he has to keep one eye open to watch for wayward students. Could he know something I don't? Have I forgotten my own words? Am I actually being deceitful?

Lying is a big deal in the Wilson home. Not long ago, Dad was convinced I was leaving the toilet unflushed and lying about it. This left more work for Mom, he said, more residue. When my brothers peed, they didn't use TP, so clearly I was the guilty party. "Heidi, this is the third time this week," he said. "Now, flush it down." "But I didn't go." My arm was nearly yanked from its socket, my bottom kicked a time or two, as Dad goaded me up the stairs. Seething, he administered a flurry of spanks until even I questioned my honesty. Only later did Shaun admit he was the one dropping TP in the toilet to get me into trouble.

What about now at my new school? Am I lying?

No. I am positive I'm telling the truth.

Alone in the teacher's lounge, I'm aware of the clock ticking on the wall and a newspaper headline flashes through my mind: *Pastor's Daughter Booted from Christian School.* My doom seems certain.

Footsteps sound in the hall. Principal Shear reenters with Mr. Rice, who sits on the couch. The principal's voice is stilted. "Now I am going to ask this for all to hear. Mr. Rice, is it true that Heidi said you would no longer be teaching seventh graders because you couldn't handle the class?"

Mr. Rice nods. "That's true."

"There," Principal Shear barks. "Heidi, it's time to confess."

"I mean, yes," Mr. Rice jumps in, recognizing the point of conflict. "I did tell you what Heidi said. But it wasn't Heidi Wilson. It was the other Heidi."

Principal Shear doesn't even hesitate or make Mr. Rice repeat himself. He doesn't come up with excuses or command me to keep quiet about this whole fiasco. No, he drops to his knees before me, a perfect picture of repentance.

"Oh, Heidi, I'm so sorry. Please forgive me. I didn't know, Heidi. I didn't know. I am so very, very sorry."

I'm still too stunned by this turnaround to respond.

Afterward, the principal seems in my debt. He knows I held to the truth even when faced with expulsion. And I know he apologized instantly when faced with his own mistake. Later, he will even share regrets that he and the school resorted to using the paddle so quickly with other students.

Our respect for each other is mutual, and when Principal Shear takes over as my seventh-grade teacher he pretty much gives me free rein.

I'm not only popular, but also a leader.

I like this new responsibility. Truly, I have arrived.

41

Shaun

Passion describes me, for better or worse. It moves me forward and sets me back. Whether I'm talking about music, friendships, sports, or spiritual matters, I go at it with conviction. Of course, I'm not always humble in my approach.

Maybe that's why some people won't listen.

This passion gets me in hot water during a chapel session at school.

Typical chapels at Christ's Center have all grades seated in folding chairs or on the gym floor for songs, sermonettes, and announcements. We sometimes have special sessions for sixth graders and up, which makes me feel like a big kid now. One session involves a guest speaker who rails at us about the evils of rock music. Not only is the beat demonic, he claims, but the bands are often living hedonistic lives revolving around sex and drugs. My stomach turns as he shows a film and gives examples. His presentation is dirtier than anything I'm allowed to watch at home.

"Even worse," he growls, glaring down, "is the backward masking."

Apparently, some of the world's most popular bands—the Beatles, Queen, Pink Floyd—are sneaking evil lyrics into their music by recording them in reverse beneath the regular tracks. And for the sake of all that's holy, we are warned, never listen to Led Zeppelin's "Stairway to Heaven" because it mentions 666 backwards.

He plays it over and over and over just to convince us.

Is it really there? Hmm, I guess so. If I use my imagination.

The morning on which I cause trouble is just a regular chapel session, nothing too weird, before we all go to class. The leadership isn't happy with us, though. We're supposed to show some enthusiasm during worship time. Don't we love God? Do we think He is pleased when we just sit here and go through the motions?

We're kids, I think. Many of us are dealing with puberty. We're tired. Hungry. Wondering if anyone notices our smelly armpits.

The leaders wait for a response as we all hang our heads.

I'm sure they have good intentions. Principal Shear, for example, has a soft heart for God. Pastor Jon is like me, passionate and intense. Pastor Gordon is always sincere. Mr. Perry hides a great sense of humor behind his heavy jowls.

Whatever. Right now, their judgment grates on me.

Doesn't the Bible say all have sinned and fallen short of God's glory? Why, then, does humility seem so hard to find? People want to believe their Christian leaders have all the answers and no real problems, but this shoves them toward hypocrisy, trying to look like they have it all together when they don't.

As a pastor's kid, I know leaders have faults of their own. While Dad was on staff at Faith Center, I spent hours stuffing church mailers into envelopes, setting up tables for bake sales in the Fireside Room, and observing other pastors' behavior. Our dad wasn't perfect. Neither were any of them. Even Roy Hicks, Jr., who joked and smiled while preaching in public, could be harsh and dismissive in private.

Tap-tap-tap...

One of the Christ's Center leaders raps a knuckle on the podium. "None of you have anything to say?" he asks. "Tell us what's going on instead of slouching in your chairs, looking like you've been sucking on lemons. Who in here loves God?"

A few high schoolers straighten up, my brother included.

"We'll open the floor," the leader says. "You can be honest with us."

Nobody speaks. Younger kids fidget.

Tap-tap-tap...

At Faith Center and NFC I have been taught my voice matters. Mom says Jesus can speak through a child as clearly as through Billy Graham, Jack Hayford, or Roy Hicks, Jr. My hand shoots up. This is probably a bad move, but my brother's reputation might give me a little leeway.

"Yes, Shaun?"

Everyone turns my way.

Here goes. I stand and say, "You tell us you want us to hear from the Lord, but you act like what you hear from Him is better than what we hear."

"Excuse me, young man. Is there a question in there somewhere?"

"Do you hear the Lord better than us?"

"Yes," he states, leaving no room for debate.

"Really? I mean, in the Bible, God spoke through children, adulterers, murderers, even a donkey." Somehow, I keep myself from saying Balaam's ass, which is the way it's told in the King James. That word choice would fail me now. "Doesn't He speak to anyone who will listen? Can't any of us hear His still small voice?"

"I suppose so, Shaun, but Scripture also tells us He opposes the proud and gives grace to the humble."

I was thinking the exact same thing.

Oh, but I guess he means me.

While overseas, Eric, Heidi, and I saw things and places many kids never see. For the most part it was a great adventure, even with all the moving and transitioning, but change was my only constant.

I'm okay with switching to Christ's Center. I like it here, for the most part. But I've been pulled away from my other friendships, respected teachers, and the soccer team at Eugene Christian. Christ's Center doesn't have a soccer team or full music program. Its motley choir and tutors don't come close to the caliber of Ms. Norland.

We do have some nice girls in our sixth-grade class, though. One girl and I seem to like each other off and on, just never at the same time. Another is too standoffish, even if she is adorable with her round glasses and short dark hair.

Am I too short, I wonder, to be noticed by the opposite sex?

On Christ's Center's junior-high basketball team, I wear number three on my jersey and soon the girls are calling me Three Foot. Hey, at least they know I exist.

Jill Mulkey, my first true girlfriend, is cute and talkative. Her family attends NFC, and both sets of parents seem amused by our innocent romance. We go to the Mulkeys' for dinner. After dark we play flashlight tag in their orchard, a game called *Russia*, which gives me a chance to tell Jill about our Bible-smuggling adventures.

After a basketball game one evening, she and I kiss on the school's back steps. It isn't any raging physical experience, but if feels special to me—even holy.

Five minutes later, her friends make us kiss again just to prove it to them. For me, this cheapens the relationship. Soon after, we break up.

~ ~ ~

When Dad hears about the special chapel regarding backward masking, he throws his head back and laughs. "You have *got* to be kidding me. The *Beatles*?"

"They played the songs over and over."

"And you heard these hidden messages yourself?"

I shrug. "Maybe. I don't know. The speaker was kind of scary."

"C'mon, Shaun. As if there aren't enough bad lyrics being played frontwards these days. I mean, who has time to go playing records backwards for some garbled proof of Satan? It's *asinine*. We don't need a rock band to tell us what the Bible has already made abundantly clear."

"So we can listen to the Top Forty? You say to avoid secular music."

Dad vacillates. "You know, most of it's not bad. In fact, there are some songs I love. Just don't tell your mom, okay? She doesn't appreciate them the way I do." He beckons me out to the Dodge Colt beneath the carport. We roll up the windows, lock the doors, then flip through radio stations and bob our heads to the latest hits.

"Thing is, Shaun, a lot of lyrics reduce the love between a man and woman to just sex. There's *always* someone more attractive out there. You better believe it. But that's not what a relationship's about. It's about commitment, you understand?"

I nod. I'm still sad about Jill's and my second kiss.

"Just use some common sense when listening to music. Being *secular* isn't what makes it bad, per se. Musical talent comes from God, which you know as well as anyone. You've got to be *wise* in how you use it. Garbage in, garbage out."

This is an age of religious paranoia. Christian parents wring their hands over pop songs, movies, books, and even certain toys. A boycott goes out against Procter & Gamble because of rumors they use a satanist logo. TV preachers capitalize on anger and fear, begging for donations in exchange for trinkets. Eyes open, people. Pay attention. The soul of a nation is at stake and moral values are more vital than ever.

After all the hysteria at school, Eric and I pull out a favorite vinyl record and turn on the turntable in our room. We run Petra's "Judas Kiss" backwards under the needle and listen for hidden messages, knowing Mom doesn't like the song's dark, foreboding sound. In the clearest of voices, it says: *What are you looking for the devil for, when you ought to be looking for the Lord.*

Our mouths drop and we stare at each other.

Yep, that pretty much sums it up.

42

Eric

Pastor Jon marches into the gym one afternoon during basketball practice. Mr. Perry, our high-school teacher and coach, raises his hand and calls us to the half-court line, over a dozen huffing and puffing teenage boys. Tim and I glance at each other, not sure what this is about.

"We've been praying," Pastor Jon says. "As men and as athletes, many of you on this team are leaders in our student body. You set an example here at Christ's Center, as well as at other schools where we play."

What about the girls? I wonder. Isn't my sister a leader too?

"The Lord's been doing mighty things in this school," the pastor continues. "We believe this should carry over to all of you. He's told me to pray right now to empower each of you, and when I do, you will be slain in the Holy Spirit."

Tim and I now exchange worried looks.

Seriously? In the gym? In our sweat-drenched uniforms?

Being slain in the Spirit is a popular yet controversial phenomenon in the evangelical world at this time. We've seen it before, ministers touching or blowing on people's foreheads and watching them fall. Elders usually stand behind to lower limp bodies to the ground. The idea has some precedent in the Old Testament, with priests falling in God's presence, unable to stand before His holiness and glory. While I'm not into flashy demonstrations, I don't want to stand in God's way.

"Who is willing to let the Lord touch them?" Pastor Jon asks.

A few kids step forward, the ones who sit in front during chapel, as well as an upperclassman who often leads worship from the piano. He is someone I respect and I wonder if I should respond.

"Anyone else?"

Despite our preoccupation with girls, Tim and I truly hunger for deeper spiritual knowledge. Mr. Perry sometimes leads us in song at the start of class and he has taught us "As the Deer," which pictures us panting for God the way a deer pants for water. We have high regard for our leaders, Pastor Jon and Pastor Gordon. We know these are men of God, and if this is how the Lord wants to move today, who are we to disagree? As awkward as the moment seems, Tim and I shrug and step forward. This spurs others to join in until the whole team has responded.

Pastor Jon and Mr. Perry move down the line, praying and catching.

One by one, teammates fall.

My turn.

I press my eyelids shut. Though I feel the weight of cold palms and the breath of bold prayers, nothing happens. Pastor Jon promises to come back to me and slides over to the next player. While God's Spirit seems to move among my teammates, I am left standing with only one or two others. The peer pressure is intense as Pastor Jon returns and prays no hidden areas of my life will hinder what God is doing.

"Move, Lord. Move. Break any chains upon this young man."

I pray silently. Still nothing.

"Free Eric from his past. Forgive him, Lord, for his sins."

Sheesh, of course I have sins. What fifteen-year-old boy doesn't struggle with masturbation and a half-dozen other issues? Lust is the primary topic of many youth pastor sermons. Guilt and condemnation are common tactics and I'm sure I've relented to some form of evil in the past twenty-four hours.

Does the pastor sense my dirty deeds? Are they written all over my face?

I let myself fall. I lie motionless on the gym floor.

Not because anything genuine has come over me but because I don't want to be the only one left standing in my basketball shorts, stinking up the place with guilt. I want to please God. I want to surrender myself to whatever He has for me.

Trying not to peek at the others, I remain still. I take a shot at praying in my spiritual language, but it feels forced. Grains of dirt dig into my back. How long am I supposed to stay here on the cold floor? If I get up too soon, will I seem less godly?

Eyes still closed, I vow to never again surrender to the pressure of a religious experience. I feel angry and frustrated, knowing the blame is mine as much as anyone's. In the future, if it is really God doing something, great.

Otherwise, forget it.

~ ~ ~

My faith is shaken again when the summer of 1982 comes around. I've completed my freshman year at Christ's Center, earned my driver's permit, and grown two more inches. I'm now at Clark Creek Campground with high schoolers from both the NFC and Faith Center youth groups joined together for a few days away.

In the warm July sun, guys in cutoffs and girls in tight swimsuits take turns running and launching off the flat rock high above the creek. Heidi's on the bank below, sunbathing with Karma, Anna, and some of their friends.

I'm next.

Oh, boy. Can't back down now.

Unable to see the green pool of water from where I stand, I sprint across the rock. Most of my friends have jumped feet-first, so I decide to show off with a swan dive. I'm high in the air before I spot the previous jumper still in the creek below. Plummeting, I tuck my head and flip over.

My lower back collides with the boy's skull.

Pain fires off in every direction.

The boy comes up gasping beside me. He is flapping his arms, complaining his head hurts. I drag myself onto the rocks, worried I've caused him permanent brain damage. Then I comprehend my own injury.

"I can't feel my legs," I call out. "My legs aren't working!"

Counselors carry me up the bank to the campground. For hours I remain motionless in a large tent, bemoaning all the things I will miss out on in life. No more basketball. No more running or high jump. So much for having sex. This must be God's punishment for all the times I've jerked off.

"Please forgive me," I whisper. "I don't want to be paralyzed."

A nurse steps in later and decides my impact with the other boy has pinched nerves along my spine. With some rest, I should be back on my feet in a day or two.

By nightfall I join friends around the campfire, propped up in a canvas chair. Wayne Cordeiro, the Faith Center youth pastor, entertains us with his guitar antics and a hilarious version of *Cinderella*–or *Rindercella*—told in reverse. Next, we all worship together and counselors pray for me to get better. The evening ends with hot dogs, S'mores, and a call for lights out. My doubts are temporarily put to rest.

Heidi is the first to check on me in the morning.

"I had a bad dream," I tell her. "I feel like something bad's happened."

"Maybe back home," she agrees. "Something feels off to me too."

Soon after, campers begin sobbing as we receive news about Keith Green, acclaimed Christian singer and pianist. A private jet has crashed at his Texas ranch, killing all onboard, including Keith and two of his children. This tragedy rocks the evangelical world, and my siblings and I mark the day the way our parents remember JFK's assassination. Keith Green's influence is incalculable. A man whose music touched millions is dead at twenty-nine, leaving behind a pregnant wife and child.

How could this happen to one of God's anointed?

Didn't he pray for a safe journey? If so, why didn't the angels protect him? Is this whole Christianity thing a joke?

My own diving accident plays over and over in my head. Though my back and legs have mostly healed by the end of camp, I am scared to step back out on that rock. I'm not righteous by any means, and in the case of the Greens it seems even godly zeal doesn't shield a family from calamity. All the good deeds and human effort in the world can't hide you from danger and death.

My thoughts are muddled. My religious fervor cools.

On the last day of camp, Heidi prods me back out onto the boulder over the creek. "You have to face it," she urges. "You have to jump off."

Shuffling my feet, I perch on the edge. My mind replays my headlong plunge. My own stupid ego put me in a bad position and gave another boy a concussion.

"No one's down there, Eric. Go feet-first if it helps. Whatever works."

"I can't. I can't move."

"Remember, that's what I said before you made me swing down off that fire tower? It's your turn to make the jump," she says. "You know, you'll never conquer your fear if you don't do it now."

She's right. No more hesitation. I step over the edge and fall.

Embracing me, the water buries my fears at the bottom of the creek.

43

Shaun

At the Keith Green Memorial Concert, I meet a kid named Rich. The event turns somber. I loved Keith Green, but do I feel like sticking around? Nope. Rich and I sneak off to run high hurdles in the dark at Hayward Field, and we become instant friends.

I appreciate Rich's tender heart for God, but he gets us into some sticky situations. Wherever we go, he likes to get in fights. Provides him a rush, I guess. At home, his parents yell, drink, and watch shows not allowed under the Wilson roof. They have all the latest gadgets, games, and MTV. They take us waterskiing on Fern Ridge Lake as their daughters parade around in bikinis.

Rich knows all the girls in the neighborhood. When a thirteen-year-old propositions me for sex, he says, "Shaun's not like that. Now get the hell away."

As potty-mouthed as he can be, he defends my right to my own convictions.

It's a strange relationship, but somehow it works.

~ ~ ~

Another strange, yet wonderful relationship forms during the summer months.

My brother, sister, and I love being outdoors in the sunshine. Whether we're bounding along a river or catching eels and crawdads, we see God's fingerprints in the passing clouds and imagine His whispers in the waterfalls. Eric is usually our navigator and Heidi our explorer. Which makes me the biologist.

I'm able to identify species of salamander and snake, frog and butterfly. I know the differences between a badger, beaver, and nutria. I'm also the fisherman, thanks to the past efforts of Uncles Vinny, Frank, and Bobby. They're the unsung heroes who tied on hooks, attached sinkers, and passed me the pole whenever there was a bite.

While on a family camping trip at Blair Lake, I fish along the shore for days and barely get a nibble. I see fish out there, but they want nothing to do with my bait.

The third day, a humble pickup pulls into the campground. An old guy hobbles out, grabs his pole, and spends a good half-hour bushwacking around the lake. He makes his first cast and starts reeling. Within minutes, he is catching fish.

Older people, I've discovered, will teach you a lot if you only stop to listen. Aunt Janet, Gramps' sister, can carry on intellectual conversations with me for hours even though she's sickly and doesn't share my religious beliefs.

Here on the lake, figuring I have something to learn, I make my way toward the old fisherman. When I introduce myself, he pats at the air.

In quieter tones, I ask, "How're you catching them over here?"

"Shaun, is it? I'm Ted." A grin deepens his wrinkles. "Take a seat, if you like."

"You using your own flies? Is that a dart bobber on your line?"

He waves off my questions. "The trick, young man, is patience. See how I cast it out there? Now I reel it in slow as can be. You hear that?" The reel goes *click... click... click...* "Mighty tedious to some, but it works. Do this and you'll catch fish."

As it turns out, Ted doesn't live far from Eugene and my parents approve of him. He is a former Forestry Department employee who has charted Oregon lakes, marking locations, depths, and surrounding fauna. He takes me on expeditions to Huckleberry Lake, Gander Lake, Swan Lake, and Spirit Lake. He shows me to how find the nearest body of water and how to decipher the contents of a fish's belly. Armed with this knowledge, I start tying my own flies to match their diets.

"These are works of art," Eric states. "Seriously, I bet you could sell them."

I beam.

Sure enough, Sportsman Cafe in Oakridge starts selling my flies and I pocket the cash. The Royal Coachman is my most successful, made of lamb's tail, blue-dun rooster feather, a #12 hook, and other stuff. With it, local anglers fill their quotas.

One day, Ted tells me of an uncharted lake where he's seen fish up to two feet long. He speaks of it like it's some mystical place, a hidden treasure. "Can only get there by helicopter," he says. "I'll take you someday, I promise."

Then he stops calling. Our trips together end.

All I get from my parents are excuses: "Sorry, he's not able to make it to the phone" and "Oh, he won't be doing any fishing for a while." They hide the truth from me, afraid it will crush me—but it's their deceit which hurts me the most.

Ted is gone. My friend is dead.

And I never even get to say goodbye.

I imagine him on the shores of that uncharted lake, smiling and patient, waiting for me to join him one day.

~ ~ ~

Aware of my grieving, Dad takes me to visit many of the sites I once fished with Ted. These become special father-son times, and for my dad they also provide escape from the mounting responsibilities at NFC.

"You're busy," I say. "I don't mean to keep you away from Mom."

"What? I'm hanging out with *you*, buddy. Mom and I, we *work* together."

Dad and I spend long hours in the car, on the lake, in the woods. He drives me along rough logging roads, attacking each sharp turn, braking as little as possible, mostly scaring the crap out of me. He does the same thing to all of us at the Oregon coast, acting like he'll go right off the cliffs into the ocean. He just laughs.

"There's a big rock," I warn him on a trip to Spirit Lake.

He takes it as a challenge. "Aww, we *got* this."

Instead, we scrape over the obstacle and grind to a halt. An hour later we coast into Oakridge leaking 10W40 through a gash in the oil pan. He buys a case of Quaker State and nurses us back to Eugene, where his friend spot-welds the damage.

The times Dad and I actually do reach our fishing spots, he drags out an array of expensive equipment—poles, lures, tackle boxes, and fishing vests—the way an army stages for battle. It's a pattern of his, throwing himself 110 percent into any endeavor he undertakes. He wants to conquer this latest skill.

I fish from the bank, calm and peaceful the way Ted showed me, while my dad wrestles with his various supplies. He mutters, curses, kicks at the grass, and smacks his pole on the ground. I silently pray all his efforts will pay off.

Huckleberry Lake is a favorite spot of ours, and we paddle around one afternoon in an inflatable raft. We bask in the rays, our lines trailing along behind us, till the boat comes to a sudden stop, and my dad's pole bows behind us.

"You got something," I exclaim, hoping this will be his moment.

"An old tire, you think? Whatever it is, it's *heavy* as all get-out." Dad's reel whines as he pulls in his catch and we're both impressed by a seventeen-inch fish, shiny and swollen. She is the biggest brook trout we have ever seen.

"She's pregnant." His face drops. "It's the law, *dammit*. Got to throw her back."

"Hey, I'm your witness, Dad. Least you and I know you caught her."

~ ~ ~

Eric

Dad and Mom believe in opening our home to those in need. They teach us to be hospitable and generous. This is the way life was lived in the New Testament church, Christians looking out for one another instead of resorting to fierce individualism.

"Who's moving in with us this time?" I grumble.

"Now, honey," Mom says, "is that the attitude Jesus wants from you?"

"We never get our house to ourselves."

"Since when is it *your* house?" Dad jumps in. "We're lucky to even *have* this place. It's where we eat and sleep, that's all, and not everyone gets that luxury."

I want to be big-hearted, I do. We've opened our arms to recovering addicts, the terminally ill, and various family members. We'll even take in a foster sister named Christy for eight or nine months. Though we form close relationships with each of these people, I wonder if our parents know how to draw boundaries. I once thought Port Street would be our family refuge. It would be the Wilson home.

"Don't you want to know who's moving in this time?" Mom asks.

"Mike and Debbie Monaghan," Dad proclaims.

"Are you serious?" I smile and my worries melt away. "Okay, that's radical."

"It *is* rad, isn't it?" Dad grins. "They were in our youth group. They followed us to Europe to smuggle Bibles. Now they're looking to buy a house somewhere close by as Mike considers coming on staff at Northwest Faith Center."

"I love Mike and Debbie."

"And they love you, Eric," Mom says. "Of course, they have two toddlers of their own now, but they changed your diapers when you were only—"

"I know, Mom. Sheesh."

For the next few months, Mike works toward purchasing a house and Debbie joins us each morning before we scurry off for school. She feeds her small boys while also brightening our days with puns, practical jokes, and food fights.

"NFC has sure been growing," I say one Saturday as Dad changes the oil on our cars. He's already done the Dodge Colt. Now he slides under our Chevy Citation, which he bought after selling the Porsche. "You could really use Mike's help."

"That obvious, huh? To be honest, Eric, I haven't got a *clue* what I'm doing most of the time." He scoots from under the car with a bucket of waste oil. "Sermons, they're the *worst*. I feel so responsible coming up with a fresh word from the Lord. Sundays, I'm awake till three or four in the morning still trying to nail it down."

"I love it when you preach, Dad. You make us laugh and think. Here." I take the bucket. "What's next?"

"The new filter," he says. "In the box by the front door."

I hand it over and he slides back under. I crouch beside the car. "But don't you ever wonder if any of it makes a difference? Even though I liked your sermon, I barely remember what you preached last Sunday. And two weeks ago? No way."

"Am I just talking to the air? Yeah, I struggle with that myself."

"So why go through all the trouble?"

"When's the last time you had an unforgettable meal, Eric?"

"Maybe at Old Town Pizza. I don't know. I liked Mom's rice pilaf last week."

"We are blessed to have her, aren't we? *My* last great meal was with your mom at Café Zenon. Even better than the food was being with my sweetheart, not worried about the church or car repairs. *None* of that. Just us. It was a rare treat."

A recipe from *Global Delights*: **PERSIAN PILAF**	
2 cups white or brown rice 1 cup dried brown lentils 1 cup raisins 1/4 cup sesame seeds	*Mix and boil, then simmer until done, or cook 15 minutes in pressure cooker.

While Dad tightens the oil filter, I muse aloud, "So, a sermon's like a meal?"

"Makes sense, doesn't it? We eat to stay healthy and strong. Every meal counts, even if we have no idea what we ate last week. Then, once in a blue moon, you get something flat-out *incredible*. You taste a dish that is out of this world."

"What about all the divisions, though? Protestants, Catholics, Baptists, Lutherans. You're saying they're a bunch of different restaurants?"

"Maybe." Dad reappears, brushes off his hands, then dumps in a quart of rich, pure oil. "You know, there's good stuff I learned from Catholicism. Forget the veneration of saints and Virgin Mary, all that, but the confession of sin is something we Protestants don't talk much about. The Baptists are real *sticklers* on doctrine, even if they are a bit fuddy-duddy. And it's all experience and emotion for Charismatics, often letting our theology slide."

"If we're not careful, the food can get contaminated."

"Or poisoned," he adds.

"Wow." Metaphors are keys for me, unlocking new concepts. "But most of the time aren't we just arguing over flavors and preferences?"

"Pretty much. We've got so much food, we're spoiled. Listen, even Jesus' disciples argued over who was the greatest among them. Keep asking questions, Eric. I *love* that about you. Truth is, we all need each other. Otherwise, we're screwed."

"What about you, Dad? Who do you have?"

"Have? You kids, of course. And Mom. You know, your mother is a *wonderful* woman. We've been reading *The Far Pavilions* together, a novel about India, and we go on a date every week to buy fresh coffee beans at Sivetz Roasters, in Corvallis. In another five, ten years, it'll be just the two of us under one roof. What then? We're doing our best to keep the love alive."

"Don't you need a guy to hang out with? All your best friends are gone. Ray Kelly's in Ohio. Paul Jackson's back down in California. You can't carry it all alone."

Dad's gaze meets mine. "Thanks, bud, but I'll be fine."

As much as I admire his ability to connect with others and communicate the gospel, I know his burdens at NFC aren't going away. Heidi and Shaun never heard the word *breakdown* when we moved from India to Tehran.

I did. And it still worries me.

If anything, the pressure on our dad is getting worse these days. Expectations are growing and the screws are tightening...

Unprepared

Eugene, Oregon — 1979-1982

The pressure for Mark Wilson was constant. Was he good enough? Would he make a difference? Did his continuing struggles with sin disqualify him?

Whereas Linda seemed to float above the fray with her thick hair flowing down to her knees and eyes full of care and conviction, Mark felt inadequate. He couldn't match his wife's spirituality, not to mention the credentials of those he had served alongside at Faith Center. Sure, he'd completed correspondence Bible courses and been in high demand on the counseling calendar, but there were articulate men on staff such as Wayne Cordeiro, Jared Roth, Joe Witwer, and Steve Overman, all University of Oregon grads. They were good at sports and music and parsing Greek.

Who was he fooling? He was wholly unprepared.

"You're so gifted," Linda prodded him. "Your trust is in Jesus, honey."

Trust was still an issue for Mark. His wife claimed to know God's will as though she had a direct line to heaven. When he sent up his own prayers, they gathered like smoke on the ceiling after his morning ritual of burnt toast.

Each time Mark stumbled, Roy Hicks, Jr., gave him a swift kick in the tail and told him to keep at it. Best to learn from his mistakes and press on. The Lord worked through broken people who remained available to Him.

If being available was all it took, Mark was still onboard. The scale of lost souls had tormented him in India. He'd lost sleep, hair, weight, and even—for a brief period—his faith. These days, his goal was to impact one hurting person at a time. In this way, he believed, his stay on this planet could have purpose.

Now he was a pioneer pastor, leading Northwest Faith Center.

The thought petrified him.

He had a safety net, of course, with Faith Center only miles away. For the most part, though, he was out of sight, out of mind. As long as he didn't mess up, NFC was his to make or break.

Less than a hundred attended regularly those first few months.

Which was almost a relief.

It let him work out some kinks. Let him enlist the help of others out of necessity. This wasn't the Mark and Linda Wilson Show. They weren't trying to control and do all the ministry themselves. No, they wanted to enable and release others. Their vision, drawn straight from Ephesians 4:12, was stated in the weekly bulletin: *Equipping the saints for the work of the ministry.*

Word spread that NFC was a welcoming place—down to earth, no pretenses, no judgment, and plenty of opportunity for all who wanted to get involved. The church was a body with various parts and functions. Even a big toe played an important role, providing support and balance.

Church picnics were held out at Fern Ridge Lake. Baptisms took place in the murky reservoir waters.

As people flooded in, opportunities grew.

Programs had to be laid out, printed, and folded. Greeters had to be recruited. Chairs had to be arranged and sound equipment had to be operated. Children's teachers were paramount. Nursery workers. Youth pastors.

Ever since teenage Mark's interruption of Catholic mass with a Beatles number-one hit, he had believed in the power of music. Johnny Burke, husband of Aunt Lisa, played piano with the sincerity and heart of Keith Green. Another man in the church tinkled the ivories in a more classical style. Guitarists, drummers, and bass players did their best to make a joyful noise on the worship team. Shaun joined in, playing the melody on his clarinet. Heidi would later sing backing vocals.

Soon, NFC outgrew its space in the Clear Lake Elementary gym. An old, barnlike building was purchased on the northwest corner of Eugene. The Barn, as some called it, would become a spiritual home for hundreds upon hundreds of people in the years ahead, humble in appearance, a magnet for mill workers, truck drivers, unwed mothers, as well as lawyers, doctors, and policemen, all of them tired of being talked at for an hour each Sunday morn.

People did expect to hear God's Word, though.

Perspiring with nervous energy, Mark did his best to give down-to-earth lessons. He focused on the grace of Jesus instead of searching for demons under every bush. He read scriptures, gave insights into biblical history, and shared personal examples full of self-deprecating humor and confessions of anger, lust, and pride. The nods and amens encouraged him to go on.

For laughs, Mark would go to almost any length. His goal was to connect with each person in the sanctuary, regardless of age or circumstance. If he made them feel less alone and more understood, he believed he had succeeded.

Linda didn't always appreciate this. "Sweetie, did you have to do that?"

"Just being myself," he answered. "People need to know God's still there in the midst of their—"

She cut him off. "Please, Mark, can't we use a different word?"

"Crap. Crud. Manure. It's all the same thing. When it comes to our sin, God already knows, doesn't He? Are we really fooling anyone?"

The congregation at NFC loved him for this honesty. He was a working-class hero. His own children confirmed he was the same man at home as he was behind the pulpit—raw, real, even off-color at times.

One Sunday he invited a stout woman in a muscle shirt to join him on the platform. "During last week's service," he told the congregation, "someone asked my friend here if she was a lesbian. What if she was? She'd be more than welcome here, along with all her gay and lesbian friends. But actually, she's a competitive weightlifter. I think it's time we stop judging and making assumptions. NFC is a place for everyone."

Afterward, the woman was engulfed in hugs.

Mark noticed a disturbing pattern, though. Whenever a guest speaker delivered the sermon, weekly offerings nosedived. Did people give in support of the overall ministry or in support of him individually? Was this becoming a cult of personality?

Mark and Linda Wilson had never been about money. Not in the slightest. They didn't discuss it at home. They were not motivated by it. They even instructed the NFC financial administrator not to give them any details of who tithed and who did not. Such information could affect relationships and policy-making, No, doing God's will, they agreed, should not be dictated by dollar bills.

Nevertheless, the NFC staff and building expenses were rising. A maintenance person was now a necessity. If Mark wanted to bring in consistent offerings, he knew he must get back up there, front and center.

The show must go on.

44

Heidi

My brothers and I have regular duties at NFC. It's a family effort, and we don't mind. We gather communion cups after service, vacuum hallways, break down folding tables. Shaun and I sing duets on special occasions. I perform in Christmas and Easter plays. We all take turns in the nursery during the first service and sit in the sanctuary for the second. Dad and Mom are well loved throughout the community, and everywhere we go people stop us.

They say: "Hey, aren't you Pastor Mark's kids?"

Or: "Tell your mom hi for me. Her prayers have changed my life."

Whether we're at Skate World, Uncommon Scents, or Franz Bakery Outlet we are spotted as PKs. Half the time, we don't even know those chatting with us and giving us hugs. In a city of over a 120,000 people, we are rarely left alone.

~ ~ ~

When Anna Dale invites me over one night, we stay in the camper outside her two-story home and I am thankful for this time out of the public eye. We're both freshman at Christ's Center, and my trouble with boys is about to be rekindled.

"Man, I need some space," Anna says. "My little brother's driving me crazy."

"Oh my gosh, tell me about it."

"What? I thought you and Shaun got along. Your family seems perfect."

"Perfect?" I give a bitter laugh. "He was so mad the other day, he tried cutting through the bathroom door with a knife to get to me. Good thing it was locked."

"Hope it was just a butter knife."

"I thought he was going to kill me."

"Brothers." Anna blows her hair out of her eyes, then turns on her sleeping bag to face me. "You know, my dad was hoping for a boy when I was born. No wonder we don't get along. I was never what he wanted."

"That's not true, Anna. He loves you. Plus, he has your brother now."

"Don't remind me." She rests a hand on her hip. "Your dad's cool. I envy you."

"He won't even let me pierce my ears. He practically monitors my makeup."

A soft knock on the camper door turns her expression into something more mischievous. "Surprise," she says. "I invited over a couple guys."

We make out with our visitors before telling them it's late and they need to leave. I know Anna's hungry for affection, but what's my excuse? Feels good, I guess, taking my hormones and emotions on a thrill ride. When Anna and I are together, we seem to stoke this wild side.

Karma and I, on the other hand, tend to toe the line. Karma has grown into a natural beauty, lean and modestly dressed. She likes a boy at school, though she's too shy to say anything. At barely five feet tall, I sport the latest fashions after a shopping trip with Mom to Clackamas Town Center. I'm definitely more outgoing than my best friend and in an effort to help her, I tell her crush how great Karma is.

Afterward, some of the older girls convince Karma I was actually flirting and trying to steal her guy away.

"Why would you do that to me, Heidi?" she asks.

"Exactly. I'm already dating J.D."

"I'm really upset. I never thought you of all people would betray me."

"It's ridiculous, Karma. Those girls lied. I mean, I'm already with one of the most popular guys, and he's a junior. Why would I go for—?"

"For someone not as cool as the guy I like? Is that what you're saying? You make it sound as though I'm settling for someone inferior."

"You know that's not what I mean."

Karma is too hurt to hear my excuses and for weeks we barely speak. As a result, I turn all my attention to J.D. His older friends are dating two of my classmates, so we three couples hang out together. The boys teach us the ropes. One couple keeps an eye out as the others smooch in the school hallways. J.D.'s and my kisses turn more passionate, his body hardening as his hands wander all over me.

"If we are ever alone together..." he whispers in my ear, so enticing.

Are these feelings love, though? Is this really the next step in our intimacy?

I remember Dad drawing those pictures on an envelope. I've been taught sex is reserved for marriage, a wonderful gift from God. This all sounds nice, but who knows how much time I have? Keith Green's own death came without warning. And Eric was paralyzed for a day, worried he might never get to enjoy sex with someone he loved.

I can't wait around. There are no guarantees.

Plus, I'm almost fifteen, so I can do whatever I want.

With my decision to rebel comes the awareness of a dark presence whenever I'm alone in my bedroom. Just like in India, I speak the name of Jesus and the darkness fades—only to return the next evening. I listen to Christian music, letting Evie, Amy Grant, DeGarmo & Key, and Sweet Comfort Band fill my room with light.

One night, the darkness descends like a raven. Black wings threaten to fold me in and I cry out for help. It does no good. In fact, things get worse and the heavy breathing down my back drowns out all my music. My throat constricts. I am being choked.

Pivoting, I swing my fist through the air and force out these words: "In... Jesus'... name... *leave!*"

The presence disappears.

Even so, my dreams turn more sinister.

Afraid to even close my eyes in bed, I find it hard to sleep. Past terrors and future threats linger in my thoughts. Sometimes I knock on the wall between Eric's and my rooms and we talk until early morning. Other times, friends spend the night and their nearness affords me some rest.

One weekend, Hope comes over wearing her dangly earrings. An old friend from Eugene Christian, she now attends public high school. My brothers are gone and my parents are teaching a Friday night class at NFC. Hope and

I sit on the living room couch and take turns describing our boyfriends and physical encounters.

"He says I'm just the right size for his hands," Hope boasts.

I fire back, "Well, J.D. told me some of the things he wants to do the next time we're alone." I provide details, exaggerating just a bit, and watch in satisfaction as Hope's mouth drops and her eyes widen.

~ ~ ~

The next morning, Mom walks into my room where my friend and I are sacked out on the bed. "Hope, gather your stuff. I'm taking you home early."

"Wait." I sit up. "You can't just change the plans like this."

"Heidi, it is not up for debate." My mom's voice stays low, more sorrowful than upset. "Your father and I need to speak with you later."

What is going on? I wonder. Eric and Shaun, are they okay?

Worried sick, I wait all day for an explanation. Instead, Dad stays in his room and Mom kneels in the small flower garden she's planted in the backyard. Nothing grows there no matter how hard she tries, which leads to Dad making snarky comments about her not having a green thumb. Of course, I never see him lift a finger to help and it's usually one of my brothers who mows our lawn.

"Is Daddy sick?" I ask my mom. "Is that what's wrong?

"Not at all," she assures me.

"Why's he giving me the silent treatment?"

"He'll have to tell you himself."

The explanation comes two days later while sitting at the kitchen table.

"We *know* what you've been doing." Dad spits the words at me.

Has he heard about J.D.? Hope wouldn't have spilled anything since I have too much dirt on her. Best if I just bluff my way through this.

"It has to *stop*, Heidi. No more lies. Apparently, you and Hope, neither one of you noticed the door opening when I came home Friday night. I sat on the stairs and overheard every word of your little *brag*-fest. Oh yeah, I heard *all* about J.D."

My knees shake uncontrollably under the table.

His eyes narrow. "For starters, you will not be seeing Hope again. She is a bad influence on you."

"But she—"

"No *buts* about it, Heidi, and not another *word* out of you till I am finished." Even Mom's parakeet in his cage senses the mood and falls silent. "Next, you will break up with J.D. Actually, we've taken care of that for you. His parents are talking with him at this very moment."

My mouth drops. This is completely ridiculous.

"Freedom comes with trust," Dad says, "and *you*, young lady, have destroyed it. The final consequence is up to you. You've got two options. You either go live with the Browns, abiding by their rules, or you live under our roof and abide by ours."

The Browns? Is he kidding? They're a family we've known for years, pastors on staff at Faith Center, and they have the most severe rules of anyone. If I was stuck with them, I wouldn't see my NFC friends anymore.

"Should you decide to stay in this house, Heidi, your mom or I will be with you everywhere you go for the next year. We'll tag along to basketball games, concerts, birthday parties. We'll be your shadows. Stuck to you like *glue*, you hear me?"

How humiliating. I roll my eyes. Who do they think they are?

"You'll have to earn back our trust," Dad concludes.

"How long will that take?"

"Good question, Heidi. With your current attitude, I'd say a very long time."

It's so unfair, all of it. Mom's told me how she was pregnant before she and Dad got married. She was no angel. Of course, Grandpa Guise still won't talk to any of us, so I know there was a price to pay. In fact, I once found Mom weeping beside her bed. She told me it wasn't worth it, all the trouble her choices had brought upon her.

Maybe not, but this is my life. They can't control me. With money saved by babysitting all these years, I can run away. I know how to cook, clean, and take care of myself. Apartments, meals, and clothes add up, though. And what about my friends at school and church? Will I have any time to see them?

My best option, I figure, is to suck it up for the next year.

I deliver my decision with arms crossed. "I'll stay here."

"If you say so. You *sure* you know what you're in for?" Dad asks.

I glower and nod. Scripture says pride leads to a fall and this is proof right here. The popularity I've worked so hard to achieve is about to circle the drain. Who will invite me to anything if it means my parents get to tag along?

They're not joking, either. Dad and Mom become my shadows.

Before long, however, my friends think my parents are the coolest ever for supporting their daughter at all her events. Dad is the life of every party and Mom lends an ear to girls with their teenage troubles. No one understands I am serving a yearlong prison sentence here. I can't get any sympathy.

~ ~ ~

In December 1982, Mike and Debbie Monaghan throw an adoption party and make eleven-year-old Carolyn an official part of their family. She has been at NFC the past year with her foster family, and I know she's already gone through so much. With her come-what-may attitude, she's quickly become my good friend.

She will also marry one of my brothers.

45

Eric

I stand beside Debbie Monaghan at the party. She and I used to have so much fun when her family lived in our attic, and now they're adding a daughter to the mix.

"So, you guys found your own place?" I ask.

"Just off Royal Avenue. Mike will be going on staff at NFC in the spring."

We are lit up by Christmas decorations here at the home of Rick and Libby Lashar. The Lashars have been longtime church friends and Carolyn's foster family. Over twenty people are gathered for the unfurling of a welcome banner. Raised by a single mom with anxiety issues, Carolyn has spent most of her life in Greyhound buses and shelters from Long Beach to Tacoma. Now that her birth mother has given her up to live in a stable home, her official name will be Carolyn Rose Monaghan.

Carolyn decided to follow Jesus last year, while my dad was preaching. She will ride the bus with us out to Christ's Center. She has thick brown hair, full lips, and a soothing voice which hides a vivacious personality.

"You should go for her, Shaun," I suggest to my brother.

"If you like her so much, why don't you go for her?"

"Uh, she's four years younger than me, you ditz."

"She's my friend," Heidi butts in. "I've always wanted a younger sister."

Shaun snorts. "Not me."

"We should be thankful for our family," Heidi says, "even if Daddy and Mommy are a pain sometimes. You know, Carolyn doesn't even remember her own birth father. And Mike and Debbie are already planning to have a third baby."

I shrug. "What's wrong with that? Her brothers are rad."

Heidi rolls her eyes. "Don't you get it? With three little kids in the house, Carolyn will be changing poopy diapers for years to come."

"Hey now, Shaun and I change lots of diapers in the church nursery."

"Well, at least Daddy and Mommy trust the Monaghans. They say Carolyn and I can even hang out together, without the two of them traipsing along."

~ ~ ~

Heidi

Thanks to Carolyn, I stop feeling sorry for myself. She comes over on Saturdays and we talk as I clean my room. She provides me a fresh perspective, and my attitude shifts even further when I learn two of my classmates have gotten pregnant and are no longer allowed on campus during regular hours. This doesn't make sense to me, since Jesus reached down and showed care for the woman caught in adultery. Shouldn't we, as a Christian school, give our love and help to these girls rather than hiding them away?

It could be me in their shoes.

Probably would be, if not for my parents.

I seek out Karma and we work through our earlier misunderstanding. We decide we will never again let boys harm our friendship. Loving Jesus should be our focus, not guys. We will remind each other of this when we get off track.

Still awash in guilt, I realize I must next chat with Dad and Mom. The three of us sit down one evening for *Magnum, P.I.*, one of our favorite shows, while Shaun's at his clarinet lesson and Eric's at basketball practice.

"It's about to start," I say, fidgeting on the couch.

"Oooh, can't miss it," Mom gushes.

Though she will never admit it, she has a thing for Tom Selleck. Is it his big mustache, his broad shoulders, or his caring eyes? His poster on my closet door is there for her as much as for me, and her cheeks turn pink whenever she mentions how handsome she finds Harrison Ford.

Dad winks as he joins us. He thinks I've muted the ads to avoid the loss of TV privileges. Actually, I just want to get out my words before nerves take over.

"Daddy, Mommy, I am so sorry about everything with J.D. You wanted to protect me, but I got super mad and said some really mean stuff to you both."

Dad rests a hand on Mom's leg and waits.

"I should've listened to you guys." Moisture pools on my eyelids. "I thought you were trying to control and humiliate me. I didn't understand how wrong things could go, but I could've gotten pregnant and my... my whole life... it would've..."

"Honey, please, stop and take a breath." My mom's eyes fill with emotion. "We just didn't want you going down the same path we did."

"You could've lectured and grounded me for years. I probably deserved it. Instead, you just walked with me through it all. Literally. I hated every minute of it at first, but it was exactly what Jesus would do. Please, will you guys forgive me?"

They draw me into their arms.

"Heidi, we love you," Dad says. "We are so *proud* of you, the way you have changed in just five months. We told you it would be a year, but your mom and I don't need to go places with you anymore. You have earned back our trust."

I bite my lip. "Thanks, Daddy."

"Aww, my little princess." He swallows hard and squeezes me tighter.

"Should I tell her the other thing, Mark?" Mom whispers. He nods and she looks into my eyes, her face only inches from mine. "Heidi, we want to take you out to Valley River Center. We think it's time you for you to get your ears pierced, don't you?"

I can't help but shriek with joy.

~ ~ ~

Eric

Blame it on Michael Jackson. Even if Mom doesn't let us listen to secular music, Dad has always been a fan of soul, funk, and gospel. And Aretha Franklin? He believes she is an angel in disguise. In March 1983, Dad and I turn on a Motown special and watch Michael do his moonwalk, gliding across the stage, conquering gravity. While "Billie Jean" and "Beat It" have made him a superstar, the moonwalk turns him into an icon.

I call Tim. Anna calls Heidi. Shaun calls Paul Jackson, Jr.

The moonwalk is all anyone talks about over the weekend, and on Monday the halls at Christ's Center are filled with earnest imitators. How does he do it? The move is so fluid, so clean. It makes you believe anything's possible.

"No more excuses," I declare as summer comes around. My sophomore year is over and my future is fast approaching. "I'm going to write a full-length novel."

"You'll still need to do your chores," Mom says.

"Here's the cover." I show her my drawing of two rockets crisscrossing a swastika. "It'll be a World War II spy novel."

"Our time on this earth is so short, Eric. Do you believe this is the story Jesus wants you to write?"

"Sheesh, Mom. You know how much I love Alistair MacLean and Frederick Forsyth. Is it wrong to make someone else happy with my own books? And Robert Ludlum, one of his thrillers undermines the very basis of Christianity, so why can't I use the power of story to do the opposite and deal with questions of faith?"

"Honey, you're overreacting. Don't you think there's a reason we bought you an electronic typewriter for Christmas and encouraged your typing classes with Eben's mom? Your dad and I believe in your ability, we do. One suggestion, though… You are such a perfectionist and you always bog down trying to—"

"I just want every sentence to flow."

"I suggest you remove the correcting ribbon."

Her words land like a slap across my face.

"Just type," she adds, trailing a finger down my arm. "Finish it."

My voice falters and my arguments fall flat. She makes a valid point, of course.

Over the next ten weeks, I shut myself in my room and type. Am I wasting my energy on a spy novel? I don't know. Some days my hands shift off the home keys and make entire pages indecipherable. I am doing it, though. Page 50. Page 100. Page 200. I say no to whitewater rafting and roller-skating parties. I skip excursions to the lake with my friends. Tim lets me borrow his Sony Walkman and I listen to two new albums, Steve Taylor's *I Want to be a Clone* and The 77s' *Ping Pong Over the Abyss*. Once or twice, Tim and I make popcorn and watch rented videos.

Then, it's back to work.

Butt in chair at my rolltop desk. Paper in my typewriter.

When my junior year begins, I am sixteen and have a manuscript of 304 pages piled on my desk. I pull the rolltop down. More edits will be part of the process, I'm sure, but the novel is done. My main character has saved the world from Hitler's latest rocket technology and its payload of chemical weapons.

This achievement invigorates me. I'm no longer a teenager dreaming about being a novelist. I am one. I have 90,000 words to prove it.

Now what?

With my recently earned driver's license, I take the Dodge Colt to the Eugene Public Library, one of my favorite hangouts, and check out every book on submitting a manuscript and getting published. Per the guidelines, I stuff manila envelopes with queries, sample chapters, and return postage. All of them are addressed to New York City. I drive them down to the post office and fork over the money to send them off.

46

Eric

"You stink," Mr. Perry yells in my ear. "Your grandma wears army boots."

I'm at the free-throw line during basketball practice. It is the start of my junior season and to leave practice I must make ten free throws in a row. Nine down. One to go. If I fail, I have to start all over.

"Games are won and lost right here," Mr. Perry says. "Don't miss."

As I cradle the ball in my hands and take aim, he bumps me. My ninth shot clangs off the rim and I am sent to the back of the line. The next time through, he steps on my foot and shouts at me to sink the tenth basket anyway. Imagine I'm at an away game and the other team's fans are yelling at me. He's training me to focus, to be game-ready.

This year, however, my b-ball season ends before it even begins.

Morgan, the new girl in class, stands at Mr. Perry's desk on the first day of school, wavy blond hair drooped over smoky eyes. My heart thuds against my chest. When she turns, the pain in her heavily mascared stare only increases my interest. Plain as day, she needs someone who cares. She needs to know God's love for her.

Well, here I am. Send me.

When Morgan rides the school bus home and gets off with us at Dari Mart, I see it as a confirmation of my spiritual purpose. I mean, what're the odds?

"Do you live close by?" I check.

"There." She gives me a coy half-smile. "That apartment on the corner."

"We're right down Port Street. You can almost see our house from here."

Morgan and I spend the next few months writing notes in class, holding hands on the bus, shooting pool in our family room, making out on her couch. Her mother smokes and the odor clings to my clothes.

"Eric, have you tried cigarettes?" my mom wants to know.

"Gross. Who wants cancer?"

Mom sniffs at my hair. "Where have you been, honey? You smell like an ashtray."

"What, you think I've been sneaking out? It's probably from going into Dari Mart. You and Dad are gone all day at the church with both cars, so where would I even go?"

"You can always be honest with us," she responds. "I hope you know that."

"I'm not stupid, okay?"

But I am stupid. I don't learn from Heidi's mistakes with J.D. I allow my growing desire for Morgan to direct my choices, all under the guise of trying to help—what my youth pastors call missionary dating. We ride the bus together every day, heads down. She mentions an abusive past but won't open up about it. I think she needs my reassurance and I resort to more kissing and cuddling. Heidi and Shaun worry about me. Carolyn Monaghan sits a few seats back, staring out the window.

The shame builds up. I feel lust taking hold of me.

Does God see what I'm up to here? Do Dad or Mom have a clue?

One night while my parents are at a pastors' retreat, I trot over to Morgan's. She locks her bedroom door behind me, reveals a thong and negligee while peeling off her sweat pants, then climbs beneath the covers. Every hormone-ridden, teenage instinct in my body shouts for release.

Wait, what am I thinking? Dear Jesus, help me.

I sit at the foot of her bed. "I can't do this, Morgan."

"What, my mom? She doesn't care. Just get under the covers with me."

"I want to but I can't. My parents, they were this exact age when they got together. They went too far before they got married and ended up with me. To this day, my grandpa won't have anything to do with us. I don't want that to be how it is for you and me."

Sexual desire plagues me over the next few weeks. Morgan cries and tells me she isn't pretty and she'll never be good enough for a PK. I want so badly to convince her otherwise. I want to jump her bones. I want to make her bed my own.

I'm in a daily tug-of-war. Love for Jesus or lust for Morgan.

At my rolltop desk, I stare at my manuscript and think of the rejection letters I've received. Serious edits and rewrites are in order. Instead, I've quit the basketball team and quit writing. I can't even think straight. Though I'm still a virgin, my actions have gotten out of hand and crippled me with guilt.

Creativity? Or craving?

My sense of purpose has bowed to raging passions.

I recall Dad's warning: *Each of us has free will, Eric. If throwing temptation your way keeps you from God, then sure, Satan will try it.*

"Jesus," I pray, "You know every thought in my head. You know how crappy I feel. Nobody else has any idea. Please, Lord, I need you here with me."

Our 1983 Christmas photo gives no hint of trouble. Heidi, Shaun, and I smile in a line behind our parents. In reality, Mom accuses me that week of sneaking over to my girlfriend's place. I deny it, of course. Without Dad around, I raise my voice and drop my first F-bomb in the house. Mom is so shocked, she says nothing. I win this round.

Three days later I sneak out again.

Morgan could be mine, I think. I could give myself to her. The temptation is a hook, dragging me from one sordid emotion to the next.

Tim and I hardly get together anymore. Whole days fade away. Memories blur. When Heidi says she is worried about me, I don't buy it. I don't feel worthy of it. My relationship with Morgan is a struggle between my physical attraction and spiritual zeal. I smother her to the point she can barely stand to look at me.

Am I defective? So much for being a vessel of God's love.

One day Morgan pulls away from my attempted kiss, and this rejection sends me spiraling into a familiar dark mood. I face the wall in her hallway and bang my head against it repeatedly. I see flashes of lights, bursts of red and black. My ears ring.

"Jesus!" I scream as I march home, head still spinning.

Who can blame Morgan for pulling away from me? I'm a basket case. She refuses to talk and insists she needs time alone. I've failed at my missionary efforts and also turned down sex. Good? Bad? I'm useless at both. If I need any proof, she goes to the spring banquet with another guy and there are whispers in the halls.

My depression deepens. Darkness descends.

Heidi, Shaun, and I hop down from the school bus one afternoon and I don't even look before crossing busy Barger Drive. In the middle of the road, I watch a car barrel toward me and wonder if there will be any pain. Not that I care. Something inside hurts worse than anything on the outside. Please, put me out of my misery.

"Eric," Heidi screams. "Get out of the street!"

I sidestep the hurtling metal and hurry home. The darkness clears for a few minutes, chased off by my sister's concern. She truly cares. I am surprised.

"I love you, Jesus," I sing under my breath that night. It's a church tune I learned as a little boy. "I love you, Jesus. I love you, Jesus... And I always will."

These words are my lifeline. Beneath black, cloud-heavy skies, peace settles over me like a soothing oil. I've felt Jesus' presence during good periods in life, but now deep in my soul I know He is near even in my darkest hour. The words of Psalm 139:8 comfort me: "If I go up to heaven, you are there; if I go down to the grave, you are there." Even in this hellhole I've dug for myself, I realize I am not alone.

Still, a few evenings later, I creep out my bedroom window and climb a nearby tree. From my perch, I imagine hurling myself onto the power lines below. Grabbing hold. Electrocuting myself. Anything to numb my confusion and despair.

No one else sees my pain. No one else knows.

~ ~ ~

My parents throw me a second lifeline. With only three weeks of school left, they offer me a trip to Yosemite, Death Valley, and the Grand Canyon. The catch? Granny, my cantankerous great-grandmother, is in her mid-eighties and unable to drive. I will chauffeur her in her Winnebago camper while obeying her every whim.

"We know you'll be careful," Mom says. "It'll be a wonderful trip for you."

"Granny respects your inquisitive mind," Dad adds. "Just be patient with her. Is she *eccentric*? As all get-out. To be honest, your aunts and uncles all passed on this, not wanting to be stuck with her for days on end. You think *you* can handle it?"

As much as I want to be the godly hero who rescues Morgan from her own pain, I realize I am also drowning. If I keep reaching for her, we'll both go under.

I shrug. "I like Granny. When do we leave?"

The night before our trek, Granny ushers me into her mansion in the hills of Berkeley. She wears a Chinese robe and ornamental slippers. The scent of eucalyptus wafts through floor-to-ceiling windows and the lights of San Francisco wink across the bay. "Here, sit." She wobbles a finger at me. "Let me show you my slides."

An hour passes. Her need for affirmation seems inexhaustible.

She says, "Would you like to see more, dear? I haven't gone through my shots of Victoria Falls, have I? I'm sure you'll find them simply marvelous."

Later, Granny plays her grand piano for me. Her mother, an accomplished musician, wanted her to perform professionally. Instead, Granny encouraged Gramps as a boy in his cello playing and later bought Shaun a music stand.

"You know, Eric," she says, "your great-grandfather was a brusque man, a colonel in the Marines. The night of our honeymoon, Thornton took one look at me and said, 'My God, you're built like a battleship.' He may have meant it as a compliment, but we were never intimate after that. When he died, I realized I really did love the old fool. Naturally, this didn't stop me from carrying on an affair with a New York artist. I posed nude for him, you see?"

No, I don't want to see. Typical Wilson oversharing.

~ ~ ~

By the next afternoon, I am steering Granny's Winnebago into Yosemite Valley. The sheer scale of El Capitan and Half Dome boggles the mind. Granite cliffs soar. Birds fan over the Merced River as deer graze in the meadows. Granny waits for optimal lighting for her photos while I fetch her lawn chair, tripod, straw hat, and sunscreen.

In between, I explore paths along Horse Tail and Bridal Veil Falls. I lay on a picnic table or in the camper's forward bunk and gaze for hours at rock formations changing colors with the passing clouds. My heart and mind enlarge in this place. God's presence feels tangible, both stalwart and majestic. Tectonic activity thrust these edifices up through the earth's crust eons ago, and they will be standing long after my time here is done.

My problems feel suddenly petty and small. Chains begin to loosen.

I send my love to my family on a postcard, dated May 25, 1984, then Granny and I move on through Death Valley toward Las Vegas. She pops codeine pills to stay alert and we spend hours driving and talking.

"Abortion is a woman's right," she declares.

"But it takes two to tango, doesn't it? Seems a woman gets all the bills and the blame when it was some guy who put her in that position. As a Christian, how can I tell a teen mother to keep her child, then point a finger when she ends up on welfare or food stamps? Where's the love in that?"

"Love is not the issue, dear. The earth is entirely too crowded."

I laugh. "Granny, you and I, we've both been all around the globe. Even on this trip, we've gone hundreds of miles and seen only a handful of towns. Space isn't the problem. It's greed and gluttony. America eats half the world's food while everyone clusters together in hopes of making another buck."

She sits up. "Oh, stop here, Eric. Stop here. Isn't this spot wonderful?"

She sets up her camera near a cactus and captures the orange and purple hues of a setting sun. Las Vegas is still a mirage, blinking lights against a blackened sky. Back and forth I go for her, nabbing ISO 400, then 200 film. A filter. A zoom lens. A scarf to tie over her hair. A hat with a wide, floppy brim. I'm breathing hard and dripping sweat.

Is she playing games with me?

We park on the outskirts of Vegas, the night air hot and dry. Granny hefts herself onto piled cushions and waves at me. "I need some supper, dear. Cook me some creamed corn. I really must rest." She eyes me through her glasses. "No, not that pan. No. No. Yes, the one underneath. Nonstick is best."

I warm cans of corn and green beans and serve up two plates.

She takes one bite. "Ghastly. Whatever did you do wrong, Eric?"

"Followed the directions. Mine tastes fine."

"Bland as mush. This simply won't do. Make it again and add salt."

I stand up, my head brushing the ceiling vent. "You know, Granny, I drove over ten hours today. I carted your stuff through the heat, fetched your film and cooked you food from your own cupboards, but nothing I do is good enough. Doesn't matter how hard I try, you treat me like you're some fat sultan sitting on pillows and barking orders."

I slam the door behind me. I find a nearby theater and watch *Breakin'*.

When morning arrives, Granny tells me about a horrible dream in which I shouted that she was like a fat sultan. A dream, huh? If she says so. From that point on we actually get along, and I realize it's like making free throws while someone is stepping on your toes:

Stay focused. Make the shot. Silence the other team's fans.

~ ~ ~

Morgan calls as soon as I return to Eugene. She wants to see me. It's over, I tell her. No hard feelings. I just can't be the one to save her. I can't even save myself.

47

Shaun

We need a real getaway. We like visiting Onsen, a local hot tub rental place, but since our parents started NFC we haven't gone on a family outing without running into someone who knows us. Even at a primitive three-site campground on the other side of the Cascades, the couple in the next tent over recognizes our parents and wants their counsel and prayers. Our parents don't know how to say no.

"We never get you guys to ourselves," Heidi tells Dad and Mom.

"Hey, we're all here for dinner now, aren't we?" Dad says.

The five of us are seated around our teakwood table, enjoying Mom's *spanakopita*, a Greek dish with layers of spinach and phyllo dough. Her parakeet whistles from his nearby cage. The dining room is a family focal point for meals and homework, Bible study and art projects. I also do home improvement tasks here, using an old suitcase of tools Gramps handed down to me on my birthday.

"I'm sooo tired," Mom says. "You kids need to go to bed early tonight."

I snort. "If you're so tired, why don't you go to be bed?"

Dad comes to her defense. "You know, our church is now one of the fastest-growing in the Pacific Northwest. Your mom and I barely have a moment to think."

This is where Mom usually reminds him he needs to stop and take a breath. It is not his job to save everyone. Only Jesus saves people. Instead, she simply nods.

He goes on. "Eric, Heidi, Shaun, we will do something soon as a family, I *promise*. And I know how frustrating our phone situation has been. I *get* it. You all want turns to call your friends. Instead, we come home from church and hog the line till bedtime. All part of ministry, but I think it's time we set some boundaries. Your mom and I barely have time to deal with our own relationship."

Heidi glances across the table at me.

Boundaries? Well, this is a first.

"Of course, we can't just take the phone off the wall," Dad says, "since there are people who genuinely need to get through. Problem is, how do we *know* when it's really important or just someone wanting to *yack* until the cows come home?"

"Let's use a code," I suggest.

"You got something in mind, bud?"

"Sure. It has to stay secret, though, or it won't work. Our closest friends and family, only they can know. And maybe the staff at NFC." With my whole family listening, I continue. "They can call in, let it ring twice, then hang up and wait fifteen seconds. When they call again, we'll recognize the code."

Dad rests a hand on Mom's shoulder. "Great meal, sweetie. Thank you. So, what do you think of Shaun's idea?" When she shrugs, he says, "I'll take that as a yes. *Okay*, then, the Wilson code is now in effect."

And the code works. We've set a boundary on our landline phone.

Busy as he is, Dad still misses most of our games and events, so he does other things to show he cares. He pops up unannounced at school every few months and pulls us out for a half-day with some made-up excuse. One time, he takes us to the video arcade and hands us fistfuls of quarters. Another time, he drives us to an old abandoned house and talks us into breaking out windows with rocks from a creek.

I take out the highest one on the first try.

Crashhh...

"Hubba *hubba*." Dad shakes his head. "What an arm, Shaun."

My older brother asks if someone might still own the place, and my sister wonders if this is illegal. What's got them so worried? Our dad is with us and he'll take the fall if we get caught. He always has our backs.

"Just helping you blow off some teenage angst," Dad says. "Who's next?"

Eric shatters a picture window, then flashes a reluctant smile.

Heidi aims for the smallest pane of glass she can find.

Afterward, Dad tells us this is the balance so necessary in life—left foot and right, body and spirit, faith and good works, hard work and fun. Hmm. I wonder, does vandalism qualify as fun? Dad explains how the Bible says faith without works is dead and also says our good works cannot save us. It's a balance. I remember the three of us clinging to his legs as he clomped across the yard in Vienna. Too much weight in one direction and he came tumbling to the ground.

~ ~ ~

Dad makes good on his promise and tells us we are going on a week-long Fourth of July camping trip. This time we'll travel out-of-state. We will hike into Ruffey Lakes, nestled at over 6000 feet in the Trinity Alps. All part of Klamath National Forest.

"And we won't see anyone we know, guaranteed. Except for our old Faith Center friends, the O'Gradys. Get this, Brian saw a vision of Jesus while on an acid trip at a hippie commune. He now pastors a church in northern California and he knows a hidden access road into the range."

Sounds promising.

"We will be roughing it," Dad warns. "Got to pack in potable water, tents, gas stove, bedding, the *works*. We'll take both cars, packed to the gills."

"Daddy, you can't take any work with you," Heidi says. "You need a break."

"Sweetie, of *course* not."

We caravan south. At fourteen, I'm the only one who doesn't get a turn behind the wheel. Eric's driving makes me nervous, but Heidi is still learning how to use a stick shift and I refuse to ride with her. She's had police warnings for speeding, almost got a ticket for expired tags, and lost control on a rain-slick off-ramp.

"Shaun, you're such a meanie," she says.

"It's like riding a drunken camel, the way you make it lurch around."

"Brat."

"Enough," Dad says. "You'll go in separate vehicles."

"How will I ever learn, when all he does is make fun of me?"

"You're doing great, Heidi. Just wait till it's his turn."

After a meal with the O'Gradys, we follow the mountain fringe and turn onto a logging road with switchbacks up to our trailhead. If I thought my dad would be any less scary than my sister, I am wrong. I clutch my seat and tell him he's getting too close. Instead of slowing, he twists the wheel around a tight curve and the Colt careens toward the edge of a cliff. He slams on the brakes, the tires shudder on the dirt, and the vehicle jerks to a stop at the drop-off.

"See, bud?" He drums his hands on the wheel. "You can trust me."

My stomach is in knots.

As Dad roars up a steep incline through loose shale, he urges Eric to follow in the Citation. Sliding backward off the precipice seems like a real possibility. Does Dad think scaring us is fun? Or is he trying to prove his bravery to us? Either way, I'm not into it.

"How long's our hike in?" I want to know once we park.

"We'll have to make two trips to get everything. A mile each way."

"That's four miles, Daddy. It's already hot out here," Heidi notes.

Mom gathers her braided hair into a ponytail and wraps a bandana around her head. She offers to do the same for my sister, who rolls her eyes and grabs a pack.

"C'mon, think of it as an adventure," Dad says. "It's like we're trekking the Applegate Trail a hundred years ago. Middle of nowhere. We'll dig a toilet pit away from camp and scoop in dirt after each use. We'll live off the land, fish for our food."

Sounds great to me. I brought all my gear.

Heidi is less enthused. "My trail mix better last me."

By the time we make multiple trips in and out from the cars to our alpine destination, Dad isn't quite as upbeat. He has left behind our pegs and poles while rearranging things at the O'Gradys' house and now our big green army tent requires some creative finagling. Dad, Eric, and I keep it upright using ropes, sticks, and a rusty metal pipe we find along the tree line.

The following morning doesn't improve my sister's mood.

"I hate being a girl," she says. "I started my period. Figures."

Within hours, Dad pulls out his new Kaypro computer. I can't believe he has lugged the clunky thing all this way. He rigs it together with an inverter and battery pack, then types up a sermon while seated in the great outdoors. So this is his much-needed break? None of us grieve when the Kaypro stops working that evening.

For the next few days, we kick back in the summer heat. Heidi sunbathes in a rubber raft, while Mom wears her hair back and reclines in the shade. Mom plays games of cribbage with us. Dad's not into games. He and Eric sit on a log together and read portions of *To Kill a Mockingbird*, completely engrossed. In between, Eric, Heidi, and I explore the wilderness terrain and bound along the granite outcrops. Later, Dad and I fish various lakes and come across a patch of corn and an electric light powered by a nearby stream. Someone's living up here off nature. Pretty cool.

Aside from this mystery hermit, we are alone and undisturbed.

One night I'm peeing against a tree, staring up at a vast blanket of stars, when I hear snuffling nearby. Back in the tent, I warn everyone there might be a bear.

Heidi's eyes widen. "What do bears eat?"

"People," Dad whispers.

She gasps and the rest of us giggle, chuckle, then roar with laughter.

~ ~ ~

On the Fourth of July, I am roasting fish for lunch over a campfire when an F-14 fighter buzzes overheard like a scene out of *Firefox*, the Clint Eastwood film. Treetops whip overhead and the lake surface shivers.

Ka-boooom!

A sonic boom follows in the sleek Tomcat's wake, a hammer of sound that jars the granite mountaintop and sends us diving to the ground.

"That was so rad." Eric jumps back to his feet. "Where'd it come from?"

"Bet that pilot's just having a little fun for the Fourth, probably stationed within two hundred miles of here. Which reminds me, I have a surprise." Dad produces a large paper bag of fireworks purchased for this very occasion. He waves off Mom's concerns about forest fires and personal safety. "We're in Timbuktu, Linda, the middle of *nowhere*. We haven't seen a soul in days and this is America's birthday."

At dusk, he kicks things off. "Back up, everyone. Here goes."

We watch as he situates a small rocket on a boulder out in the open. He touches a lighter to the fuse, bounds backward, almost stumbles. The fuse burns down but nothing happens.

"Well, *that* was a dud. Let's try another one."

Again, only sparks and sputters.

"Shit," he mumbles when the third firework also fails. He snatches up all the items and tosses them back in the bag. "Sorry, guys, show's over. That roadside stand ripped me off." He tosses the bag into the fire pit, where it browns and fizzles.

Mom looks relieved.

Without warning, a high-pitched sound pierces the air and multicolored lights shoot from the coals. Incendiary items begin firing in every direction, spiraling, screaming. We dance back and forth as though dodging bullets in an old-time Western. We duck behind trees, fear turning to laughter as we ride the line between hysterical fun and sheer lunacy.

It is a week full of great memories.

Which cannot be said for our next—and final—family camping trip.

48

Heidi

In late July, the 1984 Summer Olympics are scheduled to take place in Los Angeles. Hundreds of church groups will be there, converging from all over the country. Eric and I spend the weeks prior doing bake sales and car washes for our NFC youth outreach. Even so, we don't have enough money to make the trip.

"I don't deserve it," he says. "I mean, I've mostly ignored God the past year."

"You think He's punishing you for what happened with Morgan?" I shake my head. "Don't, Eric. Don't let rejection color your view of Him."

"Just how it feels sometimes."

"What does the Bible say? 'Our hearts are deceitful above all things...' You can't trust your feelings, remember? Look at me, Eric. You are an awesome big brother. If Jesus wants you to go, it'll happen. Not because you're so bad or so good but because you are putting your trust in Him."

Days later, an anonymous donor covers both our fees.

We are going to LA.

Greater Los Angeles is swollen with international visitors, and security teams patrol the Olympic venues. A smear of smog hangs over the city.

Cockroaches the size of small mice roam the alleyways. Sunlight fries our heads and bakes our feet as we join with outreach teams from other states. We serve meals at homeless camps, pass out literature on street corners, and perform songs and skits in the parks. This is what I was born to do. In the evenings, we all worship together at Angelus Temple and recuperate after long days on the concrete terrain.

Eric appears to have it all together in his tank top, shorts, and sunglasses. He even falls for a girl on the outreach, from another congregation in Oregon. They're cute together. Inside, though, I know he is struggling. He's admitted to me his suicidal thoughts, sexual preoccupations, and blowups with Mom—many of which I saw firsthand. He thinks he is the least likely person to represent God.

As the outreach nears its end, our NFC crew files past security into the LA Coliseum for an Olympic soccer match. My brother and I jump up, cheering each time the ball gets centered and blasted toward the net. We miss playing soccer.

Our youth group volunteers along with others to clean the stadium after the match. The place is huge. Tens of thousands of souls filled these seats, many of them with no knowledge of God's love for them.

"Van's waiting. Time to go," our leader calls out.

We're headed back to Oregon soon and Eric still doesn't believe he has served any purpose here. As we hurry through the coliseum's arches, his attention goes to a cluster of young men milling around on our left. They look bored.

He steps toward them and I hear him ask, "Did you guys watch the game?"

"Naww, just selling drinks," one replies. "Making that money."

"You know what's more important than money?"

"The ladies, ha-haaa."

"I know that's right." His companion high-fives him.

Eric takes off his sunglasses. "I like making money, and yeah, I love girls. But one of my old bosses still owes me, and my last girlfriend broke my heart. The only one who hasn't let me down? His name is Jesus."

Two guys look away as the rest seem to weigh his sincerity.

"I'm sure you've been burned before," Eric continues. "Parents, teachers, cops, even friends, they all disappoint you, right? Jesus is the one who stays close through thick and thin. Come hell or high water, He loves each one of you. Believe me, I am speaking from personal experience."

A number of the guys nod.

I am proud of my brother's boldness in this moment and hope he himself will comprehend God's deep love for him.

"You can talk to Jesus right now," Eric says. "He's here with us. If you want, I can even pray with you to know Him. I'm not some wacko, I promise."

The boys glance at each other. Two or three nod.

"Eric, Heidi, we're leaving," someone yells from our van at the curb.

I turn and hold up a hand. They can wait a few more seconds.

Joining the guys in the coliseum's shadow, Eric calls on Jesus to forgive each one, give them grace, and strengthen them to do His will. As he hugs them, I see a few even wiping their eyes. When my brother turns toward the van, he is beaming.

~ ~ ~

"The Olympics were so powerful, Karma." My best friend and I are on her porch swing facing foothills to the east. "At first, I was just looking around for cute guys, but then I fell in love with Jesus. We sang this song called 'I Have a Destiny.' It talks about how each of us is born for such a time as this. God is raising us up to change our world. Eric and I are even wondering if we should go to Bible college."

"Wow, Heidi, you seem really excited. I wish I could've been there."

"I couldn't stop crying. Think about it. Even with all the stupid things I've done, no matter what I do or don't do, God won't love me any more or less than He already does. The attention from J.D. and the boys at camp, I have to admit it's all flattering, but it pales in comparison."

"It really is something to think about," Karma says. "Speaking of trips, I can't wait for our Mexico outreach. We should practice our parts."

Weeks later, Karma and I find ourselves in a Tijuana prison, where we perform with the Christ's Center drama team. Male prisoners gather in the stands to watch. Razor-wire hems us in and armed guards line the perimeter. My stomach feels hollow. My knees want to buckle. I've been at the mercy of teachers, uncles, and boys in elevators, but these tattooed inmates dwarf my previous abusers.

As our drama unfolds, the men's catcalls fade. They fall silent when I am thrown to the ground as a spurned lover. I go down hard, feeling every emotion.

I am scared and broken. Dirty and despised.

The person portraying Jesus reaches down and lifts me from the hard soil. He dusts me off, puts an arm around my shoulders. He points off to the horizon, showing me I am loved and have a destiny.

Cold stares begin to melt. The prisoners respond with whistles and cheers. Some of the men bow their heads and we pray with many of them for forgiveness, wisdom, and inner freedom. Some decide to dedicate their lives to Christ.

Karma and I are just two teen girls in a Mexican prison yard. Are we scared? Absolutely. I feel inadequate and unprepared. I do all of it anyway— acting, praying, conversing. I do all of it afraid. This, I realize, is the real key to my boldness. It isn't a feeling but an action. Acting now takes on a whole new meaning for me.

~ ~ ~

Shaun

Throughout the fall, Eric and I spend hours popping and locking, learning arm waves and body waves. It's the mid-1980s, and we are inspired by Michael Jackson and *Breakin'*. Side by side, we moonwalk on the coffee table in front of our hanging mirror. It's all for fun, of course, but we also see it as a way to use our talents for God. As a writer, Eric pens some positive lyrics. As a singer, I can rap them.

At Christ's Center one day, we get a chance to show off our moves.

"You ready to do this?" Eric is a senior now, six feet tall.

Just a freshman, I give him a nod.

We are in the gym during morning chapel, over a hundred kids gathered around. Carolyn flashes a smile at me. Anna whistles. Our current principal, Mr. Crabb, has okayed us to do a breakdancing routine, and we wear matching white painter caps and black Grand Canyon muscle shirts, which Eric bought on his trip with Granny. These are our street outfits. We are ready to take God's message to the highways and byways.

Are we actually any good?

Hmm, I'd say it's debatable.

My big brother sets down his boom box with its *Jesus Rocks* sticker. He uses this dual-cassette recorder to make Top 10 Christian countdown tapes for his friends. As rocker Larry Norman famously asked in a song: "Why Should the Devil Have All the Good Music?"

The moment Eric clicks the play button, the speakers blare Herbie Hancock's instrumental hit, "Rockit," and I rap along with our routine.

Eric and I call ourselves—please, this is just embarrassing—Dr. Popper and Coco-Pop. We start side by side on a cardboard mat in the middle of the gym, each doing an arm wave toward the middle that ends when our fingertips touch. Eric does a downward body wave as I slide under his legs into a helicopter spin. We continue with robotics, more popping and locking, and a final pose as the music fades.

Our schoolmates clap. Carolyn and Anna whoop it up. If nothing else, we're a welcome diversion from the usual chapel music and fiery-eyed guest speakers.

Pastor Jon tracks us down. "Eric, Shaun, meet me in my office."

"After school?"

"Right now."

Pastor Jon shoots baskets with us, preaches moral character and good sportsmanship, and jokes around. I bet he's happy with our chapel performance, a mix of creativity, culture, and the Good News. Our parents encourage such efforts. They're all about turning bad things into good, redeeming instead of rejecting. This is true whether we rescue stray kitties, trick-or-treat as angels and biblical prophets, or take in people off the streets who need a good night's sleep. It is certainly true when adding spiritual lyrics to a secular hit and performing it in snazzy breakdancing gear.

Eric removes his white cap and shoots me a look.

"Guess we better go," I say.

Pastor Jon is seated behind his desk, arms crossed. Standing beside him, Mr. Crabb peers down through thick glasses. He is an even-tempered man with light red hair and freckled skin. Loved by all, he doesn't look pleased at the moment.

"I know your hearts," he tells us. "You're both good young men."

"But," Pastor Jon cuts in, "we're not happy with what just happened. There was nothing godly about what we witnessed."

Is he for real? Chin down, I peek at my brother.

"Honoring God was the whole point of it," Eric says.

"No, don't even start. The move you did at the beginning—"

"The arm wave?"

"It looked like a snake, which is how the devil appeared to Eve. I'm sorry, but people don't usually move that way unless they are demon-possessed."

I stifle a laugh.

"Something funny?" Pastor Jon's tone goes cold.

"There's nothing demonic about it. It just looks weird because it's not a natural motion." I step forward. "See, you put your arm out like this, then act like you're pushing down with your hand while you angle your elbow up and—"

"No, stop right there. I don't want to see that. It's not of God."

Eric elbows me and we both go silent.

"You're done, you understand," says the pastor. "No more of these moves in the halls or on school premises. If Mr. Crabb or any of the teachers catch you at it, you will be suspended from Christ's Center. Is that clear?"

To me, it seems ridiculous.

"Is that clear, Eric? Is that clear, Shaun?"

We both nod.

Mr. Crabb addresses my brother. "You graduate in a few months, Eric. You're studious, with a good head on your shoulders. Do you plan on going to college?"

"Not sure," he says. "I've thought of applying for grants for LIFE Bible College, but after twelve years of prison, I'd like to travel first."

The principal frowns and mulls this over. "You know, you might consider signing up with YWAM. They're a good organization. You'd fit in well, I think."

Youth With a Mission draws many young people who want to dedicate their lives to the Lord. Sincere as they are, I know my brother has something else in mind. He's spoken with me about it, mentioned it to our sister. Will he share it here?

"If you ever want to come talk," Mr. Crabb says, "my door is always open."

"Thank you."

Back home our parents discuss the chapel situation with us. They've watched us rehearse. Dad's helped us clear out the garage for our cardboard mats. Mom, of all people, likes much of the rap music we play and has shown off her old-fashioned dance moves—the Twist and the Mashed Potato. Even though we laugh, it's cute.

"Can we still breakdance at home?" I ask.

"Of course," Dad says. "If you can control all that snake charmer stuff."

Mom groans. "Mark, honey, it's not funny."

He faces me and my brother. "Here's the deal. As long as you two are at Christ's Center, I want you to respect Pastor Jon and Mr. Crabb's authority. Can you do that? They have good intentions, whether or not we agree with their methods."

We obey. We toe the line.

Later, Pastor Jon apologizes for letting assumptions cloud his view. "Listen," he says, "we all have our baggage, don't we? Roy Hicks, Jr., used to warn me against being too religious, and my reaction to your routine, that was just ugly old religion rearing its head."

Religion and rules.

To me they seem like twin fangs, often dripping with poison.

49

Eric

I have big plans. Worried that Gramps, Grandma Guise, and my parents might try to talk me out of them, I keep them to myself and tuck my money away. My muscles are taut from swinging hammers and hanging drywall. My forearms bear scars from operating a sheet-metal press. I work weekends delivering Domino's Pizza to droopy-eyed security guards and to wide-eyed girls at slumber parties. The tips are great.

It is February 1985. My latest job is washing the FedEx fleet behind a building off West 11th. I split the money with my brother to cut the time in half.

"My hands are like ice," I yell to him now. "Can't even feel them."

"Why don't we use hot water?"

"These hose lines are cold water only."

A bitter wind funnels between the warehouses as we run a mobile pressure washer over mud-flecked panel vans. We get paid five dollars per vehicle and finish one every ten minutes. It is the best money we'd ever made, which makes our cracked, bleeding hands and nearly frostbitten toes seem almost worth it.

"Yahoo," Shaun yells, peeling off his shirt as I do the same.

We laugh and shout, delirious in the cold. Our chests and arms turn red, and our eyes fill with tears as we scrub and rinse. When we later hoist ourselves into the Citation, the dash heater intensifies the agony. Blood starts flowing again, and it feels as though each finger will swell and burst.

"Aghh." Shaun stomps his feet. "This must be how it feels to have bamboo shoved under your nails. Least we'll be ready if we're ever tortured for our faith."

Books about men and women of faith are recent favorites of mine. I read *Bruchko, The Hiding Place, Through Gates of Splendor,* and *Tortured for Christ.* Graduation is fast approaching, and I feel the urgency to leave my home, my school, my city, and go make a difference in the world. As my parents remind me constantly: "To whom much is given, much will be required."

With our paychecks, Shaun and I buy the latest Christian music tapes. We go to youth group dance parties at Anna Dale's house. Mrs. Dale tells us how her own mother made her feel stupid when she was growing up and never let her have any fun. She knows she sometimes loses her cool and snaps at her kids, but she wants us to be free and enjoy life. She's trying to change her family legacy.

Not long after, some of us drive up to Portland for a Stryper show. We've seen the band's makeup, long hair, and latex outfits. Are they actually honoring God? On the sidewalk outside, a local church group pickets with signs calling this a satanic event. Religion and its poison, once again on display. The moment the show begins, though, Stryper shreds their guitars, pounds their drums, and throws Bibles into the crowd. The band preaches like we're at an old-time revival service.

Shaun and I buy their album, *Soldiers Under Command*, and have those three words engraved on metal bracelets. We are committed to God, no matter what.

He is love. And His love is our weapon.

Tim and I begin frequenting downtown Eugene. We are eighteen now and we hit the teen dance clubs hard. Jesus spent most of His time with the sinners of His day—the tax collectors, drunkards, and prostitutes—and we decide to follow His example rather than hiding away in a religious bubble.

We don't drink. Don't take hits off the joints offered us. Don't give ourselves to the slithering bodies. We stick close together.

Tim wants to be a pastor someday, carrying God's flame. I want to be a writer, wielding my pen like a sword. At tables sticky with spilled booze, we field questions about our faith. God gives life its meaning, we say. This doesn't stop things from sucking at times. Hearts get broken. Addictions take hold. Corruption spreads.

And in the midst of it all, He is still here.

During a lip-sync contest at a club on Willamette Street, Tim and I take the stage. We dance, mix in some robotics, and as the beat of Farrell & Farrell's "Get Right or Get Left" thunders through the sound system, we rip open our T-shirts to reveal tank tops which read: *Jesus Saves!*

Some jeer. Others say it's cool we aren't afraid to stand for what we believe.

As much as I reek of weed and cigarettes, it makes me smile when I recall the words of my favorite poem, by C. T. Studd:

> *Some want to live within the sound*
> *Of church or chapel bell*
> *I want to run a rescue shop*
> *Within a yard of hell*

~ ~ ~

Lord God Almighty, I'm free at last. Diploma in hand, I look to the future. When my parents press me for answers, I tell them all my plans are overseas.

First stop: Hawaii.

I celebrate graduation on Kauai with a friend whose father once worked at Faith Center and now pastors a church on the island. As fellow PKs, my friend and I have a blast together. We shoot our own music videos with a monstrous camcorder. We swim, snorkel, body surf, and live in shorts as our bodies tan. It's tempting to stay here forever.

Second stop: Brazil.

Over the last year, Dad and Mike Monaghan have prepped an NFC outreach team. Ages sixteen and up are included. Since Shaun is only fifteen and Carolyn only fourteen, they don't get to go this time. Shaun stays in central California with Paul Jackson's family while Carolyn stays in Eugene with family friends. Thankfully, my sister and I are immunized for the journey—one of our rare visits to a medical clinic.

Dad, Mom, Heidi, and I fly off with the team to Rio de Janeiro. A connecting flight takes us to Belo Horizonte, a city of millions.

The largest country in South America, Brazil bursts with color, flavor, and music. The people are passionate with us, often standing nose-to-nose to talk. They wear huge smiles. They are boisterous and beautiful. We stay with local pastors and missionaries and I love the morning coffee they serve us with *pão de queijo* bread. Lunches of black beans and rice are delicious, capped with cold cans of *guarana*. In the evenings, Heidi and I enjoy pocket sandwiches at late-night stands. Even better are the *churrascarias,* where beef and pork are sliced from skewers onto our plates.

We aren't here for the sights and food, though.

For the next two weeks we scatter in taxis, buses, and cars to cinder-block churches throughout the city. We fan ourselves while leading energetic crowds in song. Heidi plays roles in skits, acting out gospel stories. I write out my testimony and share it to thousands from a platform in a field. We pray for the sick. More than once, men and women drop to the ground and froth at the mouth when we mention the name of Jesus. We are told both white and black magic are part of the culture here. Spiritualism is intertwined with local Catholicism, and it's not uncommon to see roadside shrines next to ritualistic displays.

Many of these people cry out for deliverance, begging to be free from fear. Some find freedom as we lay hands on them and pray. Others do not.

I feel love for each one. We are all created in God's image, aren't we?

During one meeting, Heidi is approached by a woman with a limp baby in her arms. Our interpreter explains the boy is actually four but cannot walk because of some degenerative muscle issues. Heidi touches the child's leg, quietly praying in her spiritual language. She figures only God knows what needs to be done here.

"*Obrigado,*" the mother thanks her.

My sister watches the woman shuffle off with the limp boy still in her arms.

Heidi and I minister together most days, our faith becoming our own. As Dad says: *Once you fully grasp God's love for you, why would you want anything else?*

Mom is adored by the Brazilians, who admire her hair and respond to her face-to-face approach and spiritual intensity. Dad's a celebrity, his gregarious nature meshing well with the locals. He is invited to numerous churches, his personality and humor endearing him to all. He and Mom discuss taking family Portuguese lessons and moving us all down here in a year or two.

A week later our team is at the Belo Horizonte airport for departure. A man runs to us, waving his arms. He is the pastor of the church we visited days ago and he says someone we prayed for is healed. Trailing behind him, the little boy with the muscular problems is on his feet and rushing our way. He throws both arms around Heidi's legs. His mom arrives in his wake, smiling from ear to ear.

"I can't believe it's the same boy," Heidi says, wiping at her eyes.

"God healed him," I say. "Your prayers meant something."

"Just wait till I get home. Karma and Anna will be so amazed."

As our departing flight lifts off from Belo Horizonte, there's already talk of another NFC trip in 1986. This makes us happy, since Shaun will be old enough to join us and he'll get to sing for the crowds. We miss my little brother. Who knows? We might all serve God together here in the future.

Our family's not perfect, but we love each other.

We love Jesus. We have a destiny.

It all sounds so idyllic, this American Dream—with its heavy Christian flavor—playing out through each one of us. Drama, music, writing, preaching. These are tools we can use for God's glory and it seems nothing can stop us now.

During a connecting flight in Panama, Mike Monaghan corrals the NFC team for boarding. Oddly, Dad misses the plane and must catch a later one all by himself.

~ ~ ~

Back home in Oregon, Dad laughs off his misadventures and sits me down for a father-son chat. "You know, Eric, when I left home at sixteen, that was it. My father and I barely stayed in contact and our relationship was about as cold as could be. If you can't tell, I've done this fathering thing on the fly. Some days I don't have a *clue*."

"You're a great dad," I tell him. "We'll never lose contact."

"Thanks, bud. Look at you now, bigger than me and with a big heart too. Have I prepared you for the real world? I don't know. I hope so. *God*, I hope so. What are your plans? Have you thought about college at all?"

"Actually, I want to follow in your footsteps."

He nods. "Correspondence courses? Northwest Christian College? There's even LIFE. Hey, I'll never discourage you from more education."

"I'm not going to college, Dad. Not yet, anyway."

"Whoa, now. Sounds like you have somewhere else in mind."

"You might say that." I grin at his perplexed look. "Tim and I have been talking, praying, and even checking on plane tickets. We're thinking of leaving in six to eight weeks. We want to fly over and smuggle Bibles in Eastern Europe."

Third stop: Vienna.

"Wow, bud. *Wow.* C'mon over here." In the privacy of our home, Dad pulls me onto his lap and we both laugh. He's only thirty-six and I am eighteen. "You know, I couldn't be more proud of you. Part of me says not to let you go, but who am I to talk? Your mom and I went over there with you three kids. Talk about *crazy.*"

"Like father, like son, I guess."

His eyes mist over. "It's all gone by so fast. I still remember carrying you around Golden Gate Park in a backpack."

"See, Dad? Not much has changed. I would still follow you anywhere..."

Unnoticed

Eugene, Oregon — 1983-1985

Mark Wilson had over a thousand people who would follow him to the ends of the earth. As pastor at Northwest Faith Center, he never pretended to be perfect. The more he peeled back the curtain to show his struggles, the more people loved him.

Linda had literally followed him around the globe. She still wore her hair long in case they ever returned to India. Ministry was their common bond.

Mark hoped to give others what he never had as a child.

Linda hoped to regain what she had lost at sixteen.

In their pursuit of love and redemption, the Wilsons focused on grassroots efforts. They weren't interested in starting a TV program or writing self-help books. They wanted to provide others with individual purpose and direction. What better way than by teaching them to function in their God-given talents and gifts? As stated in Proverbs 29:18, "Where there is no vision, the people perish…"

The doors at NFC were open seven days a week. Offerings weren't meant just to keep the lawns mowed and the lights on. Every room at the Barn was available for use by the true ministers, those in the congregation.

A five-year-old boy had a song to share with everyone?

Out of the mouth of babes.

An eighty-year-old woman had an eye for editing bulletins and lyric sheets?

What a blessing.

A younger woman hoped to run Jazzercise classes?

She could use an entire room, free of charge, twice a week.

A man wanted to teach woodworking?

Go for it. Here's another room. Surely others would like to learn.

Teen drivers and single mothers needed help with car repairs?

A mechanic who attended the church changed oil and spark plugs in the parking lot on Saturdays, giving pointers as he worked. Inside, responsible youth group kids were paid by the church to provide childcare.

It all mattered. All of it was holy.

Mike Monaghan was a master facilitator who worked alongside Mark and Linda. Together, they made Tuesday nights a focal point, with Ministry Training Center offering various classes: Counseling, Sign Language, Communion in Marriage, Biblical Languages, and more. NFC was now a family, a vibrant tapestry of believers. Services in the Barn felt more like living room gatherings.

Mark usually preached at all three Sunday morning services and the Wednesday evening service, while Linda oversaw women's Bible studies and prayer meetings. Mrs. Dale also ministered to the women, though her less structured, more dynamic style clashed at times with Linda's straight-from-God's-Word approach. Both carved out their own space, appealing to listeners from different backgrounds.

Despite all the good things happening, Mark and Linda noticed many in the church family were still hurting from wounds of the past. It wasn't enough to simply save and baptize a person. The whole being needed transformation.

Driven by a desire to be more effective, they visited various ministries, including John Wimber's Vineyard Church, Robert Schuller's Crystal Cathedral, John MacArthur's Grace Community, and Jack Hayford's Church on the Way.

What worked? What didn't?

True, Jesus was the same yesterday, today, and forever, but He wasn't opposed to working by different methods in different generations.

Brimming with ideas, Mark and Linda spent hours in deep discussion and returned to NFC to change things up. "I need a break for at least one of the services," Mark said. "I'm getting sick and losing my voice. Since when is one person supposed to have all the knowledge? We all have the same access to God's Word and His Spirit."

Wednesday services became a time for members of the congregation to put into practice all the things learned during Ministry Training Center. Time was given for repentance, reconciliation, and words of knowledge. Prayer teams waited in back rooms for those seeking physical and inner healing.

This proved to be a game-changer.

God's Spirit was at work. People were healed of bodily afflictions. Men living in shame from childhood abuse began smiling again. Women mourning abortions and miscarriages found forgiveness and peace. Marriages were restored.

The NFC family grew even larger. Even closer.

Other pastors visited to learn the secret behind NFC's success.

~ ~ ~

Caught up in all this activity, Mark and Linda had less and less time together. Time was their most valuable commodity—and with very few boundaries in place, they gave it away freely. Mark was pulled one direction. Sermons. Administration. Counseling. Reports for the district office. Linda was pulled another. Ministering in people's homes. Teaching at Ministry Training Center. Leading prayer teams.

The Barn was too small to accommodate everything.

Was it time for a larger building? Or did NFC need to have four services on Sunday mornings to pack everyone in?

For Mark, this would mean one more sermon to preach each week.

Already, he was running out of time for his own relationship with God.

One morning he found Heidi reading her Bible in bed. "Gosh," he said, "it's so good to see you doing that. These days, when *I* crack open a Bible, it's to prepare a lesson or sermon. Reading and praying feel more like a *job* to me now. Soon as I get home, all I want to do is watch a horror movie, anything to take my mind off work."

Mark and Linda stayed for hours after Sunday services, leaving their kids to drive themselves home and heat up leftovers. Eric, Heidi, and Shaun stopped counting the broken promises. So much for dinner together. So much for a movie as a family. With Mark and Linda gone so long, so often, the three siblings worried one day a police officer would knock on the door to deliver news of their parents' deaths in a gruesome car accident.

In the midst of NFC's unprecedented growth, the rumblings of trouble went mostly unnoticed. Little compromises. Little things left unsaid.

Death by a thousand cuts.

Where ministering together once created a bond, it now caused competition. Mark had his idea how things should be done. Linda often disagreed. She gave off an air of spiritual superiority while beginning to question him openly and to insist on an equal voice at council meetings.

The church and family tapestry was altered.

Strands once coiled tightly began to come apart.

50

Shaun

We know our family isn't immune to trouble. If Keith Green's plane can go down at the height of his ministry, we can go through hardships too. All part of life.

Who's to blame, though, for what happens to Mom's parakeet?

None of us know.

On our rush out the door, one of us accidentally lets my outdoor cat into the house. We drive off. We raise our hands, worship God at Wednesday night service. We pray and wait for the Holy Spirit to heal people. It's late when we get home.

Feathers are everywhere. It's like a little bird's horror movie. The parakeet's cage is knocked over, birdseed scattered across the dining room. A trail of feathers runs from the kitchen to the family room, downstairs, upstairs, into the pink bathroom, and in all of the bedrooms.

"Where is he?" Mom moans. "Where's my parakeet?"

Macaroni, my cat, hunkers behind the wood stove.

"Does anyone see him?"

"Still looking," Eric calls. "Gosh, what a mess."

I find part of the answer beneath the teakwood table, and my brother finds the other part near the pantry—two little claws, one orange beak. Goodbye, birdie.

As small as it is, this death feels like a precursor.

Mom slumps on the couch in tears. Heidi is hugging her. Dad arrives home minutes later, hears the story, and grabs Macaroni by the scruff of the neck. Before I can stop him, he shoves my poor pet into a brown paper bag, swings it around till it nearly touches the ceiling, then dumps Macaroni onto the floor. I am shaking, my fists balled. My terrorized cat gathers his feet under him, spins out on the carpet, and rockets out the sliding glass door. We won't see him again for weeks.

"Oh, Linda. *Sweetie.*" Dad pulls Mom close and smooths her hair. He catches my eye. With a nod, he indicates we should get to work on cleaning up the evidence.

~ ~ ~

Heidi

Oregon weather is cold and damp in early November. The mood isn't helped any by Eric and Tim's departure for Vienna only twelve days ago. Dad and Mom are exhausted. Shaun and I are bickering.

Now this.

Uncle John has taken his own life at only twenty-eight years of age. His body is found on the bunk of his camper with the exhaust funneled inside for a sleepy, painless death. He leaves behind a handwritten letter, dated November 7, 1985:

> The reason I killed myself is because of my abnormal sexual desires... I am doing the community I live in a favor... I have few regrets about my decision, except for the sorrow I'll leave behind... please understand, I chose to do this and am not passing blame to anyone...

There is shock and shame.

Denial. Grief.

Gramps has recently married an adorable woman we call Grams Dorene. If not for Dorene's strength, Gramps would be unable to face this day. He believes he should've been a more loving and attentive father. For the first time, we all discuss the Wilson darkness, the sudden mood swings which drag some of us down.

We must lean on each other, Gramps insists. We must do better.

Gramps and Dorene lead our family procession from Eugene to Cook's Chasm, on the Oregon coast. Here, John's ashes will be scattered. We arrive at dusk, three generations of Wilsons in mourning. Grandma Rita is present to grieve her son. Aunt Laura has flown in. Dad looks as if he has aged ten years and Mom huddles in her coat beside him. Shaun and I stand with the others, in the glow of our headlights along the bridge, and watch the tide roll in through heavy mist.

How is this possible? I wonder. Uncle John knew the Lord at one time.

For the moment, my own brushes with his *abnormal sexual desires* are buried deep beneath a mound of sorrow.

We pass around photos of our beloved relative—in his chauffeur cap, his espresso-cart apron, and his fleece-lined denim jacket. He was a wounded soul. We all loved him in different ways.

We all feel as though we failed him, too.

"Goodbye, John," Uncle Dave yells into the wind.

My dad falls apart. I've never seen him like this. Dad was already married and leaving the house when Uncle John was only nine. Recently, the two of them had been building their relationship—and now it is torn away. Dad crumples and emits a howl from the depths of his being. Anguish wracks his body. As the oldest of five children, he is the one who usually provides others comfort, but now his three remaining siblings—Uncle Paul, Uncle Dave, and Aunt Laura—gather round. They cover Dad with their arms, their coats, and their tears.

Even Jesus wept.

In this moment, I want to believe God is in the midst of our pain.

By the time we all reach a coastal diner for a meal, we are ragged and raw. While Dorene watches with an empathetic eye, Gramps and Grandma Rita join their grown children for a photograph. Daddy tries to hold himself together.

Around our two tables, I pick up snippets of conversation.

"He faced a lot of financial pressure from his businesses," Gramps says.

"That's not it," Uncle Paul reacts. "He wouldn't marry his girlfriend, and she left him. Not to mention, he didn't trust himself with younger girls and he was scared of prison. Can you imagine what they'd do to a pretty boy like him?"

"Well," says Uncle Dave, "there's a morbid thought."

Aunt Laura is smart and beautiful. She turns, her eyes full of concern. "John was so tender. He just wanted to be loved."

Uncle Paul falls quiet, eyes haunted and hollow. He is the one who lived with Uncle John at the time of the suicide. Uncle Dave fidgets in his chair, exhausted. Aunt Laura tries to be strong for her older brothers. Meanwhile, our dad is a wreck. All his years of counseling and pastoral knowledge were unable to stop this tragedy.

It isn't Daddy's fault. I know this.

I also know it's his usual desire to step in and save the day.

How can I even begin to fathom the weight he now carries? If something happened to my little brother, I wouldn't ever stop crying. No matter how much we fight, no matter how many times we've shoved and screamed and punched and kicked, he is my brother and I love him.

During the meal, our emotions surge like sets of waves—poignant memories, frail smiles, followed by deep breaths and sudden silence. Uncle Dave becomes the self-appointed jokester, throwing out funny stories from the past to lighten the mood. As his dark comedy gets louder, our laughter fills the otherwise subdued space. We are oblivious to other guests.

More sets of waves.

Still gasping for air after a particularly raucous and humorous moment, Uncle Dave leaves to use the restroom. Another diner follows him and emerges a minute later. The man's head stays down as he drops a few twenties on a nearby table, takes his date's hand, and flees this fine establishment.

We find out the reason when my uncle returns.

"I'm standing at the urinal and this guy storms in, ranting about how he was hoping for a quiet, romantic night out with his girlfriend and instead gets this rude and raunchy group taking over the whole damn place."

"Dave, that's awful," Aunt Laura says.

"I told him I was sorry, but if he really had to know, we just scattered our baby brother's ashes a few miles up the coast. We can't really be held responsible for our actions here tonight. Boy, soon as I said that, you should've seen his face. He mumbled an apology and disappeared as quickly as he could."

We all laugh about the couple's hasty retreat, too numb to appreciate their discomfort. Our own pain is all we can see. None of us want to deal with the deeper questions of eternity, forgiveness, and taking one's own life. We are riding the sets. Trying to hang on. By the time we exit the diner for the drive home, rain is coming down hard, and we are spent.

"Heidi, why don't you accompany us?" Grams Dorene beckons.

I slide into the backseat. Gramps and Dorene are in the front. It's just the three of us. Windshield wipers swish back and forth as we head inland through the coastal range. Dorene is shorter than me, strong-willed, full of hugs. She is always well put together, poised and polite. She glances back over the seat and asks if there is anything I'd like to talk about. My pulse quickens. What is she getting at?

Gramps meets my eyes in his rearview mirror. "Any questions you might have, Heidi? Anything, perhaps, regarding you and Uncle John?"

Biting my lip, I wrap my arms around myself.

"Honey," Dorene says, "you can talk to us. Family is what gives us strength. You do know John loved our savior and we hope to see him again one day."

"Certainly a nice sentiment," Gramps admits. He's still not so sure about all the religious stuff. "From here on out, Dorene and I want no more secrets among the Wilsons. I realize now, I could've done a better job communicating with my son. Sharing memories, no matter how painful, can help assuage one's grief."

"Heidi," Dorene adds, "let me be forthright with you. Your name came up in one of John's letters. No matter what you share with us, we love you, and we will still love your uncle John. Nothing can change either of those facts."

Old memories surface.

My body shudders and humiliation grips my chest.

What did his letter reveal? These are my grandparents, of all people. What do they know? Who else has read it? Have Daddy and Mommy seen it? Has anyone connected my uncle's sexual issues with my odd behavior around him? I feel outed.

"I don't have anything to talk about," I say to Gramps and Dorene, even though something in me wants to unload every last detail.

Do they think this is all my fault?

Am I, in fact, to blame for Uncle John's death?

Staring through rivulets of rain on the window, I decide to keep these secrets a while longer. My grandparents will be headed home for the Bay Area in a few days. Maybe they'll forget about whatever it is they have read.

In the darkness, my thoughts turn instead to my dad, to the image of his collapsed and wailing form on the bridge at Cook's Chasm. Eight years older than his brother, Dad only got to know him well these past few years. He reached out and tried to show his love. He wanted to be the hero for someone who meant so much to him.

Now ashes are all he has left.

PART 5

UNRAVELING

People may call what happens at midlife "a crisis," but it's not.
It's an unraveling.

Brene Brown

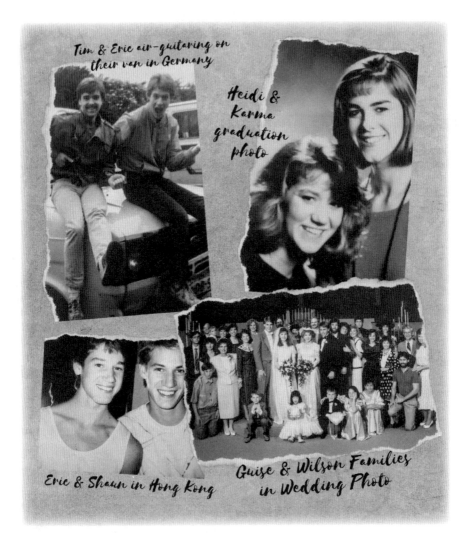

Tim & Eric air-guitaring on their van in Germany

Heidi & Karma graduation photo

Eric & Shaun in Hong Kong

Guise & Wilson Families in Wedding Photo

51

Eric

I'm back in Vienna, Austria, my old stomping grounds. When I pass the waters of the Alte Donau and knock on the door of the OM team house, memories wash over me—stolen cereal prizes, treatments for head lice, visits to the Prater, and a ride on the Ferris wheel. My heart has always been tied to this place and I ask myself:

Will I pick up the language and fit right in? Is this my true home?

So far, Tim Johnson and I have visited some of my old childhood friends in London, ridden a hovercraft across the English Channel, toured Notre Dame cathedral in Paris—wearing berets in an unfortunate attempt to blend in—and stayed at Gasthaus Lindner in the mountains of Salzburg.

The door in Vienna now opens. *"Grüss Gott,"* says the OM leader.

I recognize him right away, though he seems confused as to my identity. I return the greeting in German and switch to English. I tell him I'm Mark and Linda Wilson's son, then mention the code names they once used on the team.

He repeats the names. "Mmm, yes, I remember."

"I'm at least a half-meter taller now, so I don't expect you to remember me." I reach out to shake his hand. "Name's Eric. And this is my friend Tim."

"You were the oldest, a quiet kid. Please, come in. Are either of you thirsty?"

Tim's and my journey started two weeks ago, in late October 1985. Friends and relatives waved us off from Eugene after a Sunday-morning service. We left America with only our suitcases, one-way plane tickets, and $400 each in our pockets. Soon, we'll be smuggling Bibles into Eastern Europe, defying communist guards.

What do we know? We're just kids out of high school.

Our parents, in their thirties, still look like kids themselves.

Of course, international calls cost a fortune, and it will be another two weeks before my mom can tell me the bad news. I have no idea of my uncle's death and his suicide note, nor of the troubles already brewing back home.

~ ~ ~

Our first smuggling mission leads us into Hungary. Tim and I travel in a large van with three other English speakers. We don't even know their actual identities since code names are used from the day we join the team.

Tim is introduced as James, one of his favorite New Testament books.

I am known as Justin, a character from one of my favorite childhood books, *Mrs. Frisby and the Rats of NIMH.*

Hungary is no longer as strict as some others in the Communist Bloc and we have no problems at the border. As we traverse the countryside, we blare a tape of Bruce Springsteen's *Born in the U.S.A.* We make our drop after nightfall in the capital city of Budapest, just as my parents did years ago to a fearful veterinarian. Family lore adds weight to my every move. I am walking in my father's footsteps.

The following day, I turn nineteen. Tim and our teammates decide to make my birthday a memorable one. We all traipse up the Buda side of the city. We tour the castle-like ramparts on the bluff, then step down from a cobblestone street into an old restaurant with smoke-stained walls and candlelit tables.

"Goulash," my teammates tell the waiter. "Bowls of goulash all around."

Soup has never tasted so rich. I savor every bite.

"And a gift for you," Tim adds. He hands me a packet of Hungarian paprika, knotted shut with a scarlet string. "It's from all of us, Justin. Happy birthday."

Our first trip concludes without danger or drama and just like that we have earned our stripes. Soon, Tim is packing for East Germany, while I get ready for Romania. Neither of us divulge these details to each other. Secrecy is paramount in this longstanding operation. The less we know, the better.

~ ~ ~

"A phone call for you," the OM team leader tells me. "From the United States."

As soon as I speak into the receiver, a chorus of voices wishes me a belated happy birthday. I hear my dad, mom, brother, sister, and friends from the NFC youth group back in Oregon. I call out a thank-you and remind them of Christians around the world being tortured, even dying, for their faith.

"Don't forget to pray for the persecuted church," I tell them.

Afterwards, Mom lowers her voice and her next sentence catches my breath. "Eric, I have something to tell you." Even here, thousands of miles and multiple time zones away, I can't miss the heaviness in her tone. "Are you there, honey?"

"What's wrong?" I want to know. "Just tell me."

"It's Uncle John," she says. "He committed suicide earlier this month."

My pulse pounds and the phone digs into my ear. My mom's words carve a chunk from my chest. Numbness spreads through my shoulders, neck, and temples.

"How?" I whisper. "What happened?"

"He died from his engine's exhaust, from carbon monoxide poisoning."

I squeeze my eyes shut. Uncle John and I used to call out orders to each other in his cramped espresso cart, laughing as we worked. He once came to school in his limousine and picked up me and Morgan for a free ride through the countryside. I can still see his blond hair curling beneath his chauffeur's cap.

"He left a letter," Mom adds. "Do you want to hear it?"

My mouth opens but nothing comes out.

"Honey, are you okay with this?"

"I'm... yes, I'm listening."

By the time details are filled in, my world feels ripped apart. I hang up the phone and shuffle to the room I share with Tim. He is turned away on his bed, reading, and I don't mention the news about my uncle. Mechanically, I push clothes into a duffel bag.

The Swedish guy who will be my travel partner and fellow smuggler in Romania now appears in the doorway. "Are you ready, Justin?"

Seems safer to hide behind this code name at the moment.

"Where's your stuff?" I ask.

"In the vehicle. We're ready to go."

My partner has already packed medical supplies, children's clothing, and hundreds of New Testaments in Romanian. We meet in the team leader's office for a departing prayer, and we write farewell letters to be filed in sealed envelopes in the event our families don't hear from us again.

Uncle John's letter is the only one I can think of.

Why did you do it? I wonder. Will I see you in eternity?

Our journey is tedious, bumping over patchwork roads through regions of Serbia and Croatia. The terrain is dreary and gray, tamped down by rain-heavy clouds. Ahead lies the Moravita border crossing into Romania, one I crossed as a child while my parents were smuggling. Any cozy sense of nostalgia is undone by the sight of armed guards who now signal for us to turn off the vehicle and step out into the freezing cold.

"Weapons? Drugs? Pornography?" an official inquires.

"No." My partner shakes his head. "We are tourists to your beautiful land."

"You have Bibles?"

I keep my gaze on the guard's uniform, focused on the insignia in an effort to remain calm. What will my partner say?

"No," he answers. He tells me later he has not lied since we carry only portions of Scripture, not complete Holy Bibles.

"You come with me," the official barks at my teammate.

Left at the station, I watch our vehicle be steered onto a ramp where guards examine its underbelly with flashlights and metal prods. They take apart the headlights and back seat, keeping an eye on my partner's reactions for any signs of nervousness. With daylight fading, I can't make out all that goes on. Beside me, a guard has a rifle strapped over his shoulder and I am truly at the mercy of the situation. Even so, I feel nothing but peace.

Lord, it's up to you, I pray under my breath. Otherwise, I'm helpless here.

The New Testaments are well-hidden in the gizlis, and the men in uniform find nothing despite all their poking and prodding. By the time we are allowed into the country, it is raining. We're both exhausted, and it's my turn to drive. In the darkness, I nearly plow into a caravan of donkeys, covered carts, and children in rags. These nomadic people often travel by night to avoid cruelties perpetuated by day. Many throughout Europe view the Roma as pests and shun them.

As a five-year-old, I loved the gypsies. I remember a trio of boys doing the robber's dance for my sister and me.

So many hurting people. So many hungry, in need of compassion.

The next day, snowbanks hem us in on rutted roads as we leave the city of Timişoara. Temperatures drop below zero, and my Swedish partner warns me not to touch anything metal or it will tear off my skin. The landscape is a rolling blanket of white, dotted with trees and thatched-roof houses. Far away, Carpathian peaks claw at thick pewter clouds. Each vista is like a painting.

My sorrow pours out as the kilometers pass by: Why, Uncle John? Is there anything I could have done to intervene? Why didn't I call or write?

The notion of suicide being a solely selfish act, an unforgivable sin, seems strange to me. If I die while committing a wrong, whether suicide, gossip, or fornication, am I thus doomed forever? I don't believe this is the sort of God I serve.

According to his letter, Uncle John took his life to protect others. Heidi once told me she felt uncomfortable when left alone with him, so I simply stayed close whenever our uncle visited. I never suspected what my sister actually endured. I wanted to believe the best about my relatives.

How is Heidi handling all this? I'll check with her when I get home.

As we drive through snow-dusted forests and foothills, hot droplets spill down my cheeks. I love my uncle. I will always miss him. Real life, I decide, is so messy, and I'm in no position to start playing God.

~ ~ ~

We rendezvous with the last of our three contacts at an icy pond outside Cluj. The rural pastor meets us with hearty hugs and invites us to join him for lunch at his farmhouse a few kilometers away. When we tell him we don't want to put him in any danger, he waves off our concerns and convinces us to follow him home.

"I am in prison many times," he explains over slices of bread and bowls of thin soup. "The communists, they spy on me. They listen with bugs in radio, in walls. I am not afraid. They kill me, and what? I am in heaven, yes?" He bellows into the old radio beside him. "I am not afraid, you communists. You are small. God, He is big."

We shake our heads. How does he muster such courage?

"We Romanians think we cannot fly," he goes on. "We think we are trapped in chicken coop. But this is not true. We are eagles. We must..." He flaps his arms. "We must use wings, yes? We must fly."

On our long drive back to the border, I see birds soar above the snowy fields, wheeling shapes against a pale gray sky.

52

Shaun

I'll never see my uncle again, and I'm not sure when my big brother is coming back. Eric has no money, no return ticket, and no intention of flying home from Europe anytime soon. On my nightstand, a photo shows Eric and Tim smiling with arms raised as ocean waves crash behind them. I gaze at it each night, misty-eyed, missing my brother and feeling stuck here all alone.

Yep, alone. Least as far as my parents are concerned.

To them, I've become invisible. Dad's eyes are vacant and he stares off over my shoulder. Mom is a wreck. If she sits on the couch for even a moment, she ends up asleep in the fetal position, Bible cradled to her chest. She doesn't even make meals anymore. I cook ramen for myself or scrounge up what I can from the fridge.

Done with being stuck in the evangelical Christian bubble, I have decided as a sophomore to attend nearby Willamette High. I'm finally living in the real world, as Dad calls it, and I fit in just fine.

When I get home each day, there's no one around. Heidi's a senior at Christ's Center and drives straight from school to the NFC offices, where she helps with bookkeeping and training curriculum. Dad and Mom are busier than ever, and there's talk of a building project to make room for the growing congregation. This leads to architects, bankers, deadlines, and money topics—all things my parents have avoided in the past.

The rare evenings Dad and Mom get home early, they nitpick about schedules and staff members and whether it's appropriate for Dad to play secular music in his church office. Even when our home phone rings with the Wilson code, the two of them avoid answering it.

"Shaun, you want to get that?" Dad says.

"Probably for you."

He sighs. "Take a message, bud. We're not available."

Sometimes, my friend Rich calls. Sometimes, a girl from the youth group. When she and her mom have me over and feed me dinner, I doubt my parents even notice I'm gone. Back home, I sneak into my room, lie on my bed, and try to tune out their arguments. With their room on the other side of the wall, I can hear every word.

"Mark, honey, we cannot rewrite Scripture to fit our emotions. Your brother is gone, and we have no guarantees he repented in those final moments."

"Right. So, *you* get to judge now. Only *you* know best."

"We can't change what has happened, as much as we might like to. Do you really think wearing his jacket will bring him—?"

"He was my baby brother, okay? Just drop it. *Please.*"

I get Dad's point. I also know Mom's correct that what's done is done. I recall clinging to Uncle John's leg when I thought his being fired meant he would be killed. I loved him too. Does anyone realize how much I miss him?

"Our focus," Mom continues, "must be on Jesus, on telling others of His love. It's so crucial we speak the truth now, don't you think? If anything, Mark, it's even clearer than ever. Eternal souls are at stake."

"According to you, God's *love* would send my brother to hell."

"It's not up to me. God alone knows the intentions of the heart."

Soft footsteps. A frustrated grunt.

"Just back off, Linda. Give me some space here."

Bumps against furniture. A feeble cry.

"Dammit, Linda, I *mean* it."

"Honey, please. Why can't you let me touch you? I'm simply—"

"Enough," Dad hisses.

Sounds of tussling. Something smacks against the wall.

I flinch in my bed and jerk upright, gritting my teeth.

Who are these strangers in the other room? This has to stop. Ever since Eric's departure and Uncle John's death, things haven't been right in our house. It's as though someone has grabbed a thread of our family tapestry and started pulling—*tug-tug-tug*–until the pattern twists into something I hardly even recognize.

~ ~ ~

Heidi

My busy schedule buffers me from all the dynamics going on at home. Shaun's often left on his own and seems mad at the world. Though I wish I could be around for him, work duties, school requirements, and preparations for graduation keep the two of us apart. The thread of an older brother has always been our connection, and in Eric's absence we struggle to create our own relational pattern.

My days are hectic, filled with responsibility.

My nights are filled with skeletons.

Memories of Uncle John won't leave me alone. Long buried, they've been dug up by my uncle's letter and my grandparents' questioning. There's no use looking to my parents for guidance, since they are busier than ever.

My mom seems to seek validation through her position on the NFC staff.

And my dad? Well, he's not mad at the world, he's just gone mad.

"Daddy?" I find him sunbathing one day in front of the church in cutoff jeans, his skinny legs and bare chest exposed. Music blares through a boom box. His newly permed head rests on Uncle John's faded denim jacket, which is rolled into a pillow.

"What's up?" He turns toward me. "Something wrong?"

"Looks like you're trying to relax. I don't want to disturb you."

"No, no, I'm all ears." He lowers the music's volume and sits up.

How do I even begin? Does Dad know all that was revealed in Uncle John's suicide note? It's been years since the stuff happened between my uncle and me.

Sensing my unease, Dad pats the grass. "Sit down, sweetie."

I settle beside him. "Do you remember I rode back from Cook's Chasm with Gramps and Grams Dorene? They started asking me questions during the drive."

"Okay."

"They wanted to discuss some of the stuff in Uncle John's letter."

"Uh-huh."

"They said... they..." I want to share this weight, but the memory of Dad's howls and collapsed form make me wonder if he's ready. Then again, maybe this will be good for him, for us. We are both carrying burdens of guilt. "Remember what the letter said about sexual desires, about Uncle John not trusting himself around younger girls?"

"Mm-hmm."

How do I even say this? I wonder. The abuses I suffered at the hands of others have led me to act out. I've pushed boundaries in multiple relationships, begging for someone to love me, to show me I'm more than just a body to be had.

But the choices I've made are my own. I am not just a victim here.

Luke 8:17 says, "Nothing is secret that will not be revealed, nor anything hidden that will not be known and come to light." When given the chance with Gramps and Dorene, I kept things in the dark. As much as I've wanted to tell Karma, she is dealing with her own family revelations. If I go to Mom, she'll try to spiritualize everything, and the last thing I need is more judgment.

Uncle John's secret life destroyed him. And my own secrets will consume me if I don't bring them into the open.

Okay, maybe I just say it. Here goes.

I turn toward my dad on the grass and clear my throat. "In the car that night, Dorene asked me if Uncle John—"

"Oh, my *gosh*." Dad cranks the music and jumps to his feet. "This is *so* good."

From the boom box, Aerosmith and Run-D.M.C. belt out a song across the church lawn. The lyrics of the verse take jabs at my own shame, followed by the sing-along chorus: "Walk this waaaaay, walk this waaaaay..."

Dad drums his thigh and joins in. "Walk this waaaaay, just give me a kiss..."

I tilt my head and look away. Guess I'll stay in the shadows a while longer.

~ ~ ~

Darkness envelops me as I trudge down our gravel road. The Monaghans have bought their own home at the end of Port Street and I head there now, the weight of my abuse and trespasses growing with each step. I knock lightly due to the late hour. There's a rustling inside and Debbie appears on the threshold in her dusty-rose bathrobe, a silky nightgown peaking from beneath.

"It's almost midnight, Heidi. Everyone else is in bed."

"I need to... I need... to talk," I blubber.

"Oh, sweetheart, come in."

I follow Debbie into a sunken living room where moonlight seeps through sheer lace curtains and illuminates the furniture. She pats a powder-blue settee she has recently reupholstered and I sit next to her, curling my legs beneath me. An open Bible and journal rest on the side table. A floor lamp with a Victorian shade casts a circle of light around us.

This space feels warm. My mind and body relax. As my mouth opens, words burble forth in a stream.

Debbie doesn't interrupt, doesn't judge. She just listens.

I talk about John, describing my doubts and my desires. This leads to my pain and confusion over the incident with the teacher at public school. Then I share how fear took root as the boys in the elevator had their fun with me. Memories pour forth like a waterfall as my own willful indiscretions are revealed.

Every enticing kiss. Every touch.

Mom was right: *Many things which look nice can get you into trouble...*

Debbie and I kneel beside the couch just as Mom and I did when she first taught me how to pray. I bring every transgression to Jesus, those I've committed and those I've had perpetrated against me. I acknowledge my part in each situation. In confession, my burdens are unloaded. In repentance, weights fall from my shoulders.

The assaults, fears, and silences.

My choices, guilt, and shame.

As I walk back through each memory, I recognize Jesus has always been with me, providing avenues of escape—a nurse walking in, the scream of an elevator alarm. When cornered by my uncle, my mom and my brothers were often within calling distance, but I said nothing. I am responsible for the decisions I made, though not for the abuses endured.

I choose now to let go and to forgive.

Years of pain wash away in my flood of tears.

Dawn begins its own awakening as I walk back to my house. I feel more buoyant than I have since my initial third-grade encounter with my uncle. No more cringing in the shadows where darkness gains power from lies. From this moment on, I choose truth and light—and the disturbing dreams never return.

53

Shaun

At Willamette High, Carolyn Monaghan is my locker partner. She's nice and all, with a big heart for the loners on campus. Good for her. But she shows up to school wearing a backpack, and Rich and I are trying to forge a bold, new image for ourselves.

He and I decide one night to TP a neighbor's house. Arms stacked high with toilet paper, we emerge from the corner market and head down the street. A cop car does a U-turn, and the officer leans out the window to ask what we're up to.

"Gosh," Rich says with a smirk, "my mom's got the runs like you wouldn't believe, and if we don't get this toilet paper home, she's going to be pissed."

The officer stops and gets out. "Tell me, boys, what're your names?"

"We don't have to tell you shit," Rich says. "You've got nothing on us."

"Your names. I'm not asking."

"I'm Mickey Mouse," Rich says. "And my friend here's Donald Duck."

Such defiance shocks me. I picture us in handcuffs, shoved up against the cruiser. Rich ignores the policeman's questions and saunters away, beckoning me to come along. Livid, the officer follows us a few blocks in his car. Rich finally rips open a pack of TP, whoops at the top of his lungs, and starts stringing a house in two-ply tissue, which is more than the cop can bear.

"You're in trouble now, Mickey Mouse." The officer marches from his vehicle and pounds on the front door. "You asked for it with that attitude of yours."

The door swings wide and a large shape fills the space.

"Sir, I caught these young men on your lawn and—"

"Get the hell outta my yard," Rich's father says, stepping into view. "These here are my boys."

Rich slips inside, laughing. The dumbfounded officer drives off without a word. As for me, I am embarrassed. Eric and Tim are over in Europe trying to honor God by doing good. And what am I up to?

I'm taunting cops and killing time.

~ ~ ~

Eric

"Hashish, hashish…"

"Just ignore them," Tim says. "Don't even look their way."

He and I stroll past the drug pushers in Amsterdam's Red Light District and ring the bell at the Shelter Youth Hostel. A canal sits at one end of the cobblestone alley and a historic old church at the other. Red-lit booths display scantily clad girls who invite men in, close the curtains for a few minutes, then send them on their way.

The hostel door buzzes open.

After stints with OM in Austria, Germany, and England, Tim and I have found new lodgings. To earn a breakfast and bunk each day, we join the cleaning crew. We attend Bible studies with the hostel staff and find their faith is heartfelt and low-key.

I love it here. I wish my family could experience this.

How are they all doing? I wonder. How's life back in Eugene?

Here in Amsterdam, Tim and I meet searchers and stragglers from around the world. We play shuffleboard with Muslims, Jews, Hindus, and Rastafarians. We befriend people of all nationalities and sexualities. The potpourri of languages, customs, foods, and body odors makes my head swim.

These aren't people steeped in American Christianity who nod their heads at our evangelical beliefs. These are thinkers who won't settle for pat answers and cliches. Their questions rattle me. I spend hours poring over the Bible and C. S. Lewis' *Mere Christianity*, trying to digest this faith I've been fed since childhood.

When Easter Sunday rolls around, Tim and I can't escape our usual cleaning duties. We change beds, scrub long white sinks, and squeegee communal showers where clumps of hair and grime clog the drains. The toilets are the worst. We clear away old socks, underwear, and syringes. Drug use and sexual acts are common occurrences on the premises, strictly addressed by the Shelter's leadership.

This morning I am down on my knees, wiping toilet bowls, when I hear the Easter bells ring. This, I realize, is where Jesus would be. It feels like holy ground.

Tim and I still have goals of smuggling since underground churches are begging for God's Word. At the moment, though, we are down to a few guilders. Our combined eight hundred dollars ran out ages ago. For lunches, we grab day-old bread off bakery garbage heaps. For dinners, we eat dry corn flakes and apple sauce.

What I wouldn't give for some of Mom's cooking.

Musakka, perhaps. With homemade yogurt.

At the Shelter, we keep scrubbing, cleaning, and praying for some finances. A mail packet arrives, filled with letters from family and friends, as well as a tape from Carolyn Monaghan with songs and updates. As thankful as we are, there's no money in the packet. Nothing to alleviate our hunger.

Then I get a call at the Shelter's front desk.

"Guess what, Eric." Mom's voice crackles over the long-distance connection. "Someone here at NFC received an insurance settlement and they've deposited ten percent of it into an account for you and Tim. Isn't Jesus good?"

"Are you kidding? That's amazing."

"I'm hoping you two make it back to Vienna soon. Mike and Debbie Monaghan are leading an outreach there, and you could meet up with their team. If you fly back home with them, you could make it to Heidi's graduation in early June."

"What about our summer outreach to Brazil?" I ask. "I've been practicing my Portuguese. We still planning to go as a family?"

She hesitates, then delivers her standard response. "Pray. Just pray."

"What is it, Mom?" My blood runs cold. "Talk to me."

"Eric, I'm sooo deeply concerned. I wish you were here."

"Is it something with Dad? I've been having some weird dreams, and your last letter hinted at stuff."

"Honey, I've never seen him like this. He's been acting out since his brother's death, and if I dare say a word, he snaps at me. None of it's normal behavior from him. We need to lay it all down at Jesus' feet."

"Have you talked to Mike or anyone on staff? What about Roy Hicks, Jr.?"

"You don't understand," she whispers. "He's poisoned them all against me."

This accusation seems hard to believe. Is she okay? It's not unusual for my parents to have disagreements. Dad and Mom are human and sometimes push each other's buttons. Surely, she's misconstrued something she has seen or heard.

"Mom." I pick my words carefully. "What you're saying sounds crazy."

"See?" She clicks her teeth. "That's exactly what he wants you to think."

Unsettled by the call, I try to pray even as my mind spins. Poor Heidi and Shaun. What is going on back on Port Street? My brother and sister are trapped in the middle of a mess while I'm here in Europe playing spiritual hero.

	A recipe from *Global Delights*: **MUSAKKA**
1 can chickpeas, drained and rinsed	*In a heavy 12-inch skillet, heat 1/2 cup oil over high heat almost to smoking point.
2 medium size eggplants, washed not peeled, cut in 2-inch cubes	Drop in eggplant cubes, stirring frequently until lightly browned, about 5 minutes. With slotted spoon, remove eggplant to 9 x 14 x 2½ baking dish & spread out evenly.
3 medium onions, sliced in 1/4-inch slices	Add onions to remaining oil & cook over moderate heat 8 to 10 minutes until soft & delicately browned.
3 teaspoons salt	*Spread onions with all of their cooking oil on top of the eggplant
4 cups chopped & drained tomatoes	plus an additional 1/2 cup oil. Sprinkle onions with 1 teaspoon salt
1½ cups water	& desired amount of pepper. Scatter chickpeas over onions, top with tomatoes
1 cup oil, preferably olive	& remaining salt & pepper. Pour in the water. Bring to boil on stove top, then bake for 40 minutes at 400 degrees.

Tim and I withdrew our donated funds from a bank near Dam Square and buy a yellow Ford Transit van. We dumpster dive for supplies, then borrow the Shelter's tools to turn the hollow shell into a camper with stove, sink, and beds. We name her Dutch Baby. She's fully equipped to carry literature through communist checkpoints. We invite a trusted staff member to step inside and find the hiding places.

When he cannot, we know we are ready.

We wave goodbye to our friends at the Shelter and head for *Licht im Osten*—Light in the East—a German organization which aids the persecuted church. Despite breakdowns along the way, we reach Stuttgart and load up for a smuggling mission.

Then in late April, a nuclear meltdown occurs at Chernobyl. Radioactive contamination spreads outward from Ukraine. Nobody knows the disaster's full scale and inspectors are forced to incinerate meat and dairy supplies across much of Europe. Since our intended route leads through the danger zone, we delay the trip and instead drive down to Switzerland for a weekend along Lake Zurich.

Our minds are full of questions. With contacts waiting for us, should we press onward? Should we risk a trip despite the contamination?

"We might be glowing when we get back, but I say we go for it."

"Agreed." Tim nods and uses my code name. "No turning back now, Justin."

We angle Dutch Baby east, passing through Berlin in the dead of night. We reach Warsaw on an overcast afternoon and deliver Bibles to a family of four. They are kind, intelligent people, switching from Polish to English as they serve us a meal.

We veer south for the next few days, and if our radiation levels do spike, we don't feel it. We cross the Bratislava border into Austria. We will be here to welcome the Monaghans and NFC team when they arrive a few weeks from now. My heart still aches from the phone call with my mom and it will do me good to see familiar faces.

"After that," I tell Tim, "back to Amsterdam. Flights are cheaper there."

Tim frowns. "What about tickets? I suppose we'll have to sell Dutch Baby."

"With all the upgrades we've done, heck, we'll get double what we paid for her. Of course, we'll have to lock down all the hiding places for good. They will remain a secret. I can't miss Heidi's graduation, though. For my family's sake, I think I need to be there."

"Okay." Tim grins. "But this license plate? I'm keeping it as a memento."

54

Heidi

I'm making popcorn, shaking the kernels in our pressure cooker over the stove. I wish Eric was here so we could share our favorite treat. As I empty the batch into a big plastic bowl, I hear my parents' voices from the living room.

"Mark, that jacket is stained and dirty. If you take it off," Mom offers, "I can throw it into the warsh. It won't take more than—"

"Back off," he hisses. "It's not up to you to control me."

"You've been wearing it every day, and there's a distinct odor."

"Don't you *dare* touch it. This was my brother's."

My dad is a loose thread, his emotions catching on everything.

I slip into a chair at the teakwood table to observe my parents without being obvious. Raised voices have become more common these past few months, and I watch as Dad moves from the couch to the love seat with Mom close behind. Wearing Uncle John's denim jacket, he flips through a *National Geographic*.

"Oh, honey," Mom says. "John died over six months ago and—"

"I don't need you to remind me."

"This obsessive behavior, it's gone too far. It's not healthy."

"C'mon, Linda, you're the one I worry about. Everything's got to be your way or it's wrong. Well, I'm the one taking the flak here for your *wacky* decisions."

"All I'm asking is to warsh your coat."

"You know, I got a complaint just today from a council member. Mr. Dale tells me you plan to shut down all the women's Bible studies and merge them into your own. His wife is *not* thrilled. Her group's going strong and she suspect you are jealous."

Mom waves this off. "That's ridiculous." She drapes her hair over her shoulder and sits down. "I discussed this plan at the staff meeting. Some of the women think it's best if we all unite for a while. I'll be leading a study on

Song of Solomon, helping wives know how to love their husbands. We believe it's what Jesus wants."

"No use arguing, then. You're the one who has God's ear."

Mom is telling the truth, though. I was there at the staff meeting.

"Mark," Mom redirects, "let's go to Onsen for the evening, just the two of us. We can relax, soak in a hot tub, and forget about all this."

He skims quicker through the magazine, his knee bouncing.

"Please, honey. Some time alone together would be nice, don't you think?" She gives him a double wink and reaches out. "I can even bring some whipped cream."

He recoils and slaps at her hands. "Good *grief*, would you leave me alone?"

Stunned, I rise from my seat and step into view. "Daddy, that coat does kind of stink. I bet you've even been sleeping in it, huh?" I chuckle to lighten the mood.

"This is all I have, okay? I'm not about to let anyone take my brother's memory from me. In fact, I'm even looking at changing my name to John."

My dad is a fraying thread. He's all over the place.

"Can you legally do that?" I venture.

He throws down the magazine. "Talk about a *waste* of my time. I can't even get a little trust or understanding from my own *daughter*." He pounds up the stairs, his elbow knocking Books of Knowledge off the shelf.

Trust has become an issue between us. This started in March when I was locking up after Wednesday night service and noticed another car next to ours in the parking lot. It belonged to the Dales. Not surprising. Was Dad counseling Anna?

If so, it seemed later than normal.

Throughout our senior year, I've noticed Anna pulling away as she battles depression. She works so hard for approval. Since eleven, she's been responsible and bought her own toiletries. While she's learned lessons in stewardship, she feels isolated. She wonders how she'll cover college tuition, how she'll start this next period of her life.

For me, this period is both sad and exciting. Soon we'll be scattered—Anna at ORU in Oklahoma, Karma with YWAM in Australia, and me in Hollywood. I know LIFE is not far from there. Perhaps one day Eric and I will take a few courses together.

My plate is currently filled with school, work, drama, music, and teaching Sunday School. Since taking Time Management classes at Ministry Training Center, I've learned how to pack my schedule in fifteen-minute increments. Anna and Karma laugh at how tiny I write to fit everything on my pocket calendar.

"Are you counseling Anna?" I asked my dad that Wednesday evening.

"It's the only slot I had. Mrs. Dale scheduled the appointment."

"Just the two of you alone in your office? It's so late, Daddy."

He shot me a look. "What're you saying?"

"She's really vulnerable right now. People might get the wrong idea."

"C'mon, Heidi, out with it. Are you *accusing* me of something?"

"No, I just—"

"She needs help, and that's what I'm doing, helping her. Don't worry about it."

I am worried, though, as I prop Books of Knowledge back on the shelf. How can Dad process his brother's death while carrying the burdens of hundreds of others? He has council members upset with him. A full appointment book. Building plans. Four or five weekly services. Courses to teach at Ministry Training Center.

Here at home, the phone is constantly ringing. While the Wilson code weeds out many distractions, Dad wants to be there for everyone. He's even put in a fancy new answering machine, in case we miss any important calls.

He tries to do it all.

An hour later, Dad finds me reading my Bible in bed. As he tucks me in, he apologizes for snapping at Mom and me. "I love seeing you spend time in the Word, sweetie. It's an amazing book, a love letter straight to *you* from *God*."

I gaze up at him. "That's why we smuggled Bibles, right?"

"And why Eric went over with Tim," he adds.

"Remember how we used to read a verse out loud and you could tell us exactly where it was and what it talked about? You need a break, Daddy. Didn't Gramps take a sabbatical from teaching? Maybe that should be required for pastors, so you can have your own time with God. It's His love letter to you too, isn't it?"

"Sounds awfully nice," he admits. "Now you get some sleep."

As I pray for him over the following days, things seem to calm a little. The arguing and yelling diminish, and a truce of sorts is called.

The loose threads, for the time being, are strung back together.

~ ~ ~

Shaun

I have always looked up to Eric. He's not perfect. He sometimes says stuff which bugs me and he practically ignored me during his time with Morgan. He's still my big brother, though, and for both his sake and mine, I want to stand on my own two feet and do things better.

My opportunity comes in a class at Willamette High.

Our science teacher, Mr. Sauers, challenges us to use our brains, to interact with all synapses firing. One day he has us take turns peering through a microscope at some motionless worm-like thing on a slide.

"Is it dead?" he asks.

"Yes," the other students drone in sheer boredom.

He squirts a solution on the slide and the thing moves. "Or is it alive?"

"Yes, Mr. Sauers," the class responds in unison.

"No," I counter. "Not necessarily."

He lights up. "You know, you all need to start thinking for yourselves. Most of you are far too quick to say it's alive simply because it reacts to a bit of liquid and pressure. But what proof is there? In this class, you will learn how to come up with a hypothesis, form a theory, and establish a fact. This isn't guesswork, students. This is science."

As the weeks go by, Mr. Sauers delves into details about the ages of things ranging from amphibian fossils to sedimentary rock. He is a good teacher, but I challenge some of his statements and call them theories. Though veins bulge on his forehead, he notices how sleepy kids have come awake across the room.

"Mr. Wilson," he says, "would you like to teach our next class?"

Everyone turns my way.

"Yes," I answer.

I hit the library over the weekend, researching density of moon dust, antediluvian seas, and the sheer complexity of a single molecule. I find books which challenge the accepted theories and include overlooked details about our earth's origins. I am suddenly the complete nerd I didn't want to be, the image I've tried to avoid by distancing myself from Carolyn and her friends.

When Monday comes around, Mr. Sauers leans back in his chair with legs on his desk and watches me write one word in big letters on the white board:

WHY?

"Why what?" a girl asks from the back of the room.

I face my classmates. "Why are we all here? Isn't that the real question? For the rest of our lives we'll be trying to figure out who to love, where to live, and what work we want to do. It all goes back to how things began, and if we're honest, none of us know. We have theories but no proof. We're all taking a leap of faith."

A boy moans. "Now you're going to tell us it was God, right?"

"Nope. Can't prove that either."

Mr. Sauers tilts his chin my direction. I suspect he loves every moment of this, using me to spark conversation among his otherwise disinterested students.

"We all saw how things can change in an instant," I press on, "after watching the *Challenger* space shuttle explode a few months ago. I don't know about you guys, but it made me start asking questions. There's too much evidence on this planet pointing to a specific design for sustained life, an actual purpose behind it all. If we don't at least weigh all the possibilities, we can't say we're being scientifically honest, can we? So again, why are we here? Personally, I don't believe it's an accident."

Rich and I are among a handful of Christians in the class. Others are atheists. We have a Mormon, a Seventh-Day Adventist, and a group who call themselves Satan worshipers. They wear black and keep mostly to themselves. They aren't afraid of challenging traditional thinking, which means they're now fully engaged.

I open it for debate, and most everyone jumps in.

Opinions are shared. Theories spouted.

Mr. Sauers lets me continue the next day, and by Wednesday, word has spread throughout the school. The principal allows all who are interested to meet for science class in the theater, with three of us moderating from the stage: the Mormon kid, a Satan worshiper, and me. Sure, things get a little tense, but we don't hate on each other. Teachers grade their students on involvement. A Young Life worker and some youth pastors supply pizza and drinks during lunch so we can keep the dialogue moving.

Through it all, Rich is my sidekick, my right-hand man. Usually the person least interested in scholastic matters, he throws himself into the mix. He is stirred up about life and meaning and the whole *Jesus Rocks* thing, since I still carry around my brother's boom box with the colorful sticker.

"We're fine with believing your God is real," a Satan worshiper informs me. "He just has no power. We go out to the cemetery and I've seen things levitate."

"Nothing's more powerful than love," I point out.

"Whatever, dude. You go to church on Sunday, act nice and smile. That's all it is, a big show, one person talking down at everyone else."

"I don't like that either. You know, you can always talk to God yourself."

Over the week, Mr. Sauers and I earn each other's respect. I receive 110% on my final grade with a note that I've gone above and beyond as a student. Our church youth group grows as a result of the school discussions, and Rich and I look forward to our NFC outreach to the 1986 World Expo in Vancouver, British Columbia.

We're no angels, not by a long shot. But we have seen God at work in our school and we're ready for more.

From the photo on my nightstand, my big brother smiles at me.

~ ~ ~

Unfortunately, Eric's approval from afar is soon forgotten beneath our roof on Port Street. Dad and Mom arrive home exhausted each evening and stumble around like zombies. Are they sleep-deprived? Depressed? Burned out?

Probably all three.

I don't know the dynamics involved in their marriage or ministry. They're just Daddy and Mommy to me—and now they are barely that. I hear petty complaints. Muted curses. Slammed doors. My sophomore year is almost over and it feels as though I've become the parent these last few months, dealing with moody teens.

They are unresponsive. Whether I win over my entire school for Christ or drop F-bombs in my youth group, my parents don't seem to care. Even with four of us in the house, it often feels like an empty home.

Two more years of this.

Then, I tell myself, I'll be able to lead my own life.

55

Heidi

In May, only weeks before graduation, I call Dad to my bedroom to help with my dress. He steps in, eyes barely meeting mine, and dutifully zips up the back while I lift my hair to avoid any snags. Tonight is our parent appreciation dinner. I want to look nice since I have a special number planned for my dad and mom.

Dad steps back out, then turns to look at me from the hallway. "By the way," he says, "I'm filing for divorce tomorrow. Just wanted you to know."

"Wait. What?"

"It's time, sweetie. Things are *over* between your mother and me."

"But you... I thought... Aren't you guys trying to work things out, go on date nights and all that?"

"The love is *gone*, Heidi. We've just settled into a quiet tension."

By confiding in me, Dad makes me a co-conspirator. No. I want no part in it. Everything he's ever taught me about love flies in the face of this.

I can barely breathe. "What about my dinner tonight?"

"Oh, I wouldn't *miss* it. Just didn't want you to be blindsided later."

Blindsided is the perfect word for it. A horrible word. While I'm not blind to the issues my parents have faced, I have never heard either of them mention divorce. The D-word hasn't been an option.

An hour later, I'm in the Christ's Center gym performing a song with Anna in which we thank our parents for all they've invested in us. Anna and I sing from our hearts, trying to focus on the good. Even so, I can barely think straight. I glance at my dad and mom's table. They sit there smiling at me, so proud—as though nothing is wrong, as though their marriage isn't coming apart at the seams.

Hold it together, I tell myself. I bet Mom doesn't even have a clue.

The next morning, Dad pokes his head through my door. "Heidi, good news. No need to worry. Mom and I've talked things over and agreed to go to counseling."

What can I say? His flip-flopping is driving me crazy.

~ ~ ~

Expo '86 has already kicked off in Vancouver, British Columbia. A world's fair lasting over five months, the extravaganza draws millions from around the globe, including our outreach team in NFC vans.

Once again I put my acting skills to use, performing skits on the streets with our drama team. Shaun uses his powerful voice on the music team and we even sing some duets together. Our ministry team prays with, counsels, and comforts those who show interest in the gospel message.

With our oldest brother gone, Shaun and I now lean on each other in ways we haven't before. Despite the friction between us, we've grown closer.

And being in Canada is a nice break from the conflicts back home.

Rich sits next to Shaun, Carolyn Monaghan next to me, as we take the gondola sky-ride high over the pavilions and the crush of the crowds. An array of nations and cultures are showcased across the grounds. A huge Swatch watch is on display. The lights are eye-popping, activity all around.

"Reminds me of It's a Small World at Disneyland," Carolyn says. "My biological mom, she took me there as a little girl whenever she got her welfare checks. It was her one special thing she tried to do for us."

"Do you miss her?" Shaun asks.

"I'm glad the Monaghans adopted me, but I will always love my mom."

Shaun and I exchange a look. As much as we want to be thankful for our close-knit family, we sense a slow tearing taking place—a frazzled thread here, a tangled knot there.

"Of course," Carolyn adds, "you guys are also like family to me."

One evening after attending a B.C. Lions football game, our outreach team returns to a local church which is hosting us in their gymnasium. Carolyn, Anna, and I get ready for bed in the bathrooms at the end of the hall.

"That was so much fun," I exclaim. "What a great game."

Anna flicks light-brown hair out of her face, spits out toothpaste, and catches my eye in the mirror. "And those football players? They were hot in their uniforms."

"Anna." Carolyn chuckles.

"Like you didn't notice. You know who else looks hot? Mark in his jeans."

"Mark who?" Carolyn says.

"Who do you think?" Anna smirks. "You've got to admit, he's pretty cute."

"You mean, Pastor Mark? That's just weird."

"He's my dad," I say. "That is *not* what I want to think about."

"Whatever," Anna shoots back. "You're the ones getting weird about it."

Carolyn changes the subject. "What have you heard, Heidi? Do you think Eric will make it back for your graduation? My parents saw him in Vienna, and he told them he didn't have the money for a ticket yet."

"He'll make it," I say with more confidence than I feel. "He promised."

~ ~ ~

Eric

Tim and I sign over Dutch Baby's papers less than twenty-four hours before my sister gets her diploma. With cash in hand, we hurry to Amsterdam's Schiphol Airport and purchase standby tickets. Minutes before takeoff, we are allowed to board.

As we head west over the Atlantic, an in-flight American film lures me with its erotic scenario. This teasing sensuality catches me off guard. While we were living in the Red Light District at the Shelter Youth Hostel, the area's overt carnality was a turn-off. Toy displays in shop windows, live sex shows, and used condoms in alleyways left little to the imagination. Swinger and gay clubs. Sex for sex's sake. Raw animal lust.

Now boyhood seductions worm into my mind—colors, curves, desire.

God, no. This is not what I want.

Over the years, I've heard Americans point fingers at other nations, at their physical idols or spiritual strongholds. The United States, I realize, has idols too, but in forms more familiar to us. It's so easy to justify our own cultural hang-ups.

The past year has been incredible. Tim, as a lifelong friend, has challenged me to mature, and we've both grown in our love for God and others. There's still so much work to be done in Eastern Europe, the more hands the better.

We suspect we'll return soon, even taking along some friends from NFC. A large part of my heart remains in Vienna.

As the third leg of our flight delivers us over Eugene, I spot Green Hill Road and Barger Drive from the air. My home is down there. My family.

I picture Dad energizing crowds with his preaching. I think of Mom, so naive yet so bold in her beliefs. I imagine Heidi, eighteen and confident, acting in movies soon. And Shaun, with his strong voice and quick wit, already driving on his own. Together, the five of us may go to Brazil, Eastern Europe, or even back to India.

My hopes are high as the plane descends, but unbeknownst to me, the Wilson threads are already separating, making our larger design unclear.

Tim's mom and mine meet us at the arrivals area, never two prettier faces.

"Gosh, I forgot how little you are," I say, lifting my mom off her feet in a hug.

She giggles. "Eric, put me down." Strands of her hair cling to my sleeve.

"Where's everyone else?"

"Heidi and Shaun are already at Christ's Center preparing things for the ceremony. Dad's at the house. We're all so glad to have you back."

Only minutes away, Port Street feels small with its dust and gravel and row of leaning mailboxes. On this street I've thrown footballs with Heidi and Shaun, played hide-and-seek with Deneen, and nearly hurled myself onto power lines.

Mom stops me at our front door. "Honey, I need to tell you something."

"We'll have time later." I reach for the handle. "I need to wash my clothes for the graduation. It's in an hour and a half, right?"

"There's something wrong," she presses on.

My blood runs cold again. I shiver.

"It's like electricity." She traces long, filed nails over her arm. "I can feel it coursing under my skin. Can you see anything? I think I'm having a nervous breakdown, Eric. It's there from the time I wake up until I finally go to bed."

"Seriously, Mom. Maybe you should go to a doctor."

"Don't be silly," she says. "I already have."

"Jesus, you mean?"

She flashes a weak smile. "Let's go in and get you something to eat. Your dad will be glad to see you, I'm sure."

As the oldest, I feel a responsibility to act on my mom's words since she is clearly under duress, but pushing her to seek help may be an overreaction. Shaun calls me a people pleaser, a diplomat. He says I don't speak the brutal truth. Maybe not. I don't like conflict, and my goal is to not be a burden.

Of course, there's also a time to act. Am I already too late?

I carry my suitcase inside, expecting a loud greeting, a wiry embrace, maybe even tears in my dad's blue eyes. Instead, the house is quiet. The couch, end tables, and TV are all in their places, and our teakwood table dominates the dining area. Everything's just as I remembered, except the plants twining even higher up the dining room post.

Still, I feel disoriented. The whole pattern feels wrong.

There are wrinkles here I've never felt before.

"Dad?"

"Hey, *hey*," he calls out. "Up here, buddy."

I kick off my shoes—don't want to stink up the place—and take the stairs two at a time. I find him in his room, smoothing blankets on the other side of the bed. He doesn't even meet my eye. "I missed you, Dad. Sure feels strange being back here."

"Change is inevitable, right? You ready for Heidi's ceremony?"

I make my way around the bed. "I love you, Dad. It's been almost a year."

"Love you too, bud. *Whoa*, look at you." He squeezes my biceps. "Better watch out or you'll have all the church moms trying to set you up."

"Like those women last year?"

In the span of one week, three mothers came to me separately and claimed God had told them I would marry their daughters. Really? Wasn't polygamy against the law? Wasn't it using God's name in vain to attach His name to something so flippantly?

"Better get moving." Dad punches my arm. "We leave in thirty minutes."

~ ~ ~

Heidi

In the school hallway, Eric picks up me and Shaun at the same time and swings us around. Gramps and Grams Dorene are also present, along with Grandma Guise who drove up from California with my aunts and uncles. Grandpa Guise? Forget it. He still wants nothing to do with us. If he did show up, I wouldn't even recognize him.

Karma squeezes my hand and her eyes sparkle. "Can you believe we made it?" She smooths wrinkles from Anna's and my gowns as our graduating class forms a line for our grand entry. "A few weeks from now, I'll be in Australia."

"And I'll be in LA. Who knows? You might see me in a movie soon."

A smile tugs at Anna's lips.

Ready to take on the world, we enter the gym in tasseled caps and flowing gowns. My stomach does somersaults as I spot friends and relatives in the crowd. Each moment feels life-changing, passing in a blur of color.

Rolled diplomas. Caps in the air. Shouts and applause.

Gramps greets me afterwards with an embrace. "Why, I've never attended a more marvelous ceremony, Heidi, so personal and heartfelt. I do believe you've had a quality education, one of the finest money can buy." With a wink, he slips me a $100 bill. "I hear you'll be in Brazil again this summer, which will be its own educational experience."

"I love it there, Gramps. Thank you so much."

"Buy yourself something for posterity's sake. You've a fine head on your shoulders and I've no doubt you'll use your resources wisely. Dorene and I couldn't be prouder."

~ ~ ~

I've added to my nest egg since my early babysitting days, and I quickly multiply my savings during the summer as a full-time receptionist at NFC. I handle calls, walk-in visitors, and paperwork duties. I also put in extra hours doing data entry at the denominational district office. Tedious as it is, this trains my eyes for small, out-of-place details.

One afternoon at NFC, I carry documents up to Mike Monaghan's office for approval. His door is cracked and I hear my mom's muffled voice within.

"And it looks as though he's breaking it off," she says. "I found a letter he wrote, telling her it's over. Don't you think this is a good sign, Mike? Until this point, I really wasn't sure if he was responding to any of the counseling."

My stomach churns. What is she talking about?

I knock. "Mike, I have those reports ready."

"I'll come down in a few minutes, Heidi. Thank you."

Turning to go, I remember Dad once admitting he cheated on Mom during his pre-Christian days. He gave some story of a young woman in trouble who drew him into a complicated situation. Unable to quell my suspicions, I spin back around and burst through the office door.

"Mike, Mommy, I have to talk to you."

While they both gawk at me, I plow ahead. "Up at Expo, it was so strange hearing Anna talk about how cute Daddy is. Well, back in April, they met up in his office after a Wednesday service. Just the two of them. A counseling appointment, Dad told me, but even so, I wondered if they might've kissed or something."

"Honey, slow down," Mom says. "Take a breath."

Mike draws in a deep breath himself. "Heidi, I don't know about all that. We're very careful here in the offices, always keeping doors open when counseling women. It's true, your father has become emotionally involved with someone, a woman from California, but we've found a letter he wrote detailing how he is ending it."

"Where'd you find the letter?" I demand.

"Tucked behind a drawer in his desk. Rest assured, your parents are already meeting with a counselor and working on their marriage."

My mom is grief-stricken. "I didn't even want you to know about this, Heidi."

"Thank you," Mike says, taking the reports from my hand and ushering me out. "We'll handle this from here."

At the top of the stairs, I pause.

My mom's voice is faint. "Don't worry, Mike. Mark and I have worked through this before. As I've already said, I forgive him."

I ease down the steps, ears ringing with all I've heard. I know the words of I Corinthians 13 by heart: "Love… bears all things, believes all things, hopes all things, endures all things. Love never fails." My mom clings to love and the hope of redemption. For most of her life, she has borne the brunt of her own father's unforgiveness and seen its broader damage. Regardless, she refuses to hold a grudge.

Is mercy what Dad needs now, though? Maybe he deserves a knock upside the head. No, I scold myself. How can I even think such a thing? How can I really love my dad if I'm thinking such judgmental thoughts? How can I be so distrusting?

He's broken it off, I remind myself. He and Mom will work it out, as always. Everything will be alright.

56

Shaun

"Your dad's rad," a friend tells me as I'm leaving youth group. "I mean, how many pastors crank their rock music in the church? He doesn't even care."

"Personally, I think it's weird. He just turned thirty-seven, not seventeen."

"Well, shoot me now if I ever get old and boring."

Dad is certainly not boring. Just last week, he road-raced and angered another driver on Northwest Expressway. The man rammed our Dodge Colt from behind, turning it sideways and crumpling its panels like a tin can. Though no one got hurt, Dad was furious. The man begged him not to report the incident, and they agreed to handle it privately. With the Colt now in the shop, I'm stuck driving our clunky Citation while Dad borrows an old Porsche 911 from someone in our congregation.

What is Dad's deal these days? I hate the term *midlife crisis*.

Heading home from youth group, I crest the Maxwell Road overpass. I turn up the music on the boom box in the passenger seat. Even though it's special to him, Eric hasn't asked for it back since his return from Europe.

The stoplight on Highway 99 turns green. I punch the gas, swerve south onto the highway, then angle right onto a road around a small lake. My headlights sweep the darkness around the corner. The engine screams. I feel invincible until I'm blinded by high beams from the other direction. Roadside gravel catches my tires, and I jerk the wheel to the left while trying to keep Eric's boom box from hitting the floor.

All this over-correcting sends me into a spin.

Tall grass. Pavement. Branches whipping past.

The front end caroms off a tree trunk, and bark flies as the Citation launches off a six-foot embankment. Lights stab at the sky, then carve down through the lake's dark surface. It happens so quickly I don't even hit the brakes. The engine and tires are still racing as my head whiplashes forward. Belted in, my body is bruised by the impact. Water covers the hood and windshield, then pours in beneath the instrument panel. I yank off the seat belt, already drenched to my waist, as the car sinks like a stone. The fluorescent *Jesus Rocks* sticker glows from the boom box.

I try the door handle. Nope. Then push against the panel.

Won't budge.

The headlights shimmer green and hazy in the depths. I should be scared of drowning. Instead, I'm thinking about a girl I like. Her dad will never let me take her out again, not after this. She and I have already gone on two dates—a concert and an afternoon out at Fern Ridge—and even though I think she's gorgeous, she doesn't ever say much. I'm not sure what to do with that.

The door still won't move. The water is up to my chest. I turn and kick against the door with both feet. My neck is wet. My ears.

Is this all a bad dream? Or am I about to die?

Drawing in one full breath, I dip underwater and push again at the door. Water is now on both sides, neutralizing the outer pressure and allowing me to squeeze my head and torso upward through the buckled metal. I am free. I'm going to live, I tell myself. And then my hip snags on something.

~ ~ ~

Eric

I have no idea my brother is fighting for his life as friends throw Tim and me a welcome-home party at NFC. Bear hugs, jokes, and gifts are shared. So many of these boys. girls, and their parents offered prayers and money to aid our Bible-smuggling efforts. We are so grateful.

Being a PK used to embarrass me. Not anymore. I love this community of believers. I love all the work my parents have done, all the lives they have impacted.

From the sanctuary come the sounds of the piano. Right away, I know it's Aunt Lisa's husband, Johnny Burke. His curly black hair and radiant smile warm me as I walk in. He keeps playing, fingers dancing over the keys, while I flip through a brochure which highlights family, friends, and fellowship.

Last Sunday was my first time back at an NFC service in nearly a year. Here with hundreds of others, I lifted my hands during worship like a child reaching up for Father God. My dad knelt in response to the music. His love for Jesus is genuine, his heart moved in ways most will never understand. He's not perfect. He's never pretended to be. He's my dad—and that's all I've ever needed him to be.

Next came the sermon, with Dad's typical candor and humor. Then something strange occurred. He called the ushers forward to take a second offering, for a building fund, directing people's attention to a small-scale model of the proposed project. What was going on? I'd never heard him plead for money before.

"Hey, weirdo." A blonde's voice breaks through my ruminations.

"Hey." I give her a big hug.

As the party dies down, she and I catch up. She's a good listener, a straight shooter, and our friendship goes back to junior-high days at Camp Crestview. Over the years, we've spent hours and hours talking on the phone.

"There's something I wanted to mention to you, Eric."

"Go for it."

"It's your brother," she says. "The way he drives."

"Yeah, he's only had his license a few months."

"Tell me about it. Dude scares me." She gives a sharp laugh. "Seriously, have you been in the car with him? He takes the corners like a crazy man, and I'm scared he's going to hurt someone. Figure it's best if he hears it from his big brother."

"I'll talk to him tonight. Listen, with one of our cars in the shop and five drivers in our house, it's slim pickings right now. Think you can give me a ride home?"

She laughs again. "We're friends, dummy. What do you think?"

~ ~ ~

Shaun

The car is still sinking, dragging me down with it. I pry my hip loose, dislodge a shoe in the process, and head toward the surface. Better soaked and shoeless than dead. The submerged vehicle touches the lake bottom, cloaked in wavering light. My heart thunders against my ribs and my mind plays tricks on me. I pull myself through the reeds on the muddy bank, looking like some 1950s film monster as I stumble toward the house across the road.

The place is dumpy, a lone porch light above the steps. It's past 10 p.m. when my knocks stir someone inside, and an older man eyes me through a portal.

"I got in an accident," I tell him, "and—"

"Yeah, that happens in that lake."

"Can I please call my dad? That's all I need."

"We don't let strangers in after dark." The portal in the door closes.

Body shivering, I knock again. "Please, I can give you his number. Let it ring twice, hang up, then call again."

He huffs. "Go on, kid. Give it to me."

I do my best through chattering teeth.

A minute later the man returns. "He's been told. Now off my property."

Dad arrives in record time, the borrowed 911 screaming up Barger Drive and skidding onto the lake road. He finds me standing there, dripping wet. He lays out a towel, and I ease into the seat beside him, figuring I'm in for it now.

"Look at you," he says, voice filled with relief. "Least you're alive."

"I totaled the Citation. It was my fault."

He stares at the lake's murky glow. "Like father, like son, I guess. My own driving of late hasn't set the best example, huh? Well, Shaun, it's important you grasp the ramifications of getting behind the wheel. I'm *telling* you, it's no *game*." Wanting to make his point, he throws the 911 into gear and roars back down Barger, light posts whizzing past. Once we pass Beltline, he pushes it even faster, and the needle hits 100 m.p.h. before he brakes hard and careens onto Green Hill Road.

What is he thinking? "Why don't we just head home?" I suggest.

"First, we've got to make sure you're a confident driver. It's the *fear*, Shaun, that's what gets you. You can't overreact." He races along Green Hill, flies over a hump. We land at an angle, fishtail, and slide into a ditch.

Genius.

"Yahoo," he cheers.

This isn't even his car. Far as I'm concerned, he's acting like an idiot.

He hops out, assesses the situation. When he plops back into the driver's seat, he jams down on the accelerator, cranks the steering wheel, and pops the clutch. The 911 lurches from the dirt onto the pavement, dirty, dinged, but ready to go.

"Lookie *there*. Just like I said, bud, can't overreact. A good wash and wax, she'll be no worse for wear."

~ ~ ~

Eric

When my blonde friend drops me off, there isn't a single car in our driveway.

I've recently accepted delivery jobs with Knecht's Auto Parts and Domino's Pizza, part of my plan to earn money for the upcoming Brazil trip. I'll work at Knecht's before heading straight to Domino's. I'll switch uniforms, scarf down a few slices of pizza, and clock in for my shift. If I make it home by midnight, I'll be happy. How's all this going to work with limited transportation? We'll have to get creative, I guess.

Inside, I find Mom bundled in a robe and passed out on the couch.

"Love you," I whisper near her ear.

If Heidi is here, she's probably in bed already. She's told me she wants to discuss what is going on beneath our roof, and the thought of it makes me uneasy. I've known things were off since my return, and I feel bad for gallivanting across Europe on a spiritual adventure while my family here was struggling.

What can I do now to help, though?

First, talk to my little brother about his driving.

The throaty downshift of gears announces the 911's arrival on our street. I glance out the kitchen window. As the car passes beneath the street lamp, I spot Shaun riding beside Dad. Wait, so where's our Citation?

Dad barges through the door. "Hey, *hey*, good news. Everybody's alive."

Shaun trudges in behind him, chin down. Droplets appear at his feet. Is that a reed in his hair? Mom wakes groggily and gasps at the sight of him. Heidi pounds down the stairs. Together, we all mob dear Shaun in an embrace.

"He took a corner too fast and lost control. As we speak, the Citation's at the bottom of the pond on Barger and 99." Dad chuckles. "With the lights still on."

"Our boom box is ruined," my brother says, looking up at me.

"Like I even care, Shaun. You're still here."

"Listen," Dad says, "Eric can tell you *all about* driving mishaps. He once hit black ice on Beltline and slid backward into the grass at over forty miles per hour."

I figure my brother's already learned his lesson. No need to tell him.

"I'm freezing," Shaun says. "Dad, can I go take a shower?"

"Take as long as you want, bud. This time, ignore the three-minute rule."

57

Shaun

Aside from trips to Canada and Mexico, I haven't been out of the States since I was a kid. Varig Airlines is one of the nicest I've ever been on, and the Brazilian passengers are up out of their seats for most of the flight, jabbering and gesturing. Our team of Americans is mostly quiet, reaching for motion-sickness bags.

Heidi feels just fine. She tries to encourage the team members while also offering to finish their unwanted airline meals.

Eric and I sit next to each other, with Mom in front of us. We've worked long hours making deliveries, framing, painting, whatever was needed to cover this trip. We're toned and tan, scarred by the usual job site injuries. The two of us like pushing the limits, using our minds to keep our bodies on task.

Everything as unto the Lord, right? By the power of His might.

If we take it a little far sometimes, it's out of a righteous zeal.

Unfortunately, Dad isn't with us on this trip. He has decided he needs a break from it all, a week or two on his own in the great outdoors.

"Just don't set off any more fireworks," was my joke to him as we left.

Through much of August, my mom, brother, sister, and I have an incredible time in the city of Belo Horizonte. My translator is the local missionary's daughter. I preach and sing in front of thousands of people, not always feeling adequate at sixteen years old but amazed at people's responsiveness.

Back at Willamette High, Satan worshipers claimed my God had no power. Maybe that's how it seems to them in America, but here we see God at work. From the platform one night, I spot a wavy-haired woman in the crowd, her features contorted by an anger and pain which look more intense than anything natural. Jesus often encountered demons during his ministry. Is this what I'm seeing?

With hand outstretched, I mutter a few words in my spiritual language.

She turns, locks eyes with me, and sneers.

"In the name of Jesus," I say evenly, "I command you to leave."

She begins shaking and falls to the ground. Brazilian church elders jump in to intercede for her, holding her head so it won't shudder against the packed dirt. When at last she sits up, her face is relaxed, the convulsions gone. I'm told by the elders she has been freed tonight from demonic oppression and the scars of sexual abuse.

In America, this is the stuff of movies. We either fear or we mock it.

In Brazil, it's in our faces—evil and good, Satan and God.

Even while serving on the NFC outreach team, I succumb to the romance which seems to ooze from this place. Or maybe it's just my teenage hormones in a land of gorgeous women. Either way, girls show interest in me as one of the youngest visitors from the U.S. My affections go to the missionary's daughter, who is close to my age and has pouty lips and smoldering eyes.

She and I stand one evening on her deck, a warm breeze wafting over us. We cuddle and kiss. Down the hill, hidden by tree fronds, drums begin playing. She tells me these are part of a *macumba* ritual, the black magic in the area. When she pulls away from me, I wonder if something is wrong.

"Where do you think your dad is right now?" she says.

Through my head flashes a picture of my dad in bed with another woman. Even as I describe it aloud, the image sickens me.

"No." She shoves at my chest. "You can't say such a thing about him. He knows God. He preached here last year and everyone loves him. Absolutely not."

I try to forget it. My own thoughts are certainly not pure right now.

When our family arrives back in Eugene after an unforgettable trip, Dad doesn't even come to greet us. Weird. We catch a ride home, where I knock on his bedroom door in my excitement to share my latest stories.

"Hey, Daddy. Missed you. Where'd you go while we were gone?"

"Out in the mountains," he answers. "Lots of fresh air."

"That's cool." Having hiked so many places together, I expect him to be more specific. "Which lakes did you fish? Where else did you go?"

He stomps across the room. "In the mountains, Shaun. *End* of story."

The door slams in my face.

~ ~ ~

Heidi

Mom's emotional well-being stretches thinner by the day. Though Shaun and I suspect our dad of something, we hate to put a name to it, and Eric refuses to validate our fears. He is an optimist when it comes to others, despite his own dark moods.

"That's fine," I tell him, "but there's something fishy. I know it."

"Dad's under a lot of pressure," Eric says.

"That's crap," Shaun says. "It's no excuse for moping around in Uncle John's clothes and acting like a teenager, ignoring Mom and not even greeting us."

"He's definitely not his usual self."

"Duh," Shaun fires back. "He could've killed me in the 911."

For years, Eric has broken up bad fights between Shaun and me by punching us both once in the arm, thus diverting our anger from each other toward him. Two years ago, Shaun fought back and planted a fist in Eric's solar plexus, knocking the wind out of him. Since then, Eric pays more attention when Shaun speaks.

And this time Shaun is right. There's no excuse.

"Hopefully," Eric says, "things will be better after the reunion."

Our first Wilson family reunion is being held this weekend at Gramps and Dorene's house down in the Bay Area. Gramps insists some good should come from Uncle John's death only nine months ago. For too long, we've let the miles and years separate us. It's time to draw closer. Strength in unity.

Our family drives south on I-5, over Siskiyou Pass. Eric and Shaun chat beside me. Mom's fingernail holds open her Bible in her lap as she gazes out the window. A sign for Yreka zips by. With hours still to go, I lean forward from the back seat and tell my dad all about my recent experiences in Brazil.

"I wish you could've been there. It was even better than last year. We had one meeting in a big field packed with people. Beneath these floodlights, I had to climb scaffolding onto a rickety platform. It was scary, but I just focused on the words I was singing. The way the crowd responded, it was like I was a rock star."

"Brazil's an amazing place," Dad notes. "They are *not* shy, are they?"

"At this one church, the power went out as I stepped to the mic. People began to panic, but in the pitch black I sang 'Arms of Love' by Amy Grant: 'Lord, I'm really glad you're here. I hope you feel the same when you see all my fear...' A calm came over the crowd, and minutes later the power turned back on. It was crazy. I was reminded how God can give us joy and peace, no matter what. All we have to do is acknowledge Him in the midst of our fear and confusion."

"You certainly know how to command the stage. What about the missionary's son?" Dad inquires. "The two of you seemed to get pretty close last year, writing letters, talking on the phone every month. Was the spark still there?"

I shrug. "He was my interpreter, just like his sister was for Shaun. We also worked on some music together. I'm not really sure where it'll all lead."

"I've always liked him. You might end up in Brazil after all, Heidi. The *real* question," Dad says, eyes gleaming with mischief, "is whether or not you kissed him? Or have you turned into quite the prude?"

I wrinkle my nose. "Daddy, I decided last year, if a guy wants to kiss me, he has to put a ring on my finger first. I don't want to live with any regrets."

"Well, sweetie, that's very sensible. No, really, it is."

I switch subjects, not exactly confident in his relational advice.

~ ~ ~

On a clear summer weekend in the Bay Area, four generations of Wilsons meet at a big white house with a landscaped yard. Gramps tries to corral and to quiet everyone on a deck beneath a large maple tree—nearly impossible at a Wilson gathering—and to direct our attention to Dorene.

"I have one of these for each of you," Dorene says, handing out bright blue T-shirts which read in white lettering: *Wilson Clan—1986.*

Gramps' mother, Granny, is here. She's ninety now, surprisingly spry. She's also gone to Brazil with us, though not as part of our outreach. Instead, she hired someone to drive her to Iguazu Falls, the same waterfall seen in one of my favorite movies, *The Mission*, with Robert DeNiro. Films such as this have convinced me I can use my love of acting to make people think about spiritual things.

"Dear, I've brought my slides," Granny tells me. "And my driver, he was such a bright young man. I've arranged to move him up here and put him through college."

This doesn't surprise me. Granny likes to offer aid to those in need—usually strangers, which is a sore spot for some of our relatives. I myself am leery of her financial offerings since they often come with strings attached.

"That's great," I respond. "I bet he's excited."

Uncle Paul is also here with his new wife, Kathi. She is articulate, with bright eyes and short hair. We like her immediately.

Uncle Dave and his wife are up from San Diego with sons Ryan and Trevor in tow. Lori works with military investigations. We're always glad to see them.

Aunt Laura arrives from Hawaii with her husband and two kids. I admire their golden skin. Maybe when I move down here, I'll do more than just burn and peel.

"Micah, Terese," we exclaim, hugging our cousins. "It's been so long."

Gramps' sister, Aunt Janet, is also present for the activities, though she hovers along the periphery. Eric and I don't know her well, but she and Shaun have spent time together and share a mutual appreciation for each other. They fall into conversation.

Dorene pulls me aside, out of Shaun's earshot, and confides, "Aunt Janet is battling breast cancer. It would be good of you to send up some prayers."

When night falls, we all line up for a game on the deck. We're each handed some chewing gum for a bubble-blowing contest. Mom looks small and dejected, as though too weak to even participate. When my brothers claim they'll win, I decide to set aside my competitive nature and go find Gramps.

He isn't outside or in the kitchen. He isn't in his study. Voices draw me toward the living room, where my grandfather sits in hushed conversation with my dad. They're both leaned forward, elbows on knees, eyebrows furrowed over wire-rim glasses.

"I suspect it's a nervous breakdown," Dad says. "I need your advice."

"Certainly not my field of expertise, Mark. What is it you're asking me?"

I step into view, not wanting to eavesdrop. "Hi, Gramps."

"Hello there, sweetheart." He glances my dad's direction.

"To be continued." Dad stands. "I hear there's a contest out there. Hubba *hubba*. Guess it's time to go show these peons how to blow a *real* bubble."

I address Gramps. "Thank you again for the graduation present. I, uh…"

He tracks my dad's departure, then realizes I've stopped talking. "Forgive me, young lady. Please, come sit and tell me all about your travels in Brazil. Wonderful as Iguazu Falls may be—no disrespect to my mother, of course—I am sure you've more to share with me than a slew of color slides."

I plop down beside him. "I bought gemstones with the money."

"Gemstones. How marvelous."

"We went to a colonial town called Ouro Preto. Its architecture was exquisite. Since the sidewalks are made of slick marble, we had to exercise caution on the slopes. They say it's the only area in the world where you can find imperial topaz."

"Your vocabulary, I notice, is expanding."

I wear a satisfied grin. "Using the money you gave me, I purchased a small soapstone box, along with a topaz, a heart-shaped amethyst, and some other stones."

"Why, that's wonderful, Heidi. Tell me, did you overhear any of your father's and my conversation?" Gramps watches me shake my head, decides he believes me, then pats my knee. "Regardless of what happens, remember your father and mother love you children dearly."

~ ~ ~

A few days later we gather for goodbyes. The time has passed too quickly. Will Granny be here for the next reunion? Will Aunt Janet? This circle of life, this tapestry, twines round and round. Every colored thread adds a nuance to the design.

"One last thing," Gramps calls out. "Quiet everyone. Dorene and I've agreed we all need more moments like these together. I'm aware I didn't... didn't do enough of this before we... we lost John. I've come to understand there is power in faith, and whether a prescription or prayer helps, we mustn't let our moods drag us down. We have each other. Let's not lose hold of what we have experienced this weekend."

Dorene spots the moisture behind his glasses and slips an arm through his. "What Gramps means to say is, we would like to do reunions like this annually."

As everyone cheers, my brothers and I smile.

This is it, everything we've hoped for since our vagabond childhoods.

"Now for a final group photo," Gramps urges.

The cheers turn to groans. We join the fake protest, unaware it is one of the last times the five of us, the all-American Christian family, will be captured together in a picture.

58

Eric

We head north from the reunion along I-5, then pull off before dusk to set up camp for a night in Valley of the Rogue State Park. Mom curls up in the tent while Dad pulls on his brother's denim jacket and invites us kids to join him in the car along the pebbled riverbank. The moon hangs its head over the treetops, its silver tears washed away by the surging waters.

Then, with one sentence, our world unravels.

"I'm in love with another woman," Dad confesses.

We wait for the inevitable punchline. This isn't funny, not even close.

"C'mon," he says, "you three are smart. You've known *something* was off for months, right? Heidi's been on my case, and Shaun, buddy, I don't blame you for standing up to me when you thought I'd pushed your mother down."

I swivel in the front seat. "Pushed Mom down? When'd this happen?"

"You were in Europe," Shaun says. "I was in my bed when I heard them fighting. Mom threw Dad's briefcase against the wall, but I thought it was him hurting her. I barged into their room and tackled him to the ground."

"Now, Shaun, that's just not true," Dad retorts.

"It is true. You were mad and we ended up wrestling on the floor."

"Your accusations were what pissed me off. I hadn't even *touched* her."

Heidi cuts in. "Stop it, you guys. This isn't helping anything."

"What *matters*," Dad adds, "is your mom and I been having issues for a long time. She and I barely have anything in common, and when I started imagining the next twenty, thirty years, just her and me together, it scared the hell out of me."

I turn toward him. "Dad, you once told me hell was being cut off from God's presence. Do you really believe this is what He wants?"

"I don't know, Eric. Maybe this makes me God's enemy."

His statement hammers me back in my seat. He continues, "It's all happening quicker than I planned. I figured you and Heidi would be fine since you've already graduated, but I wanted to stick around for Shaun through his senior year."

"You still can. You and Mom love each other," I say.

"Around? Is that what you call it?" Shaun grumbles.

"No, you're right. I haven't been. And honestly, you all need to understand I would've broken up with your mother in high school if she hadn't gotten pregnant. I felt trapped. I *had* to marry her, that's what I'd always been taught. You know the real reason we left the Bankers and the OM house in Vienna when you kids were young? Your mom couldn't get along with the other OM women. Her stubborn streak, her self-righteousness, they caused conflicts no one knew how to resolve."

I clench my jaw. Even if true, this sounds like a deflection.

"Who is it?" Heidi whispers, head down. "Who are you sleeping with?"

"She's a *wonderful* lady. We met at the Eugene airport, just one of those—"

"Who, Daddy?" Heidi presses. "What's her name?"

"A businesswoman from out of town. It's not important."

"Excuse me? You just said you're in love with her. Does Mom know?"

"Why do you think she's in the tent? She wants no part in this conversation."

"I'm not buying it," I say. "Don't tell me you never loved Mom. You used to go on date nights every week. We've seen you guys kiss and hold hands."

"I've *tried*, bud. I really have."

"Then try harder," Shaun butts in. "You've been together our whole lives."

"We were just kids, Shaun. We barely knew what we were doing."

"We're your kids," I plead with him. "We've been around the world together and you've pastored and impacted thousands of lives. None of that counts?"

"I'm not saying it makes sense. Love rarely does. My feelings for her—"

Shaun shoves his way outside. "This is stupid. I don't want to hear this." He slams the door and cuts down the bank toward the Rogue River. In silhouette, he skips rocks across the water, blotting the moon's reflection.

"Daddy, you are deceived," Heidi says. "Remember that article you showed me? The feeling of falling in love releases chemicals like a drug. It's infatuation."

"It's more than that, sweetie."

"Have you cheated on Mom? Have you slept with this other person?"

"Listen, the two of you are mature enough to hear this. Your mom and I have *always* struggled in the area of intimacy. With her Catholic guilt and the troubles with her father, well, let's just say we've never had the lights on when we had sex."

"Please," I say. "Don't try blaming this on Mom."

"It's a lot to take in, I know. Plus, it's late. We'll talk more, okay? The most important thing is for you kids to know I love you. I'd never do anything to hurt you."

"This hurts us. Don't leave."

"It's tough, Eric, I know, but it feels good to tell the truth. I haven't felt this free in ages. The way you kids react here will help me make my final decision."

"So, it's on us? You already know we don't want you to go."

"I *hope* that's true, bud. I do. If you did want me to, I wouldn't blame you. You probably hate me right now, which I suppose is normal." He turns back in his seat, flashes headlights at our brother. "We should all get some sleep, don't you think?"

~ ~ ~

Shaun

Dad wants me to come back to the car and act as though everything's right with the world. Well, I'm not doing it. He's the one threatening to leave us for some woman he met in an airport. Is this even true? What are we supposed to believe?

I heft a large rock with both hands and heave it into the river.

Ka-plooosh!

I want to scream at the top of my lungs. How can the man who raised us think we'll be fine as he tears our family's fabric apart? Yep, Dad and Mom argue and say some heartless stuff, but as he likes to tell us: Welcome to the real world.

Am I going to blame God for any of this?

Not for a second. He isn't responsible for people's stupidity and selfishness. Our free will and bad choices don't alter His character in any way. Nope, I blame Dad. And this jerk of a woman, whoever she is.

A song pops into my head, Sweet Comfort Band's "You Led Me to Believe." If our dad goes through with this, he'll be violating everything he's led us to believe, everything he's taught us from God's Word and from experience. He's our dad, after all. He is the one we look to. If he goes away, where are we supposed to go?

~ ~ ~

Heidi

Dash lights cast a pall over Dad's face. Beneath starry skies, we continue north on I-5. The tent's been packed up, our final camping trip called off. Mom is in the passenger seat, her back to everyone, a bundle of short-circuited emotions.

She emits thin moans. Even when my brothers and I drape our arms around her and tell her how much we love her, she wears a pained expression and just mutters the name of Jesus.

Shaun now has his sweatshirt folded against the window, a pillow as he sleeps. I'm in the middle, my head on Eric's shoulder. He stares out into the blackness.

"Eric," I whisper. "Did I tell you about the reunion?"

He leans his head on mine, waiting.

"Daddy was talking to Gramps about a nervous breakdown. I thought he meant himself, but look at Mommy. She's not doing well."

"Maybe we should speak to the Monaghans when we get back."

"I don't know. Anytime Mom stands up to Dad at our church staff meetings, he turns it into a joke and diverts the conversation. He pushes all her buttons till she explodes, then sits back and shakes his head. He and I have gotten into arguments about it. It was so hard while you were gone."

"I'm sorry, Heidi. Mom tells me she keeps forgetting where she puts things, like she's going crazy. That's exactly how I was with Morgan. Every day was a blur."

"Do you think Daddy could be moving her stuff around on purpose?"

"Sure hope not." Eric takes my hand. "It all seems so unreal, doesn't it? I feel like we're miscast actors in a poorly written play."

"Always the writer." I nudge him. "Only you would say something like that."

"Okay, maybe you're not miscast, since you can actually act."

Dad peers at us through the rearview mirror, and we close our eyes, heads still touching, pretending we are asleep. Soon, the fog of physical and emotional exhaustion settles in. The hum of the road soothes me. As I peek one last time through heavy eyelids, I see Daddy reach toward Mommy, and hope sparks in me.

Is this a private moment between them? A point of reconnection?

But no, she is fast asleep.

59

Eric

Heidi, Shaun, and I are in limbo. The tension in the Wilson house simmers as we await our dad's decision. Will he stay true, honor his vows, and stick with us? Each breath, each step, each bite of food requires almost conscious effort.

Uncertainty, it's a knife in our sides. Ready to twist at any moment.

Tim and I walk along the ponds on the other side of Barger. He listens as I pour out my fears. Neither of my best friends, Eben or Tim, have had fathers around for most of their lives. I've been spoiled. Do I think I deserve special favor?

"This is about your dad's choices," Tim reminds me. "Proverbs 6:32 says: 'Whoever commits adultery with a woman lacks understanding; he who does so destroys his soul.' We should be begging the Lord to change your dad's heart."

I realize, of course, God won't go against my dad's own will.

Maybe just this once, Lord? Promise I won't tell.

In the meantime, Heidi and I work our jobs, and Shaun starts his junior year at Willamette High. Dad and Mom drive to the NFC offices, going through the motions, and I suspect they also meet with denominational district leaders. Will Dad tell them the truth about their marital problems? If he does so, he'll risk his livelihood and reputation. Even if he stays with us here in Eugene, we'll lose so much we hold dear. We might have to sell the house as he seeks another line of work. Our network of friends will change in ways we cannot predict.

And what if Dad takes off and leaves us all behind? Then what?

"Jump in the car, bud," Dad says to me one afternoon. He is erratic, and I now dread these moments with him almost as much as I dread the thought of ever being apart. "Old Town Pizza, bud. Your favorite."

I can't resist.

In the iconic downtown building, Dad steers me to an upstairs table. Over the radio, Peter Cetera sings his latest hit with Amy Grant, "The Next Time I Fall." Dad studies his menu and hums along. I'm glad Mom's not here to see it. In her current situation, she's not a fan of these lyrics, which highlight newfound love.

After we order and get our pizza, Dad says, "Eric, do you know the *actual* reason I first went to Europe ahead of you guys?" He lifts a slice, pulling strings of mozzarella into his mouth. "I'm not sure anyone does, except maybe Ray Kelly."

I stuff my mouth with a large bite, afraid of what I might hear or say.

"It all started just blocks from here," Dad says. "You kids were so little, and your mom and I were involved in those early days at Faith Center. So many people were in and out of our house on Barrett Avenue back then. It was an *incredible* time. Incredible." His eyes soften for a moment. "Some truly precious people."

I wash down my bite with root beer.

"Meanwhile, I was dealing with my own sexual junk, stuff from my past, stuff I didn't know how to cope with. I felt ashamed bringing it up to Roy Hicks, Jr. I mean, he intimidates me even now. Walks around like nothing fazes him."

Another bite. Where is this leading?

"So one night your mom and I get into a big fight, yelling, screaming. I still have a closing shift at a small market and I'm feeling sorry for myself. Soon as I lock up, I chug two cans of malt liquor. It's the first time I've drank that much alcohol as a Christian, so now I feel even worse. Can you *imagine* me like that, coming home and smelling like beer? It's 1 a.m., and Mom goes ballistic? No, thank you. Not interested. I head downtown, and that's when I spot the porn shop."

My appetite disappears.

"Driving through an alley of Willamette Street, I see an open second-story window. I park, creep up onto a storage shed, and crawl through into the shop. The video booths, boy, *there* is an eye opener. That occupies some of my time. Then I put a few magazines into a bag and tuck it under my arm. A light outside grabs my attention and I see a cop poking around. Guess I've set off a silent alarm."

My heart pounds as my dad tells his story. I've pocketed a few magazines in my day. Like father, like son. I feel sick to my stomach.

"So there I am," Dad goes on, "twenty-two, helping at Faith Center, taking addicts into my home, and raising three toddlers. I have a reputation to uphold and I don't want to disappoint God. This is *bad*. What if I get *caught*? I am *screwed*."

"What'd you do?"

"Went back out the window still clutching the bag of magazines. There's another cop behind the store checking ground-level doors. I'm scared to death. No *way* am I getting to my car. Instead, I drop the magazines on the shed, shimmy up a big water pipe to the third story, and slip through another window into a flop-house bathroom. I'm expecting a pistol in my face, a dog, something. But no, I just walk into the hall, down the stairs, and wander out front like I belong there."

"And it worked?"

He shakes his head. "The cops slam me down, cuff me. 'We got you, boy,' they tell me. I try to explain I was just upstairs playing cards with Joe, but they take me in, book me, fingerprint me. The next day, two detectives show up at my workplace. 'Anything you wanna confess, Wilson?' They're intimidating as all-get-out with their shades and holstered guns. They've checked out my story. There is no Joe. They've found the bag of porn mags, lifted my prints, and once these prints come back from the FBI, I'll be facing up to five years in prison."

"For stealing a few magazines?"

"That's what they say the D.A. wants. For theft, breaking and entering, evading arrest. Whatever he decides to throw at me."

"Where's the Europe connection? I thought we went into Romania and all those places to do the stuff you read about in *God's Smuggler*."

"Absolutely. That's why I already had my passport. But get this, a woman who lived a short time in our house on Barrett Avenue, she was now on staff in the D.A.'s office. She calls to tell me about a warrant for a Mark Wilson's arrest. A Christian man, a devoted husband, breaking into a porn shop? She laughs. Obviously, a different Mark Wilson. I am *freaking* out, not wanting to make Jesus look bad. I grab a few things, make some calls, and buy myself a plane ticket. I figure, Switzerland's a neutral country so I'll fly there. They won't be able to extradite me back to the United States."

"That's insane, Dad."

He sits back. "Tell me about it. I've carried this around for years."

"Mom doesn't even know?"

"How would that've helped anything? We were the perfect family, doing the Lord's work just as she always wanted. All of that was real, buddy. Believe me. When it comes down to it, though, we're all messed up on some level, aren't we? Why did God choose me to lead Northwest Faith Center? No *earthly* idea. Our staff's worked hard and we have some fantastic people, but I'm not even *remotely* qualified for it."

"We're all ministers. Isn't that what you teach us?"

"Truth is, Eric, I can't do it anymore. The building project, your mom trying to get her way, the pressures of preaching, and then carrying the burdens of all these people. It's relentless. Soon as I let others preach in my place, our offerings dry up. I lie on the floor during worship hoping to go unseen, unnoticed. Who am I? I'm not some superstar pastor like one of those grad-school guys. I'm just little ole Mark."

"Have you talked to anyone, Dad? Tried to get it all off your chest?"

"I'm talking to you, bud."

"You know what I mean. It's okay to ask for help."

"I've never felt freer. I've been exercising, suntanning, learning all of this *great* new music. Life's too short."

"We love you, Dad. We need you."

"Mm-hmm. Mm-hmm. You know, *honestly*, if it's all going to cave in at some point, I'd rather just blow things up on my own terms." He leans forward. "On the way home from our camping trip, I looked in the mirror after you'd all fallen asleep. We were going sixty, maybe sixty-five, and I thought of reaching over and unclicking Mom's seatbelt, cracking open her door and just *pushing* her out. Seemed it would solve everything, a tragic accident in the middle of the night."

"It would've killed her," I say hoarsely.

"You've seen how she is these past few weeks. She would've been out of her misery and I'd be able to move on. Eventually we would all be close again."

My breath catches in my throat. My mouth is too dry to speak. I think of my brother, who was snoozing in the backseat as my sister and I drifted off, heads touching, in the middle of the night. The three of us were this close to losing our mom and didn't even know it.

"Of course, I didn't do it." Dad chuckles. "It was just a passing thought."

This close...

Unfaithful

Eugene, Oregon — 1967-1986

No matter how close Mark and Linda Wilson's relationship seemed, there were areas of contention between them. In fact, Mark had been involved in at least three sexual encounters outside the bounds of his marriage.

The first occurred in 1967, back in Woodland before his salvation.

The second, in 1980, involved the woman from Faith Center who owned the truck with the line-painting contraption on the back.

When Roy Hicks, Jr., heard of this encounter, he was livid. In religious circles, pastors could speak of victory over alcohol, drugs, even violence, and be lauded for God's good work in them. Sexual problems were a different matter. Since pastors dealt with vulnerable people on a regular basis, the opportunities for temptation were constant. This left little room for mercy.

In a public shaming, Roy Hicks, Jr., exposed Mark's secret before nearly two hundred staff and volunteers in Faith Center's Fireside Room. He allowed Mark to stay on payroll, so long as he maintained a low profile and kept his nose clean.

Mark felt wounded and his insecurities festered.

How could he ever be on par with the U of O grads and the doctors of theology? Who was he to serve at a large, thriving church? Could he even trust himself to counsel other hurting people?

Satisfied with Mark's contrition over the year which followed, Roy Hicks, Jr., offered him an upcoming role as a pioneer pastor. The very thought terrified Mark, whereas Linda embraced this opportunity to serve others, redeem the family name, and prove themselves worthy to God—as well as to her estranged father.

"Mark, honey," she prodded, "God is the one at work in you. He's given you such gifts and people love it when you preach. They truly listen."

In mid-1981, Northwest Faith Center was founded.

Pastors: Mark and Linda Wilson

Ministers: Everyone.

Mark's doubts and loneliness were magnified by being put on a pedestal. His best friends, Ray Kelly and Paul Jackson, weren't around for support. To whom could he open up about personal deficiencies? To his surprise, the more he broadcast his weaknesses to the congregation, the more they adored him.

As NFC grew, Mark couldn't help standing a little taller. Clearly, something he was doing was working. People responded to his sermons and his openness. When asked a few years later to headline a national convention in Brazil, he glowed with pride. Who didn't like to feel wanted?

Then his brother committed suicide.

And the unraveling began.

In 1986, a third encounter occurred, this time with Anna Dale.

Mark Wilson had no ulterior motives, no previous attraction. During an earlier Super Bowl watch party at NFC, the two had passed each other in the hallway and he had noticed Anna's maturation into a young woman. He said, in reference to his duties as a pastor: "You know, one day I'm going to marry you."

Even understanding what he meant, she let her mind wander.

She could not let the thought go.

When Anna was scheduled for an appointment months later, she was depressed and unsure of her future. Mark was still grieving his brother's passing, still questioning everything. He hadn't been able to help his own family member, but perhaps he could help this young woman in some way. He had to at least try.

Anna was sullen, turning her back to him in their initial session.

Mark chipped away at her defenses. "No pressure, Anna, if you don't want to talk. I'll just share some of my own struggles from the past."

This was a tactic generally discouraged in counseling due to the potential of transference. He had no formal training, though. All he knew was, it worked like a charm. Anna began warming to him and approached him after one Wednesday evening service as others still prayed and milled about the building.

"Can we go into your office?" she prodded. "I need to talk."

He led her up the stairs. Closed the door for the sake of her privacy. This was also a no-no in the NFC offices, but she had just turned eighteen, his daughter's age—in fact, Anna and Heidi had grown up together—and he felt protective of her. All trust would be broken if she began spilling her guts only to have a stranger walk by and overhear.

Soon after he took his seat, Anna walked around the desk and sat on his lap. He saw it as an innocent move, a cry for help. Anna was trying to repair her relationship with her own father and could benefit from the emotional availability of a man she trusted. She was also upset about the rift between her mother and Mark's wife. Mrs. Dale and Linda had never got along.

"Believe me," Mark said, "Linda and I don't always get along either."

Both Mark and Anna felt needed at their most vulnerable points. In an effort to connect, he again crossed emotional and physical lines. Professional propriety was no longer a consideration. Her heart was all that mattered to him. He rested a hand on her shoulder and encouraged her to go on as he listened. It's what he did best.

As Anna concluded and headed for the door, he stopped her and planted a kiss on her forehead. "This is from Father God. You are *loved*, Anna. Don't forget it."

~ ~ ~

In August, the NFC outreach team flew to Brazil. Linda, Eric, Heidi, and Shaun Wilson were all onboard. This left Mark in America for some alleged alone time in the great outdoors. A sabbatical, of sorts.

In reality, he hoped to win Anna's love.

With his family gone, he dropped off flowers at the dentist's office where she worked on the other end of town. She was leaving soon for college in Oklahoma, and he hoped to impress her with this grand gesture. In designer clothing and a ball cap pulled low, he was sure he would go unnoticed. The dentist, however, was a longtime attendee at downtown Faith Center. He recognized Anna's visitor as a man who once served there on the counseling staff.

The dentist picked up the phone and dialed Roy Hicks, Jr.

When confronted, Mark didn't deny a thing. He would let the relationship go, if need be. He just wanted Anna to go to college, find a good guy, and be happy.

"What can I say, Roy? Linda's off her rocker, and I haven't felt anything for her in months, maybe years. She tries to coerce me spiritually. You know how she is, how it's next to *impossible* to talk to her. You do what you've got to do, but lots of wonderful stuff is happening at NFC. I'll keep pastoring if you think God's good with it."

Roy Hicks, Jr., was incensed. No, God was not good with it.

60

Shaun

Dad ushers us into the dining room. "Family announcements. Take a seat."

I'm already dreading this. Dad is at the head of the table, Mom to his right, Eric and Heidi on his left. I settle at the far end—which is probably best for now.

I stare across the teakwood surface where for years casserole dishes, pressure cookers, and pie tins have delivered up Mom's culinary creations and leftovers. This is also where we've had morning devotions with a bread-loaf centerpiece serving up daily Bible verses. I've done crafts here. Home repair projects. Gramps gave me my first set of tools, and he isn't the only one who has noticed my skills and attention to detail.

So many good things here at this table. So much history.

And for what?

"I have reached a decision," Dad tells us. "Your mom and I will be separating."

His words run against every grain in this wood, creating a dozen slivers which thrust into my chest. I've been at Willamette High long enough to learn some choice words. If my dad speaks a little French, I can speak three or four languages fluently.

"What the hell is wrong with you?" I start in.

"It's not like we won't still see each other, bud."

"Don't sit there and call me *bud* like nothing's wrong, you son of a bitch." The curses spew from my lips like sickness from an alleyway drunk. "You think it'll all be just fine, you bastard? You can screw whoever you want while we all pat you on the back?"

"Shaun," Mom bleats. "It's alright."

"What, you're going to sit there and listen to this shit?"

"That's enough," Dad says.

I glare. "You are a damn liar. Shut your mouth."

"Shaun, I expect you to be angry, a *completely* understandable step in this process. Even so, I think it's important you know who she is."

"If I ever find the slut, I'll kill her. I can't believe I'm even listening to this."

Eric and Heidi don't move, probably in shock from Dad's announcement as much as from my vocabulary dirtying their virgin ears. They are Christ's Center grads. Not me. I've done hard time. If they're not going to speak up, I sure as hell am.

Dad's voice remains level. "You're not going to kill her, Shaun. I know it's hard to understand at the moment, but eventually things will work out and we'll all move on as a family. These things happen all the time. People's feelings change, and—"

"No!" My fists land hard, rattling the table. "We will not be a family. You just told us you guys are separating, so all you're doing is lying to yourself." I jut one arm toward Mom. "She is our family." And the other toward Dad. "And you are a moron."

"C'mon, bud. We—"

"We? There is no we. You. You. It's all about you. If you leave, what's Mom supposed to do? You think you can do as you please and it won't affect any of us? It's utter bullshit. I'm not going to just sit and watch you throw all of our lives away."

"I'm starting a *new* life, Shaun, that's what you don't get. Once you kids all leave, what do I have here? Your mom and I are two *very* different people."

Seething, I jump up from the table, grateful for this wooden barrier between us. "Yours isn't the only life here. What's Mom going to do? What about us? You're not just making a fool of yourself, but dragging all of us down with you." I turn to go.

"You'll see, Shaun. I promise. Once Anna and I—"

"Anna?" My head whips around. "Anna Dale?"

His eyes brighten. "We love each other and we're going to make it work."

"You lied to us!" I want to punch that silly grin right off his face. "She's not some businesswoman, she's Heidi's friend. You're blowing up our family, her family, the church, all of it, for a girl half your fucking age?"

Silence fills the dining room, suffocating, hot, and heavy. None of us have ever before used the F-word in our dad's presence. Not that it matters to me, not now. The world could spin off its axis. The ozone layer could stretch thin and leave us all to fry in some cosmic meltdown. At this point, who cares?

"I knew it, Daddy," Heidi mutters, and we all turn toward her. "You planted that letter in your desk, didn't you? You wrote it for Mommy and Mike Monaghan to find so you could throw them off. All along, it was meant to protect Anna, wasn't I?"

"The things we do for love," Dad says.

"Or maybe," Eric says, "you are chasing something which doesn't exist."

With all three of us now on the offensive, doubt clouds our dad's eyes. His stupid little fantasy isn't going quite as planned. He drops his head, his shoulders shake, and tears roll off his sniffly schnoz. He takes a deep breath, collecting himself.

"I'll do what I have to do," he says. "Whether you believe it or not, I do love you kids and hope someday you'll understand. I have tried to be transparent."

Eric wrinkles his mouth. "Transparent? You're the one who wouldn't even let us watch *The Flintstones* and now you're lying and cheating on your own wife."

"And what good is it? Without repentance," Heidi adds, "all the honesty in the world is just bragging and blame-shifting unless you turn and change your ways."

"Listen, I've made up my mind. I don't expect you guys to get it."

"How's this even going to work, Daddy? Anna's in Oklahoma."

He lifts his head. "As soon as her parents found out about us, they yanked her out of ORU. She's coming back to Eugene. Together, we'll go find our own place."

I sneer at him. "Great plan. You two can ride off into the sunset in our family car, leaving the other car for the rest of us. Sure. I mean, what do you and your supposed girlfriend care? You are blinded by your own dick!"

~ ~ ~

Heidi

I am called into an emergency staff meeting on the first Thursday of October. As overcast skies spill gloom through the windows, a district representative informs us Mark Wilson will no longer be pastor of Northwest Faith Center. A soft-spoken man named Doug Emerson will serve as interim pastor until a replacement can be found.

A memory churns to the surface, Dad talking to me as a little girl after our truck was attacked in eastern Turkey. *If we're not careful,* he says, *our desires can lead us to hurt even those we love the most.*

It takes everything in me not to break down and sob.

The staff agrees Doug Emerson should read an explanatory letter, drafted by the district leaders, at each of three services this coming Sunday. Best to do damage control before hearsay grabs hold. Any dissenting votes?

No. Hard as this is, we all know it's the right course of action.

While Doug reads a draft of the letter out loud to the staff, a flash storm hits the northwest sector of Eugene. Hailstones pelt NFC property so hard they put divots in the parking lot and strip paint off the basketball backboard. In their fury, they drown out Doug's voice and make it impossible to concentrate. Mike Monaghan and I glance at each other, then our eyes turn toward the roof.

It would seem we're not the only ones upset.

At last, Doug calls out to us through the onslaught: "Meeting adjourned."

~ ~ ~

On Sunday, October 5, 1986, Mom, Eric, Shaun and I head for the Barn at NFC. Very few are prepared for what's to come. Already, our mom is almost catatonic. We three kids try to act normal as we enter the packed sanctuary.

Sanctuary? The word itself a mockery.

Will it ever again feel safe or sacred to us?

We find seats in the middle of the crowd. No one here is more important than anyone else. Pastors, staff, and council members are not given special parking places. We've never used our distinction as PKs to sit in designated front row chairs. Our parents don't believe it's biblical, and it's certainly not the Wilson way.

What is the Wilson way? Does such a thing still exist?

On this day of the announcement, our dad isn't allowed in the building. He is back at home in T-shirt and pajama bottoms planning his next steps.

Eric sits stoically beside me.

Shaun has his arms crossed, holding all that anger inside.

Songs. Bulletins. Offerings. Everything blurs into one colorless morning, then zooms into focus as Doug Emerson walks to the microphone. He's in a tough position, and we respect his bravery. With mournful eyes and a soothing voice, he reads the district's letter to the congregation. The air leaves the room and what's left are gasps and stunned stares.

The take-away:

Due to moral failure, Mark Wilson has agreed to step down as senior pastor of Northwest Faith Center.

Moral failure? Really? Who edited this phrase in the final draft? There are scrunched foreheads, confused looks. This ambiguous choice of words has people wondering. It leaves room for conjecture and rumor.

I want to scream for all those present to hear: He's not gambling or drinking. He's not going to anger management class. He is committing adultery. He is unrepentant and he's leaving his wife. Oh, and by the way, his new girlfriend is my age and was part of the youth group here.

A final song wraps things up, but the chorus of voices is muted at best. These people who make up our NFC family, the thousand-plus strands woven into this beautiful fabric, begin coming apart before our eyes. They twist and fray. Some people bend over in their seats, knotted at their very cores. Others cry or storm out. They've given so much and been such a part of this ministry.

We know and love so many of them. These are incredible people.

Precious. Hardworking. Dedicated.

Many of them cling now to one another in desperation. Staff and council members stand with squared shoulders, trying to be strong. If Mr. and Mrs. Dale are present, I don't see them. I can only imagine what they are going through. No, they're not perfect, but they've been faithful servants at NFC. They've tried to overcome their own upbringings to do better for their kids. And now this.

Beside us, Mom collapses in tears with her dearest friends while my brothers and I stand at the center of this jumbled tapestry and watch people thread toward us.

First come the questions:

"How could your dad do this? Has anyone talked to him about it?"

"Can you three pray for us? We sure do love your father."

"Do you know where he's going from here? Wherever it is, we'll follow."

"How can God let all this happen? What're we supposed to do now?"

A round of advice comes next:

"Be there for your mom. She needs the three of you now more than ever."

"Please, don't allow this to negatively affect your view of Father God. I hope you know it deep in your knower, God will never leave you nor forsake you."

We stay over an hour past the announcement. We soften the blow for some and take the blows from others. Eric and I try to be understanding. As the oldest, he feels the weight on his shoulders. As a staff member, I feel directly connected to the impact on this ministry. Shaun, though, has no time for diplomacy. His rage and disgust are palpable. When a woman touches his shoulder, he flinches.

"Is there anything I can do?" she says, trying to be kind.

"Yep," he blurts out. "Do you have a car?"

Her eyes widen.

"I mean, our dad's taking one of ours, so we'll probably need another one."

"Uh, okay. I mean, yes, I'll pray for you." She can't get away fast enough.

"This is BS," Shaun mumbles as he plops onto a chair.

Even as Eric and I nod and hear out people's grief, we sense the shunning from some people as they vacate the sanctuary. Their eyes flick past, not quite meeting ours, then they angle toward the exits.

"Sorry, Eric. Sorry, Shaun," one man says as he passes by. "I can't be in the same room as either of you. You remind me too much of your father."

It's the first but not the last time my brothers will hear this.

"Who are you following, anyway?" Shaun snaps. "God or my dad?"

I share my brother's frustration. This rich and vibrant tapestry has been so strong. How can people frazzle so quickly? Our hope is built on nothing less than Jesus' blood and righteousness. Isn't Christ the rock on which we stand? NFC still has a council to guide us, musicians such as Johnny Burke to lead worship, and men and women who can teach and preach. Ministry Training Center doesn't need to fold. We have a whole congregation of ministers right here.

Of course, everybody's in disbelief. This is going to take some time.

On our way out, Eric grabs a bulletin, a few brochures, and a flier regarding Ministry Training Center's upcoming classes. He's always had a thing for little mementos from around the world. Now our entire world is right here, right now, coming apart before our eyes.

"What're you doing?" I ask.

"Just some stuff for memory's sake." He tugs at my arm. "Check this out."

On the handout, Mark Wilson is listed as an instructor. The course is *Midlife Crisis and the Christian*, with the description: "Midlife crisis is all too real for many men and women today, and Christians are not exempt... This course will forge beyond merely coping, to discovering powerful solutions."

Sounds good on paper. Just a little too late.

61

Shaun

The day after the big announcement, we may as well install a revolving door at our house on Port Street. How do all these people know where we live? Seems everyone wants to see our dad, so magnanimous in their support of him:

"We love you, Mark. These district leaders, they're being so unjust."

"You made a mistake. So what? Everyone makes mistakes."

"You can start another church. We'll be there to help. Anything you need."

In the kitchen, I spread peanut butter on toast and stir a pitcher of lime Kool-Aid. I want my dad to set them straight. Instead, he just nods and thanks them. He's so charismatic, he could go start a cult and people would follow along.

"I got off *easy*," he confides to us kids. He grins like a schoolboy who has avoided the principal's office. "I was sure Roy Hicks, Jr., would step in and make me confess in front of the congregation. Few more days and I'm *out* of here."

Mom can barely get up in the mornings. She moves like a woman in physical pain. Twenty years ago she lost her relationship with her own father, Grandpa Guise, to begin this life with her young husband, and now he is dumping her for a different teenage girl. What is she feeling? It's hard for me to even imagine.

Regardless, Mom is loyal to a fault. She tells us not to disclose any details of our dad's affair to the people pounding on our door. She believes Dad will soon repent and be restored, so it's best if we don't shoot the wounded.

"Whatever," I respond. "I mean, who are we protecting here?"

"Please, Shaun," she begs. "For Daddy's sake."

It's all dumb, dumb, dumb, if you ask me.

Mom has always been there for many in this community and they now drop by unannounced, wanting words of comfort. Don't they realize she is suffering? A few ask how she's doing, but most want her prayers, encouragement, wisdom. Smiling weakly, she pulls herself together, hears them out, then bows her head with them.

I try to follow her lead. I tell myself I can be resilient, too.

~ ~ ~

A few days later, Mr. Dale shows up on our doorstep with a group of men in tow. His hands hang at his sides. "I want to keep things calm," he assures our dad as he eases through the entry. "Just want to discuss this situation regarding my daughter."

Tensions skyrocket in seconds. Mr. Dale and Dad stand nose to nose.

"What the hell do you think you're doing?" Mr. Dale growls.

"I'll say this one more time, okay? I am trying to *help* Anna."

"By sleeping with her?"

"I *love* her, Mr. Dale. It's your wife who first brought her by for counseling, and all I'm trying to do is be the father figure she needs."

That does it. Even as Dad tries to duck, Mr. Dale's fist catches him on the cheek and drops him to the carpet. As much as I hate this, it might knock some sense into my dad. Eric hears the commotion and runs in from his room. Mr. Dale's pals pull him outside. My brother throws himself against the door and I lock the deadbolt.

Heidi shows up as our heartbeats settle down. "What'd I miss?"

"Anna and I can't wait around," Dad says, ignoring her confusion. "Who knows *what'll* happen if I don't get her out by tonight?"

"You have a plan?" I ask.

He nods and tells me he's been putting things into place. "We'll take the Dodge Colt now that it's repaired and in good shape."

"Because of your road-racing incident," I point out.

"Cut me some slack, Shaun." He massages the discolored spot on his cheekbone. "Mom and you kids can have the newly replaced Citation. Need I remind you who took the old one for a swim?"

He makes a point. Guess we're even.

"What happened to your face, Daddy?" Heidi is concerned.

"Fell down the stairs. What's it matter? Listen, where Anna and I are going, all we'll need is enough to get started, a few sets of cups, plates, silverware, two or three pots and pans. Your mom, she can keep all the china and the fancy stuff." He grabs an empty box from the pantry and starts loading it up.

This suddenly feels real.

"Daddy," my sister says, "you don't have to do this."

"I'm leaving tonight. Help or get out of my way."

Eric wipes a palm across his eyes, then pulls utensils from a drawer. As usual, he thinks by joining in he might win the day. Well, not this time. He's an accomplice, that is all he is.

"What about bedding?" Heidi says.

"A few pillows, sheets, blankets. Whatever you think, cutie. Thank you."

"I'll pack some board games for you," I joke, but no one gets it.

"Games? That's Mom's thing with you guys, not mine."

"We know," all three of us respond in unison. Over the years he's scribbled reminders for himself on most of our game boxes: *Dad will not play. Too mentally aggravating.*

"Books, Shaun. I do want most of the ones on the upstairs shelf."

Sighing, I grab a box. What's the use? "Okay, but we're keeping the Arch Books, Bee Happy series, and Books of Knowledge."

"Now, hold on. Those Books of Knowledge were handed down by—"

"We're keeping them," Eric states. "You don't get to decide."

The *clangs* and *thuds* of all this packing draw Mom down from her bedroom. She drops into a dining room chair and offers weak-hearted resistance at best. The inevitable is upon us. Something about this seems more mundane, yet more devastating, than any other step in the process.

For twenty years, our parents have been joined in marriage.

For eighteen, they've been united in their love for God.

For sixteen, we've been a family of five.

"Linda, I meant to tell you." Dad doesn't even look up from his packing. "I'm signing over the papers so you can keep the house. All yours. Have at it."

"I don't want the house," she whimpers. "Not without you here."

"Get it through your head, okay? I'm *leaving*. You'll all carry on and—"

"Please, Mark," she says, "you're not being rational. None of this is Jesus' desire for you. We all want you to stay. If you do go, Eric and I will head down to Los Angeles and find an apartment. Shaun will ride the train down to join us after completing this semester at school."

"Why LA?"

"You're welcome to join us, Mark. We'll be attending Jack Hayford's Church on the Way. Jack knows and respects you. He can help us work through our issues."

"Wake *up*, Linda, for heaven's sake. I am in love with someone else."

"Stop, Daddy," I say. "Don't be a jerk."

"Heidi, you want the house?" Dad marches over to his briefcase, whips out a document. "We'll go to the bank and get this notarized. You'll have full power of attorney. Whatever you decide, I know you can be trusted with our assets."

Dad tosses stuff into the Colt and tucks in the denim jacket. Mom trails behind, murmuring verses and soft pleas. He barks at her to back off, then tells my siblings and me to hop in for an ice cream run to Garibaldi's before he is gone for good. We have to hurry so he and Heidi can dart into a nearby bank before the doors lock.

He doesn't invite Mom. As wrong as it feels to leave her behind, the three of us jump into the car anyway for a few last minutes with our dad.

"Can't you stay just one more day?" Eric reasons with him.

"You saw what happened, bud. Anna *needs* me right now. If I don't rescue her tonight, Mr. Dale could do something stupid. He's furious."

"He's not the only one," I mutter.

"I know you're mad, Shaun, and you have *every* right to be."

"Like I need your permission," I fire back.

"Do you guys still want ice cream or should we turn around?"

Heidi nudges my shoulder to let me know she understands, then replies, "We want to be with you, Daddy. Just don't expect us to celebrate what you're doing."

After getting a notary's stamp at the bank, Dad drives us over to Garibaldi's. "I hope you kids recognize I'm still your father. We'll get to do things together, hang out. None of it has to change, even with Anna in the picture."

I spot her as he speaks, seated at a booth inside. "You invited her?"

"C'mon, she's not the bad guy here."

"No shit, you moron."

He compartmentalizes, dodging my words altogether. He pulls a vanity plate from beneath the driver's seat. "Look, I have a gift for her. By tomorrow morning, she and I will be in California. Gramps and Dorene are letting me use their house for a mailing address, but as soon as we have jobs and our own place lined up, I'll let you know so you can come down and visit."

"Dad, do you think this is a midlife crisis?" Eric says. "You're running off with Anna the same way you did with Mom, reliving the days of your youth."

Dad simply turns the plate for us all to see. "Do you think she'll like it?"

It reads: *I LV ANNA*

For a guy who doesn't like games, he sure knows how to play them.

"Daddy, you... are you kidding me?" Heidi yells.

Eric shakes his head and looks out the window.

"You're a dumbass," I say. "I'm not going to help you throw your life away, so count me out of your stupid schemes. And do not expect me to call her mom."

"Shaun, buddy, all I want is—"

Exiting the vehicle, I slam the door as hard as I can.

~ ~ ~

Early the next morning, a group of men storms into our house as soon as I unlock the front door. Some are Mr. Dale's pals, and others are NFC council members. Two carry shotguns, which is no surprise since we have lots of hunters in our congregation. Another holds the .22 lever-action rifle once used by our dad to kill a possum.

"Where is he?" they shout. "Where's your dad? Is he hiding Anna?"

My chin juts out as I face them. "They're already gone."

"Get out of our way, Shaun."

The men push past, heading upstairs and downstairs. They search in closets, under beds, in the attic space. A startled gasp comes from my parents' bedroom, but our mom is never caught unclothed or indecent. The men stomp around, indignant. Far as they're concerned, they are here to retrieve Mr. Dale's daughter, who was abducted last night from her home. I almost feel sorry for them. They have followed Jesus, served the NFC family, supported our dad, probably even donated hard-earned dollars to the doomed building project.

Who can blame them for being upset?

62

Heidi

Dad and Anna have vanished. The winds of change have swept them down to central California, leaving us to scatter like leaves in their wake.

The district supervisor meets with Mom and Eric before they head to Los Angeles—where I'd hoped to be, but my acting aspirations must wait. The supervisor gives my mom a check, a pittance really, but something to help with the move. He mentions LIFE Bible College to my brother, which rekindles his interest in going.

Mom and Eric pack their bags in the Citation and drive south.

Shaun and I are left without a vehicle. He walks or rides with his friends to Willamette High, while I carpool with Mike Monaghan to the NFC offices and take the bus to fulfill my duties at the district office.

Then the district office decides it's time to clean house, sending away the few remaining leaders at Northwest Faith Center.

Mike and Debbie Monaghan have no say in the matter. They sell their home on Port Street and head for the Oregon coast along with Carolyn and their three young sons. They will pastor a small church there. For years, the Monaghans have been woven in and out of our lives and this feels like a violent ripping apart.

My heart cannot take much more.

As bitterness crops up, I try to chop it down. I won't let myself turn hard and brittle. I've seen those people. God, please don't let that be me.

Transportation is now a necessity. I ransack my savings for a 1966 Rambler Classic in mint condition. I name it My Man, mimicking the letters on the license plate. My Man carries me to work each morning. I survive on glazed donuts, hot coffee, and McDonald's drive-thru lunches. Who has time to cook and be healthy?

Then my own call comes from the district office.

I am not naive. My job at NFC is most likely over. What incoming pastor wants the former pastor's daughter sticking around? Especially when the former pastor just ran off with the daughter's friend?

Strike one, two, three. You're outta here, Heidi Wilson.

Worship has been my place of refuge since I was that little curly-haired girl entertaining communist border guards. Now, as I make the dismal drive across town for my meeting with the district supervisor, I sing, "He's got it all in control... He's put that reassurance way down in my soul... He's got it all in control."

I improvise, singing louder, "He's got my job on the line... I know I can trust Him and things will be just fine... He's got my job on the line."

A new receptionist smiles and asks my name as I enter the district office.

"Heidi," I reply.

"Full name, please?"

Though I've always worn the family name as a badge of honor, I now feel shame attached to it. Everyone seems to know my parents, and rumors of Dad's departure have spread. Some people get tongue-tied around me or cross the street to avoid an awkward encounter. Others corner me and feast on every detail. Shaun and I joke about printing handouts so we don't have to repeat the story ten times a day.

"Heidi Wilson," I mumble.

When the receptionist's smile dims, I'm not surprised.

The district supervisor appears and bails us both out. "Heidi, welcome. Come into my office." He is a calm, kind leader. He says, "We've found a new pastor for NFC. His name is Jared Roth. Under the circumstances, we would typically ask you to step down. However, Jared and his wife have requested you stay on staff."

My jaw drops. "That's great news."

"You may not remember, but they were your third-grade Sunday school teachers at Faith Center. Jared's a tall blond man, long legs, big lopsided smile. They've been praying for you and believe you are perfectly suited for the job."

"I do remember." Emotion wells up. "What about my duties here?"

"Those have never been in question, Heidi. You'll continue as you have."

My Man is waiting for me. By the time I drop into his lap, I can barely contain myself. I bellow my own lyrics as I drive home: "I'll put my trust in you, Lord... You've always been my Savior and it's you I adore... I'll put my trust in you, Lord."

~ ~ ~

Eric

Southern California's glamour relies on appearances and fake-it-till-you-make-it platitudes. The showy cars, bronzed bodies, fake boobs—all of it depresses me.

Who is real? What is true?

Right now, the answers to these questions seem more vital than ever.

Mom and I stay with friends. We're both raw and hurting and I struggle for the first time with insomnia. I save up paychecks from my new job at PacTel, where I activate cell phones for the rich and the famous. The whole fame game makes me ill.

I find a Van Nuys apartment complex only blocks from Church on the Way. I fork over first and last month's rent while Mom covers the deposit. We furnish the small place with yard-sale items. We have a fitness room and outdoor pool.

Like it or not, I'm the man of the house now. My mom's been a housewife, mother, and pastor. She's never worked in the rat race and doesn't do well there. I tell her not to worry. What she needs most is time to relax and to heal. Few have this number, and this place will be our haven. Nobody even knows us here.

When I get home from PacTel, we lay by the pool in the evening heat.

"I keep going over it," Mom says from a beach chair, "wondering where I went wrong. As much as I try, I can't understand what's going on in your dad's head."

I shrug. "If you could understand, you'd be as crazy as he is."

She laughs out loud for the first time in months.

On my walk to work each day, I stop at Church on the Way's prayer chapel. I stare up at the cross. Is God even real? Why have I given myself to this? Have I been brainwashed with evangelical thinking, befriended by others who won't disagree?

My prayers turn to Mom. She's been abandoned by the most important men in her life and she longs for her father's approval. "If you're even there, God, please bring Grandpa Guise into our lives—for Mom, if nothing else."

I wish Heidi was here with us. Honestly, we're not far from Hollywood.

And Shaun, he's supposed to be down by Thanksgiving. This has been toughest on him, with the rug yanked out while he's still in high school.

Still no word from Dad. As much as we miss him, seeing and talking to him might feel to me like salt on deep wounds. Does forgiving him mean acting like none of this ever happened? Am I supposed to just tamp down my anger? I recall Mom's words to me as a young boy: *lack of forgiveness keeps you trapped in the unpleasant memory.*

But I can't stop thinking about it. My feelings are all over the place.

~ ~ ~

Shaun

Why would I want to leave Eugene? Sure, my big brother is begging me to come live with him in Southern California, but this is where I was born. I'm sixteen now and for the last twelve years this has been the center of everything I call home.

Except we're no longer a family of five.

And this house on Port Street isn't in the best shape either.

"I'm trying to sell it," Heidi confides to me. "As much as I want to hold on, doesn't Jesus tell us to sell all and follow Him? It's too much trying to cover the mortgage and all the bills. Working two jobs, I'm only here to eat late and sleep."

"Yep. I've been pretty much abandoned by everyone."

"I'm here, Shaun. And Mom and Eric are just waiting for you down there."

"Great. I get to hop on an Amtrak and leave all my friends behind. You know, with that real estate agent's lock on the door, I can't even get into our house. Had to break through my window the other night just to sleep in my own bed."

"Oh, Shaun, I'm so sorry. I thought I gave you the combination."

As frustrated as I feel, I know many others are dealing with the ramifications of the Wilson collapse—hundreds of NFC families, couples, single mothers, staff members, friends, and relatives. So many shell-shocked. So many lives in limbo.

Each day before school, Rich and I sit on the curb and split a dozen donuts and a quart of milk. Who needs a nutritious breakfast?

Night times are depressing, so my friends and I run around doing crazy stuff. We lie flat in the middle of Barger Drive and watch cars swerve around us, drivers screaming, honking, and flipping us off. We think it's funny. I stretch out on my side in the bicycle lane and pretend I'm riding the painted bike symbol.

Does it even matter? I've been labeled. I have never stolen a car as my dad has, burned down a building, spent time in jail, slept around, or numbed myself with vodka, but I have his DNA. When teachers notice my apathy, dipping grades, and bloodshot eyes, they make me go visit the on-campus drug counselor.

Idiots. As tired and pissed off as I feel, I've never been a drunk or addict.

It's sweet, though, knowing there are people who care.

~ ~ ~

When the semester ends, my credits are transferred to Van Nuys High in Southern California where I join the track team, run high hurdles in city championships—yep, Shaun the shrimp—and receive our school's scholar-athlete award.

Eric and I share a room in our small apartment. He covers bills, Mom feeds us, and I do my best to make new friends and play nice at school.

All three of us are numb, moody, cynical.

We're trying, though. We are.

We make day trips to Zuma Beach, visit Knott's Berry Farm, and catch the Altar Boys and Undercover at local music venues. We see an SR-71 Blackbird out at Edwards Air Force Base. We sit in the audience for game-show tapings at nearby Warner Bros. At sunset we often go down to our pool, where Mom watches Eric and me try new dives. Every ninety seconds, airplanes pass overhead toward LAX, silhouetted crosses against orange-pink skies.

As much as we try to discuss day-to-day stuff, it all seems trivial. So much of our past has slipped away, our present is on shaky ground, and our hopes for the future are shattered—family ministry in Brazil, raising kids of our own, taking them to NFC and visiting Grandpa Mark and Grandma Linda on Port Street for Easter egg hunts and Christmas festivities.

Seems disrespectful to pretend and just go on.

At Church on the Way, Eric has made new friends in the college group, so when I visit the youth group I expect to do the same. I can start over. Create a new persona. I'm not a PK anymore. There'll be no prying questions, no pitying looks.

"This is Shaun Wilson," the youth pastor introduces me. "He's just moved down from Eugene, Oregon."

Nobody reacts, thank goodness.

"He's gone through some tough stuff recently," the pastor adds. "I want all of you to make him feel welcome, and please know, Shaun, we are here for you."

So much for a clean slate. Word has spread already. All of our love and prayers can't change our dad's choices, and it seems they will haunt us forever, even here in this sprawling metropolis of thong bikinis, palm trees, and Scientology.

Welcome to the land of fake-believe.

63

Heidi

I am the last of our family in Eugene. I mail a cassette tape to Karma in Australia, sharing how I feel cut off from all those closest to me. None of this seems fair, my best efforts gone to waste because of decisions over which I have no control.

"Please," I cry out in prayer, "make my dad come back to our family."

Of course, Daddy used to warn us: *God doesn't always answer your prayers... Typically He's not going to defy the laws of nature He Himself put in place.*

Righteous anger fills me.

My dad may have free will, but he's also deceived, so convinced his way is right. I wish I could have five minutes, just five, to kick the hell out of Satan. Then I remember, God is love. His love is what changes us from within, and Romans 2:4 says it is His kindness which leads us to repentance.

Dad and Anna are now in their own place near San Jose. With his new address and phone number, I call him most nights to check in.

Will he realize what he's lost? I hope so.

If not, I worry he'll end up like his younger brother.

Many times I bite my tongue and simply listen as he expresses a jumble of thoughts and emotions. As hard as it is, I try to walk alongside him in his turmoil, just as he has often done for me.

One night, something in Dad's voice sets off alarms in my soul. He is not well. He's suicidal.

"Daddy," I say, "have you listened to the tape I gave you?"

"What tape?"

"Remember, I gave it to you when you left Eugene."

"Pretty much a blur at this point."

"Listen to it, please. I left it in your car's center console."

On the cassette, I sang Benny Hester's "When God Ran," a powerful rendition of the prodigal son story, a reminder no matter how far we fall, no matter how dark things get, our loving Father is waiting for us to turn back to Him. Once we do, He runs to us with arms outstretched and celebrates our return.

I also recorded my own words: "Daddy, at some point you may wonder if life is worth living anymore. Remember, God loves you. He forgives you. Even if you can't accept God's love, please accept mine. No matter what you've done, I forgive you. You will always be my daddy and I'll always be your little princess."

My sleep is fitful. My heart is heavy.

I think of Uncle John's ashes, wafting in the wind at Cook's Chasm.

Please, no. I can't go through that again. More than anything, I want to be equipped to help my dad and others like him. The stakes are so high, a matter of life and death. We've seen the devastation in our own extended family and as much as I love acting, maybe college or even Bible college should be my focus now.

Fog hovers over Beltline as I head in early to work. I park My Man near the NFC entrance and shuffle into the Barn. Head down at the front desk, I continue my nightlong prayers. "Please protect Dad from himself, from Satan's lies, from death."

I barely hear the lobby doors open.

"Good morning, Heidi." A man from the church stands at my desk. "I came to tell you I have been praying for your dad and Anna."

"Oh, good. I know they can really—"

"I'm praying your dad commits suicide. At least that way one of them can be saved."

These words form a black cloud in the entryway. How can he say something so heartless? He is speaking death instead of life, and I want to punch the stupid right out of him. I open my mouth, ready for a fight, when the words *hurting people hurt people* flash through my head. For years to come, my brothers and I will have no closure in regards to our family. Our mom will have no closure in her marriage. We will deal everyday with the lingering pain of being torn apart at the seams, and yes, in some ways, it would be easier to have caskets and tombstones to mark this ending in our lives.

As I stare at this man before me, I'm filled with sudden empathy. He is in such pain, he can't even see straight, let alone perceive the truth. I am also hurting, and if I don't do the hard work of healing, I'll be the one who wounds others.

The man hovers over me, daring me to respond.

My eyes peer into his. "You know, I think God is big enough to save them both."

~ ~ ~

Our house hasn't sold yet, but I have interested buyers. I feel so torn. This place I believed would be a shelter for generations to come will no longer be mine. Yes, I can sleep in my car, shower early at the office, and still clock in for work, but why is all this on me? At eighteen, I'm juggling car payments, utility bills, house showings. Who has time to heal when every minute is bogged down with obligations?

I empty rooms one by one. I sell furniture, take things to Goodwill, give stuff away, and ship a few items to Mom in Van Nuys. I keep only what will fit in My Man.

It's after dark when I get home one evening and discover a new lock box on the door. The other was getting rusty and hard to open. Surely, the real-estate agent left the new combo on my answering machine—which does me no good, since the machine's inside and I'm stuck out here in the cold.

Didn't Shaun get in through his bedroom window a few weeks earlier?

In the darkness I hook my fingers, slide the glass, and hoist myself up.

A man's face appears before me, silent, disheveled.

Shock turns to rage. Still dangling from the sill, I shriek, "What're you doing in my house? Open my door and let me in."

He complies, and as I plow into the living room—my living room—I rant at this intruder. My body is trembling. He is larger than I thought, now joined by a beefy woman. She explains how they jimmied inside, seeking a warm place for the night.

"That's called breaking and entering," I shout. My family and church are in shambles, and the thought of this home violation is too much. All my pent-up rage rains upon them just as those hailstones did at our staff meeting back in October. "You have five minutes to get your junk out before I call the cops. Look at all these beer bottles. Five minutes, you hear me? Five!"

"Yes, ma'am. Sorry, ma'am," they say, gathering stuff fast as they can.

They are gone in three.

Hours pass before my limbs stop shaking, before I finally ask myself how my five-foot, 105-pound body would've fared in a brawl with those two.

I don't feel safe here anymore. This is no longer a home, not really.

It's just a house, a structure of wood and nails.

~ ~ ~

"Heidi?" The voice is thin and strident through the earpiece.

"Granny," I exclaim. "How are you?"

It is comforting to get a call from our family matriarch. Despite her mockery of my religious beliefs, I have so much respect for her and am surprised to hear from her on the NFC office line. As I switch off the coffee pot and prepare to go home, she shares her thoughts about my parents' marriage—"starting so young, they were doomed from the start"—and the importance of a college education.

"Women, in particular, must pursue higher learning," Granny states. "This is absolutely imperative, and I want you to know, dear, I will pay for you."

"What?"

"To attend college. I'll provide a car, apartment, and living expenses. You're free to choose any school you like."

My Hollywood aspirations come rushing back into focus. I can go to a performing arts school, stop worrying about bills, live the life I've often dreamed of. Does Granny feel sorry for me after everything between my dad and mom? Is she proud of me for watching over the house? Whatever the reason, this is a gift is too good to be true, and I'm taken in for a moment by the dream.

"Any school you like," Granny repeats. "Just not Bible college."

There it is.

Always a catch when it comes to Granny and her money.

With Uncle John's death and Dad's departure already tearing at the seams of the Wilson clan, I feel a strong pull toward what serves my own desires. Family and religion will fail you. Gotta look out for number one. Isn't that what people say?

I laugh aloud. Faced with the obvious, I can't help myself.

"My offer is a serious one," Granny says. "Quite serious."

"I appreciate it, Granny, but I want my life to count for something. I want to learn better ways to help others. Eric and I have talked about getting training and going into the ministry. Well, you've just helped me make my decision."

"What is that, dear?"

"I believe it's time to apply for LIFE Bible College."

Without a word, Granny hangs up the phone.

64

Eric

December 24, 1986. It doesn't feel like Christmas, so why try? I've already earned one winter sunburn here in Van Nuys and I find it difficult to get excited about anything. The good news is, Heidi is flying in for the holidays.

"We need a Christmas tree," Mom insists. "For your sister, if no one else."

"She'll love the sun and the pool. Who needs a tree and all the traditional stuff? Far as I remember, Heidi and I cried in every childhood picture with Santa."

Mom grins at that. "True, honey. But we want to make this memorable."

"Our first Christmas without Dad? I doubt I'll forget. Sorry, Mom, not pointing any fingers. Shaun and I got his new address from Heidi and sent him a card. He says he'll come see us soon as he gets the chance."

"He is living in sin, Eric."

"So we're not supposed to have any contact with him?"

"Don't be silly," she says, wrinkling her forehead. "Of course, we need to love him. Just don't be drawn in by his deception and lies. He is not in a good place."

I feel her fingernails as she squeezes my arm, pretending she herself is wonderful, in the best of all places. With my insomnia, though, I hear her weeping in her bed late at night. This woman who has spent half her life investing in her kids deserves all our support and respect. Even so, she makes me want to scream.

"Oh, Eric," she exclaims. "I have an idea. Why don't we get a small palm tree, string it with lights, and make this a festive California Christmas?"

When Shaun gets home from his track meet, he takes one look at our sad little tree and snorts. "It's even shorter than me. *Feliz Navidad.*"

Later, we pick up Heidi at LAX. We show her the city, swim in the apartment pool, and attend Christmas eve service at Church on the Way's prayer chapel. The four of us hold candles, singing "Joy to the World" with all the joy we can muster.

"I wish you'd move down and stay with us," I tell her afterward.

"I'd love to. They just need me at NFC."

"You can't fix things for everyone."

She hugs me. "It won't be forever. For now, a family in the congregation is letting me move in with them and store a few heirlooms in their garage. They've been such a blessing. It reminds me we can trust God even in the midst of all this. And just think, you and I will be freshmen at LIFE in what, eight months?"

"What about your acting? My writing?"

"We can do those too, can't we?"

"Until I've lived here in California a while longer, I won't qualify for a Cal Grant. I honestly don't think I can afford to go, Heidi." I lower my voice so neither my mom nor brother will hear. "I'm working fifty hours a week to cover food, rent, bills. There is nothing left. What about the house sale? Did you make any money?"

Heidi grimaces. "Between past-due property taxes and mortgage payments, there was barely anything left. My Man's gone too, after one of Shaun's friends borrowed it and wrapped it around a telephone pole. I'm practically broke."

"You know, I spent last Christmas in Germany. Never expected to be here."

"Don't you wish we were back in India, on our swing set in Mussoorie?"

"I've never been to Missouri," I say.

She shoves me away and we both laugh.

The next morning, we skip traditional presents around the Christmas tree. I'm twenty, Heidi almost nineteen, Shaun almost seventeen. Mom drives us to a nearly empty beach where she reads us the nativity story from her big green Living Bible. Cross-legged in the sand, we open gifts from each other, then crumple the newsprint which doubles as wrapping paper and light each bundle on fire. We set these on the surf and watch them drift away, flaming fierce and yellow on the outgoing tide.

Is it a violation of strict littering laws? Probably so.

But in the moment, we need this strangely beautiful memory.

"Sea candles," Shaun says. "Make a wish before they blow out."

Mom's eyes glisten, and we all know her wish. As much as we ourselves want Dad back, we also know he has issues to deal with and Mom has healing to do.

No, my wish is for something else, the one thing I've prayed for consistently since I was five or six years old:

A relationship with Grandpa Guise.

~ ~ ~

Heidi

I take Amtrak down to visit Grandma Guise. Usually, she's the one who comes to see us on Easters and Thanksgivings, and the few times we've been to her house our grandpa wasn't there. Grandpa Guise still wants nothing to do with us. As his grandkids, we are visible reminders that his daughter chose our dad over him.

"He's coming to pick you up at the station," Grandma tells me over the phone.

"Are you sure?" I try to hide my shock. "What if he doesn't show up?"

"He'll be there, Heidi. I told him if he doesn't come home with you in the car, he better not come home at all."

"Grandma, you're a miracle worker."

I suspect she'll pay a price for her obstinance.

As I wait outside the station, I am not sure what to expect. What if he doesn't come? If he does, will we recognize each other? I've only seen my grandpa in pictures and once on the way to Disneyland as a preteen. When we stopped by to say hi, he stormed out the door and disappeared without a backward glance.

Grandpa Guise floats into view now like a fabled, ruddy-faced creature. He is in a 1972 Cadillac painted the colors of his favorite ball team, the Oakland A's. His six-foot-two, barrel-chested frame emerges, but he avoids looking me in the eye. He simply grunts, opens the trunk, and watches me drop in my bags.

I spend the following week with my grandma, aunts, uncles, and cousins. My grandpa does his best to avoid me, with breakfast times being the only exception.

Unwilling to starve in the bedroom, he decides to put up with my beaming face. He tucks himself into a corner seat, sips orange juice from an A's glass, douses eggs in Tabasco, and eats toast with pomegranate jelly made fresh from a tree in his yard.

I greet him each time with a warm smile. "Good morning, Vince."

On the fourth morning, we sit at the table in our usual silence. He reads his paper while I read the comics. He gets up and drops his dishes in the sink.

With his back to me, he says, "My other grandkids call me Grandpa."

I'm taken aback. "Is that what you'd like me to call you?"

"That'd be alright," he mumbles before plodding out of the room.

"Well, Heidi," Grandma Guise whispers in amazement, "seems you've caused the ice to start melting."

~ ~ ~

Shaun

Easter at the Guise home. I'm pretty sure this is the first time Eric and I have ever eaten at the same table as Grandpa Guise. Eric's twenty and I've just turned seventeen. Grandpa's never said a word to me, and I've caught only glimpses of his back. He's jolly enough at the table, though, deep laughter rumbling as he shares jokes with his other grandchildren. He even tosses my sister a smile. My brother and I are mostly ignored.

Then, first contact is made.

"Can you pass the butter?" Grandpa says to me.

Grandma Guise jumps up. "He talked to you. He talked to you."

Uncle Vinny and Uncle Frank exchange a look. Uncle Bobby smiles through his big red mustache. Aunt Mary's eyes widen. As much as I don't want this first interaction to be the main event, I guess all the fanfare makes sense.

"Can you pass the butter?" he repeats.

"Here you go." I hand him the white covered dish.

Male bonding.

After this, our grandpa cannot pretend he doesn't see me.

Grandpa Guise is a season ticket holder with the Oakland A's. He takes me to some games, hands stuffed into his windbreaker, a team cap pulled over his thinning red-gray hair. We ride BART—Bay Area Rapid Transit—over to the stadium. We don't talk much. We don't know each other and I'm not even a baseball fan. Taking me to these games is probably his way of saying he's sorry, though I still think I deserve a verbal acknowledgment of what he did to us.

Sure, he's back in the picture now that Dad's gone.

Big deal.

If he does talk to me, I think it's all part of his prideful charade, trying to be the good guy again after cutting off our family all these years. If he doesn't engage with me, I'll hold that against him, too. I guess he's damned if he does, damned if he doesn't.

Still, it's a minor miracle, this chance to be with my grandfather. Despite the walls between us, something happens, a subtle connection I can't explain. While I might not ever trust him completely, I am willing to wait around for an actual apology.

~ ~ ~

Eric

Shaun believes Grandpa Guise owes us an apology—and he does. I'd love to have this self-righteous, stiff-necked Catholic look me in the eye and express his regret for punishing his three grandchildren for the sins of their father and mother.

Yes, I am the bastard child. Conceived out of wedlock.

But at least my parents made something worthwhile out of the mess.

The apology we would like never comes, not in words. Instead, Grandpa Guise drives his old Caddy down in the spring and picks up my brother and me. He drives us from Van Nuys to Long Beach, where we visit the historic Queen Mary passenger ship and the Spruce Goose H-4 Hercules. We marvel at the size of both.

"I worked at a naval airbase during World War Two," Grandpa Guise tells us. "A friend of mine got blown out of the sky, and I refused to ever fly in a plane again." He is proud of this stubborn resolve, which extends to coffee since the military swill was terrible, and to Mexican food since it once made him sick.

"I like coffee," I respond. "And I don't think I could say no to tacos."

"We've been on flights all over the world," Shaun adds.

Grandpa chuckles. "Let's get a photo together. There's a simulated Spruce Goose cockpit near the exit. We'll all climb in and say we flew together."

The picture, which he pays for, becomes a treasured memory.

When Grandpa drops us back at our apartment, he gets a quick tour and even speaks a few words to his oldest daughter. I know Mom wants his approval and love now that her husband has turned his back. She wants nothing more than to feel her father's arms around her, releasing two decades of rejection and shame.

She deserves this more than anyone.

She doesn't get it. Not directly.

For Shaun and me, though, being with Grandpa Guise is a gift and an answer to prayer. We pay visits to Grandpa and Grandma Guise's place east of Oakland, ride bikes with him, swim in his pool, and eat grapefruit growing next to his garage.

I would still trade all of it to have my dad back, in a heartbeat.

But this? It's a pretty good consolation prize.

65

Shaun

We decide we still have some smuggling to do. This time in communist China.

Despite the country's claims of religious freedom, it regularly violates human rights and holds thousands of political and religious prisoners. Are Bibles allowed? Yep, if you register your name and address with the government, a risky thing to do in a land which has cracked down on dissenters in the past.

Flying down from Oregon, Tim Johnson joins my mother, brother, and me as we catch flights from LAX to Hong Kong in the summer of 1987. The money for the trip has come from donors at NFC and Church on the Way. Now that Dad has blown up his ministry, we don't want to let our own spiritual ideals slip away.

Out to save the world. All for the glory of God.

The moment we step off the plane in Hong Kong, I feel as though we've been dropped into egg-flower soup. It is hot and muggy, assaulting my Western nose with various smells. Beneath modern skyscrapers and cruder structures with bamboo scaffolding, bicycles, taxis, and pint-sized vans vie for room on the roads.

In the meat markets, blood runs freely and turns our stomachs. Some of us discover we actually like chicken feet as a dish, and all of us love the restaurant *dim sum*—Chinese dumplings—which roll by on cafeteria-style trays. The best food, though, is in the alleyways, served by shirtless men in aprons and flip-flops who cook meat and noodles in huge woks over open flames.

We spend very little time in our rooms at the local YMCA. We become mules—our unofficial designation—transporting Bibles on trains, ferries, and night boats for a group called Open Doors, started years ago by the author of *God's Smuggler*.

"Following in our dad's footsteps," I note as we near a checkpoint.

"You ever wonder if we'll make the same mistakes?" Eric asks. "I mean, look at us. We're carbon copies of him."

"Naw, you're taller. And me, I'm definitely cuter."

"I'm serious. What if I get married? I'm worried about hurting the woman I love."

Being a mule is hard work. Dripping with sweat, we lose weight. We travel in and out of mainland China, delivering Bibles to underground churches. Each foray is an adventure. To avoid suspicion, we switch modes of transportation, switch points of entry, and switch our looks from business casual to scruffy world traveler. It's not unusual to arrive back in Hong Kong, load up our next packs, and hurry out again the same day.

Eric and I love it. Tim does too.

Mom is given slower routes more suited to her.

We rely on wit, prayer, and *chutzpah* to make it through the borders. A few times, guards stop and search us. When they see the literature in our luggage, they want to know if we speak Cantonese or Mandarin. If not, we must leave our books at the station and pay hefty storage fees to retrieve them on our way back out of the country.

~ ~ ~

Eric

After an overnight boat trip up the Pearl River, I deboard and follow Shaun toward the checkpoint's X-ray machine. The summer air is wet and humid. This border has caused troubles for previous mules, meaning fewer Chinese Bibles have reached this area of the country. My brother runs his luggage through, then gets pulled aside to the inspection bench. A female guard eyes his bag bulging with Bibles, while my mom skirts the conveyor, and I slip outside and flag down a taxi. Mom joins me. Peering back through the window, I tell the driver to wait. Other guards have gathered around my brother.

Great. He's been caught.

I must be careful since we could now be followed and lead communist spies to members of the underground church—a hand slap for us, a prison sentence for them.

Why, Lord? I wonder. Didn't we ask you to protect us this morning?

I face straight ahead, not wanting to draw attention to myself. My brother suddenly drops into the back seat of the taxi, his eyes dancing with excitement. A guard hands him his bag, bows slightly, and closes the door.

"Let's go," Shaun says and the cab driver pulls away.

Confused, I lower my voice. "I thought you were busted, Shaun."

"That was incredible," he tells Mom and me. "The woman guard, she pulls me to the side and asks, 'Do you have Bibles?' I quietly ask God what to do, because it's obviously stupid to say yes and also against my principles to say no. That would be lying. Instead, I start praying in my spiritual language."

"What'd the guard do?"

"She starts talking back in her language. She gestures to these other guards, they come over, and they join in like we're all having a conversation. The woman looks at me and says in English, 'This is amazing. I never hear American speak such perfect Chinese.' She tells the guards to carry my luggage out for me. I felt like a celebrity."

My mouth drops. "Shaun, that's rad."

"Purple Turkey Legs," he says, our silly acronym for PTL: *Praise the Lord.*

As kids, it was usually my sister and I who got our mouths washed out with soap. Yes, I may know the difference between Dial and Zest, but I'm also fairly good at discerning between truth and lies, between spiritual counterfeits and the real thing. My brother has never been a liar—if anything, his blunt honesty gets him in trouble—so I have no reason to question his story.

Lord, forgive me for doubting you.

"It's just like in the Bible," Mom notes. "In Acts, the disciples began speaking in a spiritual language, and the people around them heard the words in their own tongue."

Shaun shrugs. "All I know is, somehow God spoke through me."

Our cab takes us into a countryside bordered by shanties and terraced rice patties. We sideswipe bicycles, swerve around trucks, and send chickens fluttering.

~ ~ ~

Two nights before our return to the States, we visit Hang Fook Camp. Begun decades earlier by a British woman, Ms. Jackie Pullinger, this ministry helps opium addicts get clean and rehabilitate. We spend the evening doing kitchen duties. The next morning, we gather outside for Sunday service beneath a corrugated tin roof.

Worries fill my head. When I get back to the States, how will I pay for classes at LIFE? Heidi expects me to join her, but maybe our timing is off. Do I even belong there?

A female vocalist leads the worship, accompanied by a Hong Kong Chinese man on guitar. I sing along with the choruses I know, then watch Ms. Pullinger step to the mic. A staid and stolid person, she rarely raises her voice. She's heard it all from users and abusers. As a single woman in a culture other than her own, she has certainly earned my respect. She's done what few men would dare attempt.

She speaks to the crowd for a few minutes, then invites us all to stand. "Those who want prayer today, please raise your hands."

I raise mine.

"Now turn and minister to those around you."

Those nearest me pivot away and give their attention to others, leaving me on my own between the rows of chairs. Rejection whispers in my ear. My dad's left us and lost interest in the things of God. Perhaps my heavenly Father has also lost interest in me. I'm a box of broken pieces, full of depression, lust, and pride.

Ms. Pullinger points my direction. "Someone needs to pray for this young man. He is being anointed for service."

My ears perk up. I haven't even told her of my Bible college intentions. Faith surges through me, a reassurance things will all work out back in LA.

As hands settle on my shoulders, Ms. Pullinger speaks directly to me. "The Lord will lead you in directions you cannot imagine. Stay strong. You think you'll be with the people you know, but many times you'll be on your own and out in the cold."

I swallow hard. Okay, God, I surrender to your will.

Over the murmurs of prayer, Ms. Pullinger adds one more sentence which triggers a past frustration. "Someone move the chairs from behind him."

Now wait a sec. I know where this is headed.

Even as one hand rests on my chest and another on my forehead, I vow to stay standing no matter what. I believe in God's power but I am not about to be pressured or manipulated. If someone pushes, I will push back. Hard. As though sensing my resistance, the hands ease away from my head and chest.

I close my eyes.

If it's you, God, have your way. Otherwise, I'm done here.

The moment these words pass through my mind, my left leg starts shaking.

Oh, boy. There isn't any hot wind or physical shove, just a simple recognition of God's presence and power being greater than my own. I let myself fall. Someone lays me back gently on cool concrete. Peace blows over me with all the ease of a river breeze. My heart slows, each beat a steady pulse along my arms and through my legs.

What I guess is someone's hand slips under my head, cushioning it from the hard floor. Heat rises from the flat palm through my skull, tingling in my hair and down along my forehead to lips which go numb. I think of the vision in Isaiah 6:7: "And he touched my mouth and said: 'Behold, this has touched your lips; your guilt is taken away...'"

Peace swells through my chest, and I feel as though I will float off.

I am loved by Father God. I am not doomed to repeat my dad's mistakes, and neither is he forever condemned by them. If only he could be free of his heartache and pain. I wish he could experience this heat, this overwhelming peace, radiating up through my head. Despite the past year's uncertainties, I love my dad so deeply it hurts.

Five minutes pass, or twenty. Not sure.

I've never felt this relaxed. Who would want to leave this all-loving, all-forgiving Presence? This is goodness and light. It envelops me and I breathe it in.

A finger presses against my hip. I peek through tear-drenched lashes. No one is beside me, yet the pressure lingers, firm and undeniable. Instantly, I recall the story of Jacob, who wrestled all night with an angel only to discover he had wrestled with God. My whole life I've dealt with questions and doubts. Jacob, too, struggled, yet prevailed. His resulting limp was proof of his divine encounter.

Lord, you know how I wrestle with you. And you know it's from my sincere desire for the real thing. Nothing else will do.

Touched lips. My guilt taken away.

Pressure on my hip. Proof of prevailing.

At last I sit up. The gathering has dispersed and there's nothing holding me here, no sense of being taken over nor being out of control. Throughout, my free will has been intact, yet in surrendering I've found a will far brighter and purer than my own.

Whose hand, I wonder, was holding my head all this time? I sure felt power flowing through it, and I turn to offer my thanks to the person responsible.

But no one is there.

Instead, where my head has been, a Bible rests flat on the concrete.

66

Heidi

I awaken one morning with a jolt. Everything around me is shaking, and my college roommate yells for me to get out of bed and into a doorway. As soon as I do, a picture falls and lands where I had been lying. "It's like a roller coaster," I quip.

This is my first earthquake, though not my last. Welcome to California.

When it hits, Eric is in early morning class, able to attend school after I surprised him by covering his first semester dorm fees. Tim Johnson is also enrolled at LIFE. My brother later describes to me the quake's train-like roar, the lights swinging down from the ceiling, and the students cowering under their desks and in the doorways.

The 1987 Whittier Narrows Earthquake reveals an unknown fault line. The epicenter of the 5.9 quake is less than twenty miles from us. Eight people lose their lives. Hundreds are injured. Aftershocks continue for days, eerie ripples beneath our feet.

We call Dad just to hear his voice. He's distracted by his life with Anna, but we want to let him know we are safe.

Last year in Eugene, our family was at ground zero of a church scandal which rocked our community. The damage is hard to calculate, still rippling outward. Thankfully, it's nothing on the scale of this year's Jim and Tammy Faye Bakker fiasco, which makes international headlines. I respect my dad for not going and starting up another ministry—or even worse, a cult—in search of adulation.

My brothers and I relate to the Bakkers' son and daughter. We are reminded we are not alone and there are others with much larger troubles. We cannot let these tremors shake us apart. We must salvage what we can of our Wilson heritage. Eric and I are united in our purpose at LIFE to go deeper in our knowledge of God and His Word, learning better ways to assist people trapped in addiction and shame.

We have a destiny, just as we sang during the 1984 Olympics.

While we may not be able to control or predict the earth's shaking, we can run into doorways and avoid falling objects. What we hold onto is up to us.

~ ~ ~

According to student lore, the LIFE in LIFE Bible College stands for Living in Financial Embarrassment. Or LIFE Bridal College. Or Wife Bible College.

No, thank you. None of those appeal to me.

My trust in men isn't very high at the moment, so I see any reference to marriage as a diversion from my real purpose here. I certainly wouldn't come to Southern California to find the man of my dreams, except for make-believe in a movie. I'm used to guys from the Pacific Northwest. I want someone who will be loyal and honest and put Jesus above everything else.

When Eric and I arrived a few weeks ago at the dorms, the place was empty. We needed help hauling my stuff up the stairs, including a heavy dresser which once belonged to Granny, and we enlisted the help of the first person we found.

His name was Matthew Messner.

Since I'm a verbal processor, I asked all kinds of questions. Matt let me know he was also an incoming student from Oregon. He grew up in a small coastal town where fishing was a major part of his childhood. He ran for Track City Track Club and was the high-school state champion in cross country. In fact, he would soon be starting and coaching a team here at LIFE.

As the months go by, Matt and I form a friendship. He works at UPS and refers me to an open customer service position. Soon, we are carpooling to work and splitting gas costs with a few of our fellow students.

During an outreach to Mexico in early 1988, Matt's leadership and his love for God really get my attention. I'm twenty now, old enough to see Matt is unlike any of the guys I've known before. He is driven but not pushy, confident but not arrogant.

When he asks me to a school banquet, I hesitate. Am I ready to trust?

One chance, I decide. I'll give him one chance.

Soon we are officially dating.

~ ~ ~

Eric

Sexual scenarios from my boyhood coming roaring back to mind in a Bible college van full of basketball players.

I have no delusions being here at LIFE. Christians deal with the same struggles as everyone else. Kids at Eugene Christian and Christ's Center simply learned to hide their issues, use the accepted lingo, and wear the right masks.

There are many things I enjoy at this college. My thinking has been stretched, thanks to some excellent professors in hermeneutics, homiletics, and eschatology. One teacher has challenged me to develop my writing skills so I've joined the school newspaper staff, and when I'm not writing term papers or editing articles, I play beach volleyball in the courtyard and pull pranks on my roommates.

I also earn a spot on the LIFE basketball team.

"Why didn't you make the pass?" my coach yells at me during practice.

"Didn't see him, Coach."

"Really? He went through the key waving his arms like a hula dancer."

Turns out I'm almost legally blind. I haven't been to a doctor of any kind in ages, but a trip to LensCrafters provides me prescription contacts and a whole new perspective. My mom tells me I've now placed my trust in man instead of God. All I know is, I can see details and nuances of color I never knew existed. No more squinting to read the chalkboard in class or the road signs on the freeway.

Unfortunately, contacts don't provide me a cautionary view into the future.

Our b-ball team is on a road trip to Arizona. I'm on the middle bench seat, massaging a sore hamstring through my jeans, when one player pulls a coat over my head from behind and a second player yanks my legs up.

"Violate him, violate him," someone yells.

A third player turns from the passenger seat, bearing a whisk broom we use to sweep out the van, and jabs the handle repeatedly at my butt.

It all happens in seconds, a little manhandling from my teammates.

The moment the coat loosens from my head, I turn, ball my fist, and drive a punch as hard as I can into the groin of the guy behind me. He howls in pain and the others tell me to calm down, stop acting psycho.

Memories of prepubescent fumbling come to mind.

Mutual curiosity. Furtive experimentation.

This is entirely different, done in jest, but there's nothing comical to me about a same-sex rape scenario. It unleashes in me an intense care for the bullied and abused. No one should suffer humiliation at the hands of others. Thankfully, the enablers of this behavior won't stick around the college for long, but I know I'll do everything I can to stand up for others, even if nobody here in this van has the nerve to do so now.

More than ever, I desire a wife to have and to hold, someone with whom to share physical and emotional intimacy in all the ways I dream about. I've traveled in over three dozen countries on four continents. The world grows smaller by the day, more connected. Someday, I hope to share these travels and connections with the woman I love. The thought of committing to marriage terrifies me, though.

"You've had a different background from your father," Mom tells me. "You'll be fine. And when the time is right, you'll find her."

"What if I don't? What if I miss her?"

"Honey, without faith it is impossible to please God."

"I do have faith. I'm just not sure if a wife is the right thing for me."

"And what about your contacts? Does Jesus want you wearing those? By letting your faith waver, Eric, you've hindered Him from being able to heal."

Since Dad's departure, Mom's religious viewpoints have crystallized. When we first moved down to LA, she hoped certain leaders would step in to help her and our dad with their marital woes. Those leaders stonewalled her, and she has now set herself on a path with only room for her and Jesus.

"Do you believe He still heals today?" She leans in, inches from my face.

"Sure, Mom. I mean, of course."

"Then don't you think you should give Him a chance to do so?"

She's my mother, my spiritual mentor. Out of sincere love for her, I honor her wishes. Jesus made blind eyes see. He can do the same for me. I squeeze a contact from my left eye, from my right, then toss them and my other pairs into the trash.

Mom nudges my arm. "I'm so proud of you, honey."

The room behind her, the clock on the wall, all of it swims out of focus.

~ ~ ~

Shaun

Eric, Heidi, and I drive five hours north to see our dad on Easter before heading another hour east to Grandpa and Grandma Guise's house. Dad takes us out to breakfast, puts on his cheery voice, calls me buddy as though nothing's changed. We try to limit our verbal jabs over waffles and tell him about our daily routines. He listens. We hand him a card signed by all of us, which he props on the table next to the syrup.

Whenever we're together, his life advice sounds so good, so wise. Later, I second-guess. Should I do as he suggests? Or reject every word?

"Daddy, be honest," Heidi says with heartfelt concern. "How're you doing?"

"Been better. It's rough at the moment. Anna, well, she has her own ideas about things. You know, she's never lived on her own before."

"She barely graduated before you guys skipped town," I point out.

"True, true. Being the hopeless romantic, I thought love would conquer all. Listen, she's *incredibly* intelligent and so much more responsive than your mother ever was. In the bedroom, at least, we have *absolutely* no problems. She—"

"Dad." Eric pushes back in his seat. "You're still legally married."

"If I know Anna," Heidi says, "she's probably longing for her independence."

"Your mom was only seventeen when I married her."

"They're very different people. Mom helped raise her brothers, make meals, clean the house. She went through finishing school. Independence wasn't something women saw as an option back then."

Being the only girl, Heidi has our dad's ear in a way my brother and I don't. We polish off our bacon and hash browns while letting her do her thing. At least we get a free breakfast out of the deal. I figure it's the closest to child support I'll ever see. Will things ever be the same again? Will our family ever go back to normal?

My big brother's the writer, but I start a journal, giving shape to my thoughts.

> The stream left the river—
> > and went away...
>
> Lord—
> > help that little stream,
> > watch it each day.
> > Lead it back to the river.
> > Impassioned, I pray...

Truth is, I feel abandoned again. Eric and Heidi are hanging out at LIFE while I'm stuck with my mom in a one-room bungalow behind someone's house. Each year of my high-school experience has been in a different city, and now my senior year will end with my graduation from Burbank High.

Burbank is a wealthier area than I'm used to, tucked up against the San Gabriel Mountains. I don't exactly fit in at the school. I'm outspoken about my faith, living with a soon-to-be-divorced mom who has no job resume or formal education. I ride city buses to work in the Church on the Way bookstore. Great for discounts on music. Not so great for buying a car or the latest designer jeans.

I rely on Eric's strategy: Be cool by not caring what others think. And it works.

I befriend a kid named Tony, a tall, refined Italian who is a regular on TV's *Cagney & Lacey*. He plays Lacey's son. He also goes to Church on the Way where we bump into other celebrities, such as Lisa Whelchel, the stuck-up girl from *The Facts of Life*. She's actually sweet and petite, making me feel tall.

I go to parties with Tony, catching rides in his Mercedes convertible and rubbing shoulders with TV and film stars. Seems cool at first, then I notice they're all insecure people just trying to impress each other. Okay, so what do I have to lose? Despite avoiding auditions for years, I decide to try out at Burbank High.

Everyone seems shocked when I get the main role of Danny Zuko in *Grease*. The director says I'm perfect for it, except they'll need to recast the girl playing Sandy since the original girl towers over me.

As rehearsals progress, I change some lines and weed out the cussing. I'm trying to keep things clean. I also refuse to lip-lock with my costar. The cast mocks me for this, but the director works with me. At one point, I'm supposed to push my costar up against the car and make out. Instead, we choreograph a fall into the backseat that takes us out of the audience's view. Stagehands shake the car to give the impression we are getting busy, when really we're quietly chuckling.

The production is a hit, every show sold out. Around campus and town, people call out to me: "Hey, Danny, great job." Talent scouts come courting. One of the female cast members, a lithe dancer, asks if I want to move to New York City with her but I turn it down. Tony's agent says he can cast me in a sitcom.

"Nope," I tell him. "I'm going to be a missionary, not an actor."

Class of 1988. Burbank High. I graduate with a round-the-world airline ticket in my pocket, ready to sing and preach to all nations. I want to go live my life.

As for my brother, he's putting his energy into Bible college while his dreams of writing for New York take a back seat. My sister is also focused on LIFE, forsaking her Hollywood goals. All three of us are setting aside childhood dreams to prove ourselves through ministry.

~ ~ ~

Are we attempting to compensate for our father's sins?

I don't think so.

He's made his mistakes, but who hasn't? We all get things wrong.

Take my tooth-pulling incident, for example. I almost do something irreversible when one of my back molars starts to hurt. I have no medical insurance, no real experience with dentists, and I figure why not just pull the stupid thing myself and save some money, while also proving my pain tolerance in case I'm ever tortured for my beliefs.

With a pair of channel locks fixed around the tooth, I start to yank.

It doesn't move.

I squeeze tighter and twist. Though I can't get the molar out, relieving the pressure does seem to help. It actually feels better. The moment I stop tugging, the agony returns. What's going on? If it's rotten, shouldn't it crack or loosen?

As much as Eric, Heidi, and I pride ourselves on toughing things out, the whole operation seems suddenly like a bad idea. When I cave in and make an appointment with a dentist, she pokes at each molar with a sharp instrument until she identifies the dead and decaying culprit—the wisdom tooth behind the one I'd clamped within my channel locks.

I almost yanked the wrong tooth.

Genius.

Dad and Mom, they've taught us a lot of good stuff. Sure, they've done things we don't understand, but we want to live out those positive lessons instead of getting sidetracked by the junk. No more messing around. We've seen up close—closer than we ever imagined—how actions have serious consequences.

We just want to get it right, that's all.

67

Eric

I try to sleep, curled in the corner of a tile floor in the bustling Hong Kong airport. Good luck. It's impossible to block out the intercom, fluorescent lights, multiple spoken languages, and squeaky luggage wheels.

As usual, I am traveling on a shoestring budget. I've worked at the Los Angeles Rescue Mission, finished my freshman year of college, and hopped a plane back to Hong Kong with plans of once again delivering Bibles into China. It is early July 1988. This trip will lead to some encounters unlike any I've ever experienced.

I am exhausted after last night's flight. Where are Mom and Shaun? They're nearly two months into their round-the-world trip and coming from Seoul to meet me.

Delayed, says the arrivals board.

I nibble on the peanuts I pocketed in-flight. My mom and brother don't yet know I've been seeing a girl from Church on the Way—the first I've opened my heart to since Morgan—or that I've been youth-pastoring at a small local church. Mostly, I'm eager to hear all about their experiences. For Mom, the trip has been a chance to find her footing in a world without Dad. For Shaun, it's been a rite of passage.

When they arrive thirty hours later, I welcome them with a bear hug. The smells of *bulgogi* and *kimchi* cling to their clothes and I want to hear all their stories. Mom grins and brushes static out of her long hair. Shaun squeezes my arms, taking measure. I'm tall and lanky, while he's filled out into a man.

"You would've loved it in South Korea," Shaun says. "Mom did a great service at a church there, then I went to a bathhouse before we headed up Prayer Mountain."

"Shaun, honey, tell him what you did. It was beautiful."

He shrugs. "I sang 'When God Ran.' Always makes me think of Daddy."

The mention of our dad causes us all to fall silent for a moment.

"Who's ready to do some smuggling?" I say. "Bet our leaders at Open Doors are just waiting for their mules to arrive."

~ ~ ~

Shaun

For the next three weeks, my mom and I venture in and out of the mainland with Eric, Tim Johnson, and one of their beloved but zany college friends. We cart boatloads of literature to some of the Chinese Christians who number in the millions.

Then my brother and I are called into the Open Doors office.

"You two, very hard workers. Special assignment for you." Our leaders are some of the most precious people I've ever met. If they say jump, I'll say how high. "Eric, you go to Beijing, see Great Wall, take thousands of Bibles on train. Shaun, you short. You wear blue Mao cap like Chinese. You go with small team into North Korea, take Bibles to Christians there. Top secret. Very dangerous."

My big brother and I smile and ask, "When do we leave?"

The evening before heading separate ways, Eric and I realize we won't see each other again till next year when Mom and I complete our global trek. Assuming I make it safely in and out of North Korea.

Worst case scenario? Prison in Pyongyang.

Depressed at the thought of being apart, Eric and I attend an evening Bible study, then grab lychee fruit Slurpees at a 7-Eleven and ride a double-decker tram around Hong Kong. Nights are nice here, warm and muggy, alive with neon and color. Streets are packed with tourists, students, and shopkeepers in sweaty tank tops and flip-flops.

The tram jerks to a stop. Passengers rush to the passenger-side windows.

Eric and I peer over heads and notice pedestrians, bikes, taxis, buses all spilling into a five-way intersection. Nothing unusual. Why all the commotion?

"Look," my brother says. "A fight."

I see two Chinese men face off with bamboo poles in the middle of the intersection. They feint and thrust, managing to get in a few blows. One man's pole clatters from his hands and he is struck down. He curls and covers his head.

Sucks to be the loser.

The beating continues—*thwack, thwack, thwack*—then another man jumps in, picks up the fallen bamboo pole, and joins in. Two on one? Hang on now, that's not fair. My brother and I have agreed to never put up with bullies again. This hero-rescuer complex is one of the good things we have learned from our dad.

"Eric, you want to do something?"

"Definitely."

We don't formulate a plan. There is no time. We push through the jam-packed tram, land on the pavement, squeeze through the throng, Bibles still in hand from the study. We set them down at the fringe where spectators gasp as the downed man spills blood. He is no longer protecting himself despite the blows raining down.

I veer left. Eric veers right.

What if these guys have knives? Are we trying to break up a triad gang fight?

In one fluid motion, I accelerate from behind and throw my arms around the first attacker, lifting his body off the ground. To my right, Eric locks the other attacker in a full nelson and rears back, giving him no angle for traction or escape. We knock the bamboo from their hands and kick the poles away. Thousands watch and wait, probably expecting a knockdown brawl between all four of us, but the attackers give no resistance. Everything seems to go quiet.

Have we stumbled onto a movie set? I wait for a director to yell cut.

Instead, the fallen man rises slowly and stumbles off down an alleyway.

Good for him. Live to fight another day.

How about us? Do these men carry weapons? Are they martial arts experts? To our surprise, they remain limp in our arms. They have no idea who we are or where we came from, and neither of them wants to lose face, a big part of their culture.

"Everything cool?" I say. "Are we okay?"

Both men nod. Braced for anything, Eric and I release them and watch them scuttle off. They don't even look back. Pumped full of adrenaline, we retrieve our Bibles. We haven't taken two steps when, for the first time in all our travels through Hong Kong, the crowds part before us. It's crazy. They do nothing but nod as we pass by.

I grin at my brother. "Way to go, Batman."

"Way to go, Robin," he says.

~ ~ ~

I survive my one night in North Korea, my heart pounding after an illegal entry on the Yalu River and a clandestine rendezvous in a small village. I never learn the elderly woman's name, and in the shadows of a courtyard I barely see her face. Her form looks smaller than the huge pack of Korean Bibles I heave off my shoulders.

Mission accomplished.

My mom and I continue on to Thailand, rich in beauty and history, to Sri Lanka, full of miracles amid machetes and violence, and to India, my old stomping grounds.

The images come bubbling up from my four-year-old memory.

Funeral pyres. Scorpions and toads. Chapatis and sweet hot chai.

I go to the Domes in Ajmer and reconnect with Vikay Peter. He never does learn about the bird which revived after he swatted it down outdoors. I visit the foothills of Mussoorie and connect with a precious family doing faithful Christian work in this land.

Mom and I spend a few days in Calcutta, resting in one of the offices at a missionary hospital. As impressive as I find this ministry, I am malnourished and grumpy. Mom and are on each other's nerves. I take a walk and stumble upon a gate with *Missionaries of Charity* spelled out above, a ministry founded decades ago by Mother Teresa. I've always been impressed by her work with the sick and the poor.

I knock on the door. A panel opens.

"How can I be assisting you?" an Indian woman says.

"I have a few hours," I answer. "If you need help, I'll do anything you ask."

She tells me to wait one minute and closes the panel. A short time later, the door creaks open and Mother Teresa stands before me. She is hunched and wrinkled, not even five feet tall, adorned in a blue and white headdress, sari, and sandals.

I introduce myself and tell her I am at her mercy. She explains the work she and the nuns do here. If I want to work, yes, I can follow along. She leads me into the compound, turns left up concrete steps to the second floor. Using rags and spray bottles, we labor side by side for the afternoon, scrubbing metal-framed cribs which will be used for infants and orphans. She talks as we clean, her voice steady and quiet.

Normally I have lots to say, lots of opinions. In this woman's presence, all I do is listen. Every sentence out of her mouth seems cloaked in hard-earned wisdom. As surreal as the moment seems, it feels earthy and solid. This is real love in action.

Mother Teresa speaks of the value of every child, all of them precious in God's sight, none of them deserving a lonely, heartless death. The love of God is her main focus. God gives us the courage, she explains, to love with our hearts and our hands.

"I touch the living body of Christ," she says, "as I love the hurting and dying."

When I return to the hospital office, Mom looks up from the couch. She's been an incredible, sacrificial mother through most of my childhood. Two years ago, by her own admission, she suffered a breakdown and is now doing all she can to hang on. Meanwhile, she lives out of a suitcase and travels the world to share Jesus' love.

Who am I to hold onto my frustrations with her? Best to let them go.

~ ~ ~

Next stop? Israel. At the airport in Tel Aviv, a customs official stamps my passport and lets me through. I love the simple lifestyle here, the kibbutz-grown fruits and vegetables. Unfortunately, friction heats up again between my mom and me when she tells the friends with whom we're staying that her husband is a pastor on sabbatical.

"That's a lie," I challenge her in private.

"Oh, honey." She hugs her Bible and waves me off. Her Catholic guilt then kicks in, and she says, as though committing to be a nun, "Jesus is my husband now."

With nothing left to say, I spill words across the pages of my journal.

> *Anywhere is home—when I'm with my brother.*
> *Anywhere is home—when I'm with my best friend.*
> *When I'm with my father—anywhere is home.*
> *I'm home to stay*
> *with those who are able*
> *to cast away my cares*

As they say:
"It's not what's on the table;
it's what's in the chairs..."

Trying to create a nice memory together, Mom and I visit Bethlehem at Christmas. What better place, right? Snow lies on the shepherd's hills. Stars twinkle overhead. It is freezing cold, though, and we have no money, no place to lay our heads. Our room in the proverbial inn is a space at the end of a hallway in a local hotel. We huddle by a heater vent and try to catch some sleep while hoping we're not booted out.

I wish we were a family of five again, but there are no miracles this Christmas.

"Mom," I mutter, "would you even want Daddy back?"

"He's the only man I've ever loved. He is sooo handsome and smart. Of course, I would. Beneath it all, Shaun, your dad's just a hurting little boy. I don't think I've ever told you the things he went through as a child..."

Undone

Oakland, California — 1949-1968

Born prematurely, Mark Wilson never bonded with his mother and realized as he grew older that she had little interest in physical or emotional connection.

She never told him she loved him. Never once hugged or kissed him.

Forty-five years later, her second son, Paul, would march into her hospital room and demand those two things from her before she died: an *I love you* and a hug. She gave him both. When Mark came in and mentioned what Paul had done, his mother also told him she loved him but didn't reach out her arms.

The next day, she was gone.

Rita—known as Grandma Rita to Eric, Heidi, and Shaun—had been a single, solitary child. She was an idealist, an intellectual. She dreamed of being a traveler, a citizen of the world. Motherhood was of no real interest to her, but as a Catholic woman, what was she to do when her husband expressed his sexual needs? The pope strictly prohibited birth control.

Soon, three boys were underfoot with a daughter and son still on the way. Rita did not fit the 1950s image of a doting, dutiful housewife. All she really wanted were a few hours of peace and quiet. Her one concession was to cook nutritious morning meals for her brood. Once breakfast was over, she situated herself at her card table, poured a snifter of golden liquor, and set out a game of solitaire. She smoked unfiltered Camels between the laying out of her cards.

"Go play on the freeway," she told her kids. "Don't come back till dinner."

Mark, Paul, and Dave rode bikes and climbed trees, shot cap guns and taunted cats and dogs. Some older girls in the neighborhood convinced them to play strip poker with them, then won handily and made fun of their flaccid penises. A teen boy down the street showed Mark what it looked like to masturbate beside a row of bushes. His organ was not so flaccid.

The three Evans brothers, the real terrors of the neighborhood, lived right next door. They were older and bigger than the Wilsons. Around the block, a story was told of them laughing at their own mother, in a wheelchair with MS, as she lost control on their front steps and tumbled to the ground.

The Evans brothers used candy as bait to feed their sadistic desires, and four-year-old Paul, with his sweet tooth, was the first to fall victim.

"You want it? Fine," they said to him. "But first you have to crawl in here."

They shoved him into a built-in storage bin and locked him in the dark. He pounded on the lid until they finally let him out. Slapping their knees and laughing, they claimed it was all just for fun.

"Here you go, Paul. Here's your candy."

Over time, they ratcheted up their antics until they had Paul naked and tied to the plum tree alongside their house. They pummeled him with fallen fruit and taunted him as a car passed by. The driver either didn't see or didn't report it.

Six-year-old Mark was also invited over to play. The Evans boys shoved him down in the backyard, got his pants undone, and shoved objects into his anus. He flinched and tried not to cry. Petrified, he wondered why anyone would be so cruel.

What could he do, though?

Tattle to his parents? Call the cops?

Nobody would believe him, and these weren't the things adults discussed out loud, certainly not in the era of *Howdy Doody* and *The Roy Rogers Show*.

Confused and humiliated, Mark was nonetheless intrigued by the older poker girls and the teen boy at the bushes. Sexuality had a power which to him seemed irresistible, a cheap yet thrilling substitute for the intimacy his young life lacked.

~ ~ ~

If Rita was the distant mother, Alan—known as Gramps to Eric, Heidi, and Shaun—was the father who relied on psychological torment and unusual discipline to keep his offspring in line. When Mark once forgot to clean his room, he arrived home from school to find his bedding, toys, and clothes piled on the front lawn. When Mark and his siblings got too out of hand one year, their father canceled Christmas entirely.

Raised by Granny, Alan was a short-tempered, agnostic, liberal professor. His children were a constant source of annoyance, and he used the power of story to divert their unruly energy. He read regularly to them before bed, sharing *Aesop's Fables*, *Treasure Island*, *The Wizard of Oz*, and the hilarity of *Helen's Babies*.

When Mark was eight, Alan moved his wife, three sons, and infant daughter down to Mexico for a teaching sabbatical.

In the Jalisco region, in the town of Chapala, Mark went through a cowboy phase triggered by popular TV shows such as *Davy Crockett* and *Rawhide*. He sported chaps, spurs, and a plastic revolver. A toy whip completed the outfit. He practiced cracking the whip against the slatted fence to impress the Mexican kids next door. The seven-foot tail snaked through the slats and caught one of the boys, whose dancing around stirred swirls of dust and whose cries caught the parents' attention.

After Mark's father gathered the facts, he told his son to go to the garden shed and take off everything. Mark sulked in the dark confines. It was hot in here. He edged away from the woodpile by the wall, fearful of lurking scorpions. He removed his clothes, as ordered, and wondered what was next.

His father appeared with whip in hand. "No, Mark, I said everything." He slammed the shed door shut, his waiting shadow still visible at the threshold.

Shaking, Mark peeled off his underwear, then his socks. Tears and dust pricked at his eyes. He hadn't meant to hurt anyone. It was an accident.

"Much better," his father said. "Your turn to experience the whip."

As Mark darted about the enclosure, his father aimed that plastic tail at his exposed backside. Mark did all he could to avoid the whip's stings as well as those of any creatures which might be skittering around in the dirt.

~ ~ ~

Back in California, Rita now had five children. Once a week she dropped off Mark, Paul, David, Laura, and John for Catholic mass so she could enjoy her cards, Camels, and alcohol. In St. Bernard Church, Mark saw statues of the mother of God and heard references to a heavenly Father, though neither meant much to him as a teen who was just discovering the Beatles.

Mothers brought you into this world and fed you. That was it.

And fathers were unpredictable, even scary at times.

How could he put faith in a God whose nature was revealed through such flawed examples? No, Mark decided, he would be better off looking elsewhere.

Then he heard the story of the prodigal.

And of the Father who opened His arms. The God who ran to him.

68

Heidi

"Thanks for driving down, Daddy. I wanted you to see my new apartment."

He sets a cool, damp washcloth on my forehead. "Honey, you're *burning up.*"

"That helps. Thank you."

As much as I want to throw my arms around him, I'm in bed with a fever and feeling sick to my stomach. I was fine last night. Maybe my symptoms are more spiritual or psychological, considering this is my dad's first visit since I started at LIFE.

Dad grins. "Guess who I met pushing your laundry down the hill in a shopping cart. Says a lot about the guy. Matt seems like one of the good ones."

"I'll get my own washer and dryer soon. That's the plan, anyway."

"What do you need now, Heidi? You want some 7-Up or Saltines?"

"After all that's gone on these past few months, it's just nice to have you here. I know this isn't a great time for you either."

Dad's eyes darken beneath thick brows. He and Anna have recently separated. He made his choices and blew up his old life to escape—his words, not mine—and now his new life is also gone. I'd rather have him here with me than moping all alone.

"Still lots to process, Heidi. Why don't you tell me about your court case?"

He's followed my recent turmoil over the phone—thousands of dollars stolen from me by a roommate, a $10,000 court decision in my favor, and her failure to pay even $100 before skipping the state.

"You know, Daddy, the most frustrating part is they knew she was a kleptomaniac and let us room in the dorms together without warning me. She was the senior class treasurer, if you can believe that. Talk about a master of deception."

"Here, Heidi, lay back down." Dad props my pillow under my head. "Honestly, most organizations, even religious ones, are *horrible* at taking responsibility. There's so much at stake. It's often easier to sweep it all under the rug." His voice catches.

Is this a moment of confession for him?

"We all live and learn," he adds softly. "And just hope our kids will get it right."

"I'm trying, Daddy. Eric and Shaun are too. You know, Eric's coming by later."

"Excellent. Any word from Mom and Shaun?"

"Still in Israel, I think. I have a package from them at the post office."

"You'll get it right, Heidi." Dad gazes down at me. "I don't have any doubt."

"Being a girl doesn't make things any easier. It was a woman who started the college, and they teach that God's Spirit and His gifts are poured out on all people, but where do I see those examples? Name one or two female leaders or black pastors from our school. Don't get me wrong. Women can run children's ministries, do administrative work, or lead worship—sure, no problem—but where are the ones teaching and leading churches like we saw growing up around the world?"

"*Preach* it, Mama Bear. What are you now, twenty?"

"Twenty-one in six weeks."

"Remember, sweetie, you've seen and experienced more than many people do in a *lifetime*. We did our best with you kids. Your mom, she was willing to go all over the world with the three of you, never complaining, never fearful. A *truly* unique woman. All the stuff between her and me, I'm ninety percent at fault. I know that."

"It's not about who's at fault." I shift the cloth on my head. "Jesus turned all that guilt and religious ritual upside down. We aren't saved by our good deeds or sent to hell for our bad ones. You taught me that when I was a little girl."

He nods.

"It's His grace and His blood which cleanse us," I add.

"Mm-hmm, mm-hmm."

"Daddy, I don't condemn you. Jesus' mercy gives us the freedom to love and serve others. It's not supposed to be a job, the way it ended up for you. It should be a joy."

"Appreciate the thoughts. I do, I do. You're a *thinker*, Heidi, and you've carried a lot on those strong shoulders. I'm sorry you've had to deal with so much." He blinks hard and his Adam's apple bobs. "Now, why don't you rest so your body can heal? I'll go help Matt at the laundromat and get to know the guy a little better."

He eases the door shut on his way out.

My dad has carried a lot from his own upbringing. He's given us so much more than he was ever given. I truly want him to be free from the knotted tangles of his past and I don't want to be bound by them either.

~ ~ ~

The package at the post office bears stamps from India. It is a foot wide, a foot tall, and seems like it weighs ten pounds. What have Mom and Shaun sent me from their travels? Some dried spices, perhaps? Old photo albums?

I carry the box back to my apartment. I can almost feel Mommy's presence with me. She has so much love for other people, traversing the globe to tell them about Jesus, even as she carries her own wounds. We're all wounded healers, aren't we? As she once reminded us: '*We have this treasure in earthen vessels...*'

Opening the box on my bed, I find a heavily-taped bag inside. I work to get it loose, then gasp as the contents spill onto my lavender comforter.

"Eric," I stammer into the phone, "you need to come over here now."

When he arrives, I drag him from the front door to my bedroom.

"What is it?" he says.

"It's Mom's hair. I haven't even touched it because at first I thought she must be dead. It's so weird. Here, read the postcard I found at the bottom of the box."

"'Dear Heidi,'" he reads aloud, "'I've had a wonderful time in India. God is doing great things. Remember Vikay Peter? Lots of stories to share when I get back. Sooo many precious people. Things are different now, lots of modern conveniences, even toilet paper! This is my last trip to India. I hear there are places paying for hair in America, so I had Shaun cut it for me. He refused at first, but he did a good job. It's a bob like I had in high school. Please sell this and send me the money. Funds are low. I hope to be back for Easter. I love you so much. Mommy.'"

For nearly as long as we can remember, our mom's long locks have been her signature. There was no mistaking her from behind in a store or a crowd.

Another part of our past is gone. Again, I am letting go.

Eric lifts the thick red braid. "It's like opening an urn of her ashes."

"No wonder it was so heavy. Look, it's almost four feet long."

~ ~ ~

Eric

I see Dad briefly at Heidi's apartment, excited he's come to visit. Afterward, I turn cynical: Oh, so that's how it is? We're the second-best option now that Anna is gone? Of course, he hasn't felt comfortable coming to see me at the college or at the church where I youth pastor. He's done with that part of his life and has no interest in going back.

Meanwhile, I'm trying to live by the standards he instilled in me.

How do I reconcile the bitter and sweet, the bad and the good? My dad's not some corporation I can boycott or some book I can ban. He's the most influential man in my twenty-two years on this planet. When I shave my own patchy stubble in the mornings, I recognize his nose and his jawline in the mirror.

It's now April 1989. A Greyhound bus carries me north to the Bay Area where I'll give this another shot. Stuck near the back, I am reminded by the lingering fumes of our family trek across Europe and Asia sixteen years earlier. The dad from that time period was also skittish and vulnerable, but more affectionate and animated.

He has changed. I have too.

Cut him a little slack, I remind myself.

At the bus station, Dad zips into the parking lot in a blue Mazda RX-7. I want to make some snide remark about middle-aged men and sports cars. Instead, I toss my bag in and ask if he's heard about the new John Cusack film, *Say Anything*.

"You bet, bud. That's one Anna was anxious to see, before we, uh..."

The rawness in his tone lingers. As much as I want to forgive him for leaving Mom, part of me wants him to suffer. He left us kids too, whether or not he sees it this way. I don't carry any grudge against Anna or her family. The

Dales have suffered as much as we have, and Anna's still trying to navigate adulthood herself. Dad's the one who should be the grownup here.

"It's fine," I say. "We can do something else."

"No, no. If you're interested, Eric, let's go. We'll catch a matinee to save some money, since these theater chains, *boy*, they'll screw you for all they can get."

It's opening weekend for *Say Anything*. On the movie poster, John Cusack holds a boom box overhead. When his girlfriend realizes her father is both lying and stealing, she is devastated. This man she's trusted all her life has betrayed her, while the teenage boy she is dating sticks by her through it all.

My throat tightens. I feel her anguish. There are no simple explanations or solutions. Like the girl in the movie, I want to punish my dad for his past mistakes. This is real life, the one he always tried to warn me about. It sucks. It's messy.

Something in me breaks as Dad and I sit together in the dark theater.

Jesus, I want to love him the way you do. Help me to view him the way you do. Even if Dad and I don't see eye to eye, we can still stand side by side. Even if we don't agree on everything, we can agree we love each other. Lord, I don't want to fall into my grandfather's rut of unforgiveness. I don't want the sins of the fathers to follow me. You broke sin's curse on the cross. I'm not involuntarily trapped in some generational cycle. I can walk in freedom. And I don't want to let my dad's mistakes become my own cage.

Arms folded, I feel the heavy thuds of my heartbeat.

Truth is, I just want my dad back. He is my father, a biological fact, the man who overcame his own childhood to show me a better one. He's taught me to care for the underdogs, to put myself in others' shoes, to look deeper than skin color to the heart

Don't go burning bridges, he has warned me. Build them.

Don't expect handouts. Be willing to pay your dues.

Don't throw the first punch. But if attacked, do what you need to do.

And even then, I've been taught to forgive. The moment you lock someone up and throw away the key, you realize you're trapped in there too.

Back in the RX-7, Dad is asking me where we should eat.

"The movie was my call," I say. "You should choose the food."

In a casual bistro, Dad drinks a beer as we wait for our meal. He asks about my next summer trip. Instead of owning a car and making payments like many of my classmates, I've been saving for a school outreach to Serbia and Croatia. Heidi will be there too. Then I'll rendezvous with Mom, Shaun, and Tim Johnson in Amsterdam, and we'll apply for visas to ride through Russia on the Trans-Siberian Express.

Gorbachev and Bush are making peace. Communism is crumbling.

If all goes as planned, we'll take hundreds of Bibles to pass out for free.

"Wow, Eric," Dad exclaims. "You could've *easily* gone off the rails after I left. And who would've blamed you? Yet here you are, still dedicated to what you believe."

On the Greyhound back to LA, I press my temple to the window and feel emotion well in my chest. The sobs come unexpectedly. I don't want to hold onto this anger. I bite my lip and contain the sound, my body quivering in silence as I watch parched earth stretch toward the setting sun.

69

Shaun

"How am I supposed to get to Amsterdam?" I bark at my mom. "You refunded your own part of the airplane ticket to get some money, and now you're using mine."

"Not at all, honey. Please, let me speak with this kind ticket agent."

Gritting my teeth, I step back and stare across the departure hall. We are in Amman, Jordan. I've just come from Cairo, where a Christian friend has death threats hanging over his head.

Before this, Mom traveled to Zimbabwe with a portion of her round-the-world ticket while I stayed for months in Israel and worked at both a *moshav* and a *kibbutz*. Lodging was free, so long as I herded sheep and tilled fields—anything for the Hebrew cause. I'm not old enough to drink in America and I've never acquired the taste for alcohol. When the kibbutz leaders realized this, they put me behind the bar since I wouldn't dip into their inventory, and I served workers from assorted nations.

One hot French girl—whew!—she almost convinced me to leave it all behind.

Talk about trouble.

Now I want nothing more than to see my big brother in Amsterdam. My mom and I aren't getting along. She believes she is on a holy mission. I realize her father, her husband, and many of the men in her life have failed her. I don't want to join the list, but I will lose it if this doesn't stop. I've woken up with her hovering over me, trying to cast demons out of me. I've seen her sneak onto buses and trams without paying.

"God is my provider," she says, flicking her newly bobbed hair.

If so, don't steal someone else's seat. Which is what I catch her doing now.

"It was an error," she tells the ticket agent. "See, it was written *Mr. S. Wilson*, but it was supposed to be *Mrs. Wilson*. If you change it, I can board the flight."

"Wait." I step in. "You're taking my ticket."

"I've always held our tickets, honey. Don't worry."

"That's my ticket. *Mr. S. Wilson*."

Our voices escalate. I've ruined her little ruse to fly out of here.

What does she expect me to do? Hang onto the landing gear as we cross the Mediterranean to Europe?

A squat, olive-skinned, Jordanian airline manager finds the whole thing amusing. He leans back and listens, eyes narrowed, as though determining whom to place his bets on. Well, I'm not backing down here. I've had enough. As much as I love my mom and respect her care for others, I also know something has shifted in her. Something is broken. I'm sure I'm broken too, in ways I don't even realize.

But I refuse to be abandoned here. No, thank you.

"Mom, I am going to see Eric," I declare. "You're not going to stop me."

Eventually, the amused official calls me into his small office. He puts his feet up, listens to my story, then with only his left hand types away at his keyboard and prints out a boarding pass. I'm not about to question his motives or methods. Worried this is some kind of bad joke, I grab my bag, grab my mom's, and snap at her to follow me. We are getting on the next flight to Amsterdam.

I pull out my journal, emotions tight as a fist as I begin to write.

> *My heart beats hard,*
> > *face full of sweat,*
> > *mind pressing forward,*
> > *I'll never forget.*
> *What pain I've traveled,*
> *In just one week,*
> *Truth unraveled and*
> > *I got a peek.*
> *It's hard to take,*
> *Like the blast of a bomb.*
> *My heart aches as I talk to my mom.*
> *This episode—*
> > *I almost broke.*
> > *from all the load,*
> > *my trust was choked.*
> *Self-pity awakens from its nest.*
> *I must be blatant*
> > *and get this off my chest:*
> *My father deserted.*
> *Suicide took John.*
> *Despite all my efforts*
> > *the pain has not gone.*

The journal goes deep into my bag. Someday I'll share these poems with my brother and sister. We all care for each other. We've been through too much to just let go. When we were kids, though, things were simpler. Our steps were ordered for us, and if we argued, we had to hug and make up.

Now each day is full of dangers and unknowns.

And each day offers something new.

It's up to me, the ways I spend my time and the choices I make.

~ ~ ~

In June of 1989, we ride the Trans-Siberian from Budapest, Hungary, through Ukraine into Russia, and over the top of Mongolia. Mom, Eric, Tim, and I are joined by another student and spend nearly two weeks, round-trip, on the noisy, shaky, soot-stained journey of over 20,000 kilometers. Days before we depart, the Tiananmen Square massacre occurs in response to protests in Beijing, and the Chinese we meet on the train still sob in the aisles as they consider the situation awaiting them back home.

Peace is so elusive. Hope is a dangerous word.

Once local passengers find out we have Russian and Ukrainian Bibles, they crowd on the edges of our bunks and plead to have one. *"Biblia? Biblia?"*

We accept no money or gifts. Their huge smiles are reward enough.

"Spasibo," they say. Thank you. Or literally: *God save you.*

For us Wilsons, these renewed world travels are a return to our roots. This is how we started off, our very first memories. Home is wherever we're together. Mom's and my issues can't be resolved right now. Some never will be. I do my best to step around them and still have fun with her when I can. Eric and I have a blast hanging out with Russian soldiers on board and playing a rowdy card game called *Durak*. Younger female train officials give us rings and propose to us, hoping for passage to America.

An entire book could be dedicated to this adventure alone.

~ ~ ~

Eric

In a cowardly move, I end my latest romantic relationship by posting a letter from Amsterdam back to the U.S. Over the years I've had a number of girlfriends, all of them cute, creative, and spiritual, with big hearts for other people. Something new is in the air, though. I sense it. Summer is almost over.

When I get back to LA, I'm happy to see my youth group again and my classmates at LIFE. I'm a junior now, sharing a room with Tim and two other close friends. We're able to shake hands out our window with the girls in the room next door.

One of the girls is an incoming freshman, Carolyn Monaghan.

I pick her up in the courtyard, swing her around—and realize she is no longer a young girl. Her soft brown eyes look into mine. Her full lips part. My hands rest on the curve of her hips. I'm turning twenty-three, she's turning nineteen, and the age difference seems suddenly insignificant. I realize she is available.

Once this thought enters my mind, it scrambles my brains and makes its way to my heart. We share breakfast times in the cafeteria, study together in the stairwell, and soak in the hot tub at an off-campus apartment. Until now, I've been worried my future spouse would judge me by my father's choices, but Carolyn knows my dad and knows me. She lived through many of those choices herself. There's no judgment or fear between us, only shared understanding.

When she asks me to the Sadie Hawkins Banquet, I know I'm in trouble.

The theme is TV characters. We go as Laura and Almanzo—known as Beth and Manly—from *Little House on the Prairie*. Like Beth and Manly, our lives have been threaded together. We first met when she was ten and I was fourteen. She attended NFC, went to Eugene Christian and Christ's Center, lived at the end of Port Street. While I traveled the globe, she was growing up beneath my schnoz.

A 1975 photograph reveals yet another surprise.

The Lashars, Carolyn's foster family, camped with our family during a Faith Center outing at Honeyman State Park, on the Oregon coast. This means Carolyn was four and I was eight the first time we saw each other. How could I be so blind?

"You are blind, Eric," Carolyn notes as I drive her from the dorms to our weekly youth night. "You need to go to an eye doctor. Can you even read the signs?"

"My mom thinks I should trust Jesus to heal me."

"Sure, but until then, you're getting contacts, or else you'll kill someone."

Soon, thank God, I can see again. And the road ahead seems clearer than ever.

~ ~ ~

Shaun

When Dad hears of my conflicts with Mom, he admits his own actions have led to some of her strange behavior. "Listen, bud," he tells me during an international call, "soon as you get back to the States, you're welcome to come live with me. *More* than welcome. I have this big apartment all to myself, even got a nice hot tub downstairs."

I roll my eyes.

Anna is gone and he's lonely. What am I? Yesterday's leftovers?

Whatever his reasons, I decide I don't care. He's my dad and I want to be close to him. He and I have our issues to resolve and now my mom and I do, too. Life is complicated. My parents don't have it all figured out and neither do I.

I love them, though. That hasn't changed. Am I doomed to follow in my dad's footsteps? No, as someone who loves to dance, I don't have to fixate on his missteps. He's taken plenty of steps I am proud to walk in.

One of Dad's early struggles was the idea of a billion souls going to hell without ever hearing about Jesus. I don't take that lightly. Throughout my journeys I have talked with Sikhs, Muslims, Buddhists, Hindus, Brahmins, and plenty of others. They all have their own miracle stories. Does this mean all paths lead to God? Are all world religions using different names for the same almighty being?

Based on some pretty jarring differences, I don't think so.

Maybe, though, there is one true God who is in all and through all—art and music, science and logic. Glimmers of His truth are everywhere. If we seek

Him with heart and mind, He is ready to reveal Himself. Humility, I think, is the key.

He is our father, guiding and directing. Our mother, nurturing.

He's everything my parents tried to be and everything they aren't.

We're all leftovers in some way, aren't we? And God still has a way of concocting something good. If I had to guess, I believe I'll see people in heaven who called themselves Muslims, Mormons, Hindus, Bahá'í, even Americans who believed their truth was correct, despite the scandals and schisms throughout Christendom. And what about all those who died before Jesus came? What about all those born and raised in nations where the name of the Middle Eastern Messiah is unknown?

God refuses to remain hidden. He reveals Himself even through nature so that no one will go without a glimpse of Him. I believe God knows the heart. He sees those who are truly seeking. I imagine a Kalahari bushman staring up at the stars or watching the wonder of childbirth, then opening his heart and mind to something more powerful, more loving than anything he has ever known. He's a man I hope to be friends with in heaven.

~ ~ ~

Heidi

Matt picks up my mom at LAX as she returns from her round-the-world trip. He and I are in premarital counseling, and he wants to take her to dinner so he can share with her our plans for the future.

Will she approve? I pace my apartment alone, anxious about her response.

At a restaurant on Sunset Boulevard, Matt orders a cheese enchilada, and Mom decides on a *chile relleno*. He's heard her travel stories on their way here and now he dives into the story of our courtship. This is a big step for him, meeting her, explaining our feelings for each another. Her head is down. She hasn't eaten more than a few bites. He presses on and at last asks her blessing.

She says nothing, doesn't even move. She has fallen fast asleep.

When Matt tells me about it, I assume jet lag is part of the problem. I also know Mom is uncomfortable discussing marriage, since Dad filed papers while she was overseas and ended theirs. He will always be her husband, she insists, and she could never love another. I worry about her health, though. Something is definitely wrong.

I have long endured my own issues, including sudden fainting spells. My parents never sought medical treatment for me. If we kids were sick, we figured we either didn't have enough faith to be healed or enough money for a doctor visit.

Matt grew up differently and insisted I go to a clinic after I had more fainting incidents and hemorrhaging during my monthly cycles. The diagnosis: anemia and endometriosis. My years of waning energy and chronic pain were quickly remedied.

"I'm worried about my mom," I tell Matt. "She's had similar fainting spells, going all the way back to our days in Turkey."

"Would she agree to get a medical evaluation?"

When I ask her, she dismisses it. "I'm fine. I have Jesus, sweetie."

"But isn't it okay to do some basic maintenance? You trim your hair and your fingernails, don't you? You don't wait for Jesus to step in and do those things."

"Honey, please. Americans are so quick to turn to doctors instead of trusting in the Great Physician."

Childhood guilt rises up. Have I become the typical Westerner who turns to medicine without giving faith a chance? No, I tell myself, God isn't some vending machine who pops out healings if we deposit enough belief and good deeds. He wants me to partner with Him, to rely on His guidance and wisdom.

"Refusing to take care of yourself seems unwise, Mommy."

When she scrunches her mouth and looks away, I want to shake some sense into her. This isn't the vivacious, loving, articulate woman who raised me. Her eyes are puffy, limbs swollen, hair brittle and coarse. She often moves within inches of my face to carry on any conversation. Are her hearing and eyesight failing? Could her thyroid be off? It runs in the family, and some medication might do her good.

Despite these deficiencies—or because of them—Mom is a magnet to misfits and outcasts. She listens earnestly. They feel her sincerity. She is nothing, she tells them, without Jesus, and His love is available to them as well. Many bow with her to pray.

Who am I to judge? She's still my teacher and friend, my mommy.

~ ~ ~

Forgiveness isn't a one-time act but an ongoing decision. Yes, I need to speak truth and set boundaries, but God is my defender, and it has never been my job to punish. He gets the final say. As a child, I saw Daddy and Mommy as perfect, whereas my adult eyes spot their flaws. This doesn't mean I have to reject everything they ever taught me. "Test all things," says I Thessalonians 5:21, "hold fast what is good." Even if my parents said or did only one good thing, that is one thing I can cling to.

Sometimes one thing is enough. One truth can go a long way.

"Daddy," I say over the phone, "Matt and I have set a wedding date."

"*Excellent*, sweetie. I knew he was right for you the moment I met him."

"I used to think you'd be the one performing my ceremony. Since that's not an option, I do have a special request. You can say no, but it's important to me."

70

Heidi

On June 16, 1990, nearly five hundred people gather for back-to-back weddings at Faith Center in Eugene. Matt and I will get married first, Eric and Carolyn second. Many in the sanctuary went to Northwest Faith Center when our dad pastored there, and even four years later I'm not sure how they'll react at the sight of him.

This is my wedding, though, and he will be in it.

Not even up for debate.

Grandpa and Grandma Guise are also present. Grandpa Guise and Daddy haven't been in the same room together in over twenty years and tension fills the air.

"Are you ready?" Daddy smiles at me, eyes glistening. He's grown a beard. He waits for my nod then provides his elbow for support.

Mom is on my other arm.

The two of them have walked me through many of my struggles and today I want them to walk me down the aisle together. I am draped in quality satin, an elegant nod at generations past. Grandma Guise's dress from the 1930s has been updated to the 90s, fashioned with a sweetheart neckline, the fitted bodice laced with small pearls. A Victorian-style hat rests upon my French-rolled hair. A few loose curls caress my face.

Dad whispers, "You know, I conducted dozens and dozens of weddings as a pastor and *never* have I seen a calmer bride."

"What do I have to worry about?" I beam. "I'm marrying my best friend in front of a roomful of people I love."

As Dad and Mom escort me down, the mere presence of my father causes eyes to widen and mouths to drop. A message Matt and I recorded plays through the speakers, thanking our dads and moms for raising and investing in us. I turn to give both sets of parents hugs and kisses. Matt offers hugs and firm handshakes.

Daddy and Mommy settle side by side in the front row.

"I love you," I mouth to them.

"Love you, too, honey." Drops spill down my mom's cheeks.

"Love you, my little princess." My dad's eyes well up again. "Now go do it better than I did."

A moment of peace fills the sanctuary. I'm sure some people are holding onto their grudges and pain. We're here, though, moving on. All I can do is pray for the anguish and pain to melt away, for the healing to begin.

At the piano, Johnny Burke accompanies Shaun, who stands to sing "The Glory of Love." We exchange vows and rings and we're pronounced man and wife. Matt takes me in his strong arms and kisses me with all the passion contained in the song. My history will always be part of me, but I cannot make everything right, and I now leave the wrongs behind, giving up the Wilson name for this man before me.

Our pastor concludes: "I present to you, Matthew and Heidi Messner."

The place erupts with applause. We turn toward a sea of faces, so many who have loved, cared for, and prayed for us. I am who I am because of them. Matt and I have prayed this wedding will provide space for redemption, and I marvel at a God who can bring such beauty from ashes.

Months later, I will even receive a card which is an answer to desperate nine-year-old prayers in my closet beneath our stairs. The card is from Uncle Paul, who has suffered his own losses and heartache. It reads:

I couldn't deny the Spirit at your wedding. Back in the fold...

Matt and I hurry up the steps, aware there's another wedding still to come. This Wilson doubleheader isn't over yet.

~ ~ ~

Shaun

Boy, I made a mess of that. I sang "The Glory of Love," hoping to give the lyrics the feeling Matt and Heidi deserved, but a key change pushed me beyond my range.

Oh, well. Now for Eric and Carolyn's wedding.

I'm a best man, along with Tim Johnson. There are so many people I know in this room. Faces I haven't seen in a long time. Girls I liked. Guys I hung out with. Women who once babysat me, and men who employed me at their job sites.

Today, my big brother and sister are taking these next steps in life.

For now, I will be on my own.

Carolyn enters the sanctuary in an old-fashioned wedding gown. One of Eric's college friends plays "Jessica's Theme," from *The Man from Snowy River*, as Carolyn comes down the aisle on her father's arm.

Mike Monaghan gives her over to my brother, then steps onto the platform in his duties as pastor. I focus on keeping my eyes open and not locking my knees. I don't want to mess this up. Carolyn and Eric sing songs they wrote for each other, then invite the congregation to join them as they recite passages from Song of Solomon:

"'My beloved is dazzling... Your mouth is lovely...'"

Really? Despite my resolve, I catch myself snickering. Good for my brother, but it's all a little too sappy for my taste.

Mike Monaghan then jokes about how he knew Eric when he was two, and how Debbie changed Eric's poopy drawers but never changed her daughter's since she wasn't adopted until age eleven. A few chuckles. Nothing better than diaper jokes at a wedding.

Just hold it together, I remind myself. Keep your legs relaxed.

Then an oppressive silence fills the sanctuary—no rustling paper, no cleared throats. I glance over and see Mike Monaghan, eyes down, unable to speak. His last words have just described his family's relocation to the Oregon coast after the NFC breakup and he is now overcome by those painful memories.

The seconds pass. *Tick, tick, tick...*

C'mon, Mike. You got this.

Beside me, a body drops onto the platform—*thuddd!* The impact causes the nearby candelabra to teeter, perilously close to the flower arrangements.

~ ~ ~

Eric

Has someone just died in the middle of our wedding? I turn stiffly in my gray tux and tails and try to identify the fallen bridesmaid. She's a member of our youth group, the teen daughter of the pastor who performed Matt and Heidi's wedding. We love this pastor's family and are so honored they made the long trip.

She stirs. She's simply fainted. She's dazed but alive.

Her mother rushes to her aid and helps her down to one of the pews, while someone else rights the wobbling candelabra and spares us all a fragrant bonfire.

We turn back to listen to Mike Monaghan. Moments before, he was unable to proceed. Like many others in the sanctuary, he carries wounds from the past and we all recognize the pain in his voice.

Please, Mike, this is a day of healing. Let's do this together.

Carolyn squeezes my hand, her eyes seeking mine. She wears the wedding dress Debbie Monaghan wore at her own ceremony years ago. It's been tailored to Carolyn's shapely figure and she looks radiant. I have a bride to carry over the threshold, but there are still have photos to take, a reception, as well as a bouquet and a garter to toss.

Let's hurry this up, I think. Our honeymoon suite awaits.

Mike eases back into his wedding message and everyone takes a deep breath, despite the tension which still lingers.

In the front row, Mom presses her lips together and gives me a reassuring smile. She is cute with her short, bobbed hair. My heart aches for her, aware she is in need of some level of medical attention and emotional care. She's damaged in ways we don't fully comprehend, yet so much of who I am is rooted in her motherly wisdom. As exasperating as she can be, she is still strong in her faith and oozes love for all who will receive it.

I catch Dad's eye. Bearded and smiling, he has braved the potential anger in this room to be here for both weddings. Before the ceremony, he gave me a long hug and told me how proud he was of all three of us kids. I am my father's son.

Gramps and Grams Dorene face me from the second row. Their support means everything to me and they've even gifted us with some honeymoon lodging.

Grandma Guise is present, always our stalwart supporter—with Grandpa Guise at her side, which I never imagined possible. They drove over nine hours just to get here.

Mike Monaghan finishes his message and leads Carolyn and me to the communion table. She and I break bread, drink the juice, then light a unity candle. Our prayer is for unity for ourselves and for everyone here today. We seal our vows with the exchange of rings, then my hand cups her face and our lips touch.

Alongside us, my groomsmen hold up huge score cards to rate our kiss.

Tim and Eben encourage us with high numbers, while a third score is mediocre.

My brother wears a wry smile. He gives an abysmal rating.

Laughter ripples through the sanctuary. The harder Mike Monaghan laughs, the louder others respond. The awkward silence, the fallen bridesmaid, the years of pent-up hurt and confusion, they all give way to waves of emotion. Some hold their sides, while others slap their knees and wipe their eyes. It becomes a moment of collective cleansing.

Then the announcement: "May I introduce to you, Eric and Carolyn Wilson."

Dashing up the aisle, we are surrounded by shouts of joy.

~ ~ ~

Heidi

The photographer calls everyone in for a final photo, all the Guises and Wilsons together. Eric and Carolyn join Matt and me in the center. Nearly everyone gathers round, with flower girls and ring bearers down front.

Someone tugs at my arm. Annoyed, I turn and find my mom squinting at me.

"Heidi," she says, "is there any chance we can take separate family pictures?"

"What're you talking about? People are waiting for us to go cut the cake."

"It's Grandpa Guise. He says he won't be in a photo with Daddy."

"This is my wedding day," I respond. "Are you kidding me?"

"Honey," she pleads, then looks to Grandma Guise for support.

"No," I say. "He's not going to control my life the way he controlled yours. That's fine. He doesn't have to be in the picture."

Grandma Guise chortles. "Serves him right. A taste of his own medicine."

The photographer looks to me for direction and I return to my spot. God is all about creating something wonderful from nothing and all of these threads, these multiple generations on both sides, are being woven together into a larger, more vibrant tapestry. We've lost a few along the way—Uncle John, Aunt Janet, and others who were special to us—but their absence adds depth and dimension to the design. Each dark space, each shadow left behind, creates contrast and enhances the remaining colors.

Enough with the family drama. We are doing this.

"Whenever you're ready," I instruct the photographer.

The camera clicks, capturing this moment for generations to come. All those who remain are present this day—husbands and wives, grandparents and parents, aunts and uncles, nieces and nephews, cousins and first cousins, even our foster sister who lived with us for almost a year.

Just about everyone is pictured. Except Grandpa Guise. He stands off to the side, stern-faced and stubborn to the end. He does so by his own choice.

Daddy is here, though, right in the middle of it.

Our dad is back in the picture.

And So We Continue

Olympic Peninsula, Washington — July 2022

On the western fringes of Olympic National Park, we hike Rialto Beach for nearly two miles into gusts of wind and grit. We pass sand dollars, sea anemone, and a dead stingray pecked at by gulls.

Just the three of us, the original trio.

Our mom is gone. She died on December 15, 2008, due to heart and thyroid issues. She was only fifty-nine years old. For her last twenty years, she did what she loved, living out of a backpack, traveling to over 200 countries, telling people about Jesus everywhere she went. In 2009, a group of family and friends gathered in Israel to scatter her ashes near Jerusalem and Masada. A cluster of Sudanese refugees joined in and declared, "Your mother was our spiritual mother."

Mom, we have so many precious memories of you.

You are desperately missed.

Our dad remarried in 1994. He compiled a bestselling reference book for those seeking online degrees, served on his local police force, and taught life skills to troubled teens at a Job Corps facility. For decades we enjoyed our relationship with his wife, sweet DeeDee. She passed away on September 20, 2021, dearly loved by all.

In 2022, Dad remarried. Heidi performed the ceremony as he exchanged vows with a spunky, fun woman named Michelle. Dad and Michelle look forward to new adventures and have already made visits together to Puerto Rico and South America.

We three kids have faced our own rough patches, whether medical, financial, relational—or all of the above. Though age and gray hairs are starting to show, we're all closer than ever and at heart we're still pursuing our dreams.

Heidi has done theater in her community, producing well-received plays through her local church. Eric has penned books, including a few national bestsellers, and conducts annual writers' retreats. Shaun has fronted a Christian rock band, led worship at various churches, and served at David's Tent, a music ministry in Washington, D.C.

Our struggles with religion continue.

Heidi and Matt have served as head pastors in multiple locations, including twelve years at one of the largest churches on the coast of northern California. She earned a bachelor's degree in biblical studies at Life Pacific University–formerly, LIFE Bible College—and a master's in psychology at Northwest University. She and her husband currently serve as pastors at New Life Church in Everett, Washington.

Eric has returned to the organic faith of his childhood, meeting with friends who share his love for Jesus. He earned a bachelor's degree at Life Pacific University, but left organized religion fifteen years ago. He rarely attends Sunday service, preferring small-group settings. The mountains and rivers are his cathedral, tree stumps and boulders his front-row pews.

Though Shaun still leads worship in support of local churches, he feels a deeper connection to the Lord while worshiping on his porch or hiking through the Cascades. He holds a certificate in pastoral care and counseling and has also earned a mastery of TESL—Teaching English as a Second Language—at University of Arizona. For over twenty years, he's extended his love for the world through Agape Hosting, his Japanese exchange student program.

On this breezy Pacific shoreline, the three of us zip up our jackets. We round towering boulders shaped like dorsal fins and come upon impressive volcanic formations. Over time, waves have punched through the base. This is called Hole-in-the-Wall. It is our portal, and we don't have much time to make it through, as the opening is already lapped by the rising tide.

So much lies in the past. So much remains ahead.

The three of us dodge the surf and clamber onto the crags. Together we pass through shadows, through the rock's fissure, and reach tide pools on the other side.

The change is startling. The crashing waves and howling wind fade on this end of the promontory. Water nips at our toes. We peel off our hats and wrap our arms around each other, wearing big goofy grins. The sun's warmth kisses our foreheads.

There is plenty left to tell—heartaches, miracles, dark secrets too.

Someday, perhaps. Just not now.

We choose instead to enjoy this moment. We want to laugh and shed tears, pray and shout to the sky. Home is here in this place, in this connection of our hands on the beach. We are still here, the three of us. Yes, we are fully alive.

— *Heidi, Eric, & Shaun*

Book Group Discussion Questions

Part One: RAGAMUFFIN KIDS

1. How did travel at an early age affect the Wilson children? In what ways was it beneficial? Did any of the three kids seem damaged by it?

2. Were you aware of Bibles being smuggled into various countries around the world? Do you think this is an appropriate response to religious oppression?

3. Did you find Mark's motives in overseas work honorable or do you think he used Bible-smuggling solely as a means of escape from his troubles in the U.S.?

Part Two: RUNNING ON FUMES

4. Can you relate in any way to Heidi's fears as a young girl? Did her parents answer her questions in appropriate ways? What fears have you had to face?

5. As Mark spent time in India, he experienced physical deterioration. Do you think this was a result of his existential searching or of his dietary issues?

6. Which aspects of Mark and Linda's parenting surprised you? How did they serve their kids well? In what ways do you believe they caused their kids harm?

7. At a young age, all three kids decided to love Jesus as their savior. Was this a heartfelt response or something they did due to pressure from their parents?

Part Three: HOME FIRES BURNING

8. What does home mean to you? What did it mean to Heidi, Eric, and Shaun? How did this concept change as their story moved along?

9. As they faced different challenges in school, did you relate more to Heidi's sexual abuse, Eric's sexual exploration, or Shaun's challenges with authority figures?

10. As Eric and Shaun faced various forms of bullying, what did they learn and how did they respond? What did you think of their dad's actions when he heard of it?

11. How have relatives shaped your own life? As Heidi, Eric, and Shaun formed relationships with their extended family, how did this shape their identities?

12. What were your childhood dreams? How did the Wilson kids begin pursuing their own dreams and how did their parents encourage or discourage them?

Part Four: THE ASCENT

13. Why did Linda exhibit anger like never before? Did she know of her husband's secrets? If so, what could she have done? Who could she have turned to for help?

14. Have you ever considered the pressures pastors and their families face? What options did they have in finding help, particularly if it meant losing their job?

15. Both Heidi and Eric got involved in sexual relationships at a Christian school. Do you believe this is common? Did you ever face suicidal thoughts as a teen?

16. At school, the Wilsons were confronted with some heavy-handed religious tactics. Did their faith suffer for it? How could they have responded differently?

17. What did you think of Mark and Linda's approach to ministry and to involving everyone? Did you find Linda's spiritual fervor more helpful or harmful?

18. Just as all five of the Wilsons moved toward their dreams, a devastating event turned everything on its head. How did this play into what followed?

Part Five: UNRAVELING

19. While facing her own secrets, Heidi realized her dad was in no position to help. What forms of shame have you dealt with? How did Heidi confront hers?

20 As Mark's behavior became more erratic, his family suffered. What efforts were made to stop this downward slide? How did the kids try to help?

21. Eric returned from his own Bible-smuggling adventures to find a family barely hanging on. What was his response? In what ways did he turn a blind eye?

22. Have you ever gone through a messy breakup? Could you relate to Linda's reactions, or did you expect her be more proactive in her own defense?

23. How could the church's final announcement have been worded more specifically to avoid rumors and confusion? Or did you think it was phrased appropriately?

24. When Mark's childhood abuse and neglect was revealed, did it create in you deeper empathy for him and his decisions? Or did they simply seem like excuses?

25. How did the Wilson kids reconcile with their parents? Is there unforgiveness in your own family? If so, what steps might you take to help resolve this?

HEIDI, ERIC, & SHAUN

DURING THE WRITING OF
AMERICAN LEFTOVERS

IN OREGON,
WASHINGTON,
& NORTHERN
CALIFORNIA

FROM
2019 - 2022

PICS OF DAD

WITH ERIC, HEIDI, SHAUN, & DAD'S NEW WIFE, MICHELLE

FROM 2019 - 2022